BRITISH
OLYMPIANS
A HUNDRED YEARS OF GOLD MEDALLISTS

Acknowledgements for Illustrations

Allsport: pp. 14, 23 (top left), 29, 40, 63, 70, 76, 77, 79 (top), 84, 85, 87, 88, 91,
97, 98, 100, 102, 104, 105 (both), 107, 108–9, 111, 121, 141
British Library: p. 69
Ian Buchanan: pp. 12, 13, 22 (right), 44, 55, 73, 74, 116, 135 (top), 152
Jane Daubeny (photographer): p. 8
GSL: pp. 24, 58, 80, 95, 133
Hulton Picture Company: pp. 22 (left), 23 (bottom left), 23 (right), 32, 33, 47, 49,
78, 81, 83, 110, 128, 129, 134, 135 (bottom), 145, 146, 170, 186
ED Lacey: p. 123
RTG Mason: p. 38
Popperfoto: pp. 21, 36, 51, 79 (bottom), 93, 94

All colour illustrations courtesy of Allsport

BRITISH
OLYMPIANS

A HUNDRED YEARS OF GOLD MEDALLISTS

IAN BUCHANAN

Editor: Simon Duncan
Design: Barry Löwenhoff
Picture editor: Alex Goldberg

Copyright © Ian Buchanan 1991

Reprinted in 1992 for Shell U.K. Ltd.

The right of Ian Buchanan to be identified as the Author of this Work has been
asserted in accordance with the Copyright, Design & Patents Act 1988

Published in Great Britain by Guinness Publishing Ltd, 33 London Road,
Enfield, Middlesex

Typeset in Caledonia by Best-set Typesetter Ltd, Hong Kong
Printed and bound in Great Britain by The Bath Press, Bath, Avon

'Guinness' is a registered trademark of Guinness Publishing Ltd

British Library Cataloguing in Publication Data
Buchanan, Ian
British Olympians
1. Olympic Games British competitors, history
I. Title
796.480922

ISBN 0-85112-952-8

Contents

Introduction
8

British Olympic Champions – Biographies

Summer Games

Winter Games

British Olympic Competitors – Full Listing

Summer Games

Winter Games

Index of Biographies
190

Introduction

As the only country to have been represented at every Summer and Winter Games – including the winter sports events held as an extension of the Summer Games in 1908 and 1920 – Great Britain holds a unique place in Olympic history.

Since the 1896 Games in Athens, 379 British men and 27 women have won an Olympic title, and the story of their widely differing lives is told in this book. A total of 3534 men and 803 women have represented Great Britain at the Olympic Games, and for the first time all their names are recorded collectively.

Throughout the book, I have referred to those competitors who were placed first, second or third as Olympic gold, silver or bronze medallists respectively. This has been done for the sake of uniformity, although I am aware that medals were not actually awarded on this basis at earlier editions of the Games. Similarly, I have referred to those who represented either Oxford or Cambridge Universities in matches against their traditional rivals as 'blues', although I recognize that for some sports only 'half-blues' were awarded and for certain minor sports there was no official recognition at all.

As befits a nation with an unbroken attendance record, Great Britain played a significant role in the revival of the Modern Olympic Games. Baron Pierre de Coubertin was undoubtedly impressed and encouraged by a visit he made in 1890 to the Shropshire village of Much Wenlock, where the local doctor, W Penny Brookes, had founded the Much Wenlock Olympic Society 40 years earlier. Dr Brookes, despite the rural location of his society, had a strong sense of internationalism which particularly appealed to de Coubertin.

After a number of preliminary meetings and a great deal of lobbying, Baron de Coubertin brought together an International Athletics Congress in June 1894, and it was there in Paris that the formal decision was taken to revive the Olympic Games. An International Olympic Committee (IOC) was formed and the British founder members were Lord Ampthill and Charles Herbert.

It is not generally appreciated that London was the initial choice of the IOC to host the first Modern Olympic Games. A committee meeting held on 19 June 1894, during the Paris Congress, approved a motion put by M Duval and seconded by Viscount de Rochefoucauld, which named London as the site of the 1896 Games; but Baron de Coubertin's amendment that the decision be deferred until the arrival of the British delegate, Charles Herbert, was subsequently accepted. It is by no means certain that Charles Herbert ever actually arrived in Paris, but if he did he was evidently outmanoeuvred at the Congress by de Coubertin, who despite his Anglophile leanings favoured Athens as the appropriate site to stage the revival of the Olympic Games.

In view of the British involvement in the formation of the International Olympic Committee in 1894, it is surprising that an equivalent national body did not come into being for another 11 years. The British Olympic Association was founded on 24 May 1905, when a meeting at the House of Commons elected Lord Desborough as the first Chairman. The first British Olympic team to have any form of official endorsement, therefore, was the one which went to the Intercalated Games at Athens in 1906. British competitors had, of course, taken part on an unofficial basis in the three previous Games, and all the British Olympic champions and the competitors from 1896 onwards are recognized in this book.

Research for this work has covered a wide field and I am grateful to many academic, genealogical, military and public record sources for their help. Countless individuals, including Olympians themselves and their relatives, have responded kindly to my inquiries and I am pleased to acknowledge my debt to them all. I would like to express my particular appreciation of the assistance I have received from Harold Alderman, Dennis L Bird, Jim Creasy, Stan Greenberg, Erich Kamper, Stanley and Maria Knight, Bob Mason, Dr Bill Mallon, Peter Matthews and Ture Widlund. I would also like to acknowledge the helpful and courteous service I have received from the staff of the British Museum Newspaper Library, at Colindale; the Principal Probate Registry, Somerset House; the General Register Office, St Catherine's House; the Norwich Central Library; and the Norfolk County Library, Aylsham. Special thanks go to my wife, Jeanne, for her assistance in explaining some of the intricacies of the pc!

With the assistance of these many and varied sources, a significant amount of original information has come to light. Rather surprisingly, a 'new' British Olympic champion has been traced – the name of Algernon Maudslay (1900, Yachting) does not appear in any previous Olympic reference source. Many other errors and inconsistencies from earlier publications have also been corrected.

While much of the historical jungle which surrounded British Olympic participation has now been cleared, some of the undergrowth remains and any additional information regarding the lives of the gold medallists and the full names and relevant dates of the competitors would be welcome. Information on such matters as dates of death and number of international appearances is correct up to November 1990.

Ian Buchanan
Old Fighting Cocks
Burgh-next-Aylsham
Norfolk NR11 6TP

British Olympic Champions

Biographies

Summer Games

Archery
MEN

Dod, *William*

Born: 18 July 1867, Lower Bebington, Cheshire   Died: 8 October 1954, Earl's Court, London

GOLD: 1908 (YORK ROUND)

Willy Dod was a descendant of Sir Antony Dod of Edge, who commanded the English archers at Agincourt, so it was appropriate that he celebrated his 41st birthday by winning an Olympic gold medal for archery.

The archers at the 1908 Olympic Games competed in atrocious weather conditions, and at one stage the driving rain brought proceedings to a halt. At the end of the first day, Willy Dod of Welford Park led Reginald Brooks-King of West Somerset by 10 points. Although the weather conditions improved on the second day, eddies of wind around the stadium still provided a stern test and Dod was one of the few to master the difficult conditions. He finished the winner by the handsome margin of 47 points.

Dod was never inconvenienced by having to attend school or work for a living. He received his education entirely from private tutors, and his father, a wealthy banker and cotton broker, provided sufficient funds for him to lead a life of leisure. In addition to being a champion golfer and archer, Willy was also a fine shot and enjoyed big game hunting in the Rockies. He first took up archery as a pastime at the home of the Legh family, who had an estate close to the Dods in Cheshire and were one of the greatest names in the history of the sport.

Neither Willy nor his legendary younger sister 'Lottie' entered for any

Willy Dod, who won the 1908 archery title on his 41st birthday.

archery competitions until 1906, when the family moved south to Newbury in Berkshire and Willy and his sister joined the newly-formed Welford Park Archers. Within three years of his first competition, Willy Dod was the Olympic champion and he went on to win the Grand National Archery title, which was the British championship, in 1909 and 1911. After the fashionable Welford Park club was wound up in 1911, the Dod family quickly lost

interest in the sport; in fact, the 1911 Grand National meeting was Willy's last Open archery competition. Having previously been a scratch golfer at the Royal Liverpool Golf Club and the South of Ireland champion in 1901, he again devoted time to the sport and in 1912 he reached the fourth round of the British Amateur Championship.

Four weeks after the outbreak of war, Willy enlisted in the Sportsman's Battalion of the Royal Fusiliers and by the end of the year he was serving as a private in the trenches in France. For a 47-year-old from Dod's social background this was a particularly chastening experience and he applied for a transfer to the Navy. Surprisingly, his request was granted and he was commissioned into the RNVR in April 1915, but after spending a year back in France as an administrative officer with the Royal Naval Air Service he was invalided out.

Willy and his sister eventually settled in Devon, where they had bought a property at Westward Ho! just before the Second World War. Their lives centered around the golf club and in 1948 Willy was elected President of the Royal North Devon club; the following year Lottie was elected the Lady President. In 1950 Lottie returned to London and Willy joined her in her Earl's Court flat two years later; neither ever married and they spent their last years together.

Archery
WOMEN

Newall, *Sybil Fenton*

Born: 17 October 1854, Calderbrook, Lancashire   Died: 24 June 1929, Cheltenham, Gloucestershire

GOLD: 1908 (NATIONAL ROUND)

Fifty-three-year-old Sybil 'Queenie' Newall is the oldest woman ever to win an Olympic gold medal. Like Willy Dod, the 1908 men's champion, Queenie Newall came from one of the oldest families in England – the Newalls are recognized by the College of Arms back to the time of Henry IV in the 14th century. Queenie was the eldest of seven daughters of John and Maria (Fenton) Newall, who maintained a large country estate at Hare

Hill in Lancashire. The Fentons were also a prominent Lancashire family and Queenie's maternal grandfather, John Fenton, twice served as the Liberal MP for Rochdale.

Having left Lancashire, Queenie joined Cheltenham Archers in 1905 and made spectacular progress. In 1907 she shot at all five regional meetings, making the highest score in four of them and being placed second in the fifth. At the 1908

Olympic Games, the women archers encountered the same adverse weather conditions as the men and at the end of the first day Queenie Newall trailed the multi-talented Lottie Dod by 10 points, but Newall soon moved into the lead on the second day and went on to win the gold medal by 43 points. In less than three years, she had risen from being an obscure archer at a provincial club to become Olympic champion.

The greatest British woman archer of all-time, Alice Legh, who won 23 Grand National titles in a 41-year span between 1881 and 1922, chose not to compete at the 1908 Olympics, but the following week in the Grand National meeting at Oxford she defeated Newall by the huge margin of 151 points. Newall's successes at

these championships were to come later; she won the title in 1911 and 1912, and in 1914 she only missed a third victory by just three points. She continued shooting after the war and her last recorded score was with the Cheltenham Archers in September 1928 at the age of 74.

Queenie Newall, the 1908 archery champion and the oldest woman ever to win an Olympic gold medal.

Association Football

Bailey, *Horace Peter*

Born: 3 July 1881, Derby, Derbyshire   Died: 1 August 1960, Biggleswade, Bedfordshire

GOLD: 1908

Apart from his three games in the 1908 Olympic tournament, Bailey kept goal for England in five full and eight amateur internationals. He made his amateur international debut against Wales in February 1908 and three weeks later he won full international honours when the opponents were again Wales. His other full international caps came during England's tour of Central Europe in June 1908 and he made the last of his amateur international appearances in 1913.

Bailey, who was employed by the Midland Railway at Derby as a rating official, was rather below the average height of first-class goalkeepers but he was the outstanding amateur keeper of his time. He first signed with Derby County in 1899 and then played for Ripley Athletic and Leicester Imperial before joining Leicester Fosse in 1907. He was the first player from the Leicester Fosse club to be capped, and played a major part in their promotion to Division 1 of the

Football League at the end of the 1907–08 season. In 1910 he returned to Derby County to help them out of an injury crisis, but the following season he moved to Birmingham where he finished his playing days.

In the three Olympic matches in 1908, Bailey only conceded one goal and that was an own goal – Chapman, the English centre-half, deflected the ball into his own net in the match against Sweden.

Barridge, *JE*

GOLD: 1900

Barridge played at centre-half for Upton Park when they won the 1900 Olympic tournament.

Berry, *Arthur*

Born: 3 January 1888, Liverpool, Lancashire   Died: 15 March 1953, Liverpool, Lancashire

GOLD: 1908 & 1912

While at Denstone College, Arthur Berry captained the rugby team but when he went up to Wadham College, Oxford, he devoted his attentions to soccer and met with immediate success. He won his blue in 1908 and 1909, represented England in the full international against Ireland in 1909 and played on the right-wing for his

country in 32 amateur internationals between 1908 and 1913. Berry was one of the most brilliant amateurs of his day and a contemporary described his direct style as 'a complete art without tinsel or gaudiness'.

On leaving Oxford, Berry entered Gray's Inn and retired from football when

he was Called to the Bar in 1913. He was commissioned into the Liverpool Regiment in 1916 and served as Adjutant of the Lancashire Fusiliers before leaving the Army in 1919. After the war, he settled in Liverpool and joined the family law firm which was headed by his father Edwin, a director of Liverpool FC and

Chairman of the club from 1904 to 1909.

At the time of the 1908 Olympics Berry was still at Oxford University, but he later played for Northern Nomads, Liverpool, Fulham, Everton and Wrexham and was a member of the Oxford City team which reached the FA Amateur Cup final in 1913.

After playing in the opening match against Hungary at the 1912 Games in Stockholm, Berry was replaced by Gordon Wright for the semi-final against Finland but he regained his place for the final to become, with Vivian Woodward, one of two British players to be on the winning team at both the 1908 and 1912 Olympics.

Brebner, *Ronald Gilchrist*

Born: 23 September 1881, Darlington, Co. Durham   Died: 11 November 1914, Chiswick, London

GOLD: 1912

After qualifying as a dental surgeon at Edinburgh University, Ronald Brebner played for a wide variety of football clubs as he moved around the country establishing himself in his profession. At various times he played for Sunderland, Queen's Park Rangers, London Caledonians, Northern Nomads, Wanderers, Darlington, Elgin City, Stockton, Huddersfield Town, Chelsea and Leicester Fosse. He kept goal for England in 23 amateur internationals, but although he played in the South v North England trial match in 1912 he never won full international honours.

Brebner made just one league appearance for Chelsea in the 1906–07 season, but when he returned to Stamford Bridge four years later he was, when available, the first-choice goalkeeper and played in 17 league matches and one cup tie. He played for Great Britian in all three matches at the 1912 Olympics but two years after winning his gold medal he died, at the age of 33. In January 1914, while with Leicester Fosse, he had been carried off the field at Lincoln with an injury which ended his playing career and contributed significantly to his early death ten months later.

England goalkeeper Ron Brebner thwarts a Danish attack in the 1912 final.

Buckenham, *Claude Percy*

Born: 16 January 1876, Wandsworth, London   Died: 23 February 1937, Dundee, Scotland

GOLD: 1900

Percy Buckenham played at right-back for the Upton Park team which won the 1900 Olympic soccer tournament but he was much better known as a cricketer. After attending Alleyn's School he became a prominent sportsman in the Leyton area, playing for Leyton and Essex at football and in 1899 making his debut for the Essex county cricket team. Tall and sparely built, Buckenham was one of the deadliest fast bowlers of his time and went on the MCC tour of South Africa in 1909–10, where he played in four of the five Test matches.

His career as a county cricketer ended in 1914 when he became the professional to Forfarshire, and after serving in the war with the Royal Garrison Artillery he became the coach at Repton School.

Burn, *Thomas Christopher*

Born: 29 November 1888, Spittal, Berwick-upon-Tweed, Northumberland   Died: 25 September 1916, France

GOLD: 1912

Tom Burn played at right-back for the 1912 Olympic team. While with the London Caledonians, he won 12 amateur international caps in the seasons immediately prior to the First World War.

Like Joe Dines, his team-mate in 1912, Burn lost his life in action in France.

Chalk, *Alfred Ernest*
Born: 27 November 1874, West Ham, Essex
GOLD: 1900

Alfred Chalk was well known in London football circles at the turn of the century. He played for Ilford, Barking Woodville and Essex County and was right-half for Upton Park when they won the gold medals at the 1900 Olympics. According to the limited reports which reached London from Paris, Chalk was one of the Olympic side's outstanding players.

Chapman, *Frederick William*
Born: 10 May 1883, Nottingham, Nottinghamshire   Died: 7 September 1951, Linby, Nottinghamshire
GOLD: 1908

After attending Nottingham High School, Frederick Chapman played for Notts Magdala FC but resigned when the club decided to leave the Football Association and support the breakaway Amateur Football Association. He then joined Oxford City, where he was appointed captain; he also turned out for Nottingham Forest in league fixtures at full-back and centre-half, but at the time of the 1912 Olympics he was usually playing for South Nottingham.

In 1910 Chapman was one of the founders of the English Wanderers, a touring club whose membership was restricted to those who had won amateur international honours. The first President was Lord Kinnaird, the captain was Vivian Woodward and Chapman was joint-secretary. With 16 amateur caps for England, he easily qualified for this exclusive but short-lived club.

During the war, Chapman was initially a gunner in the Royal Horse Artillery but later, as a major, he commanded the 2nd/1st Notts Battery in Mesopotamia. He did not resume his football career after the war, concentrating instead on his business as a director of Lord & Chapman Ltd, a ladies' blouse and gown manufacturer who had a factory in Nottingham.

Corbett, *Walter Samuel*
Born: 26 November 1880, Wellington, Shropshire   Died: c.1955
GOLD: 1908

Educated locally at King Edward Grammar School, Walter Corbett played most of his football with the Birmingham club. He won three full international caps during England's tour of Central Europe in 1908 and played in 18 amateur internationals between 1907 and 1911. His later amateur honours came when he was with Wellington Town, who he joined one year after winning his Olympic gold medal. A fast and resourceful full-back, he also played occasionally for Aston Villa and once for Queen's Park Rangers.

Dines, *Joseph*
Born: 12 April 1886, King's Lynn, Norfolk   Died: 27 September 1918, Ribecourt, France
GOLD: 1912

Joe Dines won 24 amateur international caps and played at half-back in all three matches at the 1912 Olympics. After attending Peterborough Teacher Training College he became a schoolmaster at King's Lynn and earned his county colours while playing for the local team. He later took up a teaching post in Essex, where he was soon appointed captain of Ilford and also played occasionally for Millwall.

On the outbreak of war, Dines was one of three brothers to volunteer immediately and after serving in the Ordnance Corps, the Middlesex Regiment, the Machine Gun Corps and the Tank Corps, he was commissioned into the Liverpool Regiment and played one game for Liverpool before being sent to France. He survived just eleven days at the Front before he was cut down by machine gun fire. He had been leading his men in an attack on an enemy position, and although his battalion took 600 prisoners they lost six officers and 125 men.

Gosling, *William Sullivan*
Born: 19 July 1869, Hassiobury, Bishop's Stortford, Essex   Died: 2 October 1952, Hassiobury, Bishop's Stortford, Essex
GOLD: 1900

William Gosling was one of three brothers who were outstanding sportsmen at Eton and were later prominent in county affairs in Essex. William was in the Eton cricket and football XI in 1888 and won the high jump at the school sports that year. He took a commission in the Scots Guards, with whom he served in both the Boer War and the First World War. When on leave from his regiment, he played football for Chelmsford and it was through his sporting contacts in Essex that he was invited to join the Upton Park team when they went to Paris for the 1900 Olympic tournament.

In 1903 William married Victoria, the daughter of the Marquess of Lothian, and following the death of his brother Robert in 1922 he took over the family seat at Hassiobury, near Bishop's Stortford. He was appointed High Sheriff of Essex in

1927, a post which Robert, the eldest of the three brothers, had held 20 years earlier. It was Robert, in fact, who enjoyed the most distinguished sporting career. He played cricket for Eton, Cambridge University and Essex, and won his blue and an England cap at football. The youngest brother, Thomas, also won a soccer blue at Cambridge.

Hardman, *Harold Payne*

Born: 4 April 1882, Kirkmanshulme, Lancashire   Died: 9 June 1965, Sale, Cheshire

GOLD: 1908

Although not considered strong enough to play games as a boy, Harold Hardman later turned his spare physique to his advantage as an elusive and speedy outside-left. On leaving Blackpool High School, he played for Northern Nomads and a number of local clubs before joining Everton in 1903, and three years later he became one of only three amateurs this century to win an FA Cup winner's medal when Everton beat Newcastle United. In 1907 he again played in the Cup final but this time Everton lost to Sheffield Wednesday.

Hardman played four times for England in full internationals and made ten amateur international appearances. After five seasons with Everton he joined Manchester United in 1908 and subsequently played for Bradford City and Stoke before retiring in 1913.

He was admitted as a solicitor in 1907 and practised in Manchester. In November 1912 he was elected a director of Manchester United and, apart from one brief period, remained a director for the rest of his life. He was Chairman of the club from 1950, and also served as President of the Lancashire FA.

Haslam, *A*

GOLD: 1900

Haslam, an outside-left, captained the Upton Park team that won the Paris Olympic tournament.

Hawkes, *Robert Murray*

Born: 18 October 1880, Breachwood Green, Hertfordshire   Died: 12 September 1945, Luton, Bedfordshire

GOLD: 1908

Robert Hawkes was educated at Luton Higher Grade School and after playing for various local amateur sides he joined the Town club in 1901. He captained Luton Town in the 1905–06 season, played five times for England in full internationals and made 22 appearances in amateur internationals before turning professional in 1911.

Hawkes continued to play at left-half for Luton until after the war, and at the end of the 1919–20 season he had a few games for Bedford Town before retiring to his business as a straw-hat manufacturer. He had a frail physique and was a poor header of the ball, but adequately compensated for these deficiencies with excellent judgment and remarkably skilful footwork.

Hoare, *Gordon Rahere*

Born: 18 April 1884, Blackheath, Kent   Died: 27 October 1973, London, SW15

GOLD: 1912

Gordon Hoare played in all three Olympic matches in Stockholm, scoring once in the opening match against Sweden and twice in the final against Denmark. At the time of the 1912 Olympics he was playing for Glossop, but he also spent some seasons with Woolwich Arsenal and made 13 appearances for England in amateur internationals, though he was never selected for a full international.

Hunt, *Kenneth Reginald Gunnery*

Born: 24 February 1884, Oxford, Oxfordshire   Died: 28 April 1949, Heathfield, Sussex

GOLD: 1908

Kenneth Hunt was educated at Trent College and Queen's College, Oxford, and six weeks after appearing in his fourth and final match for Oxford against Cambridge he played for Wolverhampton Wanderers in the 1908 FA Cup final, scoring one of the goals which helped Wolves to a 3-1 victory over Newcastle United.

Hunt also played league football for Leyton and Crystal Palace. In 1913, while playing for Oxford City, he came close to being only the third man in history to play on the winning side in both the FA Cup final and the FA Amateur Cup final, but City lost narrowly in the Amateur final to South Shields.

A fast and fearless wing-half, he twice played for England in full internationals and made 20 amateur international appearances between 1907 and 1921. After winning a gold medal in 1908, he missed the 1912 Olympics but at the age of 36 made a second Olympic appearance at Antwerp in 1920. He was appointed an assistant master at Highgate School in 1908, was ordained in 1911, and retired from teaching in 1945 after spending 37 years at Highgate.

Jones, *JH*

GOLD: 1900

Jones had an outstanding game in goal for Upton Park at the 1900 Olympics, keeping a clean sheet against France as the English team won the inaugural Olympic soccer final 4-0.

Knight, *Arthur Egerton*

Born: 7 September 1887, Godalming, Surrey   Died: 10 March 1956, Milton, Hampshire

GOLD: 1912

While at King Edward VI Grammar School, Guildford, Arthur Knight also played for Godalming and won his Surrey county cap at the age of 17, but in 1909 he went to live in Portsmouth and was immediately signed up by the local club. After a season with the reserves, he won his place in the Portsmouth first team and played regularly until the outbreak of war. Initially, he served in India and Egypt as a Private in the Hampshire Regiment, but was later commissioned into the Border Regiment and during service in France he rose to the rank of Captain.

After the war, Knight's solid tackling and skills in the air were again welcome at Fratton Park and in the first four post-war seasons he played in 69 matches for Portsmouth at left-back. He won 30 amateur international caps between 1910 and 1923, and when he earned his only full international honours against Ireland in 1920 he was the first player to be capped from a Third Division club. Following his gold medal in 1912, Knight made a second Olympic appearance in 1920 when Great Britain were surprisingly beaten by Norway in their opening match.

He ended his playing days with the Corinthians and later gained the rare distinction of being made an honorary life member. As the manager of an insurance office in Portsmouth, he occasionally played cricket for Hampshire as an opening bat. Having served in the Army in World War I, he was a squadron leader with the RAF in World War II.

Littlewort, *Henry Charles*

Born: 7 July 1882, Ipswich, Suffolk   Died: 21 November 1934, Edmonton, London

GOLD: 1912

After playing at right-half in the matches against Hungary and Finland at the 1912 Olympics, Henry Littlewort moved to centre-half for the final against Denmark. He played occasionally for Tottenham and Fulham, but the major part of his playing career was with Glossop and he won nine amateur international caps while with the Derbyshire club. He was also a notable club cricketer and once received an invitation to play for Essex, but had to decline owing to injury.

Littlewort later became a football journalist with the *News Chronicle*. He was taken ill while preparing to leave his North London home to report on a match between Tottenham and West Bromwich, and died the following week.

McWhirter, *Douglas*

Born: 13 August 1886, Erith, Kent   Died: 14 October 1966, Plumstead, Kent

GOLD: 1912

Douglas McWhirter took over Henry Littlewort's right-half position for the 1912 Olympic final in Stockholm. McWhirter, who occasionally played for Leicester Fosse, won an FA Amateur Cup winner's medal with Bromley in 1911 and played in four amateur internationals, but was never selected for the full international side.

Nicholas, *J*

GOLD: 1900

Playing at centre-forward, Nicholas scored two goals for Upton Park at the 1900 Olympics.

Purnell, *Clyde Honeysett*

Born: 14 May 1877, Ryde, Isle of Wight   Died: 14 August 1934, Westernhanger, Kent

GOLD: 1908

After winning an Olympic gold medal in 1908, Clyde Purnell picked up an FA Amateur Cup winner's medal the following season when he scored once in Clapton's 6-0 victory over Eston United. He won four amateur caps but never played in a full international. At the 1908 Olympics, playing at inside-left, Purnell scored four goals in Britian's first-round victory over Sweden. He lived in Muswell Hill, North London, but died on Folkestone Racecourse.

Quash, *William Francis Patterson*

Born: 27 December 1868, Barking, Essex

GOLD: 1900

Bill Quash played at left-half for Upton Park at the 1900 Olympics. He also played cricket for Barking CC.

Sharpe, *Ivan Gordon*

Born: 15 June 1889, St Albans, Hertfordshire   Died: 9 February 1968, Southport, Lancashire

GOLD: 1912

During the course of his career as an outside-left with Watford, Glossop, Leeds and Derby County, Ivan Sharpe played for England in 12 amateur internationals but never won full international honours.

He was one of two members of the 1912 Olympic team who also played at Antwerp in 1920.

After his playing days were over he became a distinguished sporting journalist, serving as Editor of the *Athletic News* and with the Kemsley Group. He was also President of the Football Writers' Association and in 1952 he wrote his autobiography, *40 Years in Football*.

Smith, *Herbert*

Born: 22 November 1879, Witney, Oxfordshire   Died: 6 January 1951, Witney, Oxfordshire

GOLD: 1908

After making his debut against Wales in 1905, Herbert Smith won all four of his full international caps before making the first of his 17 appearances in the England amateur side between 1907 and 1910. He was a dashing left-back with a strong volley, and the powerful use of his left foot was always a feature of his game.

Smith attended Oxford County School and Beccles School, and began his playing career with Witney Town FC, winning the Oxfordshire Senior Cup three times in the early 1890s. He later played for a variety of clubs including Oxford City, Stoke, Derby County and Reading, where he was captain of the professional club. During his time at Oxford City, the club were losing finalists in the 1903 FA Amateur Cup and Smith also represented the South against the North. In 1910 he joined the council of the Oxfordshire FA, and he held the office of President from 1919 until his death. All his family shared his love of cricket, and his brother-in-law, Albert Lawton, was captain of Derbyshire for many years.

Spackman, *FG*

GOLD: 1900

Spackman played at inside-right for Upton Park at the 1900 Olympics. The *East Ham Echo*, which was one of the few newspapers to carry a report of the match, rated him one of the outstanding players on the team.

Stapley, *Henry*

Born: 29 April 1883, Tunbridge Wells, Kent   Died: 29 April 1937, Glossop, Derbyshire

GOLD: 1908

Harry Stapley was originally a schoolteacher and worked in various parts of the country where his footballing skills were welcomed by the local clubs. In 1904 he took up an appointment at Woodford College and became captain of Woodford Town. He joined West Ham United midway through the 1905–06 season, where he spent two and a half seasons and scored a total of 41 goals in 75 league and cup matches.

In 1908 Stapley accepted an invitation to join Glossop where their patron, Sir Samuel Hill-Wood, Bt., was spending considerable sums of money in an effort to revive the ailing Derbyshire club. Stapley's brother Will, who won amateur international honours as a centre-half, also went to Glossop but it was Harry who immediately became the favourite of the crowd as he continued to show the same high scoring capabilities which had been the feature of his game at West Ham. With 67 goals in 135 appearances he was

Glossop's leading scorer each season from 1908 to 1912. Although he won 12 amateur caps he was never selected for a full international despite the fact that during his four seasons as Glossop's leading scorer, England called on eight different centre-forwards. Further proof of his scoring ability came at the 1908 Olympics when he scored all four goals in Britain's second round win over Holland and, with a total of six goals, was Britain's leading scorer in the Olympic tournament.

However, Stapley's main duties at Glossop were as private tutor and personal football and cricket coach to the sons of Sir Samuel Hill-Wood. Stapley was clearly

particularly successful as a cricket coach as the sound grounding he gave them, later polished by George Hirst at Eton, resulted in all three of the boys winning cricket blues at Oxford or Cambridge. As the years passed, Stapley was increasingly taken into Sir Samuel's confidence and served as his private secretary after his election as the Member of Parliament for the High Peak constituency. He also served as his employer's nominee on the Board of Directors of various local companies.

Harry Stapley died on his 54th birthday.

Turner, *RR*

GOLD: 1900

Turner appeared regularly for Crouch End Vampires but joined the Upton Park team for the 1900 Olympic tournament in Paris, where he scored one goal playing as outside-right.

Walden, *Harold Adrian*

Born: 10 October 1889, Manchester, Lancashire   Died: 2 December 1955, Leeds, Yorkshire

GOLD: 1912

By concealing his true age, Harry Walden was able to enlist in the Cheshire Regiment when he was only 14 years old. He went to India almost immediately and after two and a half years his regiment returned to Lichfield where Walden first began to take football seriously. When the Cheshires were stationed in Belfast, Corporal Walden played for the Irish

Army v English Army and back in England he subsequently played for the Army v Navy in 1909–10 and 1910–11.

He was signed up by Bradford City but never played for their first team and he was later on the books of Halifax Town. At the 1912 Olympics, Walden scored six goals in the match against Hungary and a total of eleven goals in the tournament, establishing a British Olympic scoring

record which remains unbeaten. Despite his obvious prowess as a goal scorer, Walden's international honours were limited to his three matches at the Stockholm Olympics.

After his playing and Army careers were over Harry Walden became a Music Hall comedian, proving particularly popular in the north of England.

Woodward, *Vivian John*

Born: 3 June 1879, Kennington, Surrey   Died: 31 January 1954, Ealing, Middlesex

GOLD: 1908 & 1912

Universally acknowledged as one of the greatest British centre-forwards, Vivian Woodward was born, appropriately, in a house overlooking Kennington Oval, the then venue of the FA Cup final. After being educated at Ascham College, Clacton, he joined his father in his architect's practice but later became a farmer. He played for Clacton, Harwich & Parkestone and Chelmsford before joining Tottenham Hotspur in 1902 when the club was a member of the Southern League. He was with Tottenham when, in 1908, they were elected to Division 2 of the Football League and scored their first-ever goal in League football. With 19 goals in 27 matches he was Tottenham's top scorer for the season and played a

significant part in their immediate promotion to Division 1.

Woodward subsequently joined Chelsea who he helped regain First Division status in 1912. He stayed with Chelsea until the outbreak of war, when he initially joined the Rifle Brigade but later became a captain in the Footballer's Battalion of the Middlesex Regiment. He was wounded in action early in 1916 and never played serious football again.

Vivian Woodward was a skilful solo dribbler, an intelligent distributor of the ball and could play in any of the three inside-forward positions with equal facility. The England selectors readily recognised his talents, awarding him 16 of his 23 full international caps while he was

playing for a non-league club. He scored a total of 29 goals, which remained an England record until 1958 when both Tom Finney and Nat Lofthouse brought their international tally up to 30. Woodward twice scored four goals in a full international and achieved the hat trick on two other occasions.

He also played in 44 amateur internationals – including the 1908 and 1912 Olympics – scoring a total of 58 goals. His finest performances came in England's first amateur international against France in Paris in 1906, when he scored eight goals, and against Holland in 1909 when he scored six times.

Woodward won his first Olympic gold medal while serving as a director of

Tottenham Hotspur which must surely constitute a record for a director of a Football League club. When he was on the winning Olympic team for the second time in Stockholm four years later he had already passed his 33rd birthday and he remains, to this day, the oldest footballer ever to win an Olympic gold medal.

Vivian Woodward maintained his interest in football long after he ceased playing and was a director of Chelsea from 1922 to 1930.

Zealey, *James Edward*
Born: 7 March 1868, Mile End, Middlesex
GOLD: 1900

Playing at inside-left for Upton Park at the 1900 Olympics, Jim Zealey was rated one of the outstanding players on the British team and scored once in Upton Park's 4-0 victory over the French team.

The following only played in the preliminary rounds and not in the final at the 1912 Games:

Hanney, *Edward Terrance*
Born: 19 January 1889, Reading, Berkshire

Ted Hanney played centre-half in the opening match of the 1912 Olympics against Hungary when he sustained an injury which ended his participation in the tournament.

Hanney began his career with Wokingham Town before joining Reading for whom he was playing when he won his two amateur international caps. After the Olympic Games he turned professional and signed for Manchester City for the then substantial sum of £1250. After playing in 68 league matches and 10 cup ties for Manchester City between 1913 and 1919, Hanney had two seasons with Coventry before rejoining Reading for one final season as captain in Division 3 (South).

He later spent some time in Germany as coach to Stuttgart before returning to his home town of Reading where he became a publican.

Stamper, *Harold*
Born: 6 October 1889, Stockton-on-Tees, County Durham

Harold Stamper's only appearance at international level was in the 1912 Olympic semi-final when he played centre-half against Finland.

Wright, *Edward Gordon Dundas*
Born: 3 October 1884, Earlsfield Green, Surrey   Died: 5 June 1947, Johannesburg, South Africa

Although noted for his excellent ball control and tactical knowledge at outside-left, Gordon Wright played on the opposite wing against Finland in his only match in the Stockholm Olympics of 1912.

After attending St Lawrence College, Ramsgate, Wright, the son of an East Riding clergyman, went up to Queen's College, Cambridge, where he won a place in the University XI for three years (1904–06). On leaving Cambridge, he accepted a post at Hymer's College, Hull, teaching Natural History and Science. In 1906 he was elected captain of Hull City for whom he played 152 league games and became the first player from the club to be capped. Wright also played occasionally for Leyton and Portsmouth and turned out regularly for the Corinthians. He went on the Corinthians Easter tour of Europe in 1906, to North America later the same year and in 1907 he was a member of the Corinthians team which toured South Africa.

Between 1908 and 1913 he won 20 amateur caps and, unusually, he won his only full cap, against Wales in 1906, before he had been recognised by the amateur selectors. After obtaining his degree at Cambridge, Gordon Wright later graduated from the Royal School of Mines and in 1913 he went to South Africa as a mining engineer where, apart from a brief spell in America, he spent the rest of his life.

Boxing

Douglas, *John William Henry Taylor*

Born: 3 September 1882, Clapton, Middlesex   Died: 19 December 1930, At Sea

GOLD: 1908 (MIDDLEWEIGHT)

Although, ultimately, he became much better known as the cricket captain of Essex and England, Johnny Douglas was a highly successful boxer. While at Felsted, he won the 1901 Public School's middleweight championship and in 1905 he took the ABA title. In contrast to his reputation as a defensive cricketer he was a most aggressive boxer.

Representing the Mincing Lane Boxing & Athletic Club and the Belsize Boxing Club, Douglas claimed two KO's on his way to the 1908 Olympic middleweight final where he met the formidable Australian, 'Snowy' Baker. It proved to be a classic contest and after getting the verdict by a narrow margin, Douglas was presented with his gold medal by his father, the then President of the ABA.

The Douglas family owned a successful timber business and often went to Scandanavia on buying missions. In December 1930, their business completed, Johnny Douglas and his father boarded the *SS Oberon* in Finland with the intention of being home for Christmas. Tragically, their boat was involved in a collision in the Kattegat and they were among the 22 passengers who drowned.

Finnegan, *Christopher Martin*

Born: 5 June 1944, Uxbridge, Middlesex

GOLD: 1968 (MIDDLEWEIGHT)

After being ruled out of the 1968 ABA semi-finals because of a cut eye, Chris Finnegan was fortunate to be selected for the Olympic team. His critics, who maintained that only the ABA champions should be included in the team for Mexico, were silenced when Finnegan became the first Briton since Harry Mallin in 1924 to win the Olympic middleweight crown.

In the semi-finals he survived two standing counts against the American, Alfred Jones, and was involved in another

Chris Finnegan, the 1968 middleweight champion and the last Briton to win an Olympic boxing title.

close decision in the final when the judges voted 3-2 in Finnegan's favour at the end of his bout with the Russian, Aleksey Kiselyov.

A bricklayer by trade, Finnegan was awarded the MBE after his victory in Mexico City and he soon turned professional, going on to win the British, Commonwealth and European light-heavyweight titles. In September 1972 he challenged for the world title at Wembley but lost to the defending champion, Bob Foster of America, on a 14th round KO. Before the year was out he had lost his European title and was soon deprived of his British and Commonwealth crowns by John Conteh. The name of Finnegan was not, however, completely lost to boxing fans as his younger brother, Kevin, won the European middleweight title in 1974.

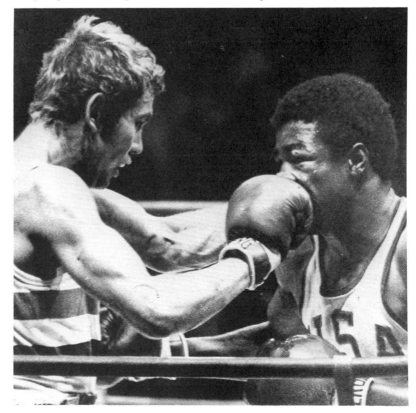

Grace, *Frederick*

Born: 29 February 1884, Edmonton, Middlesex   Died: 23 July 1964, Ilford, Essex

GOLD: 1908 (LIGHTWEIGHT)

Fred Grace of the Eton Mission BC was one of the less fancied competitors in the 1908 British Olympic boxing team. He had never won a major title and he was, by his own admission, woefully short of training. However, in the quarter-finals he scored an outstanding win over Matt Wells, who later became the British and European professional champion. In the final Grace met Fred Spiller of Gainsford

AC when, after an even first round and both boxers going down in the second round, the superior skills of Grace eventually ensured a comfortable victory.

Fred Grace went on to win four ABA lightweight titles between 1909 and 1920 but as boxing was illegal in Sweden in 1912 he was denied the opportunity of defending his Olympic title when at his peak. He did make a second Olympic

appearance in 1920 but by then he was 36 years old and after beating a Dutchman in his first bout he lost to the eventual winner, Samuel Mosberg of America.

Grace retired from his business as a heating and ventilating engineer in 1949 and while out walking one day was struck by a car, receiving injuries which proved fatal.

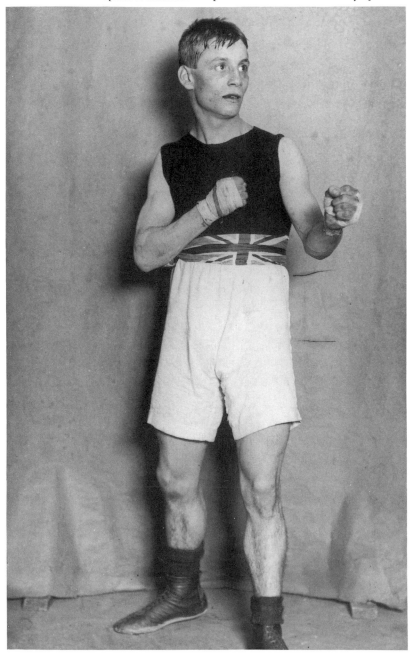

The five British boxers who took all the gold medals in 1908. Left to right: Harry Thomas (bantam), Fred Grace (light), Richard Gunn (top, feather), Johnny Douglas (middle) and Albert Oldman (heavy).

Gunn, *Richard Kenneth*

Born: 16 February 1871, Charing Cross, London   Died: 23 June 1961, Lambeth, London

GOLD: 1908 (FEATHERWEIGHT)

At the age of 37 years and 254 days Richard Gunn is the oldest ever winner of an Olympic boxing title.

In the 1908 Olympic featherweight final, Gunn met Charles Morris of the Polytechnic BC and completely out-generalled his younger opponent in the first round only for Morris to come back and take the second. The rules of the 1908 tournament provided for the third round to last an extra minute and many thought that the veteran Gunn would be hard pressed to survive a final round of four minutes. However, he drew on his vast experience and the ultimate verdict was never in doubt.

After joining his father's East End tailoring business, Richard Gunn took up boxing in 1893 at the Surrey Commercial Docks BC and, after winning the ABA championship in 1894, 1895 and 1896, he retired at the request of the authorities because of his 'acknowledged superiority over all comers'. He then served on the ABA council until 1908 when, 14 years after winning his first ABA title, he came out of retirement to win the Olympic title.

McTaggart, *Richard*

Born: 15 October 1935, Dundee, Scotland

GOLD: 1956 (LIGHTWEIGHT)   BRONZE: 1960 (LIGHTWEIGHT)

One of five boxing brothers from Dundee, Dick McTaggart earned his place on the 1956 Olympic team by winning the ABA lightweight title. After three easy victories in Melbourne, McTaggart had a difficult time in the final against the German, Harry Kurschat, but he won the gold medal and also the Val Barker Trophy as the outstanding stylist of the Games.

After completing his National Service in the RAF, McTaggart, despite his limited earnings as a labourer, declined offers to turn professional and continued in the amateur ring for many more years.

In 1958 he won his second ABA title and took the gold medal at the Commonwealth Games in Cardiff. He was again the ABA champion in 1960 and in his second Olympic appearance in Rome he won a bronze medal after losing to the ultimate winner, Kazimierz Pazdzior of Poland, in the semi-final.

By 1962, McTaggart had moved up a division and was fighting as a light-welterweight. He won silver at the Commonwealth Games in Perth that year and in 1963 took the ABA title at his new weight. In 1964 he became the only

British boxer to compete in three Olympic Games but, as in 1960, he lost to the eventual winner in the preliminaries. After many years at the top McTaggart's days as a world class boxer were inevitably numbered but he managed a fifth and final ABA title in 1965 at the age of 30 before retiring from a career that stands comparison with any amateur boxer who has ever represented Great Britain. After retirement, McTaggart continued to serve the sport and was the coach of the Scottish team at the 1990 Commonwealth Games.

Mallin, *Henry William*

Born: 1 June 1892, Shoreditch, London   Died: 8 November 1969, Lewisham, London

GOLD: 1920 (MIDDLEWEIGHT)   1924 (MIDDLEWEIGHT)

Harry Mallin, a 28-year-old London policeman and the ABA champion of 1919 and 1920, opened his bid for the Olympic middleweight title at Antwerp in 1920 by outpointing Lt Joseph Cranston of the US Army. Cranston, who later became a general, told Mallin that he could only be consoled for losing his first fight, after a 5000 mile journey, if he knew that he had been beaten by the Olympic champion. In due course, Mallin provided that consolation.

In his second bout, Harry Mallin defeated another American, Sam Lagonia, who was disqualified for persistent holding. As the US Official Report put it, the Americans were 'seething with volcanic indignation' at the decision and threatened to withdraw from the Games. The situation eventually calmed and, after a straightforward win over the Canadian, Moe Herscovitch, in the semi-finals, Mallin met another Canadian, Georges Prud'Homme, in the final. The tough French-Canadian soldier, who had won each of his three previous bouts by a KO gave Mallin a hard time throughout but the Englishman did enough to get the verdict. One of the people who helped chair him from the ring was his first round victim, Joseph Cranston.

In 1924, Mallin began the defence of his Olympic crown at the Velodrome d'Hiver in Paris. After two easy wins he met the home-town hero, Roger Brousse, in the quarter-finals with dramatic results. The bout went the full three rounds and Mallin appeared to have won comfortably, but before the decision was announced Mallin told officials that he had been

Harry Mallin, middleweight champion in 1924 and 1928, and the first boxer to retain an Olympic title.

bitten on the arms and chest, pointing to his opponent's teeth marks in support of his complaint. Neither Mallin, nor the British team managers, protested officially but when the judges awarded the fight to Brousse the Swedish officials lodged an official complaint on Mallin's behalf.

The Jury d'Appel met until the early hours of the morning and heard a great deal of evidence, including that of an American who said that he too had been bitten by Brousse in an earlier fight. No

decision was reached at the first meeting and the Jury re-convened the following evening, the boxing programme being held up until their deliberations had been completed. Finally it was announced that Brousse had been disqualified. Pandemonium followed. Fights started around the hall and the disqualified Brousse was carried shoulder-high around the ring by his supporters. Meanwhile, Mallin and his opponent in the semi-final, Joseph Beecken of Belgium, sat in the ring and watched the commotion. Eventually, the bout started, Mallin outpointed the Belgian and went on to meet his team-mate, Jack Elliot, in the final the following night.

Reports of the final are somewhat limited as, at the sight of Mallin climbing into the ring, the French crowd renewed their demonstrations and neither the press nor the spectators enjoyed an uninterrupted view of the bout. It was, apparently, a close fight with the verdict going to Mallin, who became the first man ever to successfully defend an Olympic boxing title.

This was the last fight of Harry Mallin's distinguished ring career during which he won two Olympic gold medals and five ABA titles and remained undefeated in more than 300 bouts. He was manager of the British Olympic boxing team at Berlin in 1936 and the following year he gave the first ever television sports commentary in Britain when two amateur contests were transmitted from the Concert Hall, Alexandra Palace. He was again manager of the Olympic boxing team in 1952 and in his later years held high office in the ABA.

Mitchell, *Harold James*

Born: 5 January 1898, Tiverton, Devon   Died: 8 February 1983, Twickenham, Middlesex

GOLD: 1924 (LIGHT-HEAVYWEIGHT)

Harry Mitchell of the Polytechnic BC, winner of the ABA light-heavyweight championship for four successive years (1922–5), experienced little difficulty in his quest for the 1924 Olympic light-heavyweight title until he came up against Carlo Saraudi of Italy in the semi-finals. Saraudi was an awkward fighter and a persistent clincher and it was not until the closing stages of the final round that Mitchell got the better of him. In the final, Mitchell faced Thyge Peterson of Denmark who, like Saraudi, tried to keep the fight at close quarters. The result was a disappointing fight but with Mitchell as the clear winner.

Oldman, *Albert Leonard*

Born: 18 November 1883, Mile End, Middlesex

GOLD: 1908 (HEAVYWEIGHT)

Albert Oldman, a City of London policeman who had earlier served in the Horse Guards, qualified for the final of the heavyweight division at the 1908 Olympics with a quick KO over I Myrams of Manchester followed by a bye in the semi-finals. In the final, Oldman faced Syd Evans of Reading, the current ABA champion, but unfortunately Evans had injured his shoulder in an earlier round and was no match for the aggressive policeman. Oldman won by a KO within two minutes and took the gold medal after fighting for a total of less than one round throughout the entire competition.

In 1910, he left England to join the Ceylon police.

Rawson, *Ronald Rawson, MC***

Born: 17 June 1882, Kensington, London   Died: 30 March 1952, Kensington, London

GOLD: 1920 (HEAVYWEIGHT)

At Westminster School, Ronald Rawson was an outstanding all-round sportsman and, in his last year was captain of cricket. He went up to Trinity College, Cambridge, where he came close to winning a cricket blue and took up boxing, for which he soon showed a considerable talent.

In 1913, although weighing in within the light-heavyweight limit, he won the heavyweight bout for Cambridge against Oxford and the following year, fighting in his correct division as a light-heavyweight, again beat his Oxford opponent.

In the war, Rawson served as a captain in the Royal Engineers and achieved the rare distinction of winning two bars to the Military Cross. After the war he joined the Polytechnic BC and in his first experience of open competition he won the novices heavyweight class at a tournament in January 1920. Within three months he was the ABA champion and within seven months he was an Olympic gold medallist. At the Antwerp Olympics in August, Rawson added to his reputation as a devasting puncher with none of his opponents succeeding in lasting the scheduled three rounds. He won the final with a second round KO of Soern Peterson of Denmark.

In 1921, after winning a second ABA title Rawson retired having been in top class amateur boxing for little more than a year. Since his first open contest as a novice in January 1920 he had taken part in 28 fights and won 27 of them by a KO. The other fight was won on points and the distinction of being the only man to last three rounds against Ronald Rawson goes to Harold Franks, the 1920 ABA light-heavyweight champion.

Spinks, *Terence George*

Born: 28 February 1938, West Ham, London

GOLD: 1956 (FLYWEIGHT)

It was the early ambition of East Londoner Terry Spinks to become a jockey and he gained his first ring experience in stable lads' competitions before going on to win the English Schoolboy's championship. In 1956, his first year of senior competition, he scored an exciting win in the flyweight division at the ABA championships and despite the fact that a number of selectors held the view that he was too young to be exposed to international competition, Spinks made the team for the Melbourne Olympics. In the Olympic final Spinks gave a classic display of boxing to outpoint Mircea Dobrescu, a hard-hitting Romanian, who was never quite quick enough to catch Spinks with his heavy punches.

Early in 1957, shortly after his 19th birthday, Spinks turned professional and in September 1960, in his 37th fight as a pro', he won the British featherweight title by defeating Bobby Neill in seven rounds. After successfully defending his title against Neill he lost the crown when forced to retire after ten rounds against Harold Winston in May 1961.

Thomas, *Henry*
Born: 1889, Birmingham, Warwickshire   Died: USA

GOLD: 1908 (BANTAMWEIGHT)

Within six months of taking up boxing, Harry Thomas of Birmingham BC was the Midlands bantamweight champion. After winning the 1908 ABA title, he reached that year's Olympic bantamweight final by defeating the Scottish champion, Frank McGurk, and then drawing a bye in the semi-finals. His opponent, John Condon of Lynn AC, qualified for the final with a KO against the only foreign entrant in the division, P Mazior of France, and then survived a hard semi-final against Bill Webb of St Pancras BC.

The rules for the 1908 Games provided that 'any boxer drawing a bye shall be bound to spar for the specified time with any opponent approved of by the judges and referee'. There is no evidence as to whether this condition was imposed on Thomas but he certainly entered the ring as the fresher of the two finalists. Condon, who was not noted for his aggression, surprisingly carried the fight to his opponent but after a gruelling contest it was Thomas who got the verdict.

Although Great Britain won all five boxing gold medals at the 1908 Games, Thomas was the only reigning ABA champion to succeed in winning an Olympic title. Harry Thomas turned professional in 1909 and, although he never fought for the British title, he produced some impressive performances and when he went to settle in America early in 1911 he took with him an unbeaten record. Apart from 1913, when he fought seven times in Australia, all his remaining fights were in the USA. Thomas retired from boxing in 1916 and became an American citizen. Following America's entry into the war in 1917 he served in the US Navy. He had six brothers, all of whom also served in the war with the British forces, his eldest brother, Bill, winning the DCM.

Harry Thomas paid a final visit to his home town of Birmingham in 1947 but then returned to America where he subsequently died.

Cricket

Beachcroft, *CBK*

GOLD: 1900

Beachcroft was the regular opening bat for Exeter but batted at No. 3 in the Olympic match. He played two solid innings in Paris, scoring 24 runs in the first innings and 54 in the second.

Birkett, *Arthur Ernest Burrington*
Born: 25 October 1875, St David, Exeter, Devon   Died: 1 April 1941, Hammersmith, London

GOLD: 1900

Arthur Birkett was educated at Blundell's School where he was in the cricket XI and later played for the Castle Cary club. Birkett captained the touring team which played at the 1900 Olympics.

Bowerman, *Alfred James*
Born: 22 November 1873, Broomfield, Bridgewater, Somerset   Died: 1959, Brisbane, Australia

GOLD: 1900

Having played one match as an amateur for Somerset in 1900, and another in 1905, the middle order batsman, Alfred Bowerman, was, together with Montague Toller, one of only two players in the 1900 Olympic team who played cricket at county level. A member of the Castle Cary club, he was top scorer in the Olympic match with 59 runs in the second innings.

Buckley, *George John*
Born: 1876

GOLD: 1900

Scoring only two runs and taking one catch, George Buckley did not feature prominently in the match in Paris.

Burchell, *Francis Romulus*

Born: 25 September 1873, Bristol, Gloucestershire   Died: 6 July 1947, Worthing, Sussex

GOLD: 1900

Francis Burchell's contribution to the English victory in Paris was minimal. He only batted in the first innings when he he scored 0 not out.

Christian, *Frederick William James*

Born: 1877   Died: 13 May 1941, Reading, Berkshire

GOLD: 1900

By taking seven wickets in the first innings, Frederick Christian played a significant part in the victory of the English touring team. After this success he surprisingly failed to take a wicket in the second innings.

Corner, *Harry Richard*

Born: 9 July 1874, Taunton, Somerset   Died: 7 June 1938, Radyr, Glamorgan

GOLD: 1900

Harry Corner was educated at Blundell's School and later played for Castle Cary. He was not one of the original selections for the Olympic match but was added to the team at the last minute after both teams had agreed to field twelve players each. He left his native Taunton quite early in life and became a partner in a firm of wool merchants in Wales.

Cuming, *Frederick William*

Born: 27 May 1875, Tiverton, Devon   Died: 22 March 1942, Kensington, London

GOLD: 1900

Frederick Cuming was educated at Blundell's School and later played for the Castle Cary club. With 38 runs he was top scorer in the first innings for the visitors.

Donne, *William Stephens*

Born: 2 April 1876, Wincanton, Somerset   Died: 24 March 1934, Castle Cary, Somerset

GOLD: 1900

On leaving King's School, Bruton, William Donne joined the family firm of rope and twine manufacturers which had been founded in Castle Cary in 1797.

For many years he played a leading role in civic affairs in Somerset and among the numerous appointments he held were those of Justice of the Peace, Alderman of the County Council and Governor of his old school. For a while he also held a regular commission in the Somerset Light Infantry.

William Donne was the founder of the Devon and Somerset County Wanderers, the touring side which represented Great Britain at cricket at the 1900 Olympic Games, but he was best known for his administrative work on behalf of rugby football. He was a committee member of the Somerset County Rugby Union for 38 years and served as the Hon. Secretary for nine years, immediately prior to being elected President in 1905. He represented Somerset on the Rugby Football Union committee from 1902 until he was was honoured by being elected President of the RFU for the year 1924–25. Donne's year of office coincided with the tour of the All Blacks during which Cyril Brownlie, the New Zealand back-row forward, became the first player to be sent off in an international match. The incident threatened the continuation of the tour but calm was restored as a result of Donne's tactful handling of the situation.

Powlesland, *Alfred James*

Born: 1875, Newton Abbott, Devon   Died: 25 February 1941, Newton Abbott, Devon

GOLD: 1900

As an opening bowler and batsman, Alfred Powlesland was a useful all rounder. In Paris, he failed to make a significant score in either innings but took five wickets in the match.

Symes, *John*

GOLD: 1900

John Symes opened the batting in both innings in Paris and scored the modest total of 16 runs. However, he had the foresight to bring home a scorecard of the match, completed in his own handwriting, and this valuable historical document is the only detailed record of the unique Olympic cricket match.

Toller, *Montague Henry*

Born: February 1871, Barnstable, Devon   Died: 5 August 1948, Meon Beach, Titchfield, Hampshire

GOLD: 1900

Montague Toller was in the cricket XI and the rugby XV at Blundell's School and his six matches for Somerset in 1897 as a middle order batsman and fast bowler made him the most experienced player in the Olympic team. Toller also played occasionally for Devon and, by taking seven wickets for nine runs- all of them clean bowled – in the second innings, he produced the finest individual performance of the match in Paris.

Cycling

Bartlett, *Charles Henry*

Born: 6 February 1885, London   Died: 30 November 1968, Enfield, Middlesex

GOLD: 1908 (100 KILOMETRES)

After two heats of the 1908 Olympic 100km event, the 43 competitors were reduced to 17 finalists with the favourite being Leon Meredith, the winner of the second heat and the reigning world champion at the distance. The final began with the track under water and heavy rain still falling and although the weather cleared after 30 minutes, the track remained in poor condition. There were many falls and punctures, one of which forced Meredith to withdraw. The 23-year-old Charles Bartlett, youngest of the finalists, also suffered his share of mishaps but his courageous riding eventually earned him the gold medal.

With some 30 kilometres remaining Bartlett fell and damaged his machine, he ran for a replacement and remounted but was stopped and ordered back to the point of his fall. Bartlett was, by now, almost a lap behind but he caught the field with one mile to go and somehow found the reserves to mount a sprint finish which brought him a memorable victory by two lengths.

Bartlett took up cycling in 1902 at the age of 16 with the Prince Alfred CC and won several club championships before moving to the Polytechnic CC. He won the NCU 50 miles tandem-paced title in 1908 and 1909 and broke several tandem-paced and motor-paced records. After his retirement, Bartlett built up a successful packing business but he maintained his interest in the sport and served as President of the Pickwick BC, England's premier bicycling club.

Johnson, *Victor Louis*

Born: 10 May 1883, Erdington, Warwickshire   Died: 29 June 1951, Sutton Coldfield, Warwickshire

GOLD: 1908 (660 YARDS)

Six of the 16 heats in the one-lap sprint at the 1908 Olympics were won by British riders but only Victor Johnson and Daniel Flynn survived the second round and qualified for the final. Johnson took the gold medal with a narrow victory over Emile Demangel of France and the following day he reached the final of the 1000 metres sprint. The race was declared void, as the riders exceeded the time limit of 105 seconds set by the judges but Johnson was already out of contention as he punctured early in the race.

Victor Johnson, who represented the Birmingham Rover CC, won a total of six NCU titles, including three in one day in 1911, and 11 days after his Olympic triumph he won the world amateur sprint championship in Leipzig. He also set three world and numerous British records and his best performance against the watch was a time of 28.0 seconds for the quarter-mile, standing start (unpaced) at Herne Hill in 1909. This remained a world record for 21 years until it was superseded by a slower time when the international regulations were changed.

Johnson, who worked as a carpenter and joiner, thus enjoyed a racing career that was in keeping with the family tradition. His father, Jack, a bicycle maker, had set the earliest recognised one hour record of 13 miles 600 yards on a high bicycle at Birmingham in 1870 and also made the first unicycles to be seen in Britain.

Jones, *Benjamin*

Born: 1882

GOLD: 1908 (5 KILOMETRES & TEAM PURSUIT)   SILVER: 1908 (20 KILOMETRES)

Competing in five separate events, involving a total of 11 races, the 1908 Olympic Games was a busy meeting for the Wigan collier, Ben Jones. However, with two gold medals and one silver, Jones proved to be Britain's most successful rider of the Games.

After taking second place in the 20km event, when he lost by the narrowest of margins to Clarrie Kingsbury, Jones joined Kingsbury, Leon Meredith and Ernie Payne to take the gold medals in the team pursuit. He then won his third medal, and his second gold, in the 5km and after finishing second to Maurice Schilles of France in the 1000 metres he was deprived of a fourth medal when the judges declared the race void after the pre-arranged time limit had been exceeded.

Two weeks before the Games, Ben Jones won the NCU 5 miles title and his post Olympic successes included a silver medal behind Victor Johnson in the 1908 world amateur sprint championship at Leipzig, a second victory in the NCU 5 miles championship in 1910 and four wins at the South African championships between 1911 and 1914.

Ben Jones began his cycling career with his local club in Wigan but he later based himself in the south and rode for Southwark CC and later Putney CC.

Britain's most successful Olympic cyclist – in 1908 Ben Jones won two gold medals and one silver.

Kingsbury, *Clarence Brickwood*

Born: 3 November 1882, Portsea Island, Hampshire   Died: 4 March 1949, Southsea, Hampshire

GOLD: 1908 (20 KILOMETRES & TEAM PURSUIT)

Clarrie Kingsbury of Portsmouth was a remarkably versatile cyclist. He won an NCU title every year from 1907 to 1912 at distances ranging from a quarter-mile to 50 miles and between these extremities he won the gold medal at 20km at the 1908 Olympic Games.

At the Olympics, the heats and final of the 20 km event were held on the same day and after winning the fastest of the heats, Kingsbury beat his team-mate, Ben Jones, by inches in the final. Three days later he won a second gold medal in the team pursuit. After the Olympics he went immediately to the World Championships in Leipzig and on his triumphant return to Portsmouth, Kingsbury was greeted by a vast crowd, estimated at 60 000, and honoured at a civic reception.

Clarrie Kingsbury began racing as a 12-year-old in schoolboy events and won his first open event at the age of 16. At the end of his long career he became a publican in Portsmouth which provided him with a suitable site for displaying his many valuable trophies which, it is said, his customers were constantly encouraged to admire.

After his Olympic victory one of his two infant daughters received Kingsbury's medal from the Queen. Both his daughters, Leonie and Thelma, were to become Britain's leading badminton players in the 1930s. Between 1932 and 1937 they each won the All England singles titles twice, collectively won five ladies' doubles but with different partners as they did not enjoy being paired together in major tournaments and in 1937 Thelma won the mixed doubles.

Lance, *Thomas Glasson*

Born: 14 June 1891, Paddington, London   Died: 29 February 1976, Brighton, Sussex

GOLD: 1920 (2000 METRES TANDEM)

Tommy Lance joined with his club-mate from Polytechnic CC, Harry Ryan, as a tandem pairing for the 1920 season. With Ryan steering and Lance riding behind, they set a new British quarter-mile record in June and faced the Olympic Games in Antwerp, some seven weeks later, with confidence. At the Olympics they beat a Dutch pairing in the semi-finals over a distance of 1200 metres and in the final, over 2000 metres, they covered the last 200 metres in 11.6 seconds for a comfortable victory over the South Africans.

Lance also competed in the match sprint in Antwerp but failed to reach the semi-finals and although he was an Olympic champion he never won an NCU title. After his active sporting days were over Tommy Lance became a bookmaker in Brighton.

Matthews, *Thomas John*

Born: 16 August 1884, Kensington, London   Died: 20 October 1969, Ashford, Kent

GOLD: 1906 (2000 METRES TANDEM)

At the time of the 1906 Olympics, Johnnie Matthews of Marlborough AC and Polytechnic CC and Arthur Rushen of Putney CC were a new and untried tandem pairing and their defeat of the well-atuned German brothers, Max and Bruno Gotze, was one of the surprises of the Games. The Olympic final was postponed by one day as the programme had fallen far behind schedule and the British pair objected to riding in semi-darkness. Their protest proved to be well justified as, in daylight, they beat the Germans by 20 yards.

On their return from Athens, Matthews and Rushen won the NCU tandem title, the only national championship that either of them ever won, and they set a number of British records. The best of these, a time of 49.2 seconds for the half-mile standing start (unpaced) remained on the books for many years. For the 1908 Olympics, Matthews teamed up with the great Leon Meredith and Rushen joined John Bernard, who later married Matthews' sister, but neither pairing reached the Olympic final. The partnership between Matthews and Meredith was not a happy one, they disagreed over tactics at the Olympics and at the world championships in Munich shortly after the Games, Meredith left Matthews without a ride when he withdrew from the tandem event in order to concentrate on the 100km race. At the last minute, GF Summers stood in for Meredith and Matthews and Summers took the world title, although the 1908 tandem event is not always recognised as an official world championship. Summers and Matthews had never ridden together before and were never to do so again.

After his retirement from cycling, Johnnie Matthews gave up his work as a carpenter and took over a cyclists tea house at Cippenham, near Slough, which became a popular meeting place for London club cyclists. He later became a publican in Kent before finally retiring in 1944.

Meredith, *Lewis Leon*

Born: 2 February 1882, St Pancras, London   Died: 27 January 1930, Davos, Switzerland

GOLD: 1908 (TEAM PURSUIT)   SILVER: 1912 (TEAM ROAD RACE)

Leon Meredith of Paddington CC was fortunate to enjoy the patronage of a wealthy uncle which enabled him to treat cycling as his sole occupation. He was provided with a full-time trainer, a personal pacing machine and many other facilities which were, and still are, quite beyond the means of the average amateur cyclist. His talents were seen in all the major cycling centres of Europe for almost a decade and he established a record by winning seven world championships in the amateur 100km motor-paced event. Meredith won first at Crystal Palace in 1904 and then at Antwerp (1905), Paris

(1907), Leipzig (1908), Copenhagen (1909), Rome (1911) and again at Leipzig in 1913.

It was expected that Meredith would be one of the outstanding riders at the 1908 Olympic Games but apart from his gold medal in the team pursuit he enjoyed little success. In the 20km he sustained a puncture in the first 100 yards, in the 100km he fell and later withdrew from the race and in the tandem event he and his partner, the 1906 Olympic champion, Johnnie Matthews, were eliminated in the semi-finals.

Meredith, who won seven NCU titles

at distances ranging from 5 to 50 miles, made a second Olympic appearance in 1912 but there was only one cycling race on the programme in Stockholm and the 320km road race was expected to be rather beyond his capabilities. Nevertheless, he finished fourth in the individual event and helped England take second place in the team event. At the age of 38, Meredith made the Olympic team for a third time in 1920 but he was by now well past his best and finished in 18th place in the 160km road race.

In 1912 Meredith acquired the patent rights to a new special type of racing tyre

and founded the Constrictor Tyre Company which was a huge financial success. In 1911 and 1912 he was the British amateur roller skating champion – a sport at which he subsequently turned professional – and in 1912 he built the Cricklewood Roller Skating Rink and later the Cricklewood Dance Hall. In 1913 he married Cissie Pinkham, the daughter of Mr. (later Sir) Charles Pinkham, Member of Parliament for West Willesden from 1924 to 1929.

Leon Meredith died of a heart attack while taking his annual winter holiday in Davos.

Payne, *Ernest*

Born: 23 December 1884, Worcester, Worcestershire   Died: 10 September 1961, Worcester, Worcestershire

GOLD: 1908 (TEAM PURSUIT)

Ernie Payne of Worcester St John's CC won the quarter-mile and 1 mile at the 1905 NCU championships, repeated the double in 1906 and in 1907 he won the 1 mile title for the third successive year. In

1908 he placed no better than fourth in the NCU 1 mile but three weeks later he won a gold medal in the team pursuit at the Olympic Games.

Payne was also an outstanding

footballer, winning a Birmingham League medal with Worcester City and playing 11 games for Manchester United, usually when the great Billy Meredith was on international duty.

Pett, *William James*

Born: 25 August 1873, St Peter, Derbyshire   Died: 27 December 1954, West Ewell, Surrey

GOLD: 1906 (20 KILOMETRES)

The 20km track race at the 1906 Olympics was a tandem-paced event and Billy Pett, who readily acknowledged his debt to the faultless pace-making of Johnnie Matthews and Arthur Rushen, won the gold medal with exactly half a minute to spare over the Frenchman, Maurice Bardonneau. Pett, who won three NCU titles at 50 miles, also competed in the Olympic road race in Athens and, in view of his NCU successes, was the favourite for the 84km event but he suffered a bad fall and failed to finish.

In addition to his Olympic gold medal and his NCU victories, Pett finished

second to Leon Meredith in the 100km at the 1904 World Championships but his greatest performance came at Herne Hill in September 1908 when he set a British tandem-paced record for one hour of 30 miles 1170 yards. This record withstood every attack for 20 years and it was not until 1928 that the great Frank Southall covered a greater distance inside the space of 60 minutes.

Billy Pett did not take up cycling until the age of 20 and in his early days he was associated with Southern CC and Putney AC before joining the Norwood Paragon club. Following his late start in the sport, Pett was aged 32 when he won his

Olympic gold medal and only the 38-year-old Maurice Peeters of Holland, the 1920 sprint champion, has won an Olympic cycling gold medal at a greater age.

Pett achieved all these successes despite the inhibitions imposed on him by his work. He was employed in the wine cellars at Harrods, a job that kept him on his feet from 8 a.m. to 7 p.m., and he was never able to get time off work to compete in mid-week evening meetings.

After he retired from competiton, Pett became a leading official and was one of the timekeepers at the 1948 Olympic Games.

Rushen, *Arthur*

GOLD: 1906 (2000 METRES TANDEM)

Following their Olympic victory in Athens, Arthur Rushen and Johnnie Matthews won the 1906 NCU tandem title. This was the only national championship that either Rushen or Matthews ever won, although together

they set numerous British tandem records.

In Athens, Rushen, a builders labourer who rode for Putney CC, also competed in the one-lap time trial, the 1000 metres, the 5km and the 20km but failed to place

in any of these events. He made a second Olympic appearance in 1908 when he teamed up with John Barnard for the tandem event but they were eliminated in the first round.

Ryan, *Harry Edgar*

Born: 21 November 1893, Euston, London   Died: 14 April 1961, Ealing, Middlesex

GOLD: 1920 (2000 METRES TANDEM)   BRONZE: 1920 (1000 METRES)

Harry Ryan, who was born 'over the shop' of the family business in the Euston Road, enjoyed a top-class cycling career which began in 1913 and lasted a full decade.

With this team-mate from the Polytechnic CC, Tommy Lance, Ryan steered the British pairing to victory in the tandem event at the 1920 Olympics and also won a bronze medal in the 1000

metres match sprint. Ryan won four NCU individual championships before the Antwerp Olympics and after the Games he

won the 1921 and 1922 tandem title with Tom Harvey of Catford CC as his partner.

After he retired, Harry Ryan developed the well-known family machine tool business of Buck & Ryan into a highly successful concern and became a prominent official in the cycling world, attending most of the major meetings at home and on the Continent.

Harry Ryan, who won the 1920 tandem event with Tommy Lance. They were the last British cyclists to win an Olympic gold medal.

Equestrian
MEN

Allhusen, *Derek Swithen*

Born: 9 January 1914, Chelsea, London

GOLD: 1968 (THREE-DAY EVENT – TEAM)   SILVER: 1968 (THREE-DAY EVENT – INDIVIDUAL)

Derek Allhusen made his Olympic debut in 1948 when he placed sixth in the Pentathlon, included in the Winter Games at St Moritz as a demonstration event. Twenty years later, the 54-year-old Allhusen, supported by Jane Bullen, Ben Jones and Richard Meade, led the British team to victory in the three-day event at the Mexico Olympics. He also won a silver medal in the individual event.

Allhusen's first international success

came at Copenhagen in 1957 when, riding Laurien, he was a member of the winning British team at the European Championships. He later rode Lochinvar at all the major events, including the 1968 Olympics and the European Championships in 1967 and 1969 when Great Britain won the team event.

Educated at Eton, Le Rosey and Trinity College, Cambridge, Major Allhusen served in the 9th Lancers but left the Army in 1937 to marry the Hon.

Claude Betterton. He rejoined his regiment in 1938 and competed at the International Horse Show at Olympia and at the Dublin Horse Show in 1939.

After he retired from the Army and from competitive eventing, Derek Allhusen concentrated on breeding and training top-class horses on his Norfolk estate with Lauriston, on which Richard Meade won the gold medal at the 1972 Olympics, coming from his stable.

Hill, *Albert Edwin*

Born: 7 February 1927, Devon

GOLD: 1956 (THREE-DAY EVENT – TEAM)

Bertie Hill, a West Country farmer and Devon's point-to-point champion, began his Olympic career at Helsinki in 1952 when he placed seventh in the individual three-day event. At the European Championships he won gold medals in both the individual and team events in

1954 and gained his third European gold in the 1955 team event.

At Stockholm in 1956, Hill won an Olympic gold in the three-day team event and placed 12th individually. In 1960 he was again a member of the Olympic team and became the first British rider to

compete in three Olympic Games. Hill was appointed the first official trainer of the British team in 1967 and guided them to a host of international successes. His son, Anthony, was a member of the British team which won the European Junior Championships in 1972.

Jones, *Reuben Samuel*

Born: 19 October 1932, Newport, Shropshire   Died: 3 January 1990, Melton Mowbray, Leicestershire

GOLD: 1968 (THREE-DAY EVENT – TEAM)

At Tokyo in 1964, Sergeant Ben Jones of the Royal Army Veterinary Corps became the first NCO to represent Great Britain in the Olympic equestrian events. At the Tokyo Games, Britain were eliminated in the team event but individually Jones finished a commendable ninth.

Four years later in Mexico City, Jones improved to place fifth in the individual event and won a gold medal in the team event. He was a regular member of the British team and won gold medals at the European Championships in 1967 and 1969. For many years, Ben Jones was the

staff sergeant in charge of equitation of the King's Troop of the Royal Horse Artillery at St John's Wood and on being commissioned he took charge of training of the remount depot at Melton Mowbray.

It was there that Captain Ben Jones died whilst schooling a young horse.

Llewellyn, *Henry Morton, OBE*   (Later Sir HM Llewellyn, Bt., CBE.)

Born: 18 July 1911, Merthyr Tydfil, Glamorganshire

GOLD: 1952 (PRIX DES NATIONS – TEAM)   BRONZE: 1948 (PRIX DES NATIONS – TEAM)

Harry Llewellyn, educated at Oundle and Trinity College, Cambridge, was a well-known steeplechase jockey in pre-war days, his greatest success coming in 1936 when, while still an undergraduate, he finished second in the Grand National riding his father's horse Ego. He rode Ego again at Aintree the following year and finished fourth. The war soon followed and Llewellyn saw action in Italy and Normandy and he was awarded the OBE for his work as Field Marshall Montgomery's chief liaison officer.

After the war, Lt. Col. Harry Llewellyn was a leading figure in the business world of South Wales and he

gave his time unsparingly to all equestrian causes. At various times he was a Steward of the National Hunt Committee and Chairman of the British Show Jumping Association and in 1969 he was elected a Steward of the Jockey Club. In 1953 he was awarded a CBE and, after being knighted in 1977 for his services to Wales, he succeeded to the Baronetcy the following year on the death of his elder brother.

In show jumping circles Llewellyn's name is inextricably linked with that of his horse, Foxhunter. The famous pairing represented Great Britain no less than 35 times with the performance which most

captured the public imagination coming in the final round of the show jumping event at the 1952 Olympics. After a near-disastrous first round, Llewellyn was under extreme pressure but he took Foxhunter through a faultless round and Great Britain won her only gold medals of the Helsinki Games. Unfortunately, certain uninformed sections of the British press tended to view this success in a team event as an individual victory for Foxhunter and his rider and Wilf White and Duggie Stewart, who both had less faults than Llewellyn throughout the competition, were not always given their due.

Meade, *Richard John Hannay*

Born: 4 December 1938, Chepstow, Monmouthshire

GOLD: 1968 (THREE-DAY EVENT – TEAM)   1972 (THREE-DAY EVENT – INDIVIDUAL & THREE-DAY EVENT – TEAM)

Richard Meade is Britain's most successful Olympic equestrian competitor. He is the only British rider to have won an individual Olympic gold medal and his total of three gold medals is also the best by a Briton. Meade's Olympic victories came in the three-day team event in 1968 and 1972 and in the individual event in 1972. He also competed in the 1964 and 1976 Olympics when he matched David Broome's record of being the only British rider to compete in four Olympic Games. However, Broome reclaimed the record as his own in 1988 when he took part in his fifth Olympics.

Apart from his Olympic successes, Meade was a member of the winning team at the 1967 European Championships and the 1970 World Championships and placed second individually in the 1967 and 1970 World Championships. He also won at Badminton in 1969 and 1970.

Meade, whose parents were Joint-Masters of the Corre Hounds in Monmouthshire, was educated at Lancing and Magdalen College, Cambridge, where he took an engineering degree. After Cambridge he served in the 11th Hussars and later worked in the City.

Richard Meade seated on Lauriesten after winning individual and team gold in the three-day event at the 1972 Games.

Phillips, *Mark Anthony Peter*

Born: 22 September 1948, Cirencester, Gloucestershire

GOLD: 1972 (THREE-DAY EVENT –TEAM)   SILVER: 1988 (THREE-DAY EVENT – TEAM)

Captain Mark Phillips of the 1st Queen's Dragoon Guards was educated at Marlborough and the RMC Sandhurst. After being selected as a reserve for the 1968 Olympics, his first major success came in 1970 when he was a member of the British three-day event team which won the World Championship in Chicago. The following year he was on the winning team at the European championships and in 1972 he won an Olympic gold medal in Munich. He competed in the Olympics for a second time in 1988 and although forced to withdraw before the cross-country stage because his horse sustained a pulled muscle, he won a silver medal as the fourth member of the team.

In 1973 Captain Phillips married HRH The Princess Anne but they subsequently separated. In 1974, he was appointed a Commander of the Victorian Order.

Rook, *Arthur Laurence, MC*

Born: 26 May 1921, Ednalton, Nottinghamshire   Died: 30 September 1989, Guy's Hospital, London

GOLD: 1956 (THREE-DAY EVENT – TEAM)

At the 1952 Olympics, Major Rook failed to finish in the three-day event but the following year he won gold medals in both the individual and the team events at the European Championships. On his second Olympic appearance in 1956, Rook placed sixth in the individual competition and was the second scoring member of the British team which won the gold medals in the three-day event.

After attending Oakham School and Brackley College, Laurence Rook served initially with the Maritime Artillery, which provided gunners for merchant ships, and when that regiment was disbanded in 1942 he joined the Royal Horse Guards, serving in Egypt and Italy where he won a Military Cross in 1944. After his retirement from the Army in 1954, he farmed first in Sussex and later in Gloucestershire and took an active part in the administration of the sport. He was the technical delegate of the International Equestrian Federation at the 1959 Pan-American Games in Chicago and at the Olympic Games in Tokyo, Mexico and Montreal. He also served as chairman of Britain's Horse Trials Committee from 1973 to 1980.

Major Laurence Rook's Olympic gold medal is on display at the Household Cavalry Museum at Windsor.

Stewart, *Douglas Norman*

Born: 24 June 1913

GOLD: 1952 (PRIX DES NATIONS – TEAM)

Major Duggie Stewart made his Olympic debut in 1948 in the three-day event but was eliminated after his horse pulled up lame in the cross-country stage. By 1952, Stewart had switched from eventing to show jumping and at the Helsinki Olympics won a gold medal in the team event and placed 14th in the individual competition.

Duggie Stewart was educated at Rugby and later commanded the Royal Scots Greys. On retiring from the Army he became a farmer.

Weldon, *Francis William Charles, MC*

Born: 2 August 1913, Bombay, India

GOLD: 1956 (THREE-DAY EVENT – TEAM)   BRONZE: 1956 (THREE-DAY EVENT – INDIVIDUAL)

Lt. Col. Frank Weldon had an outstanding record at the European Championships. He was a member of the winning team in the three-day event in 1953, 1954 and 1955 and after placing second in the individual competition in 1953 and 1954 he won the individual title in 1955 before again placing second in 1959.

At the 1956 Olympics, Weldon became the first British rider to win an individual Olympic equestrian medal and in addition to his bronze in the individual three-day event he won a gold medal in the team competition. Weldon would almost certainly have won the individual gold medal had he not insisted, as team captain, on a policy of strict caution in the cross-country section.

At the 1955 European Championships and at the 1956 Olympics, Frank Weldon was riding his own horse, Kilbarry, whom he had ridden earlier in the Queen's Coronation procession when he commanded the King's Troop of the Royal Horse Artillery. An Irish-bred, grey gelding, Kilbarry is almost certainly the only horse to have won international fame while still doing full daily duty as an officer's charger in a cavalry regiment.

Weldon made a second Olympic appearance in 1960 when he finished 25th individually and the British placed fourth in the team event.

Frank Weldon was educated at Wellington and the Royal Military College and won his colours in the rugby XV both at school and at Sandhurst. After he retired from the Army and from equestrian competition he continued to make a great contribution to the sport. He served as Director of the Badminton Horse Trials from 1966 to 1988 after having been asked, in 1964, to design the Badminton cross-country course. He was also a council member of the British Horse Society and was the equestrian correspondent of the *Sunday Telegraph* for many years.

White, *Wilfred Harry*

Born: 30 March 1904, Nantwich, Cheshire

GOLD: 1952 (PRIX DES NATIONS – TEAM)   BRONZE: 1956 (PRIX DES NATIONS – TEAM)

In 1964, Wilf White purchased Nizefella and the following year they scored their first major win together at Shrewsbury. At Nice in 1949 they made their debut in the British team and over the next ten years Wilf White and Nizefella were members of 12 winning Prix des Nations teams.

At the 1952 Olympics in Helsinki they won a gold medal in the team event and only lost the individual title after a jump-off. Four years later in Stockholm, White and Nizefella won a bronze medal in the team event and again placed fourth in the individual competition. At both the 1952 and 1956 Olympics, White was the highest placed of the British show jumpers in the individual classification.

Wilf White, a Cheshire farmer, was a member of the executive committee of the British Show Jumping Association and in 1958 he was awarded an OBE for his services to the sport.

Equestrian
WOMEN

Bullen, *Jane Mary Elizabeth*   (Later Mrs Holderness-Roddam)

Born: 7 January 1948, Bridport, Dorset

GOLD: 1968 (THREE-DAY EVENT – TEAM)

Educated by a private governess until the age of 14 when she entered Westwing School, Bristol, Jane Bullen later became a qualified SRN. In 1968 she was given special leave from her nursing studies at Middlesex Hospital to compete in the Olympic Games. In Mexico she became the first British woman to take part in an Olympic three-day event placing 18th individually but failing to score for the winning British team.

Earlier in 1968 Jane Bullen had won the Badminton Trials where, as at the Olympics, she rode her favourite horse, the diminutive Our Nobby.

As Mrs Holderness-Roddam she won the Burghley Trials in 1976 and ten years after her first success, she won Badminton for a second time in 1978. In later years she served the sport well as an administrator and was chairman of the selectors for the British three-day event team.

Her sister, Jenny Loriston-Clarke, competed in four Olympics in the dressage events.

Gordon-Watson, *Mary Diana*

Born: 3 April 1948, Blandford, Dorset

GOLD: 1972 (THREE-DAY EVENT – TEAM)

Mary Gordon-Watson's first major international success came in 1969 when she won the individual three-day event at the European Championships. Gold medals followed in both the individual and team event at the 1970 World Championships and in 1971 she was a member of the winning team at the European Championships. After coming close to winning a bronze in the individual competition, Mary Gordon-Watson crowned her career with a team gold medal at the 1972 Olympics.

In all her European, World and Olympic successes Mary Gordon-Watson was riding her father's horse Cornishman V which had been loaned to Richard Meade for the 1968 Olympics. In 1973 Cornishman V made his final public appearance in the film *Dead Cert*, an adaptation of the Dick Francis novel, when he was ridden by Lord Oaksey.

After her retirement, Mary Gordon-Watson became a well-known equestrian teacher and in 1976 was appointed a member of the senior selection committee for the British equestrian team.

Parker, *Bridget M*

Born: 5 January 1939, Northumberland

GOLD: 1972 (THREE-DAY EVENT – TEAM)

Bridget Parker went to the Munich Olympics as a travelling reserve and was only called into the three-day event team at the last moment after Debbie West's horse went lame. She placed 10th individually and was the third scoring member of the winning British team.

Educated at St Mary's Convent, Ascot, in 1959 married an Army officer whose overseas postings often interrupted her early equestrian career. In 1968 her husband left the Army to settle in Somerset and Bridget Parker was able to resume regular competition.

Fencing
WOMEN

Sheen, *Gillian Mary* (Later Mrs Donaldson)
Born: 21 August 1928, Willesden, London

GOLD: 1956 (INDIVIDUAL FOIL)

Since 1906, when the first British Olympic fencing team arrived in Athens aboard Lord Howard De Walden's private yacht, until 1956, Britain could claim six silver medals in Olympic fencing events; for three successive Games (1906–1912) the men finished second in the team épée and then Gladys Davis (1924), Muriel Freeman (1928) and Judy Guinness (1932) won three successive silver medals in the women's individual foil. In 1956, 50 years after first competing in the Olympic fencing programme, Britain finally won a gold medal due to the efforts of Gillian Sheen, a 28-year-old dental surgeon from University College Hospital, London.

Gillian Sheen first took up the sport at North Foreland School in Kent and won the British Schoolgirls title in 1945, the British Junior Championship in 1947 and her first British senior title in 1949. On leaving school, she attended London University, winning the British Universities title for five years and a gold

medal at the World Universities Championships in 1951.

She made her Olympic debut in 1952 and was eliminated in the second round but four years later in Melbourne she was the surprise winner of the gold medal. She edged into the final by defeating the world champion, Lydia Domolki of Hungary, in a barrage to decide the fourth place in her semi-final pool. In the final Sheen lost her

Gillian Sheen, who in 1956 became the only Briton to win a gold medal for fencing.

first bout to Olga Orban of Rumania but won her other six bouts to finish equal first with the Rumanian. The gold medal was decided on a barrage between these two and as Orban had already beaten the English girl in the opening bout of the final pool the Rumanian started as favourite. However, Sheen quickly moved into a 3-1 lead and although Orban pulled back to 3-2, in a decisive attack Sheen scored another hit to win 4-2.

Gillian Sheen went on to win the British Empire and Commonwealth title in 1958 and in 1960 she won her tenth and final British championship. Later in 1960 she competed in her third Olympics in Rome when she was eliminated in the second round. Britain's only Olympic fencing gold medallist continued competitive fencing until 1963 and then, as Mrs Donaldson, she settled in New York where she joined her husband in a dental practice.

Hockey

Atkin, *Charles Sydney*
Born: 26 February 1889, Sheffield, Yorkshire   Died: 9 May 1958, Sheffield, Yorkshire

GOLD: 1920

While at Marlborough College, Charles Atkin failed to command a regular place in the school hockey XI but on going up to Caius College, Cambridge, he won a blue and played at right-back against Oxford in 1909 and 1910. On leaving Cambridge, Atkin went on to St Bartholomew's Hospital and as a medical student he played for Beckenham and Kent and

represented England three times in 1913. He served in the war as a captain in the RAMC after which he followed his father, grandfather and great-grandfather into the family medical practice in Sheffield. After Charles Atkin's death, his son took over the practice to take the family connection into the fifth generation.

After playing at left-back in the 1920

Olympics, Atkin made his eighth and final international appearance against Ireland in 1921. Apart from his accomplishments as a hockey player, Charles Atkin was a fine all-round sportsman. He represented the Hallamshire club at lawn tennis for many years and was also an enthusiastic angler and shot.

Baillon, *Louis Charles*
Born: 5 August 1881, Fox Bay, Falkland Islands   Died: 2 September 1965, Brixworth, Northamptonshire

GOLD: 1908

Louis Baillon's father was a native of Nottingham who emigrated to the Falklands to become a sheep farmer. He married there in 1876 and Louis was the second of five children born on the Islands. Although the Crown Grant issued

to the Baillon family in 1885 for a farm known as Fox Bay West was not conveyed to the Falkland Islands Company by Louis Baillon until 1939, he had returned to England as a youth. He settled in Northampton and was married there in

1910. The marriage produced one daughter and four sons, two of whom were killed in the Battle of Britain. Baillon enjoyed a successful business career, becoming a director of Phipps Brewery.

Louis Baillon was an outstanding

sportsman. He played hockey for Northampton and won nine caps for England at left-back, he played football for Wandsworth AFC and, at the age of 50, he still held his place in the Northants county lawn tennis team.

Barber, *Paul Jason*

Born: 21 May 1955, Peterborough, Cambridgeshire

GOLD: 1988   BRONZE: 1984

Paul Barber, educated at King's School, Peterborough, won 99 caps for England and played 67 times for Great Britain at left-back. For England he won a bronze medal in the European Cup in 1978 and silver medals in the 1986 World Cup and the 1987 European Cup. He was selected for the Great Britain team for three Olympics but missed making his Olympic debut in 1980 due to the boycott of the Moscow Games. After winning a bronze medal at Los Angeles in 1984, Barber was vice-captain of the team which won gold in 1988. He played in all seven of Britain's matches in Seoul and, as the corner striker, scored in each of the first five matches. Paul Barber, a quantity surveyor who played for Slough, is considered to be one of the best defenders in world hockey.

Batchelor, *Stephen James*

Born: 22 June 1961, Beare Green, Dorking, Surrey

GOLD: 1988   BRONZE: 1984

In 1980, shortly after leaving Millfield School, Stephen Batchelor made his international debut for England as a 19-year-old. He went on to play 48 times for England winning silver medals in the 1986 World Cup and the 1987 European Cup.

Batchelor, who played for Southgate, represented Great Britain 66 times, winning an Olympic bronze medal in 1984 and a gold in 1988. At the Seoul Olympics, he either started or came on as a substitute in all seven matches but despite his reputation as a striker he failed to score in the tournament.

Bennett, *John Hadfield*

Born: 11 August 1885, Chorlton, Lancashire   Died: 27 May 1973, Budleigh Salterton, Devon

COLD: 1920

John Bennett was educated at Harrow, where he made the football XI, and then went up to Magdalene College, Oxford, where he won a hockey blue in 1907 and 1908. After graduating, he played for Hampstead and Surrey and was called to the Bar of the Inner Temple in 1911. He made the first of his 34 appearances at right-back for England that year but, despite being wounded while serving with the Royal Warwickshire Regiment, the majority of his international honours came after the war.

An all-round sportsman, Bennett represented Magdalene at cricket, association football, rugby football and hockey, played cricket for Berkshire and had a golf handicap of five.

Bhaura, *Kulbir Singh*

Born: 15 October 1955, Jullundur, India

GOLD: 1988   BRONZE: 1984

The only match in which Kulbir Bhaura did not take part at the Seoul Olympics in 1988 was that against his native India.

Bhaura, centre-forward for Hounslow and the Indian Gymkhana, won 84 caps for England and 61 for Great Britain. After winning an Olympic bronze medal in 1984, he was a member of the England squad which won silver medals at the 1986 World Cup and the 1987 European Cup.

Cassels, *Harold Kennedy*

Born: 4 November 1898, Paoling, China   Died: 23 January 1975, Taunton, Somerset

GOLD: 1920

Born of missionary parents in the Far East, where his father became the first Bishop of West China, Harold Cassels, was sent to England for his schooling. At St Lawrence College, Ramsgate, Cassels became school captain, football and hockey team captains and vice-captain of cricket. He left St Lawrence in the spring of 1917 and enlisted as a pilot in the Royal Flying Corps. He was mentioned in despatches at the age of 19 before becoming a prisoner of war.

In 1919 Cassels entered Queen's College, Cambridge, where he won a hockey blue playing against Oxford at left-half in 1920 and centre-half in 1921. It was during this period that he joined the England squad for the 1920 Olympic

Games, the only time he was selected to play at international level.

On graduating from Cambridge, Cassels returned to China and became the senior master at the Cathedral School in Shanghai before leaving for Australia in 1940. He returned to England in 1946 and spent two years lecturing troops in the Middle East before becoming a housemaster at Millfield School.

Clift, *Robert John*

Born: 1 August 1962, Newport, Monmouthshire

GOLD: 1988

Robert Clift, who was educated at Bablake School and Nottingham University, won the first of his 75 England caps in 1982 and was a member of the team which won silver medals in the 1986 World Cup and the 1987 European Cup. He also played 52 times for Great Britain, winning a gold medal at the 1988 Olympics in Seoul.

Clift was a member of the Southgate club when he won his Olympic gold medal but moved to East Grinstead for the 1989 season. A bank official by profession, he plays at inside-forward or mid-field.

Cooke, *Harold Douglas*

GOLD: 1920

Harold Cooke's international experience was limited to four caps for England, including the two matches he played at the 1920 Olympic tournament in Antwerp. He played for Warwickshire and graduated from Birmingham University in 1920 with a degree in metallurgy.

The only known photograph of England's winning hockey team in 1920. Left to right: CSW Marcon, JH Bennett, HE Haslam, CTA Wilkinson, RW Crummack, HK Cassels, SH Shoveller (captain), HD Cooke, GF McGrath, WF Smith, AF Leighton, EB Crockford, CS Atkin, unknown official, JCW McBryan, unknown official.

Crockford, *Eric Bertram*

Born: 13 October 1888, Wylde Green, Warwickshire   Died: 17 January 1958, Sutton Coldfield, Warwickshire

GOLD: 1920

After leaving Eastbourne College, Eric Crockford returned to his native Warwickshire where he later practised as a solicitor. He played hockey for Sutton Coldfield and Warwickshire and won the first of his 17 international caps in 1920. Crockford was also an accomplished cricketer, playing 21 first-class matches for Warwickshire as a middle-order batsman between 1911 and 1922.

Crummack, *Reginald William*

Born: 16 February 1887, Salford, Lancashire   Died: 25 October 1966, Stockport, Cheshire

GOLD: 1920

On leaving Rossall School, Rex Crummack trained in the cotton business in London, during which time he played football for Middlesex. On his return home, he joined St Anne's Hockey Club in 1908 and represented Lancashire for the first time that year. He played football, hockey and golf for the North but his career as fine all-round sportsman was interrupted by the war, during which he was mentioned in despatches while serving as a captain in the Prince of Wales Volunteers (South Lancs).

In addition to playing for St Anne's, Crummack also represented Alderly

Edge, and won five caps for England between 1913 and 1926. In 1920, at the age of 33, he won an Olympic gold medal as an inside-forward.

Although he became an international hockey selector in 1931, Rex Crummack's main sporting interest was as a golfer. As a successful cotton broker he had the time to play frequently and as a member of the Royal Lytham St Anne's Golf Club he was the amateur champion of Lancashire three times. Crummack was a regular competitor in the Amateur Championship beating the defending champion, John Ball, in 1911 and reaching the quarter-finals in 1925. As he first played in the Amateur Championship in 1909 and made his last appearance in 1946, Crummack holds the incredible record of being the only man to compete in the Championship both before World War I and after World War II.

Not surprisingly, he was an outstanding figure in the amateur golfing world and in 1953 he was appointed to the General Committee of the Royal & Ancient.

Dodds, *Richard David Allan, OBE*

Born: 23 February 1959, York, Yorkshire

GOLD: 1988   BRONZE: 1984

After learning the game at the notable hockey nursery of Kingston Grammar School, Richard Dodds went on to win the highest honours. He won a Cambridge blue while attending St Catherine's College and also played for St Thomas's Hospital. After winning an Olympic bronze medal in 1984 and silver medals at the 1986 World Cup and 1987 European Cup, the highlight of his career came when he captained the British team to victory at the 1988 Olympics.

Dodds, a mid-field player with Southgate, won 79 caps for England, played 65 times for Great Britain and was awarded the OBE for his services to hockey. Today he is a surgeon at St Peter's Hospital, Chertsey.

Faulkner, *David Andrew Vincent*

Born: 10 September 1963, Portsmouth, Hampshire

GOLD: 1988

David Faulkner formed a formidable full-back pairing with Paul Barber and they played alongside each other in every one of Britain's seven matches in Seoul at the 1988 Olympics. In the same year, Faulkner was voted 'Player of the Year' by the Hockey Writer's Club, finishing one vote ahead of Sean Kerly and Richard Dodds in the balloting. Apart from his Olympic gold medal, Faulkner won silver medals in the 1986 World Cup and the 1987 European Cup. In 1988 he also led his club, Havant, to second place in the National League and to the semi-finals of the Hockey Association Cup.

After making his England debut against West Germany in 1982 and first playing for Great Britain the following year, Faulkner went on to win 69 caps for Great Britain and 81 for England.

Freeman, *Harry Scott*

Born: 7 February 1876, Staines, Middlesex   Died: 5 October 1968, Bourne End, Buckinghamshire

GOLD: 1908

As a young man, Harry Freeman's main sporting interests centred around the river sports to be found in his home town of Staines and he did not take up hockey until 1894 when he was 18 years old. Despite this rather late start he showed a remarkable aptitude for the game and soon commanded a place in the Staines team. It later became apparent that the Freeman family had an unusual talent for hockey, Harry being the first of five brothers who played for Staines between 1894 and 1922 and his son, Robert, played nine times for England.

Freeman first played for England in 1903 and, although he was not a regular choice at full-back, won a total of ten caps never being on the losing side.

Following his successful captaincy of Staines, Middlesex and the South he was chosen to captain England at the 1908 Olympics when England were comfortable winners. He was also selected to represent England at bandy at the 1908 Games but the event was abandoned due to the lack of any foreign-entries.

After the 1908 Olympics, Harry Freeman retired from international hockey but continued to captain Staines and Middlesex until after the war. He later became a member of the International Hockey Board and served as the Honorary Treasurer of the Hockey Association for many years.

Despite his successes at hockey, Freeman never forsook his love of the river and in 1897 he won the Amateur Doubles Punting Championship of the Thames with EHH Green as his partner. As a solicitor, his services were much in demand by many sporting bodies which had an affiliation with the Thames; at various times he served as Captain of the Staines Boat Club, Honorary Secretary of the Thames Amateur Rowing Association, President of the Thames United Sailing Club, Commodore of the Upper Thames Sailing Club and Honorary Secretary of the Sailing Boat Association.

Garcia, *Russell Simon*

Born: 20 June 1970, Portsmouth, Hampshire

GOLD: 1988

The 18-year-old Portsmouth hairdresser, Russell Garcia, is the youngest hockey player ever to have represented Great Britain. A mid-field player with Havant, Garcia came on as a replacement in three of the preliminary round matches in Seoul but did not play in the semi-final or the final.

Although his playing career is still in its relative infancy he has played 32 times for Great Britain and represented England 28 times.

Green, *Eric Hubert*

Born: 28 August 1878, Epsom, Surrey   Died: 23 December 1972, Stanford Dingley, Berkshire

GOLD: 1908

On leaving St Mark's School, Windsor, Eric Green joined the Staines club and played at outside-left for their unbeaten team for several seasons. He won 16 caps for England between 1902 and 1908 and after his playing days were over became hockey correspondent of *The Times*.

Grimley, *Martyn Andrew*

Born: 24 January 1963, Halifax, Yorkshire

GOLD: 1988

Martyn Grimley, a Hounslow mid-field player, made his international debut in 1984 and won silver medals in the 1986 World Cup and 1987 European Cup. He played in all seven matches at Seoul in the 1988 Olympic Games and has won 60 caps for England, 40 for Great Britain and also represented England in 40 indoor international matches. He is currently a schoolmaster at Dulwich College.

Haslam, *Harry Eustace*

Born: 7 February 1883, Aston, Worcestershire   Died: 7 February 1955, Ilford, Essex

GOLD: 1920

Harry Haslam started his representative hockey career with Worcestershire but moved south in 1905 and for many years, both before and after the war, was goalkeeper for Ilford, Essex and the East. He won the first of nine England caps in 1920 and was awarded the OBE the same year for his work with the Special Constabulary. Haslam worked for a firm of sports goods manufacturers and toured the country with the first-ever hockey instructional film. He held numerous posts as an administrator of the game and wrote regularly for the *News Chronicle*. He died on his 72nd birthday.

Kerly, *Sean Robin*

Born: 29 January 1960, Herne Bay, Kent

GOLD: 1988   BRONZE: 1984

After scoring seven goals for Britain's bronze medal winning team in Los Angeles in 1984, striker Sean Kerly went one better with eight goals at the 1988 Olympics in Seoul. Kerly also won silver medals at the 1986 World Cup and the 1987 European Cup and was a member of the Southgate team which won the English Club Championship in 1987 and 1988.

In his 74 matches for Great Britain he scored 57 goals and also played for England in 58 outdoor and nine indoor internationals. Extensive television coverage focused attention on his scoring

feats and, unusually for a hockey player, he became one of Britain's best known sportsmen. The strictly amateur nature of the game precluded Kerly from benefiting financially from the publicity and shortly before the 1988 Olympics he lost his job as a buyer for a fashion chain due to the demands made on his time by training and competition. The necessity of earning a living, coupled with a certain loss of form, eventually obliged him to take a break from international hockey, although he continues to play for Southgate in the National League.

Striker Sean Kerly whose eight goals in Seoul helped Britain to the 1988 gold medals.

Kirkwood, *James W*

Born: 12 February 1962, Lisburn, Northern Ireland

GOLD: 1988

Jimmy Kirkwood did not play in a complete match but came on as a replacement against South Korea and India at the 1988 Seoul Games.

As a forward with the Lisnagarvey club he was capped 48 times by Ireland and played 31 times for Great Britain.

Leighton, *Arthur Francis, MC*

Born: 6 March 1889, Esk, Queensland, Australia   Died: 15 June 1939, Walsall, Warwickshire

GOLD: 1920

Australian-born Arthur Leighton was the first pupil from Bishop's Stortford College to win a hockey blue. After going up to Caius College, Cambridge, he played against Oxford in 1908, 1909 and 1910 and captained the Cambridge team in his final year. While at Caius, Leighton made his international debut in 1909, going on to win 27 England caps.

During the war, Leighton won a Military Cross as a lieutenant in the Royal Field Artillery and despite being severely gassed continued to play top class sport after the war. Although playing occasionally for Hampstead, he was the regular centre-forward for Walsall and the East Midlands and won his final England cap in 1921. On giving up the sport in 1927 he was appointed an England selector.

After his war service, Arthur Leighton took up a post with AS Smith & Sons, a firm of hardware manufacturers in Walsall, of which he later became a director.

Leman, *Richard Alexander*

Born: 13 July 1959, East Grinstead, Sussex

GOLD: 1988   BRONZE: 1984

After attending Gresham's School in Norfolk, Richard Leman returned to Sussex and joined the local club in his home town of East Grinstead where he developed into an outstanding forward. In the 1990 World Cup in Lahore he became England's most capped player when he played in his 106th match, thereby surpassing Norman Hughes' record of 105 caps. He also represented Great Britain 70 times and won 40 further caps for England in indoor internationals. After the 1990 World Cup he retired having amassed a record total of 216 selections for international matches.

Apart from winning bronze and gold medals at the 1984 and 1988 Olympics, Leman also won silver medals at the 1986 World Cup and the 1987 European Cup.

Logan, *Gerald*

Born: 29 December 1879, Copse Hill, Wimbledon, Surrey

GOLD: 1908

At Kingston Grammar School, Gerald Logan and Stanley Shoveller were contemporaries. Logan played at inside-right and Shoveller at centre-forward and their close understanding of each other's play took them from the school XI into the Hampstead, Surrey and England teams together. They were team-mates at the 1908 Olympic Games and with Logan scoring five goals and Shoveller seven, between them they accounted for exactly half the 24 goals scored by England in their three matches in the Olympic tournament. Logan played nine times for England before emigrating in 1909.

McBryan, *John Crawford William*

Born: 22 July 1892, Box, Wiltshire   Died: 14 July 1983, Cambridge, Cambridgeshire

GOLD: 1920

After a brief spell at Cheltenham College, Jack McBryan attended Exeter School and the RMC Sandhurst, where he earned a reputation as an outstanding cricketer, rugby footballer and hockey player. While still at Sandhurst he made his debut as a county cricketer for Somerset in 1911. He was commissioned into the Prince Albert's Somerset Light Infantry in 1912 but on his 21st birthday resigned his commission and enrolled at St Bartholomew's Hospital with the intention of following his father as a doctor. The war soon interrupted his medical studies and after rejoining his regiment, McBryan had the misfortune to be taken prisoner in France just three weeks after the outbreak of hostilities.

After the war, McBryan went up to Jesus College, Cambridge, and won a cricket blue in 1920. Although he also played hockey for Cambridge he was not selected for the match against Oxford. The 1920 Olympic Games was the only occasion that he played hockey at international level. Apart from his obvious cricket and hockey talents he was an accomplished golfer, playing to a handicap of four at Sunningdale and at Prince's Club, Sandwich, and also played rugby for Richmond. McBryan represented Somerset at all four sports but cricket was undoubtedly his main love.

On leaving Cambridge, he served for two years as the private secretary to Sir Francis Towle but then took a job on the Stock Exchange which did not interfere with his cricketing summers. He was one of the mainstays of the Somerset team from 1911 to 1931 and in 1924 he played for England against South Africa at Old Trafford but, because of rain, little play was possible and McBryan did not bat. However, the opportunity to show his batting talents to the South Africans was not long delayed and he went on the unofficial MCC tour that winter, playing in four of the five 'Tests'. He scored more than 1000 runs in a season five times, coming close to scoring 2000 in 1923, and in 1925 *Wisden's* named him as one of the Cricketers of the Year.

Sadly, Jack McBryan's good fortune as a sportsman did not embrace his whole life. His marriage to the Gaiety Girl, Myrna Thompson, was short-lived and in his old age he suffered severe financial distress. After retiring from the stockbroking house for whom he had worked for many years he joined another firm which soon failed and McBryan was faced with the tragedy of being 'hammered' at the age of 80.

He spent his last years in very modest circumstances in Cambridge and the Memorial Service held there one week after his death, on what would have been his 91st birthday, was attended by only 14 people.

McGrath, *George F*

GOLD: 1920

George McGrath was the captain of Wimbledon Hockey Club and although he never played for England in the home internationals he won an Olympic gold medal, playing at inside-left, at Antwerp in 1920. As an administrator, he served as Honorary Secretary of the Wimbledon club and the Southern Counties Hockey Association.

Marcon, *Charles Sholto Wyndham*

Born: 31 March 1890, Headington, Oxfordshire   Died: 17 November 1959, Tenterden, Kent

GOLD: 1920

On leaving Lancing, Sholto Marcon went up to Oriel College, Oxford, where he won a hockey blue as a freshman in 1910. He played against Cambridge for the next two years and was captain of the Oxford team in 1913. His father had been one of the pioneers of hockey at Oxford and was the founder of Marcon's Hall.

In 1913, Sholto Marcon made the first of his 23 appearances for England and in the early 1920s the inside-forward trio of Marcon, Shoveller and Saville were virtually automatic choices for England.

After war service, Marcon taught at Cranleigh until 1936 when he left to be ordained at the age of 46. He served as a chaplain in the RAF from 1943 to 1945 and later became the vicar of Tenterden.

Martin, *Stephen A*

Born: 13 April 1959, Bangor, Co. Down, Ireland

GOLD: 1988   BRONZE: 1984

Stephen Martin and James Kirkwood were the only Irish players in Great Britain's 16 man squad which won the gold medals at the 1988 Olympics. Martin, a sports development officer who played defence for Holywood, won 62 caps for Ireland and played for Great Britain 53 times.

Noble, *Alan H*

GOLD: 1908

Alan Noble played for Huyton, Formby, Bebington and Alderley Edge and was the left-half on England's winning team at the 1908 Olympics. All of Noble's six England caps were won in 1908 and consisted of the three matches in the Olympic tournament plus appearances against Ireland, Scotland and Wales.

Page, *Edgar Wells*

Born: 31 December 1884, Wolverhampton, Staffordshire   Died: 12 May 1956, Wolverhampton, Staffordshire

GOLD: 1908

In an international career that lasted from 1907 to 1920 Edgar Page represented England 15 times as a centre-half. He had shown great sporting versatility at Repton and after leaving school he played cricket for Staffordshire, football for the Old Reptonians and hockey for Wolverhampton, Penn Fields, Northampton and England.

Page, a chartered accountant by profession, won a Military Cross in World War I.

Pappin, *Veryan Guy Henry*

Born: 19 May 1958, Henley on Thames, Surrey

GOLD: 1988 BRONZE: 1984

Veryan Pappin went to the Seoul Olympics as the reserve goalkeeper and as the tournament progressed it became apparent that he had little chance of replacing the brilliant Ian Taylor. However, Pappin was called on for the last minute of the final and as he had, therefore, actually played in the Olympics he was awarded a gold medal as a member of the winning squad. A physical education officer in the RAF, Pappin has won 37 caps for Scotland and 17 for Great Britain. He currently plays for Hounslow.

Potter, *Jonathan Nicholas Mark*

Born: 19 November 1963, London

GOLD: 1988 BRONZE: 1984

As a 20-year-old geography student at Southampton University, Jon Potter was the youngest member of the team which won the bronze medals at the 1984 Olympics. After graduating, Potter joined Hounslow and at the Seoul Olympics played at centre-half in every match, scoring once in Britain's 3-0 win over India.

Potter won silver medals at the 1986 World Cup and the 1987 European Cup and played 69 times for England and 84 times for Great Britain.

Pridmore, *Reginald George*

Born: 29 April 1886, Birmingham, Warwickshire   Died: 13 March 1918, Piave River, Italy

GOLD: 1908

Reggie Pridmore attended the now defunct Elstow School, Bedford, which was closed down permanently in 1916 when it was requisitioned as a school for Army officers. At school he was a notable hockey player and cricketer and later achieved distinction in both sports.

At hockey, Pridmore played inside-left for Coventry, and represented England 19 times between 1908 and 1913. At the 1908 Olympics he was England's leading scorer with four goals against Ireland and hat-tricks against both France and Scotland.

As a cricketer he played 14 times for Warwickshire as a middle order batsman between 1909 and 1912 and also appeared occasionally for Hertfordshire.

During the war, Pridmore served as a major in the Royal Horse & Field Artillery, winning a Military Cross on the Somme before being killed in action in Italy.

Rees, *Percy Montague*

Born: 27 September 1883, Camberwell, London   Died: 12 June 1970, Wonersh, Surrey

GOLD: 1908

Percy Rees played outside-right for Barnes, winning 14 international caps. Rees and the goalkeeper, Harvey Wood, were the only players to represent England in all their seven matches in the 1908 season.

Robinson, *John Yate*

Born: 6 August 1885, Burton-on-Trent, Staffordshire   Died: 23 August 1916, Roehampton, London

GOLD: 1908

John Robinson, the only University blue in England's 1908 Olympic hockey team, came from a family with an outstanding record in the sport. Robinson was in the Oxford XI for four years (1906–09) and in his first three matches against Cambridge his twin brother, Laurence, was on the opposing team. Laurence captained Cambridge in 1908, John was the Oxford captain the following year and in 1912 a third brother, Hugh, captained Cambridge. John went on to play nine times for England between 1907 and 1911 with Laurence being capped three times.

John Robinson went up to Merton College, Oxford from Radley and when he left University he was a schoolmaster at Broadstairs for a short while before being commissioned into the North Staffordshire Regiment. He was soon promoted to the rank of captain but in the campaign in Mesopotamia he received injuries which were to prove fatal.

SCOTT FREEMAN, see FREEMAN

Sherwani, *Imran Ahmed Khan*

Born: 9 April 1962, Stoke-on-Trent, Staffordshire

GOLD: 1988

After missing the 1984 Olympics through injury, Imran Sherwani made a significant contribution to Britain's victory in 1988. He played on the left-wing in all seven matches in Seoul and scored two of the three goals against West Germany in the final.

Sherwani won silver medals at the 1986 World Cup and the 1987 European Cup and has won 49 England caps and represented Great Britain 45 times. He is a newsagent in Stoke and plays for Stourport.

Shoveller, *Stanley Howard, MC*

Born: 2 September 1881, Kingston Hill, Surrey   Died: 24 February 1959, Broadstone, Dorset

GOLD: 1908 & 1920

Playing on the winning team in 1908 and 1920, Stanley Shoveller was the first man in Olympic history to win two gold medals for hockey.

Shoveller was one of the boys who introduced the game to Kingston Grammar School and was the greatest of the many fine players who attended the school. He joined Hampstead in 1899 and first played for Surrey the following year. After being selected to play for the South in 1901 he won the first of his 35 England caps in 1902. As a centre-forward he scored in 26 of these matches and accumulated a total of 76 goals for England. He captained the England side from 1910 until his retirement in 1921.

During the 1908 Olympic tournament he scored a total of ten goals and although he celebrated his 39th birthday during the 1920 Olympic Games he added to his reputation as a prodigous scorer with eight goals in England's 12-1 victory over Belgium.

During the war Stanley Shoveller won the Military Cross serving as a captain in the Rifle Brigade.

England's greatest centre-forward – Stanley Shoveller won two Olympic gold medals and scored 76 goals in 35 international matches.

Smith, *William Faulder*

Born: 14 November 1886, Carlisle, Cumberland   Died: 3 March 1937, Marylebone, London

GOLD: 1920

On leaving Marlborough College, Faulder Smith went up to Trinity Hall, Cambridge and won his hockey blue in 1909 playing at outside-right in the match against Oxford. After University he joined Beckenham and also played for Blackheath, Lowestoft and the East before making his international debut. He first played for England in 1911 and won a total of 26 caps in an international career which ended in 1921. He served as lieutenant in the army during the War and then followed his father, Sir Henry Smith, DL, JP, into the family businesses, serving as a director of the textile manufacturers, Stapley & Smith, and the insurance brokers, Smith & Burns.

Taylor, *Ian Charles Boucher*

Born: 24 September 1954, Bromsgrove, Worcestershire

GOLD: 1988   BRONZE: 1984

Ian Taylor, who was educated at Queen Elizabeth's Grammar School, Hartlebury and Borough Road College, was, at his peak, the outstanding goalkeeper in world hockey. He made his international debut in 1977 and went on to play for England 91 times and Great Britain on a record 80 occasions. Taylor won gold and bronze medals at the Olympics, a silver medal in the World Cup and a silver and bronze medal in the European Cup.

A marketing manager, Taylor played for East Grinstead for the major part of his career.

Wilkinson, *Cyril Theodore Anstruther*

Born: 4 October 1884, Durham, Co. Durham   Died: 16 December 1970, Honiton, Devon

GOLD: 1920

For many years cricket was Cyril Wilkinson's main sporting interest. He was in the Blundell's school XI before joining Surrey in 1909 and captaining them to the County Championship in 1914. He played his last game for the county in 1920 but continued as a club cricketer for many years. In August 1952, he played his final game at the age of 67 and after scoring 50 runs he took all 10 wickets for 27 for Sidmouth against the visiting Nondescripts XI.

At hockey, Wilkinson played for Norwood, Hampstead, Surrey and the South but he did not win the first of his four England caps until 1920 when he was 35 years old. Cyril Wilkinson went on to serve the sport well as an administrator. An international umpire and a member of the International Hockey Rules Board for 27 years, he was also a vice-president of the Hockey Association and in 1954 was awarded the CBE for his services to the sport.

By profession, Wilkinson was a civil servant and from 1936 to 1959 held the post of Registrar of Probate and Divorce.

Wood, *Harvey Jesse*
Born: 10 April 1885, Beverley, Yorkshire

GOLD: 1908

Standing 6′4″ (1.93m) tall and weighing 14 stone (89kg), Harvey Wood was an unusually large man for a goalkeeper. After understudying the international, LH Gurney, at West Bromwich, the 23-year-old Wood won a regular place in the club team in 1908 and in his first season of top class hockey won international and Olympic honours. He played for England in all their matches in 1908 and, including the Olympic Games, he only conceded six goals in seven games. Despite a successful first season at international level, Harvey Wood did not play for England again.

Lawn Tennis
MEN

Barrett, *Herbert Roper*
Born: 24 November 1873, Upton, Essex   Died: 27 July 1943, Horsham, Sussex

GOLD: 1908 (MEN'S DOUBLES – INDOORS)   SILVER: 1912 (MIXED DOUBLES – INDOORS)

Roper Barrett learnt his tennis at Merchant Taylor's School and the Forest Gate Club and was able to devote a great deal of time to the game. He won the Belgian Open singles title for four successive years from 1900, the Austrian title in 1904 and a vast number of tournaments at home. He was most successful in the Suffolk Championships at Saxmundham which he won no less than 17 times between 1898 and 1921. Barrett also reached the final of the All-Comers singles at Wimbledon four times, going through to the Challenge Round in 1911 when he was forced to retire against Tony Wilding with the score level at two sets all.

Despite these considerable successes, Roper Barrett must, in retrospect, be considered as a better doubles player. With his Olympic partner, Arthur Gore, they made up one of the more formidable doubles combinations of their era, winning Wimbledon in 1909 and reaching the All-Comers final on three other occasions. They won the Olympic covered court title in 1908 and the following year took the British indoor title.

Barrett and Gore went to Stockholm in 1912 to defend their Olympic indoor crown but after winning the first two sets were beaten by a Swedish pair in the semi-finals. Barrett, however, had the consolation of winning a silver medal in the mixed doubles with Helen Aitchison as his partner. Apart from his win at Wimbledon with Gore in 1909, Barrett was also successful in 1912 and 1913 when he was partnered by Charles Dixon, who, like Barrett, was a solicitor by profession. Additionally, he won the covered court mixed doubles in 1910 with Mrs O'Neill.

Roper Barrett played in the first Davis Cup match at Boston in 1900 with his last appearance coming in 1919. Although he did not have a particularly distinguished playing record in Cup matches he did, as non-playing captain, lead the British team to four consecutive victories in the thirties.

He served as Chairman of the Lawn Tennis Association in 1924 and was active in civic affairs, being twice Master of the Worshipful Company of Farriers and Chief Commoner of the City of London in 1924. He was also a keen footballer, playing regularly for Corinthian Casuals and Weybridge.

Boland, *John Mary Pius*
Born: 16 September 1870, Dublin, Ireland   Died: 17 March 1958, Westminster, London

GOLD: 1896 (SINGLES & MEN'S DOUBLES)

In 1894, John Boland of Christ's College, Oxford invited a Greek acquaintance, Thrasyvoalos Manaos, to speak at the Oxford Union. His guest chose as his subject the revival of the Modern Olympic Games. Boland and Manaos subsequently became close friends and Boland was invited to spend the Easter holidays of 1896 in Athens. Although John Boland had no intention of competing in the Olympic Games, his host, who was a member of the Organizing Committee, prevailed upon the 26-year-old Irishman to enter the lawn tennis tournament. Boland had little experience of domestic tournament play and none whatsoever of international competition but, surprisingly, he succeeded in winning two Olympic gold medals.

Boland took the singles title by beating Dionisios Kasdaglis of Egypt in three sets and then joined with Fritz Traun of Germany, whose original partner had withdrawn because of injury, for a comfortable victory in the men's doubles.

John Boland benefited from a broad educational background. He attended the Catholic University School in Dublin and Edgbaston Oratory and then studied at the Universities of Oxford, London and Bonn, a fine academic grounding which put him in good stead later in life. Boland was called to the Bar in 1897 and was the Member of Parliament for South Kerry from 1900 to 1918. He was General Secretary of the Catholic Truth Society for 21 years and a member of the Commission for the foundation of the National University of Ireland. Up until his death which, appropriately, occurred on St Patrick's Day, he was a keen advocate of the Irish language being an essential subject in the matriculation examination of the National University which he had

helped to establish some 50 years earlier.

Boland's two daughters also achieved recognition in their chosen fields. As Mrs Crowley, Honor became a national political figure as the Dail Eireann

representative for East Kerry and Bridget was a notable playwright who will be best remembered for her highly-acclaimed work, 'The Prisoner'.

Dixon, *Charles Percy*

Born: 7 February 1873, Grantham, Lincolnshire   Died: 29 April 1939, West Norwood, London

GOLD: 1912 (MIXED DOUBLES – INDOORS)   SILVER: 1912 (SINGLES – INDOORS)
BRONZE: 1908 (MEN'S DOUBLES)   1912 (MEN'S DOUBLES – INDOORS)

In an all-British final, Charles Dixon and Edith Hannam beat Roper Barrett and Helen Aitchison to take the mixed doubles covered court title at the 1912 Olympics in Stockholm.

Mrs Hannam had earlier won the women's singles and Dixon had already made his mark on the tournament with an outstanding win over the reigning Wimbledon champion, Tony Wilding of New Zealand, in the semi-finals of the men's singles. In the singles final, Dixon went down in straight sets to Andre

Gobert of France but completed his set of Olympic medals by winning a bronze in the men's doubles.

Charles Dixon reached the All-Comers final of the singles at Wimbledon in 1901 and 1911 but he did not win a Wimbledon title until two months after the 1912 Olympics when the 39-year-old veteran won the Wimbledon doubles with Roper Barrett. He then took the 1912 Australian doubles title with James Parke and concluded a memorable year by captaining the team which recaptured the Davis Cup from Australasia. In 1913

Dixon and Roper Barrett successfully defended their Wimbledon title.

Charles Dixon was educated at Haileybury and Clare College, Cambridge before becoming a solicitor. He played in four Davis Cup ties and while at Cambridge won a blue for Rackets but, surprisingly, not for lawn tennis. He was also a scratch golfer and his sporting talents were shared by his brother, John, who captained Nottinghamshire at cricket for many years and won an England cap at soccer.

Doherty, *Hugh Laurence*

Born: 8 October 1875, Wimbledon, Surrey   Died: 21 August 1919, Broadstairs, Kent

GOLD: 1900 (MEN'S SINGLES & MEN'S DOUBLES)

The Doherty brothers, Laurie and Reggie, reigned supreme in the tennis world at the turn of the century and were one of the finest doubles pairings in the history of the game.

Both educated at Westminster School and Trinity Hall, Cambridge, they won the Wimbledon doubles a record eight times, took the US title twice and were unbeaten in the five Davis Cup rubbers they played together. When they were at their peak, the Dohertys lost only four of the countless doubles matches they played together.

The younger of the two, Laurie, had slightly the better record as a singles player, winning Wimbledon five times to Reggie's four and also winning the US singles in 1903, being the only overseas player to do so between 1881 and 1925. Laurie also enjoyed an impeccable record in the Davis Cup, winning all twelve of his rubbers. Reggie won the Wimbledon singles from 1897–1900 and Laurie took the title from 1902–1906, with Arthur

Gore being the only person able to prevent the brothers from completely monopolising the Championship for a full decade when he beat Reggie in the 1901 Challenge Round. Their feats are commemorated by 'The Doherty Gates' at the south-west entrance of the All England Club.

In the Olympic singles in 1900, Laurie Doherty was scheduled to meet Reggie in the semi-finals but Reggie conceded a walk-over so that Laurie met the Irishman, Harold Mahoney, in the final. Mahoney reputedly had the best volley and the worst forehand in the game and at times this was clearly an adequate enough combination as Mahoney had won the 1896 Wimbledon singles. But in Paris, Mahoney's assets and liabilities failed to meet the searching demands of Doherty's audit and the Englishman won the gold medal in straight sets.

Laurie won a second gold medal in the men's doubles with Reggie as his partner. The Official Report indicates that the

scratch pairing of Max Decugis (France) and Spalding de Garmendia (USA) gave the Dohertys a good match before losing 6-3, 6-3, 7-5 but *The Field* reported that the British pair had a rather more comfortable victory at 6-1, 6-1, 6-0.

Laurie also played in the Mixed Doubles at the 1900 Olympics with the American, Marion Jones, as his partner but they were beaten in the semi-finals by Reggie and Charlotte Cooper, winner of the Women's singles.

After poor health forced Laurie to retire from top class tennis in 1906 he turned to golf and with a handicap of plus two at Royal St George's he played several times in the Amateur Championship. His best performance was on his home course in 1908 when he reached the last sixteen.

In 1914, Laurie Doherty joined the Royal Naval Reserve but the rigours of service in an anti-aircraft unit hastened the breakdown of his delicate constitution and he died, aged 43, after a long illness.

Doherty, *Reginald Frank*

Born: 14 October 1872, Wimbledon, Surrey   Died: 29 December 1910, Kensington, London

GOLD: 1900 (MEN'S DOUBLES & MIXED DOUBLES)   1908 (MEN'S DOUBLES)   BRONZE: 1900 (SINGLES)

At the 1900 Olympics in Paris, Reginald Doherty won the men's doubles with his brother and then partnered Charlotte

Cooper to win the mixed doubles without dropping a set in either event.

The successes of the brothers as a

doubles pairing have been noted in the preceeding biography on Laurie Doherty and although they shared much good fortune together in was also their tragic lot to share the burden of indifferent health.

After winning four successive Wimbledon singles titles, Reggie faced an agonizing decision in the 1901 Challenge Round. He was again in poor health and his doctor had forbidden him to play but as Laurie had been beaten in an earlier round, Reggie felt that if the Wimbledon title was to leave the family it should not be by default. Against all advice, he decided to play and after winning the first set and leading 5-2 in the second he simply did not have the strength left to cope with the relentless baseline game of Wentworth Gore who went on to win by three sets to one.

Despite this warning, the Doherty's did not end their career as major championship contenders until five years later in 1906. Seeking their ninth successive Wimbledon doubles title, they came up against the Gloucestershire pair, Sidney Smith and Frank Riseley, in the final. After taking an early lead, Reggie and Laurie were too frail to maintain their challenge and their mother, who had watched the match in tears, made her sons

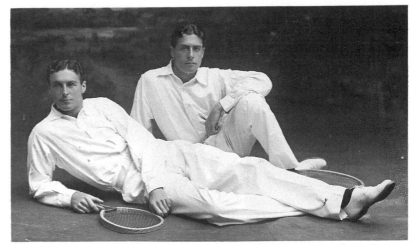

Reggie and Laurie Doherty, winners of the men's doubles in 1900 and the first brothers to win an Olympic title.

promise never to overtax their strength again.

Laurie immediately turned to golf but Reggie continued to play in selected major events. In 1908, with George Hillyard as his partner, he won his second Olympic gold medal in the men's doubles and in 1909 he won two titles at the South African Championships. The following year he died at his home at Albert Hall Mansions just a few hours after returning from a Swiss nursing home.

Gore, *Arthur William (Wentworth) Charles*

Born: 2 January 1868, Lyndhurst, Hampshire   Died: 1 December 1928, Kensington, London

GOLD: 1908 (MEN'S SINGLES – INDOORS & MEN'S DOUBLES – INDOORS)

The covered court singles matches at the 1908 Olympic Games began at the Queen's Club immediately after the English Championships had been held on the same courts. Regrettably, the Olympic tournament drew a poor entry and Wentworth Gore had to play only two singles matches to add an Olympic gold medal to the English title he had won the previous week. In his first match, Gore came from behind to beat Major Ritchie, who later in the summer won the Olympic outdoor title, and in the final the 40-year-old Gore was relieved to beat George Caridia in straight sets after his five set opening match.

With Roper Barrett as his partner, Gore won a second Olympic gold in the

indoor men's doubles thereby confirming their position as one of the leading doubles pairings of the day. They reached the Wimbledon All Comers final in 1899 and 1908 before winning the Challenge Round in 1909 when they also won the British covered courts title. But possibly their greatest victory came on the only occasion they played together in the Davis Cup. In the 1907 Challenge Round, Gore and Barrett lost the first two sets to the Australasian pair, Norman Brookes and Tony Wilding, but after squaring the match they took the final set 13-11.

In 1900, Gore beat the great Laurie Doherty at Dublin, Beckenham and Wimbledon and was honoured with the captaincy of Britain's first Davis Cup

team. The following year he won the first of his three Wimbledon singles titles.

Despite his many successes, it is really the longevity of his career that places Wentworth Gore among the lawn tennis immortals. He played at every Wimbledon from 1888 to 1927, a remarkable span of 39 years; he is the oldest winner of the Wimbledon singles (aged 41 in 1909) and he also holds the record of being the oldest Wimbledon singles finalist (aged 44 in 1912).

Wentworth Gore learnt his tennis on the sand courts of Brittany and although many sources indicate that he was educated at Harrow this is incorrect and he was, in fact, educated abroad.

Hillyard, *George Whiteside*

Born: 6 February 1864, Hanwell, Middlesex   Died: 24 March 1943, Pulborough, Sussex

GOLD: 1908 (MEN'S DOUBLES)

To reach the final of the 1908 Olympic men's doubles George Hillyard and his partner, Reggie Doherty, had to survive seven match points in the fourth set of the semi-finals before finally defeating Charles Cazelet and Charles Dixon. In the final, Hillyard and Doherty faced Major Ritchie, the new Olympic singles champion, and James Parke, who had won 20 caps for

Ireland at rugby. After their scare in the semi-finals, Hillyard and Doherty were relieved to take the gold medals in straight sets.

At the time of his Olympic victory, Hillyard was 44 years old and had been married to Blanche Bingley, six times winner of the Wimbledon singles, for 21 years. He was in the second year of his 17

year tenure as the Secretary of the All England Club and his best playing years were already behind him. He had won the English covered courts doubles in 1890 and 1891 with Harry Scrivener and again in 1904 and 1905 with Laurie Doherty as his partner. Hillyard's outstanding achievement outdoors was to win the German Championship in 1897 and 1898 when this was still one of the major international tournaments.

As a young man, George Hillyard spent some time in the Navy and served on the same ship as the Prince of Wales. He developed a close personal friendship with the future King George V, the basis on which the still surviving interest of the Royal family in lawn tennis is founded. Upon the outbreak of war, Hillyard rejoined the Navy and rose to the rank of Commander.

Hillyard also excelled as a golfer and in 1903 he defeated Harry Hilton, the Open champion of 1892 and 1897 and the reigning amateur champion. It was, however, cricket and not golf that was really George Hillyard's second sport. He played for Leicestershire, Middlesex and the Gentlemen of England and went with Lord Hawke's team to America in 1891 and 1894.

Ritchie, *Major Josiah George*

Born: 18 October 1870, Westminster, Middlesex   Died: 28 February 1955, Ashford, Middlesex

GOLD: 1908 (MEN'S SINGLES)   SILVER: 1908 (MEN'S DOUBLES)   BRONZE: 1908 (MEN'S DOUBLES – INDOORS)

Major Ritchie learned his tennis on the family court at home in Putney but when he went to Brighton College he chose not to specialise in the game remaining active in many sports most notably as a particularly fine gymnast.

It was not until early in 1892 that Ritchie, by then aged 21, began to take lawn tennis seriously. Seven years later, he won the French covered courts singles championship and from then on he compiled an impressive record of successes both at home and on the Continent.

At the 1908 Olympics, with Ritchie meeting the German, Otto Froitzheim, in the final the 22-year-old German surprisingly elected to take on Ritchie, 15 years his senior, from the baseline. Ritchie had few peers at this type of game and as Froitzheim was not one of them he lost to the English veteran in straight sets. Ritchie also won an Olympic silver medal in the doubles with John Parke as his partner and earlier the same year had won a bronze in the covered court doubles.

Major Ritchie won the Wimbledon doubles in 1906 and 1910, partnering the New Zealander, Tony Wilding, with his best performance in the Wimbledon singles coming in 1909 when he won through to the Challenge Round only to lose to Arthur Gore in five sets.

His son, Richard, was also an accomplished player but became better known for having served as Secretary of the Queen's Club for some 30 years.

Turnbull, *Oswald Graham Noel, MC*

Born: 23 December 1890, Highgate, London   Died: 17 December 1970, Whitby, Yorkshire

GOLD: 1920 (MEN'S DOUBLES)

On leaving Charterhouse, Noel Turnbull joined the family firm of shipowners but his business career was soon interrupted by the war. After serving as a driver he was then commissioned into the RASC and during the Battle of the Somme he won the Military Cross and was mentioned in despatches.

He first came to prominence as a tennis player in 1919 and made his Davis Cup debut that year. He played again in the Davis Cup in 1921 but then virtually gave up the game for four years to concentrate on golf in which he played off scratch at St George's Hill and West Hill. On resuming serious tennis, he again made the Davis Cup team in 1926 and won the singles at the Portugese Championships in 1927 and 1928. He was, however, essentially a doubles specialist and his victory with Max Woosnam in the 1920 Olympic doubles was undoubtedly his greatest achievement.

Woosnam, *Maxwell*

Born: 6 September 1892, Liverpool, Lancashire   Died: 14 July 1965, Westminster, London

GOLD: 1920 (MEN'S DOUBLES)   SILVER: 1920 (MIXED DOUBLES)

Max Woosnam was a man of such talent and versatility that he must be ranked as one of the greatest all-rounders in the history of British sport. He was an international or first-class player at association football, lawn tennis, golf, cricket, real tennis and rackets.

Woosnam himself said 'If I was any good at anything, it was football' but such were his achievements that it is advisable to review them chronologically rather than try to assess their respective merits.

Max Woosnam was educated at Winchester where he was captain of cricket and golf and played for the College at football and rackets. When he went up to Trinity College, Cambridge he played against Oxford at football, golf, lawn tennis and real tennis with perhaps the only surprise of his wonderful University career being his failure to win a fifth blue at cricket: in his freshman year, 1912, he played for the University in every game before losing his place at the last minute for the Oxford match and went to Lord's as 12th man.

After his sporting commitments at Cambridge were complete for the 1914 season, Woosnam went on the Corinthians FC tour of Brazil but no sooner had the team arrived in South America than the news arrived of the outbreak of war in Europe. The touring party spent just one night in Rio and took the next boat home. Within 24 hours of docking at Tilbury every man in the team was with the Colours, Woosnam joining the Montgomeryshire Yeomanry before transferring to the Royal Welch Fusiliers. After service in France, Woosnam left the Army early in 1919 and returned to Cambridge.

He was elected captain of cricket that summer but he again failed to hold his place in the team for the match against Oxford and it was then that he decided to concentrate on lawn tennis. His victory in the men's doubles with Noel Turnbull at the 1920 Olympics was his first major success and in Antwerp he also won an Olympic silver medal in the mixed doubles partnering Kitty McKane. Woosnam was also selected as a member of the association football squad for the 1920 Olympics but as the soccer tournament began as soon as the lawn tennis programme ended, he felt he could not spend any more time away from his work and so withrew.

In 1920 he made a winning Davis Cup debut in the doubles against Spain with Randolph Lycett as his partner. The same pair went on to win the Wimbledon title in 1921. Woosnam was again a member of the Olympic team in 1924 but failed to repeat his successes of four years earlier, being eliminated in the early stages of the singles and the men's doubles.

During this golden era, Max Woosnam turned to football when the summers were over. Before the war, he had played for Chelsea while still an undergraduate but when he left Cambridge in 1919 he joined the staff of ICI in Manchester and remained with the company until his retirement in 1954. He made 89 appearances for Manchester City between 1919 and 1925 and captained the team when they were runners-up for the First Division championship in 1920–21.

Woosnam won three international caps in the 1921–22 season, playing against Wales and Ireland in the amateur internationals and captaining the full international team also against Wales. Woosnam was a dominating centre-half with a ferocious shoulder charge and in his three international appearances, England did not concede a single goal. Shortly after the game against Wales a broken leg ended his football career.

Lawn Tennis
WOMEN

Cooper, *Charlotte Reinagle*   (Later Mrs AE Sterry)
Born: 22 September 1870, Ealing, Middlesex   Died: 10 October 1966, Helensburgh, Scotland
GOLD: 1900 (WOMEN'S SINGLES & MIXED DOUBLES)

The distinction of being the first woman ever to become an Olympic champion goes to the 29-year-old Charlotte Cooper of Ealing who won the women's singles at the 1900 Olympic Games. In Paris, 'Chattie' Cooper defeated the French champion, Helene Prevost in straight sets and then won a second gold medal in the mixed doubles with Reggie Doherty as her partner.

Miss Cooper won the Wimbledon singles five times, the last occasion being in 1908 when, at the age of 37, she became the oldest winner of the title. She also won the All England mixed doubles seven times and the women's doubles twice although this was before these events became part of the official championship programme. Other major successes

included eight Irish championships, including a triple win in 1895, the Scottish singles in 1898 and the British covered court singles in 1895. She was also a three-time winner of the covered court mixed doubles.

In 1901, Charlotte married Alfred Sterry, who later became President of the Lawn Tennis Association, and their daughter, Gwen, represented Great Britain in the Wightman Cup. Gwen's husband, Max Simmers, won 28 rugby union caps for Scotland and their son – Charlotte's grandson, Brian, also played rugby for Scotland.

The world's first Olympic woman champion died at the age of 96 thus establishing a longevity record for all British Olympic gold medallists.

Charlotte Cooper playing at Wimbledon in 1908. At the 1900 Games she won the ladies' singles and mixed doubles and was the first woman Olympic champion.

Eastlake-Smith, *Gladys Shirley*   (Later Mrs WH Lamplough)
Born: 14 August 1883, Lewisham, London   Died: 18 September 1941, Middleham, Yorkshire
GOLD: 1908 (WOMEN'S SINGLES – INDOORS)

There were only seven competitors in the 1908 Olympic covered court women's singles and in only her third match of the tournament, Gladys Eastlake-Smith met Alice Greene in the final. After two sets the match was level but Eastlake-Smith won the final set 6-0 to take the gold medal.

Neither of the finalists were in the absolute top flight of British players but Eastlake-Smith certainly had the better indoor record of the two. She won the All England covered court singles in 1907 and was again a finalist in 1908 when she lost to Mrs Lambert Chambers who did not enter for the Olympic event. Miss Eastlake-

Smith also won the All England covered court mixed doubles in 1905 with Reggie Doherty and again in 1908 with Tony Wilding.

Two days after her Olympic victory, Gladys Eastlake-Smith married Wharram Lamplough and in 1913 they won the now defunct Married Doubles championship.

Hannam, *Edith Margaret* (née Boucher)
Born: 28 November 1878, Bristol, Gloucestershire   Died: 16 January 1951, Bristol, Gloucestershire
GOLD: 1912 (WOMEN'S SINGLES – INDOORS & MIXED DOUBLES – INDOORS)

As the outdoor lawn tennis events at the 1912 Olympics coincided with Wimbledon, Great Britain was not represented in this part of the programme but they did send a strong team to the Olympic indoor events in May. The most successful member of this team was Edith Hannam who won two gold medals. In the singles final, she beat Thora Castenschiold of Denmark in straight sets and then joined Charles Dixon to take the mixed doubles title.

Edith Boucher came from a prominent Gloucestershire family and her four brothers were all notable sportsmen in the area. In May 1909 she married Francis Hannam, after which she gave up tennis for a while when the newly married couple settled in Canada where her husband pursued his business interests as a timber merchant.

The Hannam's did not stay long in Canada and on their return Edith became an outstanding figure at the Welsh Championships, winning a total of ten titles between 1912 and 1923. She enjoyed mixed fortunes at Wimbledon, her best years being 1911, when she reached the All Comers singles final, and 1914 when, with Ethel Larcombe as her partner, she was a finalist in the women's doubles. Her husband was killed in action in 1916 when serving as a captain in the Gloucestershire Regiment.

Lambert Chambers, *Dorothea Katharine* (née Douglass)
Born: 3 September 1878, Ealing, Middlesex   Died: 7 January 1960, Kensington, London
GOLD: 1908 (WOMEN'S SINGLES)

As all the foreign entrants withdrew from the women's singles at the 1908 Olympics, the field eventually consisted of five British players. Dora Boothby drew a series of byes into the final where she met 'Dolly' Lambert Chambers and won a silver medal for losing the only match she played. Lambert Chambers and Boothby met again many times after the Olympic final, the most notable re-match being in the 1911 Wimbledon final when Lambert Chambers won 6-0, 6-0 and Dora Boothby earned the unenviable distinction of being the only Wimbledon singles finalist who has failed to win a single game.

Dorothea Douglass was born and raised in Ealing, where her father was the vicar of St Matthew's Church, and she was educated locally at Princess Helena College where she first took up the game of tennis. As the 1900 Olympic champion, Charlotte Cooper, also came from the same neighbourhood, the Olympic title returned to Ealing in 1908 with Dorothea's victory.

Before her marriage to Robert Lambert Chambers in 1907 she won three Wimbledon singles championships and was to win four more as a married woman. Her total of seven Wimbledon singles victories has only been surpassed by Helen Wills Moody and Martina Navratilova and had it not been for the interruption caused by the war it is not unreasonable to assume that Lambert Chambers would have won further honours. In fact, she very nearly claimed an eighth title in 1919 when she held two match points against Suzanne Lenglen. She also lost the 1920 final to Lenglen.

In 1927, at the age of 48, Dolly Lambert Chambers played at Wimbledon for the last time and the following year became a professional coach. During the course of her outstanding playing career she had, in addition to her seven Wimbledon singles title, won the All England women's doubles in 1903 and 1904 and the mixed doubles in 1903 and 1906. Hence, in 1903 she became the first woman to win all three titles at the All England Championships.

The talent of this great sportswoman was not confined to the tennis courts and she won two All England badminton titles and played hockey for Middlesex.

McKane, *Kathleen* (Later Mrs LA Godfree)
Born: 7 May 1896, Bayswater, London
GOLD: 1920 (WOMEN'S DOUBLES)   SILVER: 1920 (MIXED DOUBLES)   1924 (WOMEN'S DOUBLES)
BRONZE: 1920 (WOMEN'S SINGLES)   1924 (WOMEN'S SINGLES)

With a bronze in the singles, a silver in the mixed doubles and a gold in the women's doubles, Kitty McKane acquired a full set of medals at the 1920 Olympic Games. Her bronze medal in the 1920 singles was won in unique circumstances: as she wished to be at her best to partner Winifred McNair in the doubles she conceded a walk-over in the semi-final of the singles but still qualified to play in the match between the losing semi-finalists to decide third place, a match which she duly won against Sigrid Fick of Sweden to take the bronze medal.

She won two more medals at the 1924 Games in Paris but despite a total of five Olympic medals she will be remembered for more notable successes in wider fields.

Although London-born, Kitty McKane learned her tennis at St Leonard's School in Scotland and made her tournament debut at Roehampton in April 1919. A few weeks later she reached the quarter-finals on her first appearance at Wimbledon and soon took over the role of Britain's number one player from 'Dolly' Lambert Chambers. By 1924 she had established herself as a world class player and confirmed her status by beating the great Helen Wills in the Wightman Cup, repeating the feat at Wimbledon a few days later. In a classic Wimbledon final, McKane lost the first set and trailed 1–4 in the second but came back to hand Helen Wills her only defeat in a singles match in nine appearances at Wimbledon.

In January 1926, Kitty McKane married Leslie Godfree while they were on a tennis tour of South Africa and later that year they achieved the ultimate in familial success by becoming the only husband and wife pairing ever to win the mixed doubles at Wimbledon. In 1926 she also won her second Wimbledon singles title and reached the final of the women's doubles for the third time, the first time having been in 1922 when she was partnered by her sister, Margaret Stocks. Although she never succeeded in winning the women's doubles at Wimbledon, McKane had a fine record in other major championship doubles, winning the US title in 1923 and 1927 and the US mixed doubles in 1925.

Kathleen McKane Godfree's record as a tennis player was matched by her success at badminton. She won eight All England titles (4 singles, 2 doubles and 2 mixed doubles) her victories in the doubles coming with her sister, Margaret, as her partner. Her sporting talents were not restricted to racket games: as a nine-year-old she cycled 600 miles from London to Berlin on a family 'outing', the following year she was awarded the bronze medal of the National Skating Association and in 1914 she was selected to play for England against Scotland in the lacrosse international but the game was called off due to the outbreak of war.

McNair, *Winifred Margaret* (née Slocock)

Born: 9 August 1877, Donnington, nr. Newbury, Berkshire   Died: 28 March 1954, Kensington, London

GOLD: 1920 (WOMEN'S DOUBLES)

At the 1920 Olympics, Winifred McNair, who had recently celebrated her 43rd birthday, partnered Kitty McKane in the doubles and as they were expecting a hard match in their semi-final against the French pair, Suzanne Lenglen and Elisabeth D'Ayen, McKane sportingly withdrew from the semi-finals of the singles in order to give her partner maximum support in the doubles. After losing the first set, McNair and McKane won their semi-final and then took the final against the British pair, Geraldine Beamish and Edith Holman.

Although Winifred McNair's playing record could not match that of her distinguished partner she was not without successes of her own. She reached the finals of the All Comers singles at Wimbledon in 1913 and won the doubles that year when partnered by Dora Boothby after their opponents, Dolly Lambert Chambers and Charlotte Sterry, were forced to retire through injury when leading 6-4, 4-2. Like her Olympic partner, Winifred McNair also had a second string to her sporting bow. In 1921 she was runner-up in the English Ladies Golf Championship and played for England in the international matches at Turnberry that year.

In 1908 she married Roderick McNair who later became the first President of the International Lawn Tennis Federation.

Modern Pentathlon

Fox, *Jeremy Robert*

Born: 19 September 1941, Pewsey, Wiltshire

GOLD: 1976 (TEAM EVENT)

Jim Fox is one of the most influential figures in the development of the Modern Pentathlon in Britain. He won the British title a record ten times and is the only British pentathlete to have competed in four Olympic Games. His fourth place in the individual event at Munich in 1972 was the best placing by a Briton up to that time and has only subsequently been matched by Dick Phelps in 1984.

Fox made his Olympic debut in 1964, when he placed 29th in the individual event, and in his second Olympic appearance in 1968 he improved to finish eighth. After the 1968 Games, Fox, then a sergeant in the REME, announced his retirement but he was dissuaded by his coach, Ron Bright, and remained in the sport for another eight years. During that period he set a fine example to the tyros of the sport and following his fine individual effort at the 1972 Olympics he won a gold medal in the team event in 1976. Fox, who was later commissioned in the REME, was first awarded the MBE and subsequently the OBE for his services to the sport.

Nightingale, *Robert Daniel*

Born: 21 May 1954, Redruth, Cornwall

GOLD: 1976 (TEAM EVENT)

Danny Nightingale, a 22-year-old engineering student at the University of Sussex, was the youngest member of the team which won the Olympic team gold medals in 1976. In the individual event, Nightingale finished in 10th place. He made a second Olympic appearance in 1980 when, as captain of the team he finished 15th individually. He was the British champion in 1976, 1977 and 1978 and in 1979 became the only westerner ever to win the Spartakiad. Danny Nightingale later served as the Development Officer for the Modern Pentathlon Association.

Britain's winning team in the 1976 Modern Pentathlon receive Royal congratulations. Left to right: Mike Proudfoot (manager), Jim Fox, Adrian Parker, HM Queen Elizabeth, Prince Edward (aged 12), Andy Archibald (reserve), Robert Nightingale, Ron Bright (coach).

Parker, *Adrian Philip*
Born: 2 March 1951, Croydon, Surrey

GOLD: 1976 (TEAM EVENT)

With only the cross-country event remaining, Great Britain were in fourth place in the Modern Pentathlon team event at the 1976 Olympics with all hopes resting on Adrian Parker, rated as one of the best run-swimmers in the world. If all went well, the bronze, or perhaps the silver medals, seemed a possibility. With an outstanding run, Parker won the cross-country discipline and against all probabilities, Britain won the gold medals.

Parker, a director of the family music firm, had been the British champion in 1975.

Motor Boating

Field-Richards, *John Charles*
Born: 10 May 1878, Penzance, Cornwall   Died: 18 April 1959, Christchurch, Hampshire

GOLD: 1908 (CLASS B & CLASS C)

Although Capt. John Field-Richards is not mentioned in the Official Report of the British Olympic Association on the 1908 Games, his participation is confirmed by many reports in the national press and sporting magazines which show that he joined Bernard Redwood as a crew member aboard Tom Thornycroft's *Gyrinus II*. Redwood and Field-Richards later purchased the winning Olympic boat and raced her successfully as co-owners.

John Field-Richards was the son of a Cornish clergyman and was educated privately and at Keble College, Oxford. During the war he served as a major with the Hampshire and the Yorkshire Regiments and was awarded the OBE for his work as a Staff Officer. On leaving the Army in 1920 he retired to Jersey but later settled in Hampshire.

Redwood, *Bernard Boverton*
Born: 21 November 1874, Finchley, London   Died: 28 September 1911, Hampstead, London

GOLD: 1908 (CLASS B & CLASS C)

Due to poor weather conditions, Tom Thornycroft enlisted the help of Bernard Redwood and Capt. Field-Richards to bail out *Gyrinus II* in the 1908 Olympic motor boating events. This proved to be a sound tactical move as in both the Class B and Class C races neither of the other two entries completed the course and consequently Redwood and Field-Richards won two Olympic gold medals for their skills with a bucket!

Despite his bizarre success at the Olympics, Bernard Redwood was, in fact, well known in the world of motor boating. He was a member of the Royal Motor Yacht Club and was awarded the medal of the Royal Society of Arts for a paper on high speed motor boats.

After attending Bath College, he went up to Peterhouse College, Cambridge and represented the University in the 1894 cycling match against Oxford. He was the son of Sir Boverton Redwood, Bt. but he never succeeded to the title as in 1911, at the age 36, he died of pneumonia and so pre-deceased his father.

Thornycroft, *Isaac Thomas*
Born: 22 November 1881, Basingstoke, Hampshire   Died: 6 June 1955, Basingstoke, Hampshire

GOLD: 1908 (CLASS B & CLASS C)

Tom Thornycroft's motor boat, *Gyrinus II*, won both the Class B and Class C events at the 1908 Olympics against scant opposition – in fact, the only other entry in both events failed to complete the course.

Tom Thornycroft was the second son of Sir John Thornycroft, the founder of the engineering and boat building firm which took his name, and *Gyrinus II* had been designed by Tom and built in the family boatyards. On leaving St Paul's School, Tom Thornycroft joined the family firm but resigned from the Board in 1934 following differences of opinion over future company policy.

Many of the Thornycroft family were distinguished sculptors and following the tradition of his parents and grand-parents Tom himself became a sculptor of considerable note. Although he was never a professional yacht designer, he had much to do with the development of the Swallow class. His greatest success as a helmsman came in 1931 when he won the Prince of Wales Cup. He was also a keen motor racer and in 1908 he placed fifth in the Tourist Trophy on the Isle of Man.

Tom Thornycroft came very close to making a second Olympic appearance in 1952. At the age of 70, and 44 years after winning his two gold medals, he was an official reserve for the yachting team and although he went to Finland for the Games he was not called on to compete.

Polo

Barrett, *Frederick Whitfield*

Born: 20 June 1875, Co.Cork, Ireland   Died: 7 November 1949, Swindon, Wiltshire

GOLD: 1920   BRONZE: 1924

Captain 'Rattle' Barrett of the 15th Hussars captained the 1914 Westchester Cup team when Britain regained the trophy by winning both matches in America. After winning an Olympic gold medal in 1920, he again played in the 1921 Westchester Cup, when both matches went to the Americans, and in 1924, on his second Olympic appearance, he won a bronze medal.

Barrett was an accomplished steeplechase rider and only took up polo when his regiment went to India in 1902. After his return to England a bad fall at Sandown put an end to his steeplechasing career and he then concentrated on polo, with considerable success.

In 1904, Captain Barrett married the Hon. Isobel Caroline, daughter of Lord Kensington, and they acquired an estate at Wroughton Hall, Wiltshire. On retiring from the Army, Barrett began training under National Hunt rules in 1929 and saddled winners for three Kings, George V, Edward VIII and George VI. His greatest success as a trainer was Annandale's victory in the 1931 Scottish Grand National.

Beresford, *Hon. John George*

Born: 10 June 1847, Ireland   Died: 8 May 1925, Ireland

GOLD: 1900

Captain The Hon. John Beresford of the 7th Hussars played one game for the Foxhunters in the 1900 Olympic tournament when he replaced Foxhall Keene in the semi-final match against a French team. Three weeks later, Beresford, who was a prominent figure at the Hurlingham Club, was a member of the Westchester Cup team which defeated the Americans by eight goals to two.

Daly, *Denis St George*

Born: 5 September 1862, Co. Galway, Ireland   Died: 16 April 1942, Chipping Norton, Oxfordshire

GOLD: 1900

Denis Daly won his Olympic gold medal as a member of the Foxhunters team but despite being one of the more accomplished polo players of his time never played in the Westchester Cup. He was the son of the Irish Peer, Lord Dunsandle, and served with the 18th Hussars until his retirement from the army in 1893. At the age of 52, Daly rejoined the army on the outbreak of World War I and served as a major in the Army Remount Department.

He was a keen huntsman and on the death of his father in law, Albert Brassey, Denis Daly succeeded him as Master of the Heythrop.

Keene, *Foxhall Parker*

Born: 18 December 1867, Oakland, California, USA   Died: 25 September 1941, Ayre's Cliff, Quebec, Canada

GOLD: 1900

The informal nature of the 1900 Olympic polo tournament is best illustrated by the fact that only three weeks after winning a gold medal with the Foxhunters team, Foxhall Keene played for America against Great Britain in the Westchester Cup.

As an 18-year-old, Foxhall Keene played in the first Westchester Cup match at Newport, Rhode Island in 1886 when he had the distinction of scoring the first ever goal in international polo. Although the visiting British team won 10-4, Keene scored for the home team after only 24 seconds of play. Keene was the only player to appear in all of the first six Westchester Cup matches, in 1886, 1900 and 1902, and

he only missed the 1913 series after breaking a collar bone in the final workout. He was the first American to be given a ten goal handicap and he maintained that rating for 14 of the next 28 years.

Keene spent two years at Harvard as a special student with the Class of '91 before transferring to the Law School, where he stayed only one year. He then joined his father and helped direct the family's substantial business interests. During this period he was a familiar figure on the hunting and polo fields of England and the Keene's Castleton Farm in Kentucky enjoyed many successes on the turf on both sides of the Atlantic.

Foxhall Keene was a talented and versatile sportsman. In 1897 he finished 31st in the US Open Golf Championship and the following year reached the quarter-finals of US Amateur Championship before losing to the great Walter Travis. After being badly injured when his car crashed into a telegraph pole in the 1905 Vanderbilt Cup races, he gave up motor racing and devoted himself to other sports as a result of which he played in the 1914 World Rackets Championships. Keene never married and in 1913 he went to live with his sister in Canada where he eventually died.

Lockett, *Vivian Noverre*

Born: 18 July 1880, New Brighton, Cheshire   Died: 30 May 1962, Norwich, Norfolk

GOLD: 1920

Vivian Lockett was educated at Wellington and Trinity College, Cambridge and the Royal Military College, Sandhurst. Whilst at Cambridge he failed to win a polo blue which is something of a surprise as he had the most distinguished Westchester Cup record of any of the 1920 British Olympians, playing in a total of five matches in 1913, 1914 and 1921. His record in Army polo was even more noteworthy: he maintained a ten goal handicap for many years, was a member of the team which won the inter-regimental tournament in India in 1913 and 1914, and, when polo re-started in England after the war, played on the winning team in the inter-regimental championship every year from 1920 to 1930, with the exception of 1927.

On leaving Sandhurst, Lockett initially joined the Royal Field Artillery before transferring to the 17th Lancers. After the regiment had become the 17/21 Lancers he succeeded his fellow Old Wellingtonian and Olympic gold medallist, Tim Melvill, as Commanding Officer in 1927. Colonel Lockett retired from the Army in 1933 but was recalled in 1940 and commanded the Cavalry Training Centre in Edinburgh. In 1915 he married, Violet, the daughter of Russell Colman, an East Anglian land owner, and they made their home in Norfolk. They had three children, one of whom was killed in North Africa in World War II while serving with his father's old regiment.

Mackey *Frank Jay*

GOLD: 1900

Although originally from Chicago, Frank Mackey played much of his polo in England and was one of two Americans on the Foxhunters team which won the 1900 Olympic polo tournament. He did not take up polo until he was 40-years-old and, along with Foxhall Keene, played for America against Great Britain in the Westchester Cup soon after the 1900 Games.

Melvill, *Teignmouth Philip, DSO*

Born: 13 February 1877, Cape Town, South Africa   Died: 12 December 1951, King's Lynn, Norfolk

GOLD: 1920

After leaving Wellington College, Tim Melvill went to Sandhurst and in 1896 was commissioned into the South Wales Borderers, the regiment with which his father had won a posthumous VC for saving the colours at Isandlwana in 1879. His love of riding led him to transfer to the 17th Lancers and after winning the DSO while serving in France he was appointed Assistant Military Attaché in Madrid in 1921. Following the amalgamation which led to the formation of the 17/21 Lancers he was appointed colonel of the regiment.

Apart from his Olympic gold medal the highlight of Melvill's polo career came in 1924 when he played in the second Westchester Cup match against America at Meadowbrook. After leaving the Army, Melvill was for many years polo correspondent of *The Field*.

Miller, *Charles Darley*

Born: 23 October 1868, London   Died: 22 December 1951, Putney, London

GOLD: 1908

After attending Marlborough and Trinity College, Cambridge, Charles Miller went to India to work for the family merchant trading house. In India, he took up polo for the first time and played regularly during his summers back in England. While on leave in 1901, he founded the Roehampton Club and after resigning his post in India became managing director at Roehampton, a position he held until 1950.

Miller played in one Westchester Cup match, in 1902, and was a member of the Roehampton team which won the Olympic tournament in 1908. During the war, Charles Miller commanded the Remount Depot at Rouen and on being demobilised in 1919 with the rank of Lt. Colonel resumed his duties at Roehampton.

Miller, *George Arthur*
Born: 6 December 1867, London   Died: 21 February 1935, At Sea
GOLD: 1908

Apart from playing with his younger brother, Charles, on the winning Roehampton team at the 1908 Olympics, George Miller's other successes included six Champion Cup victories and two wins in the Ranelagh Open Cup. He also captained England in the 1920 Westchester Cup matches.

Like his brother, he was educated at Marlborough and Trinity College, Cambridge and also served in a Remount Depot in the war. He assisted in the management of the Roehampton Club together with a third brother, Edward. He died while on a cruise in the West Indies.

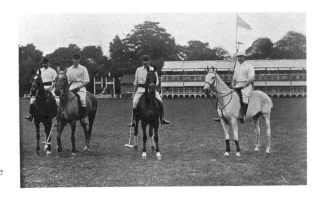

The Roehampton team which won the 1908 polo tournament. Left to right: Charles Miller, Patteson Nickalls, George Miller, Herbert Wilson.

Nickalls, *Patteson Wormersley*
Born: 23 January 1876, Widdington, Essex   Died: 10 September 1946, Rugby, Warwickshire
GOLD: 1908

Patteson Nickalls went up to New College, Oxford from Rugby where he played polo against Cambridge in 1895, 1896 and 1897, thus making him the only blue on the Roehampton team which won the gold medals at the 1908 Olympics.

At the outbreak of the Boer War, Nickalls was gazetted to the Durham Light Infantry and took part in the Relief of Ladysmith. In 1901 he became a member of the Stock Exchange but rejoined the Colours in 1914, winning a DSO in 1918.

Rawlinson, *Alfred*   (Later Sir A Rawlinson, Bt., CMG, CBE, DSO)
Born: 17 January 1867, London   Died: 1 June 1934, Clapham, London
GOLD: 1900

Although he spent less than two years at Eton, Alfred Rawlinson can claim the distinction of being the first of a remarkable thirty two Old Etonians who have won an Olympic gold medal. After playing on the winning Foxhunters team at the 1900 Olympics he led an interesting and varied life.

Rawlinson was the son of Major-General Sir Henry Rawlinson, Bt., and he first served with the 17th Lancers but resigned when still a lieutenant. He rejoined the forces at the outbreak of World War I, serving initially as a despatch rider but later receiving a commission in the RNVR, and in 1915 he was appointed second-in-command of London's aerial defences with the rank of Lt. Commander. In 1916 he was awarded the CMG and the following year he left his post at ariel defences to rejoin the Army as a Lt. Colonel with the Royal Garrison Artillery. In 1919 Rawlinson was awarded the DSO for his role as the leader of a special mission to Ezerum. He was also appointed a CBE that year. In 1920 he was taken prisoner by the Turks and, after his release in 1921, was much feted on his return to London.

Before the war, 'Toby' Rawlinson had been a prominent figure in the pioneering days of motoring and aviation. He invented an internal combustion engine from which he made a great deal of money, most of which was spent on experiments in aviation. Flying was one of his great passions and he held International Pilots Certificate No. 3.

Rawlinson succeeded to the Baronetcy on the death of his brother in 1925.

Wilson, *Herbert Haydon, DSO*
Born: 14 February 1875, London   Died: 11 April 1917, Ypres, France
GOLD: 1908

Captain Herbert Wilson was a figure of much influence in polo circles and maintained a fine home at Hurlingham, where he served as a member of the Hurlingham Committee, the governing body of polo. He often played at the neighbouring club, Roehampton, and it was with their team that he won his Olympic gold medal in 1908.

Of the winning Olympic team in 1908, only Wilson had not already played in the Westchester Cup although he was to do so in 1909 and 1911. He was also a keen huntsman and rode with the Quorn, the Cottesmore and the Belvoir from his country residence at Ashley Folville in Leicestershire.

The son of Sir Samuel Wilson of Ercildoune, Victoria, Australia, Wilson was educated at Eton and New College, Oxford. Soon after leaving Oxford, he joined the Notts. Imperial Yeomanry, winning a DSO in the Boer War. The fighting in South Africa, and later in France, took a cruel toll on the Wilson family: Wilfred lost his life in the Boer War, in which his brother was also severely wounded, and, in the 1914–18 War, Herbert and his eldest brother, Lt. Col. Gordon Wilson, MVO of the Royal Horse Guards, were both killed. Hence, only one of the four brothers survived the two wars, and he was gravely wounded.

Wodehouse, *Lord John, MC*   (Later the Earl of Kimberly, CBE, MC)

Born: 11 November 1883, Witton Park, Norfolk   Died: 16 April 1941, London

GOLD: 1920   SILVER: 1908

Although he was 36 years old, 'Jack' Wodehouse was the youngest member of the British team which won the gold medals in the 1920 polo tournament, held at Ostend. After leaving Eton, Lord Wodehouse went up to Trinity Hall, Cambridge and after being on the losing side in the polo match against Oxford in 1903 then captained the winning Cambridge team for the next two years.

He was the Liberal Member of Parliament for Mid-Norfolk from 1906 to 1910 and it was during his period in the House that he won an Olympic silver medal with the Hurlingham team at the 1908 Olympics. He also played in three Westchester Cup matches and was a member of the Old Cantab's team which won the Champion Cup six times between 1908 and 1921.

In the 1914–18 War, Lord Wodehouse served with the 16th Lancers, winning the Military Cross, the Croix de Guerre and the Italian War Cross. After the war, he was assistant private secretary to the Colonial Secretary, Winston Churchill, and was awarded the CBE in 1925.

He succeeded his father to the Earldom in 1932 and in 1941, while paying one of his rare visits to London from his Norfolk estates, he was killed in an air raid.

Rackets

Astor, *John Jacob*   (Later Lord Astor)

Born: 20 May 1886, New York, USA   Died: 19 July 1971, Cannes, France

GOLD: 1908 (DOUBLES)   BRONZE: 1908 (SINGLES)

The American, JJ Astor, came to England as a child and became a British citizen in 1889 when his father took out naturalization papers for himself and his family. His upbringing was typical of a wealthy young Englishman of the time and at Eton he opened the batting for the cricket team in 1904 and 1905. Later in 1905 he went up to New College, Oxford but his stay was brief and he left the following year to take a commission in the Life Guards. From 1911 to 1914, Astor served as ADC to Lord Hardinge, who had succeeded Astor's father-in-law, Lord Minto, as Viceroy of India after which he rejoined his regiment for active service. Although he lost his right leg in action in September 1918, amazingly this did not prevent him from winning the Parliamentary squash rackets championship in 1926 and 1927.

In 1922, Astor became Chief Proprietor of *The Times* and also entered Parliament as the Member for Dover, a seat he held until 1945. In 1924 he was President of the Royal Cinque Ports Golf Club and in 1937 became the first American-born President of the MCC. In 1956 he was created Baron Astor of Hever but six years later, in order to avoid the penal death duties in England, he took up residence in France where he subsequently died.

In the 1908 Olympic Rackets tournament, John Astor and his partner Vane Pennell scored a comfortable win over Edward Bury and Cecil Browning in the doubles. In the singles Astor drew a bye in the first round, his second round opponent withdrew and, although he lost to Charles Leaf in the only singles match he played, Astor won a bronze medal as a losing semi-finalist.

Noel, *Evan Baillie*

Born: 23 January 1879, Stanmore, Middlesex   Died: 22 December 1928, West Kensington, London

GOLD: 1908 (SINGLES)   BRONZE: 1908 (DOUBLES)

Evan Noel, the 1907 Amateur Rackets champion, qualified to meet Henry Leaf in the 1908 Olympic singles final but Leaf had injured his hand in the semi-final against John Astor and was obliged to withdraw. Noel thus won the first gold medal to be awarded at the 1908 Olympics on a walk-over. As a losing semi-finalist, he also won a bronze medal in the doubles and later played in the Olympic Real Tennis tournament where he was eliminated in the first round.

Evan Noel, who was ambidextrous but favoured the left hand, was educated at Winchester and Trinity College, Cambridge where, in addition to his talents for court games, he proved himself to be a fine cricketer, playing in the Winchester XI for three years and later captaining Trinity.

A year after leaving Cambridge in 1901, he was admitted to the Inner Temple and in 1903 he took up the post of sports editor of *The Times* but, acting on advice from his doctor that nightwork on a newspaper would be detrimental to his fragile health, in 1909 he resigned. In 1914, Noel, the leading historian of court games, was appointed secretary and manager of the Queen's Club and held this position until his death 14 years later.

His daughter, Susan, won the British Women's squash rackets title three times and, like her father, became a noted sporting journalist.

Pennell, *Vane Hungerford*

Born: 16 August 1876, London   Died: 17 June 1938, Bournemouth, Hampshire

GOLD: 1908 (DOUBLES)

After spending only one term at Eton, Vane Pennell moved to Charterhouse where he won the Public School Rackets doubles in 1893 and 1894 with Ernest Garnett as his partner. However, on going up to Trinity College, Cambridge Pennell failed to find a place in the University Rackets team and began to take more interest in the game of Real Tennis.

Although he was undoubtedly one of the outstanding players of court games of his generation, Vane Pennell only made occasional appearances in the championship events. In 1901 he was the British Rackets doubles champion, partnering a fellow Old Carthusian, Frances Dames Longworth, but Pennell did not play in the championships again until 1908 when he and Dames Longworth again won the title. His appearances in the Real Tennis championships were equally spasmodic and he only entered for the singles nine times in the twenty year period up to 1923. He was, however, a finalist seven times and won the title in 1904.

At the 1908 Olympics, Pennell played in the singles at both Real Tennis and Rackets and in each event was defeated by the ultimate winner. However, he won a gold medal in the Rackets doubles with John Astor as his partner.

Vane Pennell's sporting interests were not restricted to the dedan and he represented Great Britain, against France, at ice hockey when he was captain of the Prince's Club team. He was also the author of the first ever book written on Auction Bridge. During World War I he served overseas as a captain with the Royal Army Service Corps.

Rowing

Badcock, *John Charles*

Born: 17 January 1903, West Ham, London   Died: 29 May 1976, Petersfield, Hampshire

GOLD: 1932 (COXLESS FOURS)   SILVER: 1928 (EIGHTS)

Known throughout the rowing world as 'Felix', John Badcock made his Olympic debut in 1928 as a member of the Thames Rowing Club crew which won the silver medals in the eights. Four years later at the 1932 Olympics in California, he gave a memorable performance at stroke in the coxless fours, holding his crew together when they were hard pressed by the Germans. The British four finally finished with clear water between themselves and the Germans and Britain maintained its record of having won the coxless fours on each of the four occasions it had been held at the Olympics.

Although educated at Merchant Taylor's School, which is not noted for its rowing, Badcock had a long association with the river as his family had been in business on the Thames for almost a hundred years as boat builders and wharfingers. In 1934, 'Felix' Badcock married the swimmer, Joyce Cooper, who had won one silver and three bronze medals at the 1928 and 1932 Olympics along with three gold medals at the 1930 Empire Games. They sent both sons to Harrow, as Badcock did not want them to row as schoolboys, but eventually both became accomplished oarsmen, David winning his blue in the Oxford boat in 1958 and the elder son, Felix, rowing for England at the Commonwealth Games the same year.

Beesly, *Richard*

Born: 27 July 1907, Barnt Green, Worcestershire   Died: 28 March 1965, Ludlow, Shropshire

GOLD: 1928 (COXLESS FOURS)

On going up to Trinity College, Cambridge from Oundle, Richard Beesly won a place in the University boat and rowed at number four for the winning crew in the Boat Races of 1927, 1928 and 1929, this latter success coming when he was President of the Cambridge University Boat Club. In the 1928 Olympic four, Beesly rowed at number two when, as in 1924, Britain's crew were all from the same Cambridge college. Thus it was not only Great Britain but also Trinity College, Cambridge who successfully defended their Olympic coxless fours title in 1928.

In 1932, Richard Beesly joined Guest Keen and Nettlefold as a management trainee and enjoyed a successful business career which was only interrupted by the war when he served with the Ministry of Supply.

In 1945 he acquired a controlling interest in a light engineering firm and pioneered the introduction of mobile forestry saws and mechanical hedge cutters. He also farmed, at Ashford Hall, Shropshire, and it was there that Richard Beesly met his death when attacked and instantly killed by a bull.

Beresford, *Jack, Jr.*

Born: 1 January 1899, Chiswick, Middlesex   Died: 3 December 1977, Shiplake-on-Thames, Oxfordshire

GOLD: 1924 (SINGLE SCULLS)   1932 (COXLESS FOURS)   1936 (DOUBLE SCULLS)
SILVER: 1920 (SINGLE SCULLS)   1928 (EIGHTS)

Generally considered to be the finest British oarsman of all-time, Jack Beresford was born into a rowing family with his father, Julius, having won an Olympic silver medal in the coxed fours in 1912. Jack first showed his inherent talent at Bedford School where he stroked the eight and also captained the rugby football XV.

After serving in the Liverpool Scottish Regiment, his Olympic career began in 1920 when he placed second to the American, Jack Kelly, in the single sculls. At the Paris Olympics four years later, Beresford met another fine American sculler, William Gilmore, and after losing to Gilmore in the heats Beresford reached the final via the repechage which had been introduced into Olympic competition that year. In the final, Beresford gained revenge for his earlier defeat in the heats by defeating Gilmore quite comfortably to win the first of his three Olympic gold medals.

At the 1928 Olympics, Beresford demonstrated his versatility by winning a silver medal in the eights. He then won a

gold in the coxless fours in 1932, won his third Olympic gold medal in the double sculls in 1936 and was in training for a sixth Olympic appearance when war intervened in 1940. No other British oarsman has come close to matching his record of competing in five Olympics and winning a medal in each.

Away from the Olympics his record was no less impressive: he won the Wingfield Sculls seven times, the

Diamond Sculls four times and the Grand, the Stewards' and the Silver Goblets twice each. Beresford, who rowed for the Thames, Kingston and Leander clubs, was awarded the Olympic Diploma of Merit in 1949 and was honoured with the CBE for his services to the sport in 1960.

With three gold and two silver medals, Jack Beresford is the greatest Olympic oarsman of all time.

Bevan, *Edward Vaughan*

Born: 3 November 1907, Chesterton, Cambridgeshire   Died: 23 February 1988, Storey's End, Cambridgeshire

GOLD: 1928 (COXLESS FOURS)

Edward Bevan was educated at Bedford School and Trinity College, Cambridge but despite rowing at bow in the coxless four which won the Olympic title at Amsterdam in 1928, he was unable to

command a place in the Cambridge boat. On leaving Cambridge, Bevan qualified as a doctor at St Mary's Hospital after which he returned to Cambridge where he joined a practice with the Olympic shot

putter, Rex Salisbury Woods. He maintained his contacts with the University, serving as senior treasurer of the Cambridge University Boat Club for many years.

Blackstaffe, *Henry Thomas*

Born: 28 July 1868, Islington, London   Died: 22 August 1951, West Wickham, Kent

GOLD: 1908 (SINGLE SCULLS)

Three days after his 40th birthday, Harry Blackstaffe of the Vesta Rowing Club met Alexander McCulloch of Winchester and University College, Oxford in the final of the single sculls at the 1908 Olympics, a race that brought together the two men who were undoubtelly the best scullers in England. Although McCulloch was exactly half Blackstaffe's age, the final proved to be the finest race of the Olympic Regatta and it was impossible to pick the winner

until the last 50 yards when Blackstaffe held on to his slight advantage to become the oldest sculling champion in Olympic history.

After this great victory, Blackstaffe retired and ended a career which had brought him nine victories in the London Cup, five wins in the Wingfield Sculls and one victory in the Diamond Sculls. All these successes proved particularly gratifying to a man who, because he was a

butcher, initially experienced great difficulty in having his entry accepted for Henley.

Following his Olympic victory, Blackstaffe was made a Freeman of the City of London and at the time of his death he was the Senior Life Vice-President of the Amateur Rowing Association. Blackstaffe was also a useful cross-country runner and represented South London Harriers in the National Championships.

Bucknall, *Henry Cresswell*

Born: 4 July 1885, Lisbon Portugal   Died: 1 January 1962, Dumfries, Scotland

GOLD: 1908 (EIGHTS)

Henry Bucknall was stroke of the Eton boat before going up to Merton College, Oxford where, in 1905 and 1906, he stroked the Oxford eight. In 1907, when President of the Oxford University Boat Club, he elected to row at number two but then reverted to stroke in the Leander crew which won the eights at the 1908 Olympics. On leaving Oxford, Bucknall joined a ship building firm in Newcastle-on-Tyne.

Budgett, *Richard Gordon McBride*

Born: 20 March 1959, Glasgow, Scotland

GOLD: 1984 (COXED FOURS)

Prior to the 1984 Olympics, Richard Budgett competed in three world championships. In 1981 he won a bronze medal in the coxed pairs and in the coxed fours he placed fifth in 1982 and sixth in 1983. Budgett was educated at Radley and Selwyn College, Cambridge before qualifying as a doctor in 1983.

Burgess, *Edgar Richard*

Born: 23 September 1891, Kensington, London   Died: 23 April 1952, Tangier, Morocco

GOLD: 1912 (EIGHTS)

Edgar Burgess was educated at Eton and Magdalen College, Oxford and rowed at bow in the 1912 Olympic eight. He was the only man in the crew who had not already won a blue but the following year stroked Oxford to victory in his only appearance in the Boat Race.

Burgess was a member of the Inner Temple and spent many years with the Sudan Political Service. On retirement, he stayed on in Africa where he died, at his home in Tangier.

Burnell, *Charles Desborough*

Born: 13 January 1876, Beckenham, Kent   Died: 3 October 1969, Blewbury, Oxfordshire

GOLD: 1908 (EIGHTS)

Charles Burnell, who was educated at Eton and Magdalen College, Oxford, is one of the select group who have rowed in the winning crew in the Boat Race on four occasions (1895–98). As a member of the Leander crew he also won the Grand for four consecutive years (1898–1901) and was a three time winner of the Stewards' at Henley.

Serving as a captain in the Rifle Brigade, Burnell won a DSO in 1918 and, after the war, rejoined the family firm of stockbrokers in the City. He was Chairman of the Wokingham Rural District Council for 35 years and was awarded the OBE in 1954 for Public Service in Berkshire.

Both his son, Richard (1939), and his grandson, Peter (1962), rowed in the Boat Race with the former also winning an Olympic gold medal, in 1948.

Burnell, *Richard Desborough*

Born: 26 July 1917, Henley-on-Thames, Oxfordshire

GOLD: 1948 (DOUBLE SCULLS)

Richard Burnell and his father, Charles, winner of a gold medal in the 1908 Olympic eights, are the only father and son in Olympic history to have won gold medals for rowing. Both were educated at Eton and Magdalen College, Oxford.

After rowing in the Oxford boat in 1939, Richard Burnell's rowing career was interrupted by military service but he soon regained his form after the war, winning the Wingfield Sculls in 1946. In 1948 he joined with Bert Bushnell for the Olympic double sculls and although they lost to France in the first round they then won the repechage followed by the semi-final before beating Denmark and Uruguay in the final.

After the Olympics, Burnell won a bronze medal in the eights at the 1950 Commonwealth Games and in 1951 he won the Double Sculls Challenge Cup at Henley. He married the daughter of Arthur Garton, a gold medallist in the 1912 Olympic eights, and their son rowed in the Boat Race in 1962. Richard Burnell later became a distinguished rowing journalist and the leading historian of the sport.

Bushnell, *Bertie Thomas*

Born: 7 May 1909, Woking, Surrey

GOLD: 1948 (DOUBLE SCULLS)

As the winner of the Wingfield Sculls in 1947, Bert Bushnell was disappointed not to be selected for the single sculls at the 1948 Olympics. However, teaming up with Richard Burnell he won the Olympic double sculls. Bushnell had prepared well for the Olympics and toured South America the previous winter, where he maintained an unbeaten record.

Bert Bushnell had been educated locally at Henley Grammar School and his family owned a boatyard at Wargrave, with a branch at Henley, but had Bert worked in the family business his amateur status might have been in jeopardy, so he was apprenticed as an engineer to the firm of Thornycroft's.

Clive, *Lewis*

Born: 8 September 1910, St George's Hospital, London   Died: 2 August 1938, Gandesa, Spain

GOLD: 1932 (COXLESS PAIRS)

After winning the Goblets at Henley in 1931 and 1932, Lewis Clive and 'Jumbo' Edwards were selected to compete in the coxless pairs at the 1932 Olympics where the pair, from Christ Church College, Oxford, scored a comfortable victory in the Olympic final at Long Beach, California.

On leaving Eton, where he achieved the rare distinction of being captain of both the Oppidans and Boats, Clive rowed for Oxford in 1931 and 1932 but, most unusually, he declined an invitation to become a member of the Leander Club.

Lewis Clive, whose father, Lt. Col. PA Clive of the Grenadier Guards, died on active service in 1918, was himself killed in action whilst fighting in the Spanish Civil War. He was a man of strong political views, serving as a Labour member of Kensington Borough Council and writing books and pamphlets for the New Fabian Society. He had plans to stand for Parliament and it was his political convictions that took him to Spain where he met his death at the age of 27.

Cross, *Martin P*

Born: 21 July 1957, London

GOLD: 1984 (COXED FOURS)   BRONZE: 1980 (COXLESS FOURS)

Martin Cross of the Thames Tradesmen Rowing Club made his Olympic debut in 1980 when he won a bronze medal in the coxless fours. Four years later he won a gold in the coxed fours and on his third Olympic appearance at Seoul in 1988 he was a member of the crew which placed fourth in the coxed fours.

Cross, a history teacher at Hampton School, also won a gold medal in the coxed fours at the 1986 Commonwealth Games and bronze medals in the coxless fours at the World Championships in 1978 and 1979.

Cudmore, *Robert Collier*   (Later Hon. Sir CR Cudmore, Kt.)

Born: 13 June 1885, Wentworth, New South Wales, Australia   Died: 16 May 1971, Adelaide, South Australia, Australia

GOLD: 1908 (COXLESS FOURS)

In July 1908, Collier Cudmore was member of the crew from Magdalen College, Oxford which won both the Stewards' and the Visitors' at Henley and was then given the honour of representing Great Britain in the coxless fours at the Olympic regatta later the month same month.

Before coming to England, Cudmore attended St Peter's College, Adelaide and Adelaide University and while at Magdalen rowed in the Oxford boats of 1908 and 1909. He was Called to the Bar in 1910 and then returned to his native Australia to practise law. Before too long he was back in Europe for the war in which he was wounded twice while serving with the Royal Field Artillery in France. In post-war years his legal practice in Adelaide flourished and he had ample time to devote to politics. He rose to become leader of the powerful Liberal and Country Party and in 1958 he was knighted for his political services.

Edwards, *Hugh Robert Arthur*

Born: 17 November 1906, Woodstock, Oxfordshire   Died: 21 December 1972, Southampton, Hampshire

GOLD: 1932 (COXLESS PAIRS & COXLESS FOURS)

'Jumbo' Edwards went up to Christ Church College, Oxford from Westminster School and rowed in the Oxford boat as freshman in 1926 when his brother was also a member of the crew. Unfortunately, Edwards collapsed when the Dark Blues held a slight lead and Cambridge went on to win by five lengths.

In 1927, Edwards was rusticated for failing his examinations and he then spent two years as a schoolmaster although he continued to row regularly with the London Rowing Club. While he was teaching, Edwards decided to follow his brother into the Royal Air Force and the only avenue open to him by which he could secure a permanent commission was to return to Oxford and obtain a University degree. So in 1930, Edwards went back to Oxford, took his degree and then joined the RAF the following year. During his second period at Oxford, he devoted more time to flying than to rowing and obtained Proctorial Licence

No. 1, which enabled him to keep his private plane at the University. However, he was still good enough to command a place in the Oxford boat and five years after his first appearance he rowed again in the 1930 Boat Race. Referring to the 1930 race, Edwards later wrote, 'I was incomparably the best oarsman in either crew' but apparently his Oxford colleagues could not match his talents as Cambridge won by two lengths.

Later in 1930, Edwards was in the London Rowing Club crew which won the Grand and the Stewards' at Henley and he then went to Canada for the British Empire Games where he won gold medals in the coxless fours and the eights. In 1931

he won three events at Henley, the Grand, the Stewards' and the Goblets. At the 1932 Olympics he became only the second man in Olympic history to win two rowing gold medals on the same day. Firstly, he won the coxless pairs with Lewis Clive and then he was a member of the winning crew in the coxless fours, having been brought in as a late substitute for Thomas Tyler who contracted influenza after arriving in California. All these victories added up to a remarkable display of stamina for a man who had collapsed in the 1926 Boat Race.

After being commissioned into the RAF in 1931, Edwards became a well-known racing pilot and, in his own plane,

finished second in the King's Cup of 1935. During the war, he served with Coastal Command, winning the AFC in 1943 and the DFC the following year. In 1943 his rowing ability literally saved his life. Being forced to ditch his Liberator off Land's End he rowed a dinghy for four miles before getting clear of the minefield in which he had landed. He was the only survivor of his crew.

Group Captain Edwards retired from the RAF in 1946 and soon developed a reputation as an innovative coach. He advised his old University on a number of occasions, including 1959 when his son was in the Oxford crew, and he also coached Britain's Olympic eight in 1960.

Eley, *Charles Ryves Maxwell*
Born: 16 September 1902, Samford, Suffolk   Died: 15 January 1983, East Bergholt, Suffolk
GOLD: 1924 (COXLESS FOURS)

Britain's coxless four at the 1924 Olympics were a remarkably well atuned crew. Maxwell Eley, James Macnabb, Robert Morrison and Terence Saunders had all rowed together at Eton and continued their partnership when they went up to Trinity College, Cambridge.

At Henley in 1922 this notable four won the Stewards', having entered as Eton Vikings, and then won the Visitors'

representing Third Trinity. They won the Stewards' again in 1923 and 1924 and maintained their unbeaten record with an easy victory at the Olympic Games. Maxwell Eley, who sat at bow in the Olympic four, first rowed at Henley in 1921, when Eton won the Ladies' Plate. He was a member of the winning Cambridge crew in the 1924 Boat Race and won the Goblets that year, partnered

by his fellow Olympic gold medallist, John Macnabb. He was also a member of winning Leander crews in the Grand.

After a working life spent with ICI, Maxwell Eley retired to the family estate at East Bergholt in Suffolk where he developed the impressive grounds and arboretum which had been created by his father into one of the finest private gardens in England.

Ellison, *Adrian C*
Born: 11 September 1958, Solihull, Warwickshire
GOLD: 1984 (COXED FOURS)

The London radiologist, Adrian Ellison, of the Tyrian Boat Club was Britain's leading cox in the years leading up to the 1984 Olympic Games. In 1981, he won a bronze

medal at the World Championships in the coxed pairs and he also took part in the next two World Championships, competing in the coxed fours in 1982 and

the eights in 1983.

At the 1984 Olympics he steered Britain to their first Olympic rowing gold medal for 36 years.

Etherington-Smith, *Raymond Broadley*
Born: 11 April 1877, Putney, London   Died: 19 April 1913, Smithfield, London
GOLD: 1908 (EIGHTS)

Raymond Etherington-Smith was educated at Radley and Trinity College, Cambridge but before going to university competed for the London Rowing Club and was a member of their Thames Cup crew in 1895. After being in the eight which finished second in the Grand in 1896, 1899 and 1900 he finally achieved success in 1901 when he stroked Leander to a memorable victory over the University of Pennsylvania. In 1903 and 1905, Etherington-Smith was again in the

winning Leander crew in the Grand and in 1905 and 1906 he was in the Leander boat which won the Stewards'. He rowed against Oxford in 1898, 1899 and 1900 and in his last year, when he was President, a unique record was set when his brother, Thomas, was also in the Oxford boat.

To counter the strong challenge of the Belgians, who had won the Grand in 1906 and 1907, Great Britain chose a vastly experienced Leander crew for the eights at the 1908 Olympics. The 31-year-old

Etherington-Smith rowed a fine race at number seven and after one of the great races in Olympic rowing history, Leander won by two lengths.

On leaving Cambridge, Raymond Etherington-Smith qualified as a surgeon but after performing an operation at St Bartholomew's Hospital on a gangrenous lung he contracted peritonitis which sadly, caused the death of both patient and surgeon.

Fenning, *John Reginald Keith*

Born: 23 June 1885, Fulham, London   Died: 3 January 1955, Coventry, Warwickshire

GOLD: 1908 (COXLESS PAIRS)   SILVER: 1908 (COXLESS FOURS)

At the 1908 Olympics, John Fenning and Gordon Thomson won the coxless pairs, representing Leander, and later in the afternoon they were both in the Leander crew which lost the final of the coxless fours to Magdalen College, Oxford.

Fenning, who was also a member of the London Rowing Club, was a medical student at London Hospital at the time of his Olympic victory but he did not qualify as a doctor until 1917. He had entered London Hospital Medical College in January 1904 and the records of London Hospital indicate that 'his prolonged, 13-year medical course was the result of failing examinations rather than war service'. When he eventually qualified, the 32-year-old Dr John Fenning initially practised in the Home Counties but he moved to the Midlands in 1937 where he spent the rest of his life.

Fleming, *Philip*

Born: 15 August 1889, Newport-on-Tay, Fife, Scotland   Died: 13 October 1971, Woodstock, Oxfordshire

GOLD: 1912 (EIGHTS)

Philip Fleming, who was educated at Eton and Magdalen College, Oxford made only one appearance in the University Boat Race when he rowed at number seven in the winning Oxford boat of 1910. At Stockholm in 1912, he stroked the Leander eight which beat the crew from New College, Oxford by one length in the Olympic final.

During the war Fleming served as a subaltern with the Queen's Own Oxfordshire Hussars where one of his fellow officers was Winston Churchill. He was one of the founders of the merchant bank which bears his name and he held numerous directorships, many of which he only relinquished shortly before his death. He married, Jean, the daughter of Sir Philip Hunloke, the 1908 Olympic yachting bronze medallist, and they were a prominent couple in Oxfordshire society. Philip Fleming often rode with the Bicester and the Heythrop hunts and after serving as a Deputy Lieutenant he was appointed High Sheriff of the County in 1948.

Garton, *Arthur Stanley*

Born: 31 March 1889, Epsom, Surrey   Died: 20 October 1960

GOLD: 1912 (EIGHTS)

When he went up to Magdalen College, Oxford in October 1908 there was little doubt that Stanley Garton, who had been an outstanding member of the Eton crew, would win his blue the following spring. He rowed in the winning Oxford boat in 1909, 1910 and 1911, was in the Magdalen boat which won the Grand in 1910 and 1911 and, as a member of Leander scored a third win in the Grand in 1913. After leaving university, he maintained a close interest in the sport and coached the Oxford eight in 1925 and 1930.

Stanley Garton's daughter married Richard Burnell, the 1948 Olympic gold medallist, and their son, Peter, who was Garton's grandson, rowed for Oxford in 1962.

George, *Roland David*

Born: 15 January 1905, Bath, Somerset

GOLD: 1932 (COXLESS FOURS)

Roland George first took up rowing when he went up to Lincoln College, Oxford from Wycliffe College in 1922. He did not succeed in winning a blue and on leaving Oxford began his business career with a firm of printers and packing manufacturers in Bristol which left him with no time to devote to rowing. In 1929 his employers transferred him to their London office and the following year George joined the Thames Rowing Club where he rapidly developed into one of the finest oarsmen in Britain. He was in the Thames eight which lost narrowly in the final of the Grand in both 1931 and 1932, although he was not completely without success at Henley, winning the Wyfold in 1931 and the Stewards' in 1932. Later in the year he rowed at bow in the coxless four which won the Olympic title at Long Beach, California.

In 1933 Roland George married the daughter of Lord Rathcreedan, a marriage which produced three sons and one daughter. In the war, George served in the RAF, rising to the rank of wing commander. He was awarded the OBE in 1943 and at the Salerno landings in 1944 he became the first, and possibly the only, member of the RAF's Equipment Branch to be awarded the DSO.

Gillan, *James Angus*   (Later Sir JA Gillan, KBE, CMG)

Born: 11 October 1885, Aberdeen, Scotland   Died: 23 April 1981, Leigh, Surrey

GOLD: 1908 (COXLESS FOURS)   1912 (EIGHTS)

Angus Gillan was a member of the Magdalen College crew which won the Visitors' and the Stewards' at Henley in 1908 before going on to win the Olympic coxless fours title. Four years later he was a member of the Leander crew which won the eights at the Stockholm Games and so became the first oarsman from any country to win two Olympic gold medals.

Gillan was educated at Edinburgh Academy and Magdalen College, Oxford and rowed in the Oxford boat in 1907 and 1909, having missed the 1908 race because of a severe attack of influenza. He was also in the Leander crew which won the Grand in 1911.

His successes at Henley in 1911 and

Stockholm in 1912 were achieved while he was on leave from the Sudan Political Service, which he had joined in 1909. Gillan served with distinction in the Sudan for thirty years, becoming Civil Secretary in 1934. He was appointed a CMG in 1935 and a KBE in 1939 and after the war headed the British Council's Empire Division, playing a major part in

the organisation of the 1948 Olympic Games. After his years in Africa, office work in London held little appeal and in 1949 he left to become the British Council representative in Australia. Gillan returned to England in 1951 and served as Chairman of the Royal Overseas League from 1955 to 1962.

Gladstone, *Albert Charles* (Later Sir AC Gladstone, Bt., MBE)
Born: 28 October 1886, Cheshire   Died: 2 March 1967, Fordingbridge, Hampshire
GOLD: 1908 (EIGHTS)

Albert Gladstone was a descendant of the former Prime Minister and at the age of 21 was the youngest member of the Leander crew which won the eights at the 1908 Olympics. Gladstone went up to Christ Church College, Oxford from Eton and rowed in the Oxford boat for four years (1906–09) but only in his last year were Oxford the winners. He was also a member of the Christ Church eight which

won the Grand at Henley some four weeks before the 1908 Olympics.

During the war, he served in Mesopotamia and Gallipoli and was mentioned in despatches three times. He was awarded the MBE in 1919 and then enjoyed a successful business career which, among the many important positions he held, included a directorship of the Bank of England from 1924 to 1947

and the senior partnership of the East India merchants, Ogilivy, Gillanders & Co. In 1929, Albert Gladstone was appointed Deputy Lieutenant for Flintshire and High Sheriff for the County of London and in 1935 became Chief Constable of Flint Castle. In 1945, on the death of his cousin, he succeeded to the Baronetcy.

Holmes, *Andrew John*
Born: 15 October 1959, Uxbridge, Middlesex
GOLD: 1984 (COXED FOURS)   1988 (COXLESS PAIRS)   BRONZE: 1988 (COXED PAIRS)

At the World Championships, Andy Holmes competed in the coxed fours in 1981 and the eights in 1982 and 1983 but, for the 1984 Olympics, he reverted to the coxed fours and won a gold medal. His second Olympic gold came in the coxless pairs at Seoul in 1988 when he also won a bronze in the coxed pairs.

Holmes first major success came in 1982, when he was a member of the Leander crew which won the Grand and, between his two Olympic victories, he won the Goblets in 1986 and, in the same year, the gold medals in the coxless pairs and the coxed fours at the Commonwealth Games.

Andy Holmes (right) and Steve Redgrave, winners of the coxless pairs in 1988. Four years earlier they were both members of the winning crew in the coxed fours.

Horsfall, *Ewart Douglas*
Born: 24 May 1892, Toxteth, Liverpool, Lancashire   Died: 1 February 1974, Devizes, Wiltshire
GOLD: 1912 (EIGHTS)   SILVER: 1920 (EIGHTS)

Ewart Horsfall went up to Magdalen College, Oxford from Eton in October 1911 with an outstanding reputation and five months later was in the winning Oxford boat against Cambridge. Oxford were again successful in 1913 with Horsfall as stroke but in 1914, when Horsfall rowed at number four, Cambridge enjoyed a comfortable victory. He also rowed number four in the Leander eight which won the gold medals at the 1912 Olympics when, at the age of 20, he was the youngest member of the crew.

Ewart Horsfall will go down in history as one of the great strokes of English rowing: in 1913, he became the first stroke to win the Boat Race after being behind at Barnes Bridge, he won the Grand four times – three times as stroke – and he stroked the winning crew in the Stewards' on the only two occasions he competed.

At the outbreak of war, Horsfall initially joined the Rifle Brigade but later transferred to the RAF, attaining the rank of squadron leader and achieving the distinction of being awarded the rare

'double' of a Military Cross (1916) and a Distinguished Flying Cross (1918). After the war, he was invited back to Oxford to help re-establish rowing at the University, a task which enabled him to keep in training and, in 1920, make a second Olympic appearance, stroking the Leander eight which came within half a length of winning their third successive Olympic title. Horsfall always maintained his interest in the sport and in 1948 he was manager of the British Olympic rowing team.

Johnstone, *Banner Carruthers*

Born: 11 November 1882, Pool Bank, Bebington, Cheshire   Died: 20 June 1964, Bournemouth, Hampshire

GOLD: 1908 (EIGHTS)

After Eton, 'Bush' Johnstone went up to Trinity College, Cambridge and was in the Cambridge boat for four years (1904–1907), being President of the Boat Club in his last year. The following year he rowed in the Leander eight which won the gold medals at the Olympics. His other notable successes included wins in the Grand in 1904 and 1905 and the Goblets in 1906, 1907 and 1909.

In 1909, Johnstone joined the Government Survey Department in Ceylon but in 1913 he moved to the Administration of Zanzibar and on the outbreak of war initially served with the Carrier Corps in East Africa. After transferring to the Black Watch, he was awarded the OBE for services in France and Belgium. In his later years, Banner Johnstone was the rowing correspondent of the *Daily Telegraph*.

Kelly, *Frederick Septimus*

Born: 29 May 1881, Sydney, New South Wales, Australia   Died: 13 November 1916, Beaucort-sur-Ancre, France

GOLD: 1908 (EIGHTS)

Frederick Kelly enjoyed a remarkable rowing career and was equally competent as a sculler or in an eight. He won the Diamonds in 1902, 1903 and 1905, the Wingfield in 1903, when he was also in the Oxford eight, was member of the Leander crew which won the Grand in 1903, 1904 and 1905 and was in the Leander eight which took the 1908 Olympic title.

In 1914, Kelly, who was educated at Eton and Balliol College, Oxford, joined the Royal Naval Division and served in *HMS Hood* together with the poet, Rupert Brooke. He won the DSC at Gallipoli but later in 1916, when with his unit in Fance, was killed instantly when rushing a German machine gun post.

Had he survived, Kelly would certainly have achieved fame as a musician. He had shown considerable talent for the piano as a child but did not take up music seriously until he left Balliol in 1903. He studied for five years at Dr Hoch's Conservatory at Frankfurt-on-Main, made his concert debut in his native Sydney in 1911 and, the following year, gave a series of concerts in London. However, contemporary critics were of the opinion that Kelly's true forte was as a composer and his best remembered work is his 1915 composition dedicated to his late friend and entitled 'Elegy for String Orchestra in Memoriam to Rupert Brooke'.

Kinnear, *William Duthie*

Born: 3 December 1880, Laurencekirk, Scotland   Died: 5 March 1974, London

GOLD: 1912 (SINGLE SCULLS)

Wally Kinnear worked in the drapery trade in his home town, an experience which enabled him to obtain a position with the Debenham Company when, in 1902, like many other young Scots of the time, he headed south to seek employment. He was introduced to sculling by his colleagues at work and initially joined the Cavendish Rowing Club. In 1903 he won the West End ARA sculling championship and repeated this success in 1904 and 1905, after which he joined the more prestigious Kensington Rowing Club. Over the next five years, Kinnear won numerous sculling events along the Thames and in 1910 he won the Diamonds and the Wingfield and, with both these victories being repeated in 1911, became firmly established as one of the world's leading scullers.

For 1912, Kinnear had as his target a hat trick of victories in the Diamonds and a gold medal at the Stockholm Olympics. He was surprisingly beaten in the first heat of the Diamonds, various reasons being given for his defeat, the most plausible being that his favourite boat was already on its way to Stockholm and that he had sculled at Henley in an unfamiliar craft. At the Olympics he won his heat, semi-final and the final without being extended, so retaining the Olympic sculling title for Great Britain. After a short break, he was back on the Thames and in August 1912 won the Wingfield Sculls for the third successive year. Although no more major championships came his way, Wally Kinnear continued rowing until the outbreak of war. He served with the Royal Naval Air Service for the duration and after the war took a keen interest in coaching.

Kirby, *Alister Graham*

Born: 14 April 1886, Brompton, London   Died: 29 March 1917, France

GOLD: 1912 (EIGHTS)

Alister Kirby went up to Magdalen College, Oxford from Eton and although he was in the Oxford boat for four years (1906–9) it was not until his last year, 1909, when he was President that Oxford avenged three successive defeats by Cambridge. Kirby was captain of the Leander eight which won the gold medals at the 1912 Olympics. On the outbreak of war he was commissioned into the Rifle Brigade and later died of a war illness.

Lander, *John Gerard Heath*

Born: 7 September 1907, Liverpool, Lancashire   Died: December 1941, Hong Kong

GOLD: 1928 (COXLESS FOURS)

After his fine performance as stroke in the coxless fours at the 1928 Olympics, John Lander of Shrewsbury and Trinity College, Cambridge seemed assured of a blue in 1929. However, Richard Beesly, the Cambridge President and Lander's fellow gold medallist in Amsterdam, called on Tom Brocklebank as stroke for the centenary year Boat Race, which Cambridge won by four lengths.

On leaving Cambridge, Lander took up a business appointment in Hong Kong where he was killed in defence of the colony during the Japanese invasion. While no less than thirteen British Olympic gold medallists lost their lives in World War I, John Lander was the only one to be killed in action in World War II.

Laurie, *William George Ranald Mundell*

Born: 4 May 1915, Granchester, Cambridgeshire

GOLD: 1948 (COXLESS PAIRS)

'Ran' Laurie, who was educated at Monkton Combe and Selwyn College, Cambridge, established a fine reputation as stroke when he was an undergraduate. He was in the winning Cambridge eight for three successive years and in the last two years, 1935 and 1936, he was the stroke. Later in 1936 he stroked the British eight which finished fourth at the Berlin Olympics but possibly his greatest performance came in the Grand in 1934, when he stroked the winning Leander eight as they set a Henley record which was to last until 1952.

After the 1936 Olympics, Laurie joined the Government Service in Sudan where his friend and future Olympic partner, John Wilson, was already serving. In 1938 they took their leave together and won the Goblets at Henley. Ten years later they again travelled to England from the Sudan and won the Goblets for a second time before going on to win the Olympic title. When 'Ran' Laurie finally retired to England he qualified as a doctor.

Mackinnon, *Duncan*

Born: 29 September 1887, Paddington, London   Died: 9 October 1917, Ypres, France

GOLD: 1908 (COXLESS FOURS)

Duncan Mackinnon, who was educated at Rugby and Magdalen College, Oxford, had not yet won his blue when he won an Olympic gold medal in the coxless fours in 1908, although he subsequently rowed in the Cambridge boat in 1909, 1910 and 1911.

In the five years he competed at Henley, Mackinnon lost only two races winning the Grand and the Visitors' twice each and the Stewards' and the Wyfold once.

On leaving Oxford, McKinnon became a partner in the family business in Calcutta but returned to England on the outbreak of war. After initially being commissioned into the Royal North Devon Hussars he transferred to the Scots Guards before being killed in action.

Maclagen, *Gilchrist Stanley*

Born: 5 October 1879, Chelsea, London   Died: 25 April 1915, Pilken Wood, France

GOLD: 1908 EIGHTS

Gilchrist Maclagen was one of six Old Etonians in the Leander Olympic eight in 1908 and an Olympic gold medal was a fitting reward for his outstanding career as a cox. While he was at Magdalen College, he coxed the Oxford boat for four years (1899–1902) and he steered the Leander boat at Henley from 1899 to 1908, during which period he set the record of being the only man to be in the winning crew in the Grand six times.

Maclagan was killed in action while serving as a lieutenant in the Royal Warwickshire Regiment.

Macnabb, *James Alexander*

Born: 26 December 1901, Keighley, Yorkshire   Died: 6 April 1990, London

GOLD: 1924 (COXLESS FOURS)

James Macnabb, whose distinguished rowing career began at Eton and continued at Trinity College, Cambridge, made his first appearance at Henley in 1920 as a member of the Eton crew which reached the semi-finals of the Ladies' Plate. In 1922 he won the Stewards' with Eton Vikings and the Visitors' with Third Trinity and, the following year, he again won the Visitors', this time with Third Trinity, and rowed for Eton Vikings in the Grand. 1924 was probably his finest year. He began as a member of the Cambridge crew which scored an upset victory over Oxford in the Boat Race, at Henley he won the Goblets partnering Maxwell Eley and the Stewards' with Third Trinity and finished the year on a winning note when the Third Trinity crew won the coxless fours at the 1924 Olympic Games.

Macnabb was a qualified accountant and served the cause of charitable housing for many years. In 1972 he was awarded the OBE for his work with the Peabody Trust. He was the Chief of Clan Macnabb but later relinquished his claim to his uncle although he remained president of the Clan Society. He also gave invaluable service to the sport of rowing. He was honorary treasurer of the Amateur Rowing Association for 20 years, honorary secretary and treasurer of Leander and a steward at Henley. He coached the winning Cambridge crew from 1931 to 1933 and, following an interruption for the war when he commanded a regiment in the Royal Artillery in Burma, the Oxford crew from 1949 to 1951, making him one of the few people to have coached both Universities.

Morrison, *Robert Erskine*

Born: 26 March 1902, Richmond, Surrey   Died: 19 February 1980, Cambridge, Cambridgeshire

GOLD: 1924 (COXLESS FOURS)

Like all the other members of the coxless four which won the gold medals at the 1924 Olympics, Robert Morrison was educated at Eton and Trinity College, Cambridge. He rowed in the Cambridge boat in 1923 and won a total of eight events at Henley, his most successful year being 1925 when he won the Stewards', the Visitors' and the Goblets.

Morrison followed a career as an engineer and lived in many parts of the country before retiring to Cambridgeshire four years before his death.

Nickalls, *Guy*

Born: 13 November 1866, Sutton, Surrey   Died: 8 July 1935, Leeds, Yorkshire

GOLD: 1908 (EIGHTS)

There could not have been a more fitting close to the outstanding career of Guy Nickalls than an Olympic gold medal. Rowing in the winning Leander eight at the 1908 Olympics at the age of 41 years and 251 days, Nickalls is the oldest rowing champion in Olympic history.

Educated at Eton and Magdalen College, Oxford, Nickalls rowed in the University Boat Race five times (1887–91) and was the Oxford President in 1890. He also had a remarkable record at Henley, losing only 13 of the 81 races in which he took part and winning the Stewards' seven times, the Goblets six times, the Diamonds five times and the Grand four times. He also won the Wingfield four times.

At the outbreak of war, Nickalls was approaching his 50th birthday but he enlisted in the Army and served in France as the superintendent of bayonet training with the Royal Engineers. After the war, he resumed his career as a stockbroker. While motoring to Scotland on his annual fishing holiday he was involved in a car crash near Leeds and died in hospital the following day.

His son, Guy Oliver Nickalls, won an Olympic silver medal in the eights in 1920 and 1928.

Redgrave, *Steven G*

Born: 23 March 1962, Amersham, Buckinghamshire

GOLD: 1984 (COXED FOURS)   1988 (COXLESS PAIRS)   BRONZE: 1988 (COXED PAIRS)

Steven Redgrave was a dominant figure in British rowing and after winning the Diamond Sculls in 1983 he won an Olympic gold medal in the coxed fours the following year. He won the Diamonds again in 1985 and in 1986 he won the coxed pairs at the World Championships along with three gold medals at that year's Commonwealth Games. Redgrave was again a world champion in 1987, this time in the coxless pairs, when he was partnered by Andy Holmes, and they then went on to win the Olympic coxless pairs in 1988. Redgrave and Holmes also competed in the coxed pairs at the 1988 Olympics when they were joined by Patrick Sweeney as cox. In their sixth race of the Games they did well to take the bronze medals, particularly after competing in the semi-finals of the two pairs races within an hour.

Apart from his successes in international championships he won the Wingfield Sculls for the championship of the Thames for five consecutive years from 1985, setting a course record with his fifth win in 1989.

Steve Redgrave was a member of the Marlow Leander Rowing Club and his wife, Ann, was a member of Britain's women's eight at the 1984 Olympics and later became the first woman President of the Marlow club.

In 1989, Redgrave took up bobsleighing and in his first season in the sport he was a member of the crew which won the British 4-man championship.

Sanders, *Terence Robert Beaumont*

Born: 2 June 1901, Ireland   Died: 6 April 1985, Dorking, Surrey

GOLD: 1924 (COXLESS FOURS)

Terence Sanders, who was educated at Eton and Trinity College, Cambridge, stroked the Cambridge boat in 1923, won the Stewards' in 1922, 1923 and 1924 and was in the Leander eight which won the Grand in 1929.

In 1925 he took up a post as a lecturer in engineering at Cambridge University and maintained his interest in rowing by serving as honorary treasurer of the University Boat Club from 1928 to 1939. He joined the Ministry of Supply in 1941 and in 1946 he was appointed Principal Director of Technical Development (Defence). After being awarded the CB in 1950 he left the Army the following year with the rank of colonel. He later became Chairman of the Buckland Sand & Silica Co. and in 1967 he was appointed High Sheriff and Deputy Lieutenant of the County of Surrey.

Sanderson, *Ronald Harcourt*

Born: 11 December 1876, Uckfield, Sussex   Died: 17 April 1918, Gonnercourt, France

GOLD: 1908 (EIGHTS)

Ronald Sanderson was the son of the Reverend Canon E Sanderson who rowed in the Cambridge boat in 1862. Ronald rowed for Cambridge in 1899 when Oxford's nine-year winning streak was ended and he was again in the winning Cambridge boat in 1900. Sanderson was educated at Harrow and Trinity College, Cambridge. He was killed in action while serving with the Royal Field Artillery.

Somers-Smith, *John Robert*

Born: 15 December 1887, Walton-on-Thames, Surrey   Died: 1 July 1916, Gonnercourt, France

GOLD: 1908 (COXLESS FOURS)

John Somers-Smith attended Eton and Magdalen College, Oxford and continued the strong family sporting traditions at both establishments. His father, also an Old Etonian, ran for Oxford against Cambridge in 1868 and 1869 and was twice the AAA half-mile champion, whilst his brother, Richard, of Eton and Merton College, rowed against Cambridge in 1904 and 1905. John never won a blue himself and apart from stroking the winning Olympic four, his greatest success was as a member of the Leander crew which won the Grand in 1910 and 1911.

Somers-Smith won a Military Cross in 1916 and was killed in action exactly one year and one day after his brother had lost his life at the front.

The varying fortunes of Olympic champions cannot be more poignantly illustrated than by the fate of the four young men from Magdalen College, Oxford who won the coxless fours at the 1908 Olympic Games. Two were killed in the war and the two who survived became Knights of the Realm.

Southwood, *Leslie Frank*

Born: 18 January 1906, Fulham, London   Died: 7 February 1986, Bury St Edmunds, Suffolk

GOLD: 1936 (DOUBLE SCULLS)

On leaving Latymer Upper School, Dick Southwood initially joined the Auriol Rowing Club where his sculling potential was spotted by Jack Beresford. He then joined Beresford at the London Rowing Club and made his Olympic debut in 1932 when he reached the final of the single sculls only to finish in last place following an attack of cramp in his shoulder. Four years later in Berlin, Southwood partnered Jack Beresford in the double sculls and they scored a sensational victory over the Germans in the final. Beresford and Southwood got together again in 1939 when a double sculls event was introduced to mark the centenary of the Henley Regatta and they dead-heated with the Italian pair, Scherli and Broschi, who were the reigning European champions. This was Dick Southwood's only success at Henley but in 1933 he won the prestigious Wingfield Sculls for the sculling championship of the Thames and his time of 21 minutes 11 seconds stood as a course record for many years.

Swann, *Sidney Ernest*

Born: 24 June 1890, Sulby, Isle of Man   Died: 19 September 1976, Minehead, Somerset

GOLD: 1912 (EIGHTS)   SILVER: 1920 (EIGHTS)

Sidney Swann, who was educated at Rugby and Trinity Hall, Cambridge, was a member of a family rich in sporting talent. His father rowed in the Boat Race three times, won the 25 mile bicycle race against Oxford in 1884 and rowed across the Channel single-handed at the age of 49. His brother, Arthur, was equally versatile, winning a blue for athletics in 1913 and for rowing in 1920.

On his first appearance at Henley in 1910, Sidney Swann stroked Trinity Hall to victory in both the Visitors' and the Wyfold and he was in the Cambridge boat in 1911, 1912 and 1913. In 1913 he was also in the winning Leander eight in the Grand and won the Goblets that year partnered by his brother, Arthur, a victory the Swann brothers were to repeat in 1914. A unique record was set in the eights at the 1912 Olympics when, of the 18 men in the final, Sidney Swann was the only one who had not attended Oxford University.

Following the family tradition, Sidney Swann entered the Church and after war service won an Olympic silver medal in the eights at Antwerp. His clerical duties took him to Africa from 1926 to 1933 and in 1941 he was appointed Chaplain to King George VI.

Thomson, *Gordon Lindsay*

Born: 27 March 1884, Wandsworth, London   Died: 8 July 1953, Staplehurst, Kent

GOLD: 1908 (COXLESS PAIRS)   SILVER: 1908 (COXLESS FOURS)

After attending University College School, Hampstead, Gordon Thomson went up to Trinity Hall, Cambridge where he won his rowing blue in 1909. The previous year he had won the coxless pairs, with John Fenning as his partner, at the 1908 Olympics and both Thomson and Fenning also won silver medals as members of the Leander crew in the coxless fours.

During the war, Gordon Thomson served with the RAF and was awarded the DSC for his photographic work at low altitudes over enemy lines in Gallipoli. He also won the DFC and was thus honoured with a rare 'double' of gallantry medals.

Thomson was also a fine rugby player and represented UCS Old Boys, London Scottish and Surrey.

Warriner, *Michael Henry*

Born: 3 December 1908, Chipping Norton, Oxfordshire   Died: 7 April 1986, Shipston-on-Stour, Warwickshire

GOLD: 1928 (COXLESS FOURS)

Michael Warriner went up to Trinity College, Cambridge from Harrow and was in the winning Cambridge boat in 1928, 1929 and 1930, his last year as President of the Cambridge University Boat Club. Other successes included victories at Henley in the Visitors' in 1928 and the Stewards' and the Ladies' in 1929.

In 1930, like many rowing blues of the time, Warriner joined the Sudan Government Service but returned to England in 1934 and entered the business world as an engineer. In the war, he was, at first, with the Indian Army but he then served in Greece and the Middle East as a Lt. Colonel in the REME. He was awarded the MBE in 1945.

Wells, *Henry Bensley*

Born: 12 January 1891, Kensington, London   Died: 4 July 1967, Newton Abbott, Devon

GOLD: 1912 (EIGHTS)

After coxing the Oxford boat from 1911 to 1914, Henry Wells was called to the Bar by Gray's Inn in 1914. Shortly afterwards, on the outbreak of war, he joined the 6th London Brigade and was awarded the MBE in 1919. Wells, who was educated at Winchester and Magdalen College, Oxford, was appointed a County Court Judge in 1934 and retired in 1958.

Wilson, *John Hyrne Tucker*

Born: 17 September 1914, Bristol, Rhode Island, USA

GOLD: 1948 (COXLESS PAIRS)

Jack Wilson was born of English parents in America and went to school in Texas before entering Shrewsbury School in 1924. He subsequently went up to Pembroke College, Cambridge and rowed in the winning Cambridge boat from 1934 to 1936. While at Cambridge, Wilson met his future Olympic partner, Ran Laurie, and from then on their lives were closely knit.

Jack Wilson would almost certainly have been selected for the 1936 Olympics had he not already taken up a post with the Sudan Government Service. Later in 1936 Ran Laurie joined him in the Sudan. Their friendship was soon re-established and on one occasion Laurie received news that Wilson had been speared through by a crazed woman with an assegai but, after speeding to see Wilson before he died, Laurie found the victim of the attack playing tennis with his nurse! Although training opportunities were limited, Wilson and Laurie ensured that their leave in 1938 coincided with Henley week where they surprisingly won the Goblets. Ten years later, this unusual pairing from Africa scored their second win in the Goblets and then went on to take the Olympic title.

Wormwald, *Leslie Graham*

Born: 19 August 1890, Cookham, Berkshire   Died: 10 July 1965, Knightsbridge, London

GOLD: 1912 (EIGHTS)

Although he only rowed in the second eight at Eton, Leslie Wormwald showed considerable improvement when he went up to Magdalen College, Oxford. In 1910 he was in the Magdalen boat which finished at the Head of the River and won the Grand at Henley. The following year Magdalen won the Grand for a second time and in 1913, Wormwald was in the winning Oxford crew in the Boat Race.

Wormwald won a Military Cross while serving in France in 1918 and died at the Hyde Park Hotel, London while visiting England from his retirement home in Spain.

Shooting

Amoore, *Edward J*

GOLD: 1908 (SMALL BORE RIFLE – TEAM)   BRONZE: 1908 (SMALL BORE RIFLE – DISAPPEARING TARGET)

Edward Amoore, a member of Southfields Rifle Club, competed in four small bore events at the 1908 Olympics and won medals in two of them. He had the worst score of the winning British foursome in the team event but in the individual competition with a disappearing target was one of eight marksmen to score a maximum of 45 points and took the bronze medal on the count-back.

Amoore also placed fifth in the individual small bore event but in the competition with a moving target he scored only three out of a possible 45 points and, not surprisingly, finished in last place.

Britain's winning team in the 1908 Small Bore team event. Left to right: (Standing) MK Matthews, EJ Amoore. (Seated) WE Pimm, W Milne (non-competing captain), HR Humby.

Braithwaite, *John Robert*

Born: 28 September 1925, Scarborough, Yorkshire

GOLD: 1968 (CLAY PIGEON)

Bob Braithwaite made his Olympic debut in 1964 when he placed seventh in the Clay Pigeon shooting. Four years later, at the Games in Mexico City, he became the first Briton to win an Olympic shooting gold medal for 44 years.

At the 1968 Olympics, Braithwaite, a 42-year-old veterinary surgeon, was in second place at the end of the first day but hit all hundred clays on the second day to take the Olympic title with a score of 198 points out of a possible 200. On the first day, Braithwaite missed only the fifth and thirteenth clay, so this meant that he scored 187 consecutive hits, an incredible achievement considering that the clays came from the traps at any height and angle and at speeds in excess of 100mph.

His daughter, Norine, was a nationally ranked middle distance runner but did not succeed in making the Olympic team.

Carnell, *Arthur Ashton*

Born: 21 March 1862, Somers Town, London   Died: 11 September 1940, Bedford Park, London

GOLD: 1908 (SMALL BORE RIFLE)

The 1908 Olympic small bore rifle title was decided at Bisley over rounds at 50 yards and 100 yards. After the opening round at 50 yards, Carnell was in joint fifth position but moved into the lead during the second phase at 100 yards, finishing one point ahead of Harry Humby, the half-way stage leader. Carnell finished with a total of 387 points* out of a possible 400 and in view of this fine performance in the individual event he was asked to compete in the team event, for which he had been named as reserve. Not wishing to deprive another marksman of the chance of Olympic competition, Carnell declined selection for the team event but despite his absence, Britain still won the gold medals by a comfortable margin. Both Arthur Carnell and his wife, who was also a champion shot, were members of the Mansfield (Highgate) Rifle Club.

* Philip Plater actually set a world record score of 391 points but was then disqualified in unusual circumstances. (See page 161)

Cooper, *Malcolm Douglas*

Born: 20 December 1947, Camberley, Surrey

GOLD: 1984 (SMALL BORE RIFLE – THREE POSITIONS)   1988 (SMALL BORE RIFLE – THREE POSITIONS)

Malcolm Cooper first took up shooting as a 14-year-old in New Zealand, where his father was stationed as a lieutenant in the Royal Navy. He soon earned a place in the Auckland City team and when he returned to England, after three years in New Zealand, he immediately established himself as a marksman of county standard. From then on, Cooper progressed steadily to become the finest small bore rifle shot in the world.

After placing 18th at both the 1972 and the 1976 Olympics, Cooper missed the 1980 Games in Moscow because of the boycott by the British shooting team but in 1984 he won the gold medal by ten clear points. He repeated his victory at Seoul in 1988 although this time he only had one point to spare over his team-mate, Alister Allen.

Apart from his two Olympic gold medals, Cooper established himself as the best in the world with numerous wins at the World and European championships. Possibly, his outstanding performances came at the 1985 European Championships when he won all five individual titles and at the 1986 World Championships when he set five world records. In all, Cooper has set 17 world records and shooting is now his full time occupation. His wife, Sarah, was also a member of the Olympic shooting team in 1988 and together they run a shooting supplies business in Hayling Island.

Malcolm Cooper, winner of the Small Bore Rifle (three positions) in 1984 and 1988.

Easte, *P*

GOLD: 1908 (CLAY PIGEON – TEAM)

Great Britain entered two teams for the clay pigeon event at the 1908 Olympics and Easte was a member of the team which finished two points ahead of the Canadians to take the gold medals. Easte was undoubtedly off-form for the competition as he posted the worst score for his team and all six members of the second British team, who won the bronze medals, also bettered Easte's score for the first team. He did, however, perform rather better in the clay pigeon individual event and finished in eighth place.

Fleming, *John Francis*

Born: 26 August 1881, Keswick, Cumberland   Died: 9 January 1965, New Malden, Surrey

GOLD: 1908 (SMALL BORE RIFLE – MOVING TARGET)

The standard of shooting in the small bore rifle (moving target) event at the 1908 Olympics was disappointing and John Fleming was one of four British competitors who tied for first place with a modest score of 24 points out of a possible 45. After the targets had been examined, Fleming was awarded the gold medal on the count back.

John Fleming, a civil servant, was for many years a member of the City Rifle Club and during the 1914–18 War was an instructor at the NRA School of Musketry. He was in the King's Hundred in 1934 and was a life member of the National Rifle Association.

Humby, *Harry Robinson*

Born: 8 April 1879, West London   Died: 23 February 1923, Muswell Hill, Middlesex

GOLD: 1908 (SMALL BORE RIFLE – TEAM)   SILVER; 1908 (SMALL BORE RIFLE)   1912 (CLAY PIGEON TEAM)

After placing second in the small bore rifle individual event at the 1908 Olympics, Harry Humby had the best score of the British marksmen in the team event, although Arthur Carnell, who had beaten him for the individual title, did not compete in the team event.

At the 1912 Olympics, Humby competed only in the clay pigeon competition, when he won a silver medal in the team event and was the leading Briton in the individual competition, finishing in fourth place. A captain in the Middlesex Regiment and member of the Alexandra Palace Rifle Club, Humby made a third Olympic appearance in 1920 when he was a member of the fourth-placed team in the clay pigeon team event.

Lessimore, *Edward John*

Born: 20 January 1881, Clifton, Gloucestershire   Died: 7 March 1960, Bristol, Gloucestershire

GOLD: 1912 (SMALL BORE RIFLE – TEAM 50 METRES)

Two separate small bore rifle team events were held over distances of 25 metres and 50 metres at the 1912 Olympics. Lessimore won a gold medal in the event at the longer distance and also placed fourth in the individual small bore rifle prone event.

Mackworth-Praed, *Cyril Winthrop*

Born: 21 September 1891, Mickleham, Surrey   Died: 30 June 1974, Ringwood, Hampshire

GOLD: 1924 (RUNNING DEER – DOUBLE SHOT TEAM)   SILVER: 1924 (RUNNING DEER – SINGLE SHOT)
1924 (RUNNING DEER – DOUBLE SHOT)

With three medals, Cyril Mackworth-Praed was the most successful British marksman at the 1924 Olympics, an appropriate reward for the man who raised and led the British team for the Games.

In addition to his gold medal and two silver medals, both of which were won after a shoot-off, Mackworth-Praed also placed fourth in the running deer, single shot, team event and eighth in the clay pigeon event. He made a second Olympic appearance 28 years later when he placed 11th out of the 14 entries in the individual clay pigeon event at Helsinki in 1952.

Mackworth-Praed's enthusiasm for the sport began at an early age and he was a member of the Eton Ashburton VIII from 1908 to 1910, captaining the team in his final year. Later in 1910 he was also captain of the Imperial Cadet team which went to Canada. After Eton, Mackworth-Praed went up to Trinity College, Cambridge and during the war he served with the Scots Guards.

He was a Fellow of the Royal Geographical Society and the Royal Zoological Society and the author of several papers on African ornithology. As a wealthy stockbroker he was able to visit East Africa in pursuit of his hobby and on these expeditions he collected for the British Museum.

Cyril Mackworth-Praed reached the final of the King's Hundred on six occasions between 1921 and 1938 and in the 1930s he ended a long run of German successes by winning the unofficial World Clay Pigeon Shooting Championship in Berlin. In World War II, he commanded the Commando Training School in the Western Isles and was awarded an OBE for his services. Throughout his life he was a generous supporter of the National Rifle Association and was made a life member in May 1924.

Matthews, *MK*

GOLD: 1908 (SMALL BORE RIFLE – TEAM)   SILVER: 1908 (SMALL BORE RIFLE – MOVING TARGET)

With some consistent performances, MK Matthews of the Mansfield (Highgate) Rifle Club won a gold and a silver medal at the 1908 Olympics, placed fourth in the small bore rifle individual event and ninth in the small bore rifle, disappearing target, competition.

As Matthews always felt that his showing in team events was inferior to his form in individual competition he tried to withdraw from the small bore team event but his opinion was over-ruled by the selection committee, whose decision was vindicated when Matthews made the highest individual score of the team.

Maunder, *Alexander*

Born: 3 February 1861, Loxbear, Devonshire   Died: 2 February 1932, Bickleigh, nr. Tiverton, Devonshire

GOLD: 1908 (CLAY PIGEON – TEAM)   SILVER: 1912 (CLAY PIGEON – TEAM)   BRONZE: 1908 (CLAY PIGEON)

Alex Maunder and Charles Palmer were the only members of the winning clay pigeon team at the 1908 Olympics who also won silver medals in Stockholm four years later. In the 1908 team event, Maunder made a vital contribution to the British success by beating the Canadian, Walter Ewing, who won the individual title, by two points – the margin by which Britain defeated Canada for the team title.

Additionally, Maunder won a bronze medal in the 1908 individual clay pigeon event.

Although Alex Maunder was not a member of the 1920 Olympic team, he was selected, at the age of 63, for the 1924 Games but asked for his name to be withdrawn in order to give a younger person a chance.

Alex Maunder was a long-time resident of Palmers Green and a member of the North London, Ealing, Middlesex and National Gun Clubs. He won the championship of the Clay Pigeon Shooting Association three times during the years when the event was considered to be the world championship. Maunder died of a heart attack while taking part in a billiards tournament at the local institute of the Devon village to which he had retired in 1929.

Merlin, *Gerald Eustace*

Born: 3 August 1884, Piraeus, Greece   Died: 1945, India

GOLD: 1906 (CLAY PIGEON – SINGLE SHOT)   BRONZE: 1906 (CLAY PIGEON – DOUBLE SHOT)

Although Greek-born and a resident of Athens, Gerald Merlin was of British parentage and elected to represent Great Britain at the Olympic Games.

There were eleven separate individual shooting competitions at the 1906 Olympics and Gerald Merlin took part in ten of them. Apart from his medals in the clay pigeon events, his best performance was in the duelling pistol at 25 metres, where he finished fourth shooting at dummies dressed in frock coats.

In 1906 the clay pigeon, single shot, competition consisted of 30 clays from four traps at a distance of 16 metres and as Merlin and John Peridis of Greece each hit 24 clays, a shoot-off was necessary.

Peridis was the first to make a mistake when he missed the fourth clay and the gold medal went to Gerald Merlin.

One of Merlin's infrequent visits to England coincided with the 1908 Olympic Games when he took the opportunity to defend his Olympic title but he was not successful and finished in 19th place.

Merlin, *Sidney Louis Walter*

Born: 26 April 1856, Piraeus, Greece   Died: 1952, Athens, Greece

GOLD: 1906 (CLAY PIGEON – DOUBLE SHOT)   BRONZE: 1906 (CLAY PIGEON – SINGLE SHOT)

Sidney Merlin was the only British marksman to take part in the first Modern Olympic Games in 1896 and ten years later he competed in all eleven individual shooting events at the 1906 Games. He won the gold medal in the clay pigeon, double shot, with 15 hits out of a possible 20 and he also won the bronze medal in the single shot event.

The considerable fortune of the Merlin family and their native-born knowledge of the Greek language placed them among the leaders of Greek Society at the turn of the century. The family were substantial landowners and one of the main thoroughfares of Athens is still known as Merlin Street. Sidney Merlin married Zaira, the daughter of George Theotokis, the Greek Prime Minister, and when they were later divorced Zaira married John Rollis who, like his father-in-law, also became Prime Minister.

Gerald and Sidney Merlin are invariably referred to as brothers but this is not correct. A search of the British Consular Birth Register reveals that Gerald was the son of Charles EP Merlin and his wife Irene (neé Stournare) whereas Sidney was the son of the British Vice-Consul for Athens, Charles LW Merlin and his wife Isabella (neé Green). However, they were certainly related and were, in all probability, cousins.

Millner, *Joshua Kearney*

Born: c. 1849, Ireland   Died: 16 November 1931, Dublin, Ireland

GOLD: (1908 FREE RIFLE – 1000 YARDS)

The 58-year-old Jerry Millner is the oldest Briton ever to have won an Olympic gold medal*, a distinction he achieved at Bisley in 1908 when he won the free rifle event with a score of 98 points out of a possible 100.

Millner first took a serious interest in competitive shooting in 1871 and in 1874 he was a member of the Irish team which visited the United States. In the match against the Americans, Millner began with a bullseye but unfortunately it was on the wrong target and the four points deducted for Millner's error virtually cost the Irish the match as the host country won by only three points.

Jerry Millner visited America again in 1887 when the British team lost the Palma Match at Creedmore by 93 points. He also represented Ireland in the Elcho Match for thirty years and captained the team in 1919, although he did not actually compete that year.

Millner was a distinguished figure in the Territorial Army. He served as a lieutenant in the Finsbury Rifles from 1882 to 1887 and then joined the famous Carlow Militia which was by then a territorial regiment of the King's Royal Rifle Corps. The Carlow Militia was finally disbanded in 1908 with Millner as their last Commanding Officer, having been Colonel of the Regiment for the past 15 years. Colonel Millner served as a member of the Council of the National Rifle Association from 1907 to 1914. In his later years he devoted much of his time to the breeding of sporting dogs and published a well received book on the subject.

Jerry Millner, winner of the Free Rifle in 1908 and at 58 Britain's oldest gold medallist.

* Millner was born before the Registration of Births became a legal requirement in Ireland. However, as it is known that he died at the age of 82, it can be calculated that when he won his gold medal on 9 July 1908 he cannot have been younger than 58 years 237 days of age. It is possible that he could have been as old as 59 years 238 days.

Moore, *FW*

GOLD: 1908 (CLAY PIGEON TEAM)

FW Moore was the captain of the six-man team which won the gold medals in the 1908 Olympic clay pigeon team event. He also placed equal seventh in the individual event.

Murray, *Robert Cook*

Born: 18 February 1870, Edinburgh, Scotland

GOLD: 1912 (SMALL BORE RIFLE – TEAM 50 METRES)

Robert Murray was the founder of the first small bore rifle club in Britain and later served as chairman, secretary and treasurer of the Urmston Miniature Rifle Club.

Apart from his gold medal in the team event at the 1912 Olympics, Murray also placed fifth in the small bore individual event with disappearing targets and sixth in the small bore individual event from any position.

Neame, *Philip, VC, DSO*   (Later Lt. General Sir P Neame, VC, KBE, DSO, DL)

Born: 12 December 1888, Faversham, Kent   Died: 28 April 1978, Faversham, Kent

GOLD: 1924 (RUNNING DEER – DOUBLE SHOT TEAM)

On leaving Cheltenham College, Neame went to the RMA Woolwich and was commissioned into the Royal Engineers in 1908 which marked the start of an outstanding military career. In December 1914 he won the Victoria Cross at Neuve Chappelle, two years later he was awarded the DSO and after filling various commands with distinction attained the rank of lieutenant general in 1940. He was knighted in 1946.

Neame was a fine all-round sportsman, his interests embracing not only target shooting but also hockey, mountaineering, polo, hunting, skiing and big game shooting. None of these sports made excessive demands on his time to the detriment of the others and he looked on each strictly as a pastime. In fact, his autobiography, which he wrote in captivity before escaping from an Italian prisoner of war camp, reveals that at the 1924 Olympic Games he was under the impression that he was representing the British Empire rather than Great Britain. Unlike his team-mates in the running deer, double shot, team event who defeated Norway by a single point, Neame did not take part in any other event at the Paris Olympics but he has the distinction of being the only man to win an Olympic gold medal and be awarded the Victoria Cross.

Neame was a versatile shot and represented the Army in both revolver and rifle competitions. Although overseas postings meant that his appearances at Bisley were spasmodic, he reached the King's Final in 1929.

Like many other Olympians, it was a love of sport that led Philip Neame into matrimony but the particular circumstances of his meeting his future wife are, fortunately, not commonplace. After being badly mauled by a tiger while big game hunting in India he married Miss Alberta Drew who nursed him in hospital.

Lt General Sir Philip Neame VC, KBE, CB, DSO, a member of the Running Deer team in 1924 and the only man to have won both a Victoria Cross and an Olympic gold medal.

Palmer, *Charles*

Born: 18 August 1869, Old Warden, Bedfordshire

GOLD: 1908 (CLAY PIGEON – TEAM)   SILVER: 1912 (CLAY PIGEON – TEAM)

Charles Palmer was the only member of the medal winning teams of 1908 and 1912 to compete again in the clay pigeon team event in 1920 where, with the British team finishing in fourth place at the Antwerp Games, Palmer came close to winning a third Olympic medal.

Pepé, *Joseph*

Born: 5 March 1881, Manchester, Lancashire

GOLD: 1912 (SMALL BORE RIFLE – TEAM 50 METRES)   SILVER: 1912 (SMALL BORE RIFLE – TEAM 25 METRES)

Joseph Pepé, of Wimbledon Park Rifle Club, and William Pimm were the only Britons to win medals in both the small bore rifle team events at the 1912 Olympics.

Perry, *Herbert Spencer*

Born: 23 January 1894   Died: 20 July 1966, Bridport, Dorset

GOLD: 1924 (RUNNING DEER – DOUBLE SHOT TEAM)

Herbert Perry was commissioned from the Special Reserve into the Royal Artillery in 1916 and retired from the Army in 1920 as a lieutenant with the honorary rank of captain. At 30 years of age he was the youngest member of the team which won the gold medals in the running deer – double shot team event at the 1924 Olympics and he played a significant role in Britain's narrow victory. With only Perry left to shoot, Norway led Britain by 67 points and as Perry only managed 29 points with his first 10 shots, victory seemed assured for the Norwegians but with his final 10 shots Perry scored 39 points to give Britain a dramatic one point win. Perry's second series was the best 10 shots of the entire competition. He also placed 13th in the individual double shot event.

Pike, *JF*

GOLD: 1908 (CLAY PIGEON – TEAM)

In the 1908 clay pigeon team event only the leading Briton, Alex Maunder, and the Canadian, Walter Ewing, had higher scores than Pike. However, in the individual event, Pike finished back in 12th place.

Pimm, *William Edwin*

Born: 10 December 1864, London

GOLD: 1908 (SMALL BORE RIFLE – TEAM)   1912 (SMALL BORE RIFLE – TEAM 50 METRES)
SILVER: 1912 (SMALL BORE RIFLE – TEAM 25 METRES)

Until Malcolm Cooper claimed his second Olympic title in 1988, William Pimm of the Wandsworth Rifle Club was the only British marksman to win two Olympic gold medals. He also competed in the various small bore rifle individual events in 1908 and 1912, his best performance being in the moving target event in 1908 when he placed sixth.

Postans, *JM*

GOLD: 1908 (CLAY PIGEON – TEAM)

After the first two stages of the clay pigeon team event at the 1908 Olympics, Postans had the worst score of the six-man British team. However, he shot well in the third and final stage and eventually finished ahead of FW Moore and P Easte in the British team.

Styles, *William Kensett*

Born: 11 October 1874, Islington, London

GOLD: 1908 (SMALL BORE RIFLE – DISAPPEARING TARGET)   SILVER: 1912 (SMALL BORE RIFLE – TEAM 25 METRES)

William Styles won his Olympic gold medal in 1908 on a count-back after nine competitors – eight of them British – had scored the maximum 45 points in the small bore event with a disappearing target. In 1912 he went to Stockholm to defend his title but disappointed by finishing back in 13th place.

Although Styles was not at his best in the 1912 individual event he was the fourth scoring member of the team which won the silver medals in the small bore team event at 25 metres.

Whitty, *Allen, DSO*

Born: 5 May 1867, Martley Hillside, Worcestershire   Died: 22 July 1949, Aldermaston, Berkshire

GOLD: 1924 (RUNNING DEER – DOUBLE SHOT TEAM)

By concealing his true age*, Allen Whitty joined the Worcestershire Regiment as a 13-year-old boy and soon saw service in India where he developed his skills as a marksman. He returned home as a regimental sergeant major in 1897 and became a well-known figure at Army and national rifle meetings. He was a member of the Army VIII at various times between 1897 and 1920 and he shot in the King's Hundred five times, the last time being in 1938 as a 71-year-old.

Allen Whitty was gazetted to a quartermaster's commission in his county regiment in June 1916 and, later that year, won a DSO after which he was soon promoted to lieutenant colonel.

At the 1924 Olympics, Whitty only competed in the running deer, double shot, events and after finishing in 18th place individually, he won a gold medal as a member of the team which defeated Norway by a single point.

The date of birth given for Whitty in Army and Olympic records is 16 April 1866 but the correct date, as given above, is from his birth certificate.

Swimming

MEN

Derbyshire, *John Henry*

Born: 29 November 1878, Manchester, Lancashire   Died: 30 July 1938, Forge Baslow, Derbyshire

GOLD: 1900 WATER POLO   1908 (4 × 200 METRES FREESTYLE RELAY)
BRONZE: 1906 (4 × 250 METRES FREESTYLE RELAY)

Between 1898 and 1904 'Rob' Derbyshire won a total of ten individual ASA titles, including six victories in the 100 yards freestyle; he became the first Briton to break one minute for that distance in 1907. In addition to his three Olympic medals events he also competed in the 100 metres freestyle in 1906, 1908 and 1912, and the 400 metres freestyle in 1906. The only time he reached the final was in the 100 metres of 1906 when he finished fifth.

Derbyshire began his career with Manchester Osborne SC and was the only star swimmer who remained with them following a major disagreement within the club in 1901. Eventually he too left Manchester Osborne, joining the Old Trafford SC in 1908, and later competed for the London-based Amateur SC.

After working as a baths manager in the Manchester area, Derbyshire took up a similiar post at the Lime Grove Baths in London.

Foster, *William*

Born: 10 July 1890, Bacup, Lancashire   Died: 17 December 1963, Fylde, Lancashire

GOLD: 1908 (4 × 200 METRES FREESTYLE RELAY)   SILVER: 1912 (4 × 200 METRES FREESTYLE RELAY)

Exactly two weeks after his 18th birthday, William Foster was on a winning relay team at the 1908 Games and is the youngest-ever British winner of an Olympic gold medal. He originally competed for his home-town club Bacup SC before joining Hyde Seal and although he never won an ASA title he was in the top flight of British swimmers for a number of years.

Goodhew, *Duncan Alexander*

Born: 27 May 1957, Marylebone, London

GOLD: 1980 (100 METRES BREASTSTROKE)   BRONZE: 1980 (4 × 100 METRES MEDLEY RELAY)

While still a student at Millfield School, Duncan Goodhew made his Olympic debut in 1976 and finished seventh in the 100 metres breaststroke. At the 1978 Commonwealth Games he won silver medals in both individual breaststroke events and the medley relay, while at the World Championships that year he finished fourth in both individual events and won a bronze medal in the medley relay.

A training spell at an American University under the great coach David Haller provided the final preparation for the 1980 Olympics, and in Moscow Goodhew won the gold medal in the 100 metres breaststroke and a bronze in the medley relay.

After his competitive career was over, the shaven-headed Goodhew became a familiar and easily distinguishable media personality.

Duncan Goodhew after winning the 100 metres breaststroke in 1980.

Holman, *Frederick*

Born: March 1885, Dawlish, Devon   Died: 23 January 1913, Exeter, Devon

GOLD: 1908 (200 METRES BREASTSTROKE)

Fred Holman was an outstanding junior swimmer, winning age-group races from the age of 11. As a senior he won numerous Devon county and Western Counties championships but never succeeded in winning an ASA title.

Holman only took up the breaststroke towards the end of his career but he still succeeded in winning an Olympic gold medal and set the inaugural world record in the process. On his return to Devon from his Olympic triumph in London he was given civic receptions in both Exeter and Dawlish, and announced that his ambition was to become the chef in his own restaurant. Sadly, this ambition was short-lived as Britain's first Olympic breaststroke champion died at the early age of 27 as a result of complications following typhoid and pneumonia.

Jarvis, *John Arthur*

Born: 24 February 1872, Leicester, Leicestershire   Died: 9 May 1933, St Pancras, London

GOLD: 1900 (1000 METRES FREESTYLE & 4000 METRES FREESTYLE)   SILVER: 1906 (1 MILE FREESTYLE)
BRONZE: 1906 (400 METRES FREESTYLE & 4 × 250 METRES FREESTYLE RELAY)

Jack Jarvis won his first Olympic title in 1900 when he beat the Austrian Otto Wahle by more than a minute in the 1000 metres freestyle. Eleven days later he won a second gold in the 4000 metres freestyle with an even more resounding victory, finishing almost 11 minutes ahead of the Hungarian Zoltan von Holmay. The fact that both races were swum with the benefit of the downstream current in the River Seine made a significant contribution to the fast times recorded.

Jarvis won three more medals at the 1906 Games in Athens and made his third and final Olympic appearance in 1908. By this time he was 36 years old and after winning his heat in the 1500 metres freestyle he failed to finish in the semi-final.

Between 1897 and 1906 Jarvis won 24 ASA swimming titles representing Leicester SC, and in 1904 he was also the plunging champion. He won 108 major international races using a right overarm sidestroke with a special kick he had developed with Joey Nuttall, a leading professional of the time. This effective technique, known as the Jarvis-Nuttall Kick, enabled Jarvis to set many world records although none were ever officially recognised by FINA. Jarvis was also a water polo international for 11 years, from 1894 to 1904, but never played for Great Britain in the Olympic Games.

After his retirement from competitive swimming, Jarvis devoted himself to life-saving techniques and was respectfully referred to as 'Professor' Jarvis. He personally saved many lives including a well-publicised rescue when he brought in twin sisters. His sister Clara was chaperone to the British women's swimming team at the 1912 Olympics and three of his daughters, all swimming teachers, went to Florida in 1968 to represent their father at his posthumous induction into the Swimming Hall of Fame at Fort Lauderdale.

Moorhouse, *Adrian David*

Born: 24 May 1964, Bradford, Yorkshire

GOLD: 1988 (100 METRES BREASTSTROKE)

Adrian Moorhouse achieved his first major international success when he won the 200 metres breaststroke at the 1983 European Championships. The following year he made his Olympic debut, finishing fourth in the 100 metres breaststroke and winning the 'B' final in the 200 metres breaststroke at Los Angeles. Wins in the 100 metres breaststroke at the 1985 and 1987 European Championships followed and at the 1988 Olympics he won the gold medal by the narrowest of margins over Karoly Guttler of Hungary.

In addition to his successes at the Olympic Games and European Championships, Moorhouse won individual gold medals at the 1982, 1986 and 1990 Commonwealth Games. Although he constantly threatened the world record, he seemed destined to miss

adding this honour to his impressive list of achievements until in the heats of the 1989 European Championships in Bonn he clocked 61.49 sec and shaved 0.16 sec off the world 100 metres breaststroke record set by the American Steve Lundqvist at the 1984 Olympic Games. Moorhouse could not make a further improvement on his record in the final but he duly took the gold medal, his fourth successive European title. At the 1990 Commonwealth Games in Auckland, he equalled the world record he had set in Bonn and later that year, at the National Championships at Crystal Palace, he equalled his own world record for a second time.

RADMILOVIC, Paul – see *Water Polo*

Adrian Moorhouse, 1988 Olympic and 1990 Commonwealth breaststroke champion.

Taylor, *Henry*

Born: 17 March 1885, Oldham, Lancashire   Died: 28 February 1951, Chadderton, Lancashire

GOLD: 1906 (1 MILE FREESTYLE)
1908 (400 METRES FREESTYLE, 1500 METRES FREESTYLE & 4 × 200 METRES FREESTYLE RELAY)
SILVER: 1906 (400 METRES FREESTYLE)   BRONZE: 1906 (4 × 250 METRES FREESTYLE RELAY)
1912 (4 × 200 METRES FREESTYLE RELAY)   1920 (4 × 200 METRES FREESTYLE RELAY)

Henry Taylor's total of eight Olympic medals is a record for a British Olympian in any sport and his feat of winning a medal in the same event, the freestyle relay, at four successive Games remains unique in British Olympic history.

Born in poor circumstances, Taylor worked in the mills in his native Lancashire and trained in the canals and streams around his work-place; he only used the local swimming baths on 'dirty water day' when admission was cheaper. As it happened, this proved to be an admirable preparation for the 1906 Olympics in Athens where the swimming events were held in the open sea at Phalerum Bay.

Taylor was the surprise of the Games and won two gold medals, although he had yet to win an ASA title. On his return home he set about remedying this omission and by the end of the season he was the British champion at 440 yards, 500 yards, 880 yards and 1 mile. His winning time of 11 min 25.4 sec for the 880 yards was recognised as the inaugural world record and he claimed further world records at the 1908 Olympics in the 800 metres and 1500 metres. In all, Taylor won 15 ASA titles, the last being the long distance event in 1920 when he was 35 years old and still playing water polo for England.

Having originally competed for Chadderton SC, he later joined the Hyde Seal club. He found his lack of formal education a considerable handicap in a variety of ways and while on tour it fell to Jack Jarvis to write Taylor's love letters home. Taylor pawned his swimming trophies to buy the Nudger Inn at Doleross, but the business venture failed and he never redeemed his prizes.

In 1969 Taylor, one of the greatest of all British Olympians, was posthumously inducted into the Swimming Hall of Fame at Fort Lauderdale, Florida.

Swimmer Henry Taylor is chaired after Britain win the relay in 1908. Taylor is Britain's most successful Olympian, winning eight medals between 1906 and 1920.

Wilkie, *David Andrew*

Born: 8 March 1954, Colombo, Sri Lanka

GOLD: 1976 (200 METRES BREASTSTROKE)   SILVER: 1972 (200 METRES BREASTSTROKE)
1976 (100 METRES BREASTSTROKE)

David Wilkie, Britain's most successful international swimmer since the heyday of Henry Taylor some 70 years earlier, first learned to swim in Sri Lanka, where he was born of Scots parents. He returned to Scotland in 1965 to attend Daniel Stewart's College in Edinburgh and although he had no serious competitive aspirations he joined Warrender Baths SC, where he was fortunate to meet an understanding coach in Frank Thomas.

On a modest training schedule, Wilkie won a bronze medal in the 100 metres breaststroke at the 1970 Commonwealth Games and a silver in the 200 metres at the 1972 Olympics; it was these performances which inspired him to raise his sights. In January 1973 he went to the University of Miami to study marine biology and now had the time, the facilities and the self-motivation to establish himself as the best breaststroke swimmer in the world. By the summer of 1973 he had, in part, fulfilled his ambition by winning the 200 metres at the World Championships with a new world record.

His subsequent record at major championships remains unmatched by any other British swimmer. In 1974 he won the 200 metres breaststroke and the 200 metres individual medley at both the Commonwealth Games and the European Championships and his winning time in the individual medley at the latter event was a new world record. These outstanding performances earned him an

MBE in the Queen's Birthday Honours list. At the 1975 World Championships he won both individual breaststroke events and took a bronze medal in the medley relay.

Wilkie opened the 1976 Olympic season by becoming the first Briton ever to win an American Championship title. In fact, he won three – the 100 and 200 metres breaststroke and the 200 metres individual medley. Then at the Montreal Olympics, his greatest ambition was fulfilled. After finishing second to John Hencken of the USA in the 100 metres breaststroke he gained ample revenge by taking the gold medal in the 200 metres. In an event which is measured in hundredths of a second Wilkie finished more than two seconds ahead of Hencken, and in beating the world record by more than three seconds he put up what most experts judged to be the finest performance in the Olympic pool at Montreal in 1976.

David Wilkie was the world breaststroke champion over 200m in 1973 and 1975 and Olympic champion in 1976.

Swimming

WOMEN

Fletcher, *Jennie*

Born: 19 March 1890, Leicester, Leicestershire   Died: 1968, Canada

GOLD: 1912 (4 × 100 METRES FREESTYLE RELAY)   BRONZE: 1912 (100 METRES FREESTYLE)

Jennie Fletcher of Leicester Ladies SC won a bronze medal in the 100 metres freestyle at the 1912 Games to become Britain's first woman Olympic swimming medallist. She later contributed an outstanding second leg in the relay which assured Great Britain of the gold medals and a new world record.

One of 11 children in an underprivileged family, she was only able to train after working 12 hours a day, six days a week. Despite their impoverished circumstances, her parents refused an offer for Jennie to tour as a professional with Annette Kellerman in 1907. She therefore remained an amateur, winning six ASA 100 yards freestyle titles between 1906 and 1912 and in 1909 setting a world record for the distance.

Grinham, *Judith Brenda*   (Later Mrs P Rowley)

Born: 5 March 1939, Hampstead, London

GOLD: 1956 (100 METRES BACKSTROKE)

Judy Grinham's first success came in 1953 when she won the Middlesex girls 100 yards backstroke as a member of Hampstead Ladies SC. She never reached the final of an ASA Junior event, but had already won two international races for Britain when she won her first national title in 1955. A successful round of international galas and the retention of her ASA title in the summer of 1956 secured her place in the team for the Melbourne Olympics.

At the Games, Judy won the 100 metres backstroke in 1 min 12.9 sec, which was the first world long-course record for the event, and she was the first British woman swimmer to win an Olympic gold medal for 32 years.

As a relief from the pressures of world class backstroke swimming, Judy Grinham turned to the freestyle event in 1957, winning the ASA 220 yards title, but the following year she reverted to her former style and enjoyed an outstanding season. At the Commonwealth Games she won the 110 yards backstroke with a new world record of 1 min 11.9 sec and this was also ratified as a record for the marginally shorter 100 metres distance. She then won a second gold medal and shared in a second world record in the medley relay, before completing her medal haul

Judy Grinham, winner of the 100 metres backstroke in 1956.

with a bronze in the freestyle relay. Later in the season, she won the 100 metres backstroke at the European Championships to become the first woman ever to hold the Olympic, European and Commonwealth titles. At the European Championships she also won a silver in the freestyle relay and bronze medals in the individual 100 metres freestyle and the medley relay.

Judy, who in addition to her international championship honours won seven ASA titles, retired from competitive swimming on her 20th birthday and married the journalist Peter Rowley soon afterwards.

Lonsbrough, *Anita*   (Later Mrs HW Porter)

Born: 10 August 1941, York, Yorkshire

GOLD: 1960 (200 METRES BREASTSTROKE)

Although born in Yorkshire Anita Lonsbrough first learned to swim in India, where her father was serving as a Regimental Sergeant-Major with the Coldstream Guards. After the family's return to England, Anita began her swimming career with the Huddersfield Borough Club, where she was an average freestyle performer but for the 1958 season she turned to the breaststroke and almost immediately became a world class performer.

At the 1960 Olympic Games and the Commonwealth Games and European Championships of 1958 and 1962, she won a total of seven gold, three silver and two bronze medals. The highlight of this impressive series of performances was her gold medal in the Olympic 200 metres breaststroke when she set the second of her four individual world records. At the ASA Championships she won a total of eight titles in the breaststroke, freestyle and individual medley. Her eighth and last ASA victory came in the individual medley in 1964 and this was the event she contested at the Tokyo Olympics, in preference to defending her breaststroke title. She reached the final of her new event but finished seventh.

Anita retired after the 1964 Games and was awarded the MBE at the end of the year. She later married Hugh Porter, MBE, an Olympic cyclist who, on turning professional, became the only man to win the world pursuit championship four times. Anita followed a career in journalism and is currently the swimming correspondent for the *Telegraph* newspapers.

Moore, *Isabella*

Born: 23 October 1894, Tynemouth, Northumberland   Died: 7 March 1975

GOLD: 1912 (4 × 100 METRES FREESTYLE RELAY)

At the age of 17 years and 226 days, Bella Moore was a member of the winning relay team at the 1912 Games and is the youngest British woman ever to win an Olympic gold medal at the Summer Games.

Moore, who competed for the Premier Club, Glasgow, was a Scottish champion and record holder but never won an ASA title. As well as competing in the relay at the Stockholm Olympics she also swam in the individual 100 metres freestyle, but was eliminated in the heats.

Morton, *Lucy*   (Later Mrs H Heaton)

Born: 23 February 1898, Blackpool, Lancashire   Died: 26 August 1980, Blackpool, Lancashire

GOLD: 1924 (200 METRES BREASTSTROKE)

Weakened by illness, Britain's world record holder Irene Gilbert only finished fifth in the 200 metres breaststroke at the 1924 Olympics, but in a major upset her second string Lucy Morton became the first British woman to win an Olympic gold medal in an individual swimming event.

Lucy Morton had a long career at the top of British swimming. She won her first Northern Counties title as a 15-year-old in 1913 and three years later set the inaugural world records for both the 150 yards backstroke and the 200 yards breaststroke. After winning both these events when they were added to the ASA championship schedule in 1920, she was denied a chance of Olympic honours as there were no backstroke or breaststroke events for women at the Antwerp Games. But after a four-year wait, Lucy was a surprise winner of the breaststroke event in Paris when she broke the monopoly of the American women, who won the other four swimming events and both diving competitions.

After her marriage to Henry Heaton in 1927, she became a well-known coach and official.

Lucy Morton winning the 200 metres breaststroke in 1924.

Speirs, *Annie*

Born: 14 July 1889, Wallen, Liverpool, Lancashire   Died: October 1926

GOLD: 1912 (4 × 100 METRES FREESTYLE RELAY)

The day after celebrating her 23rd birthday, Annie Speirs of the Liverpool Ladies SC won a gold medal in the relay at the 1912 Olympics. She also finished fifth in the individual 100 metres freestyle in Stockholm

Steer, *Irene*   (Later Mrs W Nicholson)

Born: 10 August 1889, Cardiff, Glamorgan, Wales   Died: 18 April 1947, Cardiff, Glamorgan, Wales

GOLD: 1912 (4 × 100 METRES FREESTYLE RELAY)

At the 1912 Stockholm Games, a collision in the heats of the 100 metres freestyle robbed Irene Steer of the chance of individual Olympic honours but she later won a gold medal in the relay, swimming the anchor leg for the British team which set a new world record.

Steer was unbeaten in the 100 yards freestyle at the Welsh Championships, winning the title for seven successive years from 1907 before retiring at the end of the 1913 season. She represented Cardiff Ladies Premier SC and won her only ASA title in 1913 when she equalled the world record in the 100 yards freestyle. After she retired, Irene married William Nicholson, a director and Chairman of Cardiff City FC.

Track & Field
MEN

Abrahams, *Harold Maurice*

Born: 15 December 1899, Bedford, Bedfordshire   Died: 14 January 1978, Enfield, Middlesex

GOLD: 1924 (100 METRES)   SILVER: 1924 (4 × 100 METRES RELAY)

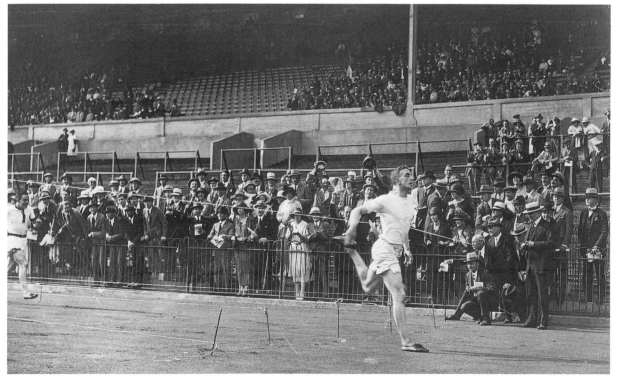

Harold Abrahams wins the 220 yards for Oxford & Cambridge against Harvard & Yale in 1923. The following year he became the first European to win an Olympic sprint title.

From an early age, Harold Abrahams set out to emulate his two elder brothers who were both excellent athletes. As a schoolboy at Repton, Harold won the 100 yards and the long jump at the 1918 Public Schools championships and then went up to Caius College, Cambridge, where during his four years' residence he won a total of eight events in the annual match against Oxford.

During his years at Cambridge, Abrahams had his first experience of international competition and his debut, in the 1920 triangular match between England, Ireland and Scotland, saw him win the 220 yards. The following month he competed, without success, in the Antwerp Olympics. After a successful tour of America with the combined Oxford & Cambridge team in 1921, Abrahams confined himself to the domestic scene for the next two seasons and in 1923 set an English long jump record of 23ft 8¼in (7.19m) before improving the record to 23ft 8¾in (7.23m) with his first victory at the AAA Championships.

Throughout the winter of 1923–24 Abrahams trained assiduously under the eye of the brilliant coach Sam Mussabini – their relationship was one of the many fascinating themes of the award-winning film Chariots of Fire. Reward for a winter

of hard work came early in 1924 when Abrahams ran a wind-assisted 9.6 sec for 100 yards and again improved the English long jump record to 24ft 2½in (7.38m). After an interval of two weeks, he won the 100 yards and long jump at the AAA Championships and then went to Paris for the Olympic Games.

Following a near-disaster at the start of the semi-finals of the 100 metres, he ran magnificently in the final to beat the American Jackson Scholz by two feet. His time was officially given as 10.6 sec, although the electric timer showed no more than 10.52 sec. In Paris, Abrahams also reached the final of the 200 metres and was a member of the relay team which ran progressively faster at each outing before taking the silver medals with a time of 41.2 sec, which was to remain a British record for 28 years. There were no presentation ceremonies at the Paris Olympics and one month after the Games, Abrahams received his medals through the mail; but as the French authorities had not put sufficient stamps on the package, he had to pay the excess postage himself!

Abrahams had certainly not fulfilled his potential, particularly as a long jumper, when a severe leg injury put an end to his active career in May 1925, but he went on to render unsurpassed service

to the sport as an administrator, journalist, broadcaster, historian and statistician. He was the athletics correspondent of the Sunday Times from 1925 to 1967, a founder member of the Association of Track & Field Statisticians, and for many years a commentator for BBC radio.

He became a member of the AAA General Committee in 1926, being appointed Secretary in 1931 and President in 1976. He was the first Secretary of the International Board, which was the forerunner of the British Amateur Athletic Board, and in 1963 he was appointed Chairman of the BAAB after serving as Treasurer for 21 years. Abrahams was not universally popular within the sport and his sometimes brusque manner became rather more pronounced in his later years, but many people can bear witness to the gentler and more generous side of his character. Somewhere within the differing aspects of his personality probably lies the answer to the question as to why he never received any official recognition for the enormous amount of voluntary work he undertook on behalf of the sport. He was, however, awarded the CBE in 1957 as Secretary of the National Parks Commission, which he joined after practising as a barrister for 13 years.

Ahearne, *Timothy*

Born: 18 August 1885, Athea, Co. Limerick, Ireland   Died: November 1968, USA

GOLD: 1908 (TRIPLE JUMP)

Disappointed by his eighth place in the long jump three days earlier, Tim Ahearne fought hard for his victory in the 1908 Olympic triple jump. He had trailed Garfield McDonald throughout the competition but on his very last jump he beat the Canadian's best effort by six inches to take the gold medal. Ahearne's winning mark of 14.91m (48ft 11¼in) was a new world record with the by now standard hop-step-jump technique,

although a number of athletes, mostly Irish, had jumped further using the hop-hop-jump method. Ahearne was also the Irish champion in the high hurdles and he competed in this event – and the standing long jump – at the 1908 Olympics.

On returning to Ireland after the 1908 Games, Ahearne revealed his true form in the long jump and came within two inches of Peter O'Connor's world record of 24ft 11¾in (7.61m). In 1909 he cleared a

magnificent 25ft 3½in (7.71m) in his home town of Athea but the record was disallowed because of a downhill runway. Five days later Tim won the AAA long jump title, and then followed his younger brother Daniel to America. Earlier in 1909, Dan Ahearn, who dropped the final 'e' from his name on emigrating, had taken over from Tim as world record holder in the triple jump when he cleared 50ft 11in (15.52m) in Boston on 1 August.

Ainsworth-Davis, *John Creyghton*

Born: 23 April 1895, Aberystwyth, Cardiganshire   Died: 3 January 1976, Stockland, Devon

GOLD: 1920 (4 × 400 METRES RELAY)

Having initially only been selected for the relay at the 1920 Olympic Games, Jack Ainsworth-Davis also ran in the individual 400 metres after Cecil Griffiths had withdrawn because of illness. Jack finished a surprising fifth in the individual final and then ran the third leg on the winning relay team.

On leaving Westminister School, Ainsworth-Davis served both as a captain in the Rifle Brigade and, after receiving

his 'wings' in Egypt, as a pilot in the Royal Flying Corps. After the war, he went up to Christ's College, Cambridge, where he was rather over-shadowed as a quarter-miler by Guy Butler and in his only appearance in the University match, in 1920, he finished third. On leaving Cambridge, he studied medicine at St Bartholomew's Hospital and supported his family by playing in a band at a fashionable nightclub. He could no longer spare much time for sport and after finishing fourth

in the 440 yards at the 1921 AAA Championships he virtually retired.

Ainsworth-Davis subsequently became a highly qualified and much respected doctor and urological surgeon, and served as Secretary of the Royal Society of Medicine. On the outbreak of World War II, he gave up a lucrative practice to return to the RAF where he was appointed head of the surgical division at the RAF Hospital in Cosford.

Applegarth, *William Reuben*

Born: 11 May 1890, Guisborough, Yorkshire   Died: 5 December 1958, Schenectady, New York, USA

GOLD: 1912 (4 × 100 METRES RELAY)   BRONZE: 1912 (200 METRES)

Willie Applegarth made his debut in the AAA Championships in 1910 when, as a 20-year-old Post Office worker representing Polytechnic Harriers, he finished third in the 100 yards. Two years later he won the 220 yards and finished second in the 100 yards, and these performances won him a place in the 1912 Olympic team in both the individual sprints and the relay.

Applegarth was eliminated in the semi-finals of the 100 metres in Stockholm, but after some great running in the early stages of the 200 metres final he held on to take the bronze medal; then, as lead-off man, he put Britain on their way to the gold medals in the relay. He maintained his brilliant form in post-Olympic meetings, setting a world best of 19.8 sec for 200 yards and equalling the world 100 metres record of 10.6 sec. He also claimed a new British record of 21.8 sec for 220 yards and equalled the British 100 yards record of 9.8 sec.

In 1913 he twice equalled his British 100 yards record and set a world best of 14.6 sec for 150 yards, but the high-light of the season came at the AAA Championships where he became the first home athlete to take the sprint double. His winning time of 21.6 sec in the 220 yards was yet another British record. 1914 was Applegarth's last season as an

amateur, and after equalling his own British records in both the 100 yards and 220 yards he won his second AAA double, with the finest performance of his career coming in the 220 yards as he set a world record of 21.2 sec, which was to remain unbeaten for 18 years.

In November 1914, Applegarth turned professional and twice beat the Australian Jack Donaldson, the reigning 'world champion'. He continued to run as a 'pro' after the war but in 1922 he emigrated to America, where he took up an appointment as a soccer and track coach at

Mercersburg Academy in Pennsylvania. During his early days in the US he played for Brooklyn in the American Soccer League and took part in a few exhibition races. On one notable occasion, at Fordham University, he beat Bob McAllister who was one of the leading American sprinters of the time.

Willie Applegarth's coaching appointment at Mercersburg was relatively short-lived and in 1925 he joined the General Electric Company as a welder. He remained with the company for 30 years until his retirement in 1955.

British Olympic 100 metres Trials in 1912. The four finalists later made up the winning relay team in Stockholm. Left to right: HM Macintosh, DH Jacobs, WR Applegarth, VHA D'Arcy.

Barrett, *Edward*

Born: 3 November 1880, Ballyduff, Co. Kerry, Ireland

GOLD: 1908 (TUG-OF-WAR)   BRONZE: 1908 (WRESTLING – HEAVYWEIGHT FREESTYLE)

After winning an Olympic gold medal in 1908 as a member of the City of London Police Tug-of-War team, Edward Barrett won a bronze medal in the heavyweight freestyle wrestling. He also competed in the shot, discus and javelin at the 1908 Games but wrestling was undoubtedly his

premier sport and he was the British heavyweight freestyle champion in 1908 and 1911. Barrett also competed in the Greco-Roman style wrestling events at the 1908 and 1912 Olympics but lost in the early rounds on each occasion.

In addition, he won an All-Ireland gold

medal for hurling as a member of the London Irish team which beat Cork in the 1901 All-Ireland final. In July 1914, Barrett resigned from the City of London Police and there is no trace of him in sporting circles after that date.

Bennett, *Charles*

Born: 28 December 1870, Shapwick, Nr Wimborne, Dorset   Died: 9 March 1949, Bournemouth, Hampshire

GOLD: 1900 (1500 METRES & TEAM 5000 METRES)   SILVER: 1900 (4000 METRES STEEPLECHASE)

Charles Bennett of Finchley Harriers, a railway engine driver at Bournemouth Central Station, won the AAA 4 mile title in 1897 and in 1899 he was the National cross-country champion and won both the AAA 4 miles and 10 miles on the track. Early in 1900 he retained his cross-country crown, but by the summer he had developed a certain measure of speed and defeated a rather undistinguished field to

take the AAA 1 mile title. His winning time of 4 min 28.2 sec did not augur well for his Olympic chances but 1900 was not a vintage year for milers and the best time recorded in the world that year was a modest 4 min 24.4 sec by the American John Cregan. Cregan withdrew from the 1500 metres at the Paris Olympics on sabbatical grounds and Bennett's main challenger was Henri Deloge, the local

idol and the world record holder at 1000 metres. There were no heats for the 1500 metres and after a close race Bennett beat Deloge by two metres in 4 min 6.2 sec. This was said at the time to be a 'world record', although clearly many athletes had passed the 1500 metres mark in a faster time during the course of a 1 mile race. Nevertheless, Bennett achieved the distinction of being the first British athlete to win an Olympic track & field event.

Bennett won a second gold medal and set a second world record seven days later when he led Britain to victory in the 5000 metres team race and he had, in the interim, won a silver medal in the longer of the two steeplechase events. Despite his two world records and his two Olympic titles, Charles Bennett remains a much under-rated athlete, particularly in historical rather than temporal terms. His

performance at Paris in July 1900 was possibly the finest double by a British athlete since Fred Elborough achieved the remarkable feat of breaking the world record for both the 220 yards and the 880 yards in one afternoon in October 1876.

Bennett's Olympic season closed in October with a challenge match against Alfred Tysoe at Bellevue, Manchester. Tysoe was the AAA and Olympic champion at 880 yards/800 metres and

Bennett held identical titles at the 1 mile/ 1500 metres distance, and a meeting was arranged over three-quarters of a mile, which was mid-way between their championship distances, to decide which of these two fine athletes was Britain's leading middle-distance runner. Tysoe won a close race in 3 min 13.0 sec but Bennett's British record of 3 min 10.6 sec survived.

Brasher, *Christopher William*
Born: 21 August 1928, Georgetown, Guyana
GOLD: 1956 (3000 METRES STEEPLECHASE)

Before the 1956 Olympics, Chris Brasher, who was educated at Rugby and St John's College, Cambridge, had enjoyed a long track career, winning the 3 miles for Cambridge against Oxford in 1950 and the 5000 metres at the World Student Games in 1951. It was in 1951 that he made his debut as a steeplechaser and he did well to reach the Olympic final the following year. In 1955 he represented Britain in three of their five international matches, finishing second to John Disley on each occasion, and in 1956 he clinched his place in the Olympic team with a personal best of 8 min 47.2 sec in the match against

Czechoslovakia when he was again second to John Disley. With Disley, Brasher and Eric Shirley all qualifying for the Olympic final, British hopes ran high in Melbourne with Brasher perhaps the least fancied of the three. But from 300 metres out, Brasher launched an unanswerable attack and came home the winner with 12 metres to spare in 8 min 41.2 sec, a new British and Olympic record. However, some hours were to pass before he received his gold medal as he had to survive a protest that he had impeded the Norwegian Ernst Larsen.

After the Melbourne Olympics, Chris

Brasher retired from athletics and from his job with Mobil Oil to take up the post of Sports Editor of the *Observer* which had been offered to him before the Games. In 1961 he joined the BBC as a reporter on the *Tonight* programme and in 1969 was appointed Head of General Features, Television, but he did not renew his contract in 1972. In more recent times he has been the organizer of the hugely successful London Marathon. Chris is married to the lawn tennis player Shirley Bloomer, and their daughter was also a successful tournament player.

Chris Brasher clears the final water jump on his way to the gold medal in the 1956 steeplechase.

Brown, *Arthur Godfrey Kilner*

Born: 21 February 1915, Bankura, India

GOLD: 1936 (4 × 400 METRES RELAY)   SILVER: 1936 (400 METRES)

Twenty-one-year-old Godfrey Brown was the youngest member of the British 4 × 400 metres relay team at the 1936 Olympics. Despite his youth he was given the responsibility of running the testing anchor stage but he had already shown that he had the ability and the experience for this formidable task.

Brown had been an outstanding athlete at Warwick School and when he went up to Peterhouse College, Cambridge, he was awarded his blue in his freshman year, gaining the first of his three successive victories in the 440 yards in the match against Oxford. Later in 1935 he set a Fenner's ground record of 48.1 sec before making his international debut against Germany in Munich, where he finished second to Bill Roberts.

Prior to the Berlin Olympics, Brown only ran four serious quarter-miles in 1936, all of which he won, but he had also run 9.7 sec for 100 yards and 1 min 56.0 sec for 880 yards; this combination of speed and stamina boded well for his Olympic chances. After running 47.3 sec in the semi-finals, Brown failed by inches to take the Olympic title but his time of 46.7 sec was a new European record and

one second faster than he had run before the Games began. In the 1600 metres relay, Freddie Wolff, Godfrey Rampling and Bill Roberts handed Brown a six-metre lead over the American Al Fitch and with a fine run Brown stretched the advantage to 15 metres, breaking the tape in 3 min 9.0 sec for another European record.

In London, one week after the Olympics, Brown produced an even greater relay leg, when he snatched victory with his last stride for the British Empire in the match against the Americans. Brown's 440-yard stage was unofficially timed at 45.9 sec, and he made up a three-yard deficit on the Olympic bronze medallist Jimmy Lu Valle.

In 1937, Godfrey Brown brought his personal best for 880 yards down to 1 min 52.2 sec in America and later ran a relay leg of 1 min 51.2 sec in the match against Germany when he comfortably held off the future world record holder Rudolf Harbig. Brown was unbeaten in 1938 and was possibly the world's leading quarter-miler that year; he was the AAA and European champion and could count among his victories a win over the

American champion Ray Malott.

After a strenuous season, Brown only indulged in light training the following winter and this neglect showed when the 1939 track season arrived. Apart from winning the AAA 880 yards title in a modest time, he had an undistinguished season and in the last major race of his career he finished fourth and last in the 400 metres in the match against Germany in Cologne. After the war, he attempted a comeback but met with little success and soon retired completely.

Godfrey Brown was the most distinguished member of a notable sporting family. His sister Audrey (later Lady AK Court) was a silver medallist in the relay at the 1936 Olympic Games and his brother Ralph (later Sir RK Brown) won the 1934 AAA 440 yards hurdles title and finished third in the Empire Games later that season.

Brown, who was the son of the Reverend Arthur Brown, taught at Bedford School, King's School, Rochester, and Cheltenham College and was the Headmaster of Worcester Royal Grammar School from 1950 to 1978.

Burghley, Lord, *David George Brownlow Cecil*   (Later the Marquess of Exeter, KCMG)

Born: 9 February 1905, Stamford, Lincolnshire   Died: 22 October 1981, Stamford, Lincolnshire

GOLD: 1928 (400 METRES HURDLES)   SILVER: 1932 (4 × 400 METRES RELAY)

After schooling at Eton and Le Rosey, Switzerland, Lord Burghley went up to Magdalene College, Cambridge, and although he failed to win a blue in his freshman year he competed in the 110 metres hurdles at the 1924 Olympics as a 19-year-old.

Burghley was Britain's leading all-round hurdler and was also an outstanding relay runner on the flat. At one time, he was the British record holder in all three hurdles events and the 1600 metres relay. In the high hurdles he was the first Briton to break the 15-seconds barrier, won three AAA titles, competed in three Olympic Games and was a gold medallist at the 1930 Empire Games. As a 220 yard hurdler he twice set a British record and his 1927 time of 24.7 sec was not beaten until 1950. But he was at his best in the 440 yards/400 metres hurdles, winning an Olympic gold medal in 1928, setting one world and seven British records and winning five AAA titles and the gold medal at the 1930 Empire Games. He also

Lord Burghley leads over the last flight in the 1928 400 metres hurdles.

won a relay gold medal at the Empire Games but his finest performance in this event came at the 1932 Olympic Games when he contributed a 46.7 sec stage on the British team which won the silver medals with a new European record of 3 min 11.2 sec. Earlier in the Games, Burghley had finished fifth in the 110 metres hurdles and fourth in the 400 metres hurdles with his fastest ever time of 52.2 sec.

Burghley's one world record came at the 1927 AAA Championships when he ran 54.2 sec for the 440 yards hurdles, and although the record was reduced to 52.6 sec on the same day by the American John Gibson in Nebraska, Burghley's performance was accomplished first in absolute time and his name was added to the roll of world record holders. Burghley and Gibson had, in fact, met earlier in the year at the Penn Relays with the American winning by half a yard. Later it was found that Gibson was ineligible to compete in this particular Collegiate race and Burghley was declared the winner.

Burghley entered Parliament in 1931 as the Member for Peterborough and in 1943, on his appointment as the Governor of Bermuda, he resigned from the House. He also gave many years distinguished service to the Olympic movement and to the sport of track & field. In 1933, at the age of 28, he became a member of the International Olympic Committee and in 1936 he was elected President of the Amateur Athletic Association and Chairman of the British Olympic Association. Ten years later he became President of the International Amateur Athletic Federation and in 1948 he served as Chairman of the Organising Committee for the Olympic Games.

In 1929 he married Lady Maria Theresa Montague-Douglas-Scott, the daughter of the Duke of Buccleuch, and after their marriage was dissolved in 1946 he married Mrs Diana Forbes. In 1956, on the death of his father, Lord Burghley became the 6th Marquess of Exeter.

Butler, *Guy Montagu*

Born: 25 August 1899, Harrow, Middlesex   Died: 22 February 1981, St Neots, Cambridgeshire

GOLD: 1920 (4 × 400 METRES RELAY)   SILVER: 1920 (400 METRES)
BRONZE: 1924 (400 METRES & 4 × 400 METRES RELAY)

Guy Butler enjoyed a distinguished Harrovian and sporting pedigree. His grandfather had been Headmaster of the school at the age of 26 and his father, also an Harrovian, won a cricket and athletics blue at Cambridge and was the English rackets champion in 1889.

After winning three events at the 1917 Public School Sports, Guy Butler left Harrow and spent a year at the Royal Military College, Sandhurst, before entering Trinity College, Cambridge. In 1919 he won the AAA 440 yards title at his first attempt and although he was to establish himself as Britain's leading quarter-miler, surprisingly he never won this event again.

After dead-heating with Bevil Rudd in the 1920 Oxford v Cambridge match, Butler finished second to the South African in both the AAA Championships and the Olympic final, but he won an Olympic gold medal as anchor man on the relay team. Between the 1920 and the 1924 Olympic Games, Butler won the 440 yards against Oxford in 1921 and 1922 and finished second at the 1922 and 1923 AAA Championships. Although a muscle injury forced him to use standing starts, he was in fine form at the 1924 Olympics. After setting a European record of 48.0 sec in the semi-final of the 400 metres he was third in the final and won a second bronze medal in the relay.

Following a mediocre 1925 season, Butler returned to form in 1926. He was enjoying excellent training facilities as a teacher at Lancing College and after equalling the world 300 yard record of 30.6 sec in June, he then won the AAA 220 yards title. In 1928 he became the first British track & field athlete to compete in three Olympic Games but after failing to reach the semi-finals of the 200 metres in Amsterdam he retired at the end of the season.

Guy Butler was unlucky in that he was perhaps never quite at his best in Olympic years but with one gold, one silver and two bronze medals he was one of the most successful of all British Olympic athletes. After his retirement, Butler coached some notable athletes and made a significant contribution to the techniques of filming them in action. He was also one of the advisers on the design of the White City Stadium and served as the athletics correspondent of the *Morning Post* until it was merged with the *Daily Telegraph* in 1937.

Canning, *George*

GOLD: 1920 (TUG-OF-WAR)

George Canning was a member of the City of London Police team which won the sixth and last Olympic Tug-of-War title in 1920. In Antwerp, the London policemen beat the USA, Belgium and Holland in two straight pulls and the British victory occupied, in total, less than two and a half minutes. Canning resigned from the police force in December 1935.

Coales, *William*

Born: 8 January 1886, Aldwinckle, Thrapston, Northamptonshire

GOLD: 1908 (3 MILES – TEAM)

Bill Coales of Thrapston H & AC finished in third place in the 3 miles team race at the 1908 Olympic Games and was the third-scoring member of the winning British team. The event was held in the morning, and in the afternoon of the same day Coales started in the 5 miles individual race but after his earlier efforts it is not surprising that he dropped out after 4 miles.

Like Joe Deakin and Arthur Robertson, who led the British team to their Olympic victory, Coales had a solid cross-country background. He won the Midland title in 1908 and finished second to Robertson in the National but he was below form in the International event and finished back in 22nd place. This proved to be only a temporary lapse and after opening the 1908 track season with a win in the Midland 10 miles championships, he was fifth in the AAA event before going on to win an Olympic gold medal.

Coe, *Sebastian Newbold*

Born: 29 September 1956, Chiswick, London

GOLD: 1980 (1500 METRES)   1984 (1500 METRES)   SILVER: 1980 (800 METRES)   1984 (800 METRES)

Although the brilliant career of Seb Coe included a number of disappointments, the highlights were such that he must be considered as possibly the greatest middle-distance runner of all time.

After winning the British 1500 metres title at both Youth and Junior level, his first major international championship success came when he won the 1977 European indoor 800 metres title at Dortmund with a new British indoor record of 1 min 47.6 sec. Within the next month he had twice improved on the record and later in the year he added the British outdoor record, clocking 1 min 44.95 at Crystal Palace in September. In 1978, Coe brought the British 800 metres record down to 1 min 44.25 sec in August before making a further improvement the following month with a run of 1 min 43.97.

Although this fine performance ranked no higher than eighth on the world all-time list, the breaking of the 1 min 44 sec barrier placed Coe clearly among the world's elite and he was to confirm his place in spectacular fashion the following year. Within the space of 42 days in July and August 1979, he posted new world records for the 800 metres, 1500 metres and 1 mile. In 1980 he took over as the world record holder at 1000 metres and in 1981 he improved his own world records at 800 metres and 1000 metres before

Sebastian Coe retains his 1500 metres Olympic title at Los Angeles in 1984.

twice improving his own record for the 1 mile. His only world record in 1982 came when he contributed a 1 min 44.01 sec leg on Britain's 4 × 800 metres relay team; the following year he posted world indoor records at 800 metres and 1000 metres. In all, Seb Coe set nine world records outdoors and three indoors, and this alone would have been more than enough to ensure his place as one of the legends of the sport.

But in addition to his phenomenal talents as a record breaker, Coe was also a superlative performer in major championship events. He is the only man in modern times to have won the Olympic 1500 metres title twice and his victory in 1980 when he came back from losing the 800 metres, for which he was an overwhelming favourite, was testament to his moral fortitude. In addition to his Olympic gold medals at 1500 metres in 1980 and 1984, he finished second in the 800 metres at both these Games. He also won over 800 metres at the European and World Cup in 1981 and the European Championships in 1986.

Coe missed selection for his third Olympic Games after an inexplicably poor run in the Trials and finished a disappointing sixth in his last major race, the 1500 metres at the 1990 Commonwealth Games. But these were no more than minor blemishes on a superb career.

Some ten years later, his world records for 800 metres and 1000 metres still stand and for these to have survived throughout the greatest decade of middle-distance running that the world has ever seen is a clear indication of the calibre of Coe's performances.

After retiring from top-class competition, Seb Coe entered politics and was adopted as the prospective Conservative candidate for Falmouth and Camborne. He was awarded the MBE in 1982 and the OBE in 1990; he married the show jumper, Nicola McIrvine, later in the year.

D'Arcy, *Victor Henry Augustus*

Born: 30 June 1887, Rotherhithe, London   Died: 1961, South Africa

GOLD: 1912 (4 × 100 METRES RELAY)

Vic D'Arcy of Polytechnic Harriers ran the anchor leg in the sprint relay at the 1912 Olympics and broke the tape inches ahead of the Germans, who had set a world record in the semi-finals. After the race the Germans were disqualified and the silver medals went to Sweden.

D'Arcy established himself as a top-class sprinter in 1911 when, after beating Willie Applegarth at the Kinnaird Trophy meeting, he finished second in the AAA 100 yards and closed the season by equalling the British record of 9.8 sec in Vienna. Although D'Arcy never won an AAA individual sprint title, he finished in the first 3 four times and was also on the winning medley relay team four times. At the 1912 and 1920 Olympics he was eliminated in the preliminary rounds of both individual sprints but after winning a relay gold medal in Stockholm he was again, at the age of 33, a relay finalist at Antwerp in 1920.

He concluded his career by representing the British Empire against the USA in the relay match held in London after the 1920 Olympics, and before the year-end he emigrated to South Africa where he spent the rest of his life.

Davies, *Lynn*

Born: 20 May 1942, Nant-y-Moel, Glamorganshire

GOLD: 1964 (LONG JUMP)

Lynn Davies, winner of the 1964 long jump.

After forsaking a promising career as a footballer, Lynn Davies initially specialised in the triple jump but in 1961 he was persuaded by Ron Pickering, the Welsh national coach, to concentrate on long jumping.

The wisdom of the decision soon became apparent and the following year Davies made his international debut at the European Championships. Later in 1962, he finished fourth at the Commonwealth Games with a new British record of 25ft 4in (7.72m) and after a year of consolidation Davies was ready for the Tokyo Olympics. He opened the 1964 season with a Commonwealth record of 26ft 3¾in (8.01m) in May and then raised the record to 26ft 4in (8.02m) in July. In atrocious weather conditions, Davies won a classic competition in Tokyo to become the first British athlete to win an Olympic gold medal in a field event since Tim Ahearne's victory in the triple jump in 1908. Davies' winning mark of 26ft 5¾in (8.07m) was yet another Commonwealth record.

In the post-Olympic year, Davies lost twice to Ter-Ovanesyan and traded wins with Ralph Boston; in 1966, during an early season tour of South Africa, he made two further improvements to the Commonwealth record, finishing with a win in the South African Championships with a jump of 26ft 10in (8.18m). Later in the year he added the European and Commonwealth titles to his Olympic crown to become the first athlete ever to hold all three titles.

In 1967 he won the European indoor title and in 1968 he improved the Commonwealth record to 27ft 0in (8.23m) but his hopes of retaining his Olympic title were shattered by Bob Beamon's legendary jump in Mexico. After finishing second in both the European indoor and outdoor meetings in 1969, Davies retained his Commonwealth title in 1970 and at Munich in 1972 he made his third Olympic appearance but, handicapped by injury, he failed to qualify for the final.

Sometimes overlooked are Davies' talents as a sprinter; he recorded times of 9.7 sec for 100 yards and 10.4 sec for 100 metres. At the 1964 Olympics he ran in the 100 metres and was a member the relay team which reached the final.

Davies, who ranks as one of Britain's greatest athletes, was awarded the MBE in 1967 and after retiring from competition in 1973 he was appointed technical director of Canadian athletics. He returned home in 1976 and continued to serve the sport in many capacities – he was the assistant manager of the British team at the Moscow Olympics. He is currently a BBC television sports commentator.

Deakin, *Joseph Edmund*

Born: 6 February 1879, Shelton, Stoke-on-Trent, Staffordshire   Died: 30 June 1972, Dulwich, London

GOLD: 1908 (3 MILES – TEAM)

As a young man, Joe Deakin served with the Rifle Brigade and even when stationed overseas he always managed to find time to pursue his passion for running. During the Boer War he set South African records at 880 yards and 1 mile and in 1901 he won the Irish 1 mile and 4 mile titles. On his return to England in 1903, Deakin joined Herne Hill Harriers and soon established himself as an outstanding cross-country runner, the best of his many excellent performances being second place in the National in 1907. A good showing in early season track races in 1908 earned him selection for three events at the Olympic Games and after finishing sixth in the 1500 metres he led the British team home in the 3 miles team event the following day. After winning a gold medal in the morning Deakin lined up for the heats of the 5 miles in the afternoon, but it came as no surprise when, replete with a celebratory champagne lunch, he failed to finish!

After the Olympics, Deakin transferred to Surrey AC, following a dispute with Herne Hill Harriers, and tried his luck at the marathon. In his first race he finished 20th in the 'Poly' and although he had been temporarily blinded during the war, he improved to take eighth place in 1920. The amazing Joe Deakin continued to compete until his 90th birthday and died three years after his last race.

Goodfellow, *Frederick William*

Born: 7 March 1874, Walsall, Staffordshire   Died: 22 November 1960, Croydon, Surrey

GOLD: 1908 (TUG-OF-WAR)

The 34-year-old Fred Goodfellow was a member of the City of London Police team which won the 1908 Olympic Tug-of-War title.

Green, *Thomas William*

Born: 30 March 1894, Fareham, Hampshire   Died: 29 March 1975, Eastleigh, Hampshire

GOLD: 1932 (50 KILOMETRES WALK)

Olympic history contains many stories of the handicaps which champions have overcome but few can match the adversities which Tommy Green faced before being crowned champion in one of the most gruelling events on the Olympic programme. Because of rickets, he was unable to walk at all until he was five years old; in 1906 he falsified his age in order to join the Army but he was invalided out of the Royal Hussars four years later as a result of injuries received when a horse fell on him. Then, after being recalled with the Reserve in 1914, he was wounded three times and badly gassed while serving with the King's Own Hussars in France.

Green was first encouraged to take up walking by a war-blinded friend whom he had been helping to train for the St Dunstan's London to Brighton walk and in 1926, at the age of 32, Green won the first race he entered, a 12 mile race from Worthing to Brighton. Following this surprise victory he joined Belgrave Harriers and built up an impressive record in all the major road races. Green won the London to Brighton four times and was a six-times winner of both the Manchester to Blackpool and the Nottingham to Birmingham races. Other major successes included a win in the classic Milan 100km in 1930, a year which also saw him win the inaugural British 50km title. The only significant event that Green never managed to win was the National 20 miles championship, although he finished second on five occasions.

Undoubtedly the greatest of Tommy Green's many triumphs was his victory in the 50km walk at the Los Angeles Olympics in 1932. After being troubled by the strong Californian sun he was at one stage one minute behind the leaders but, walking magnificently in the closing stages, he came through to win by more than seven minutes. At the age of 38 years and 126 days, Green is the oldest-ever winner of the event. In 1936 he made a great bid to make the Olympic team for a second time, but his fourth place in the RWA 50km was not quite good enough to earn him selection for the Berlin Games.

After his checkered early life, Tommy Green held a variety of jobs before being employed at the Eastleigh Railway Works, where he demonstrated that accident-proneness is a continuing condition by losing a thumb in an industrial accident. On retiring from the railways, Green became a publican in Eastleigh and was a prominent figure in the local sporting world.

Griffiths, *Cecil Richmond*

Born: 20 January 1901, Worcester, Worcestershire

GOLD: 1920 (4 × 400 METRES RELAY)

Nineteen-year-old Cecil Griffiths of Surrey AC is the only British Junior track & field athlete to have won an Olympic gold medal. Although illness forced him to withdraw from the individual 400 metres at the 1920 Olympics, he ran a brilliant opening leg in the 4 × 400 metres relay, handing over to Robert Lindsay well clear of the rest of the field. This enabled Britain to avoid the melee involving Sweden, South Africa, France and the USA at the first change-over and the team went on to a comfortable victory.

Cecil Griffiths finished third in the AAA 440 yards three times but in 1922 he decided to concentrate on the half-mile and developed into a remarkably consistent performer. From 1922 to 1927 he never finished out of the first three at the AAA Championships, winning the title in 1923 and 1925. This record, when taken with his earlier performances at 440 yards, meant that he was placed in an AAA Championship event for nine successive years.

Griffiths' greatest race was at the 1926 AAA Championships when the German Otto Peltzer and Douglas Lowe both beat Ted Meredith's world record of 1 min 52.2 sec. Griffiths finished a commendable but almost unnoticed third in an estimated 1 min 53.4 sec which, had it not been for Lowe finishing ahead of him, would have been the fastest half-mile ever run by a British athlete.

Halswelle, *Wyndham*

Born: 30 May 1882, Mayfair, London   Died: 31 March 1915, Neuve Chappelle, France

GOLD: 1908 (400 METRES)   SILVER: 1906 (400 METRES)   BRONZE: 1906 (800 METRES)

After a notable athletic career at Charterhouse and the RMC, Sandhurst, Wyndham Halswelle was commissioned into the Highland Light Infantry in 1901. While the Regiment was in South Africa, Halswelle's ability was noticed by Jimmy Curran, a former professional athlete who later coached at Mercersburg Academy in Pennsylvania where he guided the great Ted Meredith to Olympic honours in 1912. When the HLI returned to Edinburgh from the Boer War, Curran persuaded his young subaltern to take up the sport in earnest. The results were quick and encouraging and in his first year of serious competition, Halswelle won the 1904 Army 880 yards championship.

In 1905 he turned to quarter-miling and won the AAA and Scottish titles in addition to finishing first in the Scotland v Ireland match. The following year, Halswelle won medals in both the 400 and 800 metres at the Olympic Games in Athens and on his reurn for the British season he won the 100 yards, 220 yards, 440 yards and the 880 yards – all on the same afternoon – at the Scottish Championships. Halswelle also won the 1906 AAA 440 yards title in 48.8 sec, which was easily his finest performance to date. After winning the 100 yards and 220 yards at the 1907 Scottish Championships, Halswelle broke down in the 440 yards and did not compete again that summer but in the Olympic year of 1908 he soon showed that the setback was behind him. He set a world record of 31.2 sec for 300 yards and then posted a British 440 yards record of 48.4 sec before facing the world's best at the Olympic Games. Halswelle had the fastest time in both the heats and the semi-finals and in the final he faced three Americans, Carpenter, Robbins and Taylor.

The race was not run in lanes and the starter warned the runners against jostling, but subsequent events were to show that the warning was not heeded. Coming into the home-straight, Halswelle made a move to pass Carpenter who responded by starting on a crab-like course across the track and within 30 metres he had forced Halswelle to within 18 inches of the outside edge of the track. At this point, one of the umpires signalled the judges to break the tape and after an hour of deliberation a verdict of 'No Race' was declared and Carpenter disqualified. A re-run, in lanes this time, was ordered but Robbins and Taylor, who were both entitled to compete, sided with Carpenter and refused to run, so Halswelle appeared alone and won the 1908 Olympic 400 metres title on a walk-over.

The whole incident soured Halswelle's attitude to the sport and as he was also under pressure from his senior officers, who felt that he was being exploited, Halswelle made a farewell appearance at the 1908 Glasgow Rangers Sports and never ran again. At the age of 32, Captain Wyndham Halswelle was killed by a sniper's bullet in France.

Hampson, *Thomas*

Born: 28 October 1907, Clapham, London   Died: 4 September 1965, Stevenage, Hertfordshire

GOLD: 1932 (800 METRES)   SILVER: 1932 (4 × 400 METRES RELAY)

At Bancroft's School and St Catherine's College, Oxford, Tom Hampson showed only a passing interest in athletics although in his last year at Oxford he was selected for the match against Cambridge, finishing an undistinguished fourth in the half-mile. Later in the 1929 season, he showed dramatic improvement and after some solid performances with the Oxford & Cambridge team in America, he was a member of the team which improved the British 4 × 880 yards relay record by five seconds in the international match against Germany.

On leaving Oxford, Hampson took up a teaching post at St Alban's School and in 1930 he first revealed himself as a medal prospect for the 1932 Olympic Games. Victories in the AAA Championships, the international match against France and at the British Empire Games, where he beat a class field by 20 yards in 1 min 52.6 sec, established him as one of the world's leading half-milers. In 1931, two international victories and a second AAA title consolidated his position and in 1932, his third successive win in the AAA 880 yards was followed, later in the afternoon, by a second place in the 440 yards. Clearly, Hampson had added the essential quality of speed to his carefully acquired stamina and was now ready for the Olympics.

In Los Angeles, Tom Hampson qualified comfortably for the final where he wisely declined to follow the suicidal pace of the Canadian Phil Edwards, who led at the half-way mark in 52.3 sec with Hampson trailing by some 20 metres.

Edwards inevitably faded and Hampson then had to contend with another Canadian, Alex Wilson, but he won the battle down the home straight and took the gold medal with a new world record of 1 min 49.7 sec. Later in the Games,

Hampson won a silver medal in the 4 × 400 metres relay and then closed his track career as a member of the 4 × 880 yards relay team in the British Empire v USA match in San Francisco.

In 1935, Tom Hampson gave up his

teaching post and became an Education Officer in the RAF. After returning to civilian life in 1945, he held appointments as a Social Welfare Officer with various organizations and qualified as one of the first AAA honorary senior coaches.

Hawtrey, *Henry Courtenay*

Born: 29 June 1882, Southampton, Hampshire   Died: 16 November 1961, Aldershot, Hampshire

GOLD: 1906 (5 MILES)

Prior to the 1906 Olympics, the highlight of the track career of Lt Henry Hawtrey of the Royal Engineers, London AC and Ireland had been the AAA 1 mile championship of 1902. In a memorable race, the great Alfred Shrubb had to retire after setting too fast a pace over the first two laps and Hawtrey, who was only six days past his 20th birthday, took over and led until the final turn before Joe Binks went past him to win by two yards in a new British record time of 4 min 16.8 sec. In second place, Hawtrey was given an

estimated time of 4 min 17.0 sec, which equalled the previous British record.

Hawtrey achieved little of note in the years immediately following his great run against Binks but he was selected for the 1500 metres and the 5 miles at the 1906 Olympic Games. In the longer event, despite an injured ankle, he went to the front after 2 miles and gradually extended his lead to win by 50 yards from John Svanberg of Sweden. Hawtrey did not finish in his heat of the 1500 metres in Athens.

After an education at Uppingham and

the RMA, Woolwich, Henry Hawtrey was commissioned into the Royal Engineers in 1900 and in World War I he was awarded the DSO and the CMG. He then spent some 15 years in West Africa and India and was mentioned in despatches in the Afghan War of 1919. In 1931 Brigadier Hawtrey was appointed an ADC to King George V but relinquished the post when he retired from the Army in 1934. In September 1939 he rejoined the Colours on the outbreak of war, but in 1942 he finally retired.

Hemery, *David Peter*

Born: 18 July 1944, Cirencester, Gloucestershire

GOLD: 1968 (400 METRES HURDLES)   SILVER: 1972 (4 × 400 METRES RELAY)   BRONZE: 1972 (400 METRES HURDLES)

David Hemery was one of those rare athletes who, by a single performance, can be said to have revolutionised an event. In the final of the 400 metres hurdles at the 1968 Olympics he gave a display of power,

speed and technique that had never before been approached in the event and his reward was a new world record of 48.1 sec.

As a boy, David Hemery spent ten

years at the Thayer School in Massachusetts where his father was working as an accountant. He returned to England in 1962, but after some excellent performances as a junior high hurdler he

David Hemery (402) on his way to the gold medal and a world record in the 1968 400 metres hurdles final.

91

went back to America and enrolled at Boston University in the autumn of 1964. During the next few seasons, Hemery represented Boston with distinction at the major US collegiate meetings and regularly crossed the Atlantic to compete for Great Britain in international matches. In 1966, he set a British record for the high hurdles of 13.9 sec, won the Commonwealth title in Jamaica and had his first major win in the 440 yards hurdles at the ICAAAA Championships in New York. After missing the 1967 outdoor season, Hemery won the 1968 NCAA title and twice reduced the British 400 metres hurdles record during the course of his Olympic build-up. At the Mexico Olympics in October, he made a further reduction to the British record in the semi-finals of the 400 metres hurdles and

then came his historic run in the final, when he ran 48.1 sec to set a world record which was to last four years and a British record which remained unbeaten until 1990. Appropriately, Hemery received his Olympic gold medal from the Marquess of Exeter who had won the event for Great Britain 40 years earlier.

At the end of the 1968 season, Hemery was awarded the MBE and went up to St Catherine's College, Oxford, where he showed a remarkable talent as a decathlete, and by the end of 1969 he was ranked seventh on the UK all-time list. In 1969 he improved his own British 110 metres hurdles record to 13.6 sec, while the highlights of 1970 were the successful defence of his Commonwealth title and a win at the World Student Games. After a rest from competition in 1971, Hemery

returned to the track in 1972 and in the Olympic final in Munich he ran 48.5 sec to finish in third place. He also won a silver medal in the 4 × 400 metres relay, when Britain equalled the European record.

Hemery finished his amateur career on a winning note in the match against France in October 1972, and although he later had a few races as a professional he will always be remembered for his astonishing performance at Mexico City in October 1968. After retirement, Hemery managed the Sobell Centre in London for two years but in 1975 he returned to America and spent seven years coaching at Boston University. He settled in England again in 1982 and now runs coaching courses and works with an educational trust.

Hill, *Albert George*

Born: 24 March 1889, Tooting, London   Died: 8 January 1969, Canada

GOLD: 1920 (800 METRES & 1500 METRES)   SILVER: 1920 (3000 METRES – TEAM)

At the age of 20, Albert Hill of Gainsford AC and Polytechnic Harriers finished fourth in the 4 miles at the 1909 AAA Championships; but after he won the title the following year, little was heard of him for the next three track seasons. In 1914 he sprang a surprise by finshing a close second to the American Homer Baker in the 880 yards at the AAA Championships.

After serving in France as a signalman with the Royal Flying Corps, Hill won both the 880 yards and the 1 mile at the first post-war AAA Championships in 1919 and then in August he equalled Joe Binks' British 1 mile record of 4 min 16.8 sec when he finished second in a handicap race in Glasgow.

At the 1920 AAA Championships, Hill's Olympic aspirations received a setback when, having decided not to defend his 1 mile title in order to

concentrate on the 880 yards, he was beaten by the South African Bevil Rudd. The reaction of the British selectors was that Hill was too old to attempt the middle-distance double at the Olympics. After a vehement dispute with AAA Secretary Sir Harry Barclay, Hill won his case and with a determination to prove himself he set off for Antwerp.

After a hazardous Channel crossing, and perturbed by the inadequate accommodation, a rather bewildered Hill arrived at the stadium by lorry for the heats of the 800 metres. To add to his troubles, he found that the Belgian organisers had put all the star runners in one heat – in order, as they put it, 'to give the also-rans a chance'. Despite all the problems, Hill survived the heats and the semi-finals and after a great race he won the gold medal in the final with a new

British record of 1 min 53.4 sec. Two days later Hill concluded a magnificent double by winning the 1500 metres, and he then won a silver in the 3000 metres team race in which he himself finished seventh. Hill, at 31, is the oldest runner to win either the Olympic 800 or 1500 metres and his confidence in his own ability was well justified. He closed his long track career at the 1921 AAA Championships when he won the 1 mile in 4 min 13.8 sec, which improved his own British record by three seconds and was less than one second outside the world record.

Hill, who had been trained by Sam Mussabini and Walter George, became a coach himself on retirement and was the mentor of another outstanding miler, Sydney Wooderson. Shortly before World War II, Hill made his home in Canada, where he died some 30 years later.

Hirons, *William*

Born: 15 June 1871, Wolston, Warwickshire   Died: 5 January 1958, Nottingham, Nottinghamshire

GOLD: 1908 (TUG-OF-WAR)

Thirty-six-year-old Bill Hirons was the oldest member of the City of London Police team which won the Tug-of-War event at the 1908 Games.

Albert Hill after completing his 800–1500 metres double in 1920.

Hodge, *Percy*

Born: 26 December 1890, Guernsey, Channel Islands   Died: 27 December 1967, Bexhill-on-Sea, Sussex

GOLD: 1920 (3000 METRES STEEPLECHASE)

Hodge left the Channel Isles as a young man and took a job in Weymouth; he then moved to Bournemouth before retiring to Bexhill.

Quite apart from the competitive restrictions imposed by the war, Percy Hodge was a late developer and did not win his first AAA title until he was 28 years old. But he was the winner of the AAA steeplechase in four of the five years in which he competed in the event and his only defeat came in 1922 when he surprisingly finished back in fifth place.

In 1920 he had his shoe ripped off in the second lap of the AAA race and lost some 100 yards on the leaders but still went on to win by 75 yards, establishing himself as one of the favourites for the Olympic title. Hodge was the fastest of the heat winners at Antwerp and his time of 10 min 17.4 sec over 3000 metres represented something considerably faster

Percy Hodge winning the 3000 metres steeplechase in 1920.

than he had ever run over the 'English' distance of 2 miles. Possibly, Hodge's main concern for the final was that the race was to start at 9.00 a.m., and although his great friend and mentor Joe Binks was unable to be at the start, because of a serious accident to his father, Hodge was well supported by other members of the British team and won the gold medal by the convincing margin of 100 metres.

Hodge had a highly unusual style of hurdling, which he brought to such a fine art that he could clear the barriers carrying a tray, complete with bottle and glasses, and not spill a drop. He often demonstrated the feat on the stage and at sports meetings. Apart from his steeplechasing ability, he was an excellent performer on the flat and in the match against France in 1921 he finished third in the 5000 metres and was the first Englishman home.

Holmes, *Frederick William*

Born: 9 August 1886, Cosford, Shropshire   Died: 9 November 1944, Smithfield, London

GOLD: 1920 (TUG-OF-WAR)

Fred Holmes was a member of the City of London Police team which won the Tug-of-War at the 1920 Olympics. After retiring from the police he settled in Hadleigh, Suffolk, but he died at St Bartholomew's Hospital in London.

Humphreys, *Fredrick Harkness*

Born: 28 January 1878, Marylebone, London   Died: 10 August 1954, Brentford, Middlesex

GOLD: 1908 (TUG-OF-WAR)   1920 (TUG-OF-WAR)   Silver: 1912 (TUG-OF-WAR)

Fred Humphreys was one of three City of London Policemen who won Olympic gold medals in 1908 and 1920 and silver in 1912. At the time of the 1920 Olympics, Humphreys was 42 years and 203 days old and is the oldest ever Tug-of-War gold medallist. He also competed in the heavyweight division of both the freestyle and Greco-Roman heavyweight wrestling competitions in 1908, but in both styles he lost his first bout to the ultimate winner of the silver medal.

Ireton, *Albert*

Born: 15 May 1879, Baldock, Hertfordshire   Died: 4 January 1947, Stevenage, Hertfordshire

GOLD: 1908 (TUG-OF-WAR)

In addition to being on the City of London Police team which won the Tug-of-War at the 1908 Olympics, Albert Ireton also competed as a heavyweight boxer. His appearance in the ring was brief, as in the first round of his first bout he was knocked out by Syd Evans, the reigning ABA champion.

Jackson, *Arnold Nugent Strode*   (Later ANS Strode-Jackson)

Born: 5 April 1891, Addlestone, Surrey   Died: 13 November 1972, Oxford, Oxfordshire

GOLD: 1912 (1500 METRES)

While at Malvern College, Arnold Jackson was an outstanding runner, cricketer, footballer and boxer, and when he went up to Brasenose College, Oxford, in October 1910, he spread his sporting interests even wider. He represented his College at football and hockey, and became a useful golfer and a better oarsman; but on the advice of his uncle Clement Jackson, a former holder of the world high hurdles record and the current Treasurer of the Oxford University AC,

Arnold Jackson was a surprise winner of the 1500 metres in 1912. The 21 year-old Oxford undergraduate is the youngest ever winner of the event.

Arnold took up running again. Even by the standards of that time, his training was extremely casual; but his natural talent was such that after winning the OUAC 1 mile in 1912, he won the mile against Cambridge in a respectable 4 min 21.6 sec. On the strength of this performance alone, he was selected to represent Great Britain at the Olympic Games in Stockholm.

In the Olympic 1500 metres, seven of Britain's nine entrants were eliminated in the heats and only Jackson and Philip Baker of Cambridge (later Lord Noel-Baker) qualified for the final. In comparison with the other finalists Jackson was a complete novice, but with his long raking stride he came through from seventh place down the home straight,

overtaking, among others, the American holder of the world 1 mile record John Paul Jones and the world record holder at 1500 metres Abe Kiviat. Jackson's winning time of 3 min 56.8 sec was a new British and Olympic record.

On his return from Stockholm Jackson continued his running at Oxford, but although he was an Olympic champion and the British record holder he never even bothered to enter for the AAA Championships. He won again against Cambridge in 1913 and 1914, and in April 1914 he went to America and ran his last race at the Penn Relays, bringing the Oxford team home first in the 4 × 1 mile relay. So his brilliant track career ended after no more than half a dozen first-class races.

In the war, Jackson served with the

King's Royal Rifle Corps and achieved distinctions which more than matched his sporting honours. He became the youngest Brigadier-General in the British Army, was mentioned in despatches six times and won the DSO and three Bars; only six other officers were similarly decorated. In 1919 he adopted Strode as an additional surname by deed poll and the change was registered at the College of Arms, but he retained Strode as a forename and was known as Arnold Nugent Strode Strode-Jackson. Before settling in America in 1921, he was a member of the British delegation to the Paris Peace Conference and was awarded the CBE for his services. He became an American citizen in 1945 but his last years were spent in England.

Jacobs, *David Henry*

Born: 30 April 1888, Cardiff, Glamorganshire   Died: 5 June 1976, Aberconwy, Wales

GOLD: 1912 (4 × 100 METRES RELAY)

Although he had an impressive record at the Welsh Championships, David Jacobs never succeeding in winning an AAA title although he finished second in the 220 yards in 1912 and in the 440 yards in 1913. At the Stockholm Olympics, Jacobs ran the third leg on the sprint relay team which won the gold medals and he also performed creditably in the individual

sprints, reaching the semi-finals of both the 100 and 200 metres.

Jacobs' interest in the sport was aroused after watching the 1908 Olympic Games, and he joined Herne Hill Harriers at the end of the summer. He was at his best as a sprinter in the years immediately prior to 1914 but after the war he gradually lost interest. Herne Hill

Harriers managed to re-establish contact as Jacobs approached his 80th birthday and he once again took a keen interest in club affairs. At the time of his death, David Jacobs was Britain's oldest Olympic gold medallist; he died suddenly in his native Wales while on holiday from his London home.

Kiely, *Thomas Francis*

Born: 25 August 1869, Ballyneal, Co. Tipperary, Ireland   Died: 6 November 1951, Dublin, Ireland

GOLD: 1904 (ALL-AROUND DECATHLON)

After winning the All-Around event at the 1904 Olympics in St Louis, Tom Kiely was not, for some unknown reason, immediately recognised as an Olympic champion. It was not until 1954, following representations from Dr Ferenc Mezo of Hungary, that the International Olympic Committee rectified the mistake.

Kiely faced a monumental task in St Louis; the ten events by which all-around ability was measured were all contested in a single day, in the following order: 100 yards, shot put, high jump, 120 yards hurdles, 880 yards walk, hammer throw, pole vault, 56lb weight throw, long jump and 1 mile. Kiely won four of the events and finished 129 points ahead of the American Adam Gunn, with the hammer thrower and four-time All-American guard on the Penn Football team, Truxton Hare, in third place.

When the English authorities learned that Kiely had been invited to the 1904 Olympics they offered to pay his expenses on the condition that he represented the United Kingdom. Kiely declined the offer and travelled to America at his own expense but on his arrival in New York he was offered further financial inducements by the New York AC, the Irish-American AC and the Chicago AC to represent them in St Louis. Again Kiely declined and it should be noted that apart from the Olympic nature of the St Louis Games, they also served as the unofficial club championships of the USA; for this reason, the leading American clubs were anxious to have the Irish all-rounder on their team.

Tom Kiely was introduced to the sport and subsequently coached by his near neighbours and distant relatives the Davin brothers, Pat, Tom and Maurice, who were among the greatest all-rounders in the history of Irish athletics. Initially Kiely excelled as a triple jumper and hurdler but later, when some of his speed deserted him, he became an outstanding hammer thrower. He won the AAA title five times

and was twice runner-up in his seven appearances between 1895 and 1902 and his defeat at the hands of John Flanagan at the 1900 Championships represented one of the major setbacks of his career. Kiely had been training with the Paris Olympics in mind, but after losing to Flanagan by a margin of more than 24ft (7.32m) at the AAA meet, he abandoned his Olympic aspirations and did not make the journey to Paris. In June 1899 he had set a world record of 162ft 0in (49.38m) and although this only lasted 46 days as a world best, it was the first time that anyone had thrown beyond the 160 feet mark.

The winner of the 1904 Olympic All-Around event was also considered to be the American champion for that year, and Tom Kiely again crossed the Atlantic in 1906 and won his second US title. After his sporting travels were over, Kiely settled on his farm in his native Ballyneal where, in his competitive days, he had done much of his training.

Larner, *George Edward*

Born: 7 March 1875, Langley, Buckinghamshire   Died: 4 March 1949, Brighton, Sussex

GOLD: 1908 (3500 METRES WALK & 10 MILES WALK)

George Larner did not take up competitive walking until 1903 when he was 28 years old. In 1904, when still little more than a novice, he won both AAA titles, and he repeated the double the following year. Having won four AAA titles and set nine world records, Larner then decided to retire as he found that training interfered with his duties as a Brighton policeman. Fortunately, the Chief Constable of Brighton was persuaded to give Larner time off from

work to train for the 1908 Olympic Games and, after a two-year absence, Larner re-appeared on the track.

Although he had an exceptionally long stride, Larner was generally rated as a very fair stylist and it came as a surprise when he was disqualified in his first comeback race, the AAA 7 miles Championship in April 1908. He soon redeemed himself by winning the AAA 2 miles title in July and then won both the Olympic walking titles later that month.

After the Games, Larner retired again from race walking but he enjoyed some modest successes as a cross-country runner with Brighton & County Harriers and Highgate Harriers. In 1911 he made another comeback and won the AAA 7 miles title, but he did not stay in training for the 1912 Olympics. After he finally retired, George Larner became a respected race walking judge and when he died, at the age of 73, many of his British records were still intact.

Leahy, *Cornelius*

Born: 27 April 1876, Cregane, Charleville, Ireland   Died: 1921, USA

GOLD: 1906 (HIGH JUMP)   SILVER: 1906 (TRIPLE JUMP)   1908 (HIGH JUMP)

Con Leahy was one of seven brothers who were all outstanding athletes. Pat was a silver medallist in the 1900 Olympic high jump, Tim headed the world ranking list in the high jump in 1912, Joe was a 23ft (7.01m) long jumper, but only Con won an Olympic gold medal.

The 1906 Olympic high jump began soon after mid-day with the bar set at the absurd height of 1.37m (4ft 6in). It was then raised 1 centimetre at a time and all competitors were required to clear every height. After three hours the bar was still

only at 1.67m (5ft 5¾in) and the seven competitors who were still in contention then agreed that the bar should be raised in increments of 5 centimetres. Two hours later only Leahy and the Hungarian Lajos Gonczy remained, and after Leahy cleared 1.775m (5ft 9¾in) at his first attempt, the Hungarian failed three times and the gold medal went to the Irishman, who had celebrated his 30th birthday the previous day. The Greek officials persuaded the exhausted Leahy to continue jumping with the bar at 6ft (1.83m), but after two

failures he declined to make a third attempt.

Later in the Games, Leahy finished second to his fellow Irishman Peter O'Connor in the triple jump. In 1907 he won the high jump at the US Championships, and at the 1908 Olympics he was in a three-way tie for second place in the high jump. In August 1909, Con Leahy and his brother Pat emigrated to America, where they both eventually died.

Above *David Hemery at the start of the 400m hurdles final in Munich, 1972. He failed to repeat his 1968 success but took the bronze medal.*

Left *An unusual view of the 1968 women's 400m final in Mexico City's Olympic Stadium. Rounding the last bend, Lillian Board in the inside lane moves towards the silver medal.*

Above Steve Ovett beats Sebastian Coe to take the 800m title in 1980, but it was Coe who was celebrating victory (*right*) after the 1500m at the same Games. Pictured on the winner's rostrum with Coe and Ovett – who was third – is East German silver medallist Jurgen Straub.

Opposite Alan Wells powered his way to the 100m title in 1980, at 28 the oldest-ever winner of the event.

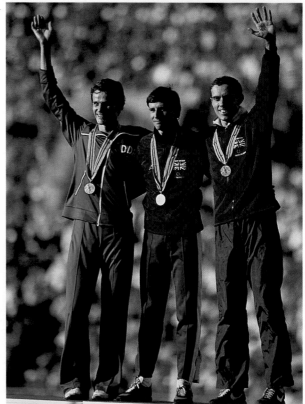

Left *British runners dominated the 1500m again in 1984 at Los Angeles. Seb Coe leads from Steve Cram and Steve Ovett on his way to retaining the title, congratulates silver medallist Cram on the victory rostrum, and shows the flag.*

Right *Tessa Sanderson became the first British woman to win an Olympic title in a throwing event when she won the javelin in 1984. Celebrating with Tessa and her coach Wilf Paish (**far right**) are her great rival Fatima Whitbread (second from left) and Finland's Tina Lillak, bronze and silver medallists respectively.*

Daley Thompson retained his decathlon title in 1984 with another superb display of running, jumping and throwing.

*A gold medal on the ice for Great Britain in three consecutive Winter Olympics, from John Curry (**above**) in 1976, Robin Cousins (**left**) in 1980 – retaining Curry's title – and Jayne Torvill and Christopher Dean (**opposite**) in the 1984 Ice Dance.*

A trio of breaststroke swimming champions. **Above** David Wilkie, winner over 200m in 1976 and Britain's only gold medallist in Montreal.
Right Duncan Goodhew, 100m champion in Moscow, 1980.
Opposite Adrian Moorhouse celebrates his gold in the 100m in Seoul, 1988.

Right *Great Britain celebrate a goal in their thrilling win over Australia in the semi-final.*

*Stars of Great Britain's remarkable triumph in the 1988 hockey tournament. Goalkeeper Ian Taylor (**right**) played in all 7 of Great Britain's matches, Sean Kerly (**left**) scored a total of 8 goals, while Imran Sherwani (**bottom left**) scored 2 of Britain's 3 goals in the final against West Germany.*
***Bottom right** The players celebrate their gold medal success.*

*More gold for Great Britain in Seoul, from yachtsmen Bryn Vaile and Mike McIntyre (**top**) in the Star Class, oarsmen Andy Holmes and Steve Redgrave (**above**), winners of the coxless pairs, and Malcolm Cooper (**above left**) who retained his title in the Small Bore Rifle (3 positions) shooting event.*

*British silver medallists on the track in Seoul. Liz McColgan leads in the 10 000m (**left**), Colin Jackson (**below**) shows impressive form in the 110m hurdles, and (**bottom**) Linford Christie takes on Ben Johnson (far left) and Carl Lewis (far right) in the 100m final.*

Virginia Holgate, winner of a team silver and an individual bronze in the 1984 three-day event.

Liddell, *Eric Henry*

Born: 16 January 1902, Tientsin, China   Died: 21 February 1945, Weihsien, China

GOLD: 1924 (400 METRES)   BRONZE: 1924 (200 METRES)

After showing brilliant promise as an all-round sportsman at Eltham College, Eric Liddell won international honours at rugby football and athletics when he went up to Edinburgh University.

Born in China in the aftermath of the Boxer rising, Liddell first entered the Scottish Championships as a 19-year-old in 1921 and scored the first of his five successive victories in the 100 yards and the 220 yards. He also won the 440 yards in 1924 and 1925. At the AAA Championships, Liddell won the 100 yards and 220 yards in 1923 and the 440 yards in 1924. His time of 9.7 sec for the 100 yards in 1923 stood as a British record for 35 years.

Liddell, who had won seven caps on the wing for Scotland, gave up rugby for the 1923–24 season in order to concentrate on his Olympic preparation. He opened the 1924 track season with a brief visit to America in April, where he finished second in the 220 yards and fourth in the 100 yards at the Penn Relays. When the programme was announced for the Paris Olympic Games, Liddell immediately forsook any idea of running in the 100 metres as the preliminaries were scheduled to be held on a Sunday. Following this decision, he naturally chose to use the AAA Championships as a final tune-up for the two events on which he had set his adjusted Olympic sights. He won the 440 yards, finished second behind the South African Howard Kinsman in the 220 yards and then went to Paris for the Olympic Games.

After winning a bronze medal in the 200 metres, he improved his personal best by more than one second in the semi-finals of the 400 metres. In a classic final, Liddell, drawn in the outside lane, set a devastating pace which, with head back and arms flailing, he somehow managed to maintain to the tape, coming home in 47.6 sec for a new Olympic, European and British record. Back at Stamford Bridge after the Games for the British Empire v USA match, Liddell again ran inside 48 seconds as he made up six yards on the Olympic silver medallist Horatio Fitch in the 4 × 440 yards relay.

After the 1924 track season, Liddell spent an increasing amount of time on his religious duties and after winning three events at the 1925 Scottish Championships he returned to China to join his father as a missionary. He did not give up athletics completely and in 1929, at a meeting in Tientsin, he clocked 49.1 sec to beat the celebrated German runner Otto Peltzer over 400 metres. Peltzer pressed Liddell to train for the 800 metres at the 1932 Olympic Games, but Liddell ran his last race in 1930 when he won the North China Championship.

Over the next decade, Liddell devoted all his energies to the Church and became a legend in the London Missionary Society, but in March 1943 he was interned in a Japanese concentration camp. The privations suffered in camp took their toll of even the fittest and Eric Liddell died in captivity at the age of 43. Although partly fictionalised, the film *Chariots of Fire* is a fitting tribute to this memorable man.

One week after winning the 1924 400 metres title, Eric Liddell anchored the British Empire relay team to victory in the match against the USA.

Lindsay, *Robert Alexander*

Born: 18 April 1890, Wandsworth, London   Died: 21 October 1958, Battersea, London

GOLD: 1920 (4 × 400 METRES RELAY)

Robert Lindsay of Blackheath Harriers was on the threshold of top-class athletics when his career was interrupted by the war. He finished fourth in the 440 yards at the 1911 AAA Championships and won three Scottish 440 yards titles in the years immediately prior to the war. In 1914 he was also the Scottish champion at 220 yards.

As a finalist in the 1920 AAA Championship 440 yards, Lindsay was selected for the relay team which won the Olympic gold medals in Antwerp, but his best performance came the following year when he defeated the Olympic champion Bevil Rudd of South Africa to take the 1921 AAA title.

Lowe, *Douglas Gordon Arthur*

Born: 7 August 1902, Manchester, Lancashire   Died: 30 March 1981, Cranbrook, Kent

GOLD: 1924 (800 METRES)   1928 (800 METRES)

Douglas Lowe was the first man to retain an Olympic 800 metres title and he surprisingly won his first Olympic gold medal, in 1924, before he had won an AAA title.

At Highgate School, Lowe won the Public Schools half-mile in 1920 and while at Pembroke College, Cambridge, he won a blue for soccer and athletics. He finished third in the 880 yards against Oxford in 1921 before winning the event for the next three years and in 1924 he also won the 1 mile.

Despite reaching the 880 yards final at the 1922 and 1923 AAA Championships, Lowe failed both times to finish in the first three; but in 1924 he was a close second to Henry Stallard. Lowe was not, therefore, Britain's first-string for the 800 metres at the Paris Olympics and was a surprise winner in 1 min 52.4 sec, which beat the British record set by Albert Hill in the previous Olympic final. He came close to winning a second medal when he finished fourth in the 1500 metres. He continued to show impressive form in the years between the 1924 and 1928 Olympics and in 1926, after setting a world record for 600 yards, he was narrowly defeated over 880 yards by the German Otto Peltzer at the AAA Championships. Peltzer set a new world record of 1 min 51.6 sec and Lowe was credited with an estimated 1 min 52.0 sec, which was also inside the old world record.

In 1927 Lowe finally won his first AAA title; in fact, he won three. He finished first in the 440 yards and 880 yards and was on the Achilles Club team which won the 4 × 440 yards relay. He also showed a surprising turn of speed as a member of the Achilles team which was third in the 4 × 110 yards relay. He retained both his 440 yards and 880 yards AAA titles in 1928 and then won his second Olympic gold medal when he devastated a world class field with a new Olympic record of 1 min 51.8 sec. Later in the Amsterdam Games

he ran a 47.6 sec leg on the 1600 metres relay team which set a new British record of 3 min 16.4 sec. to finish in fifth place.

Lowe ran two more magnificent races before he retired at the end of the 1928 season. An 880 yards relay leg, estimated at 1 min 51.0 sec, in the British Empire v USA match was probably the fastest performance of his entire career. He followed that with a victory in Berlin over Otto Peltzer with a British record of 1 min 51.2 sec for 800 metres.

Douglas Lowe was Called to the Bar of the Inner Temple in 1928, became a bencher in 1957 and took silk in 1964. He was deputy chairman of Warwick quarter sessions, Recorder of Lincoln and a Recorder of the Crown Court. Despite his busy legal career, Lowe found time to serve as Hon. Secretary of the Amateur Athletic Association from 1931 to 1938.

Douglas Lowe winning his second 800 metres title in 1928.

Macintosh, *Henry Maitland*
Born: 10 June 1892, Kelso, Scotland   Died: 26 July 1918, The Somme, France
GOLD: 1912 (4 × 100 METRES RELAY)

Henry Macintosh, who was educated at Glenalmond and Corpus Christi, Cambridge, had a poor domestic season prior to the 1912 Olympic Games. He lost to Duncan Macmillan in the 100 yards at the Cambridge University sports and in the match against Oxford, and at the AAA Championships he finished last in his 100 yards heat and did not run in the 220 yards. In Stockholm, he was eliminated in

the heats of both sprints and 1912 would have been a very lean year had it it not been for his Olympic gold medal in the sprint relay.

In 1913, Macintosh was President of the Cambridge University AC and won the 100 yards against Oxford. His vastly improved form continued when he won the Scottish 100 yards title before equalling the British record of 9.8 sec in

Vienna. In 1914, he again won the 100 yards against Oxford before leaving to serve as an Assistant District Commissioner in South Africa. After only a few months, the outbreak of war brought him home and he was commissioned into the Argyll & Sutherland Highlanders. In the summer of 1918, Captain Henry Macintosh was killed in action at the Somme.

Matthews, *Kenneth Joseph*
Born: 21 June 1934, Birmingham, Warwickshire
GOLD: 1964 (20 KILOMETRES WALK)

In 1959, Ken Matthews of the Sutton Coldfield Walking Club won the first of his six consecutive RWA 10 miles titles, and as he also won the 2 miles and 7 miles at the AAA Championships that year he was the British champion in all three walking events, a feat he repeated in 1961, 1963 and 1964.

With victories in the Olympic Games in 1964, the European Championships in 1962 and the Lugano Cup in 1961 and

1963, Matthews won four of the five major international races in which he took part and his only failure came in the 1960 Olympic Games. Starting as one of the favourites for the 20km title in Rome, he made a rare error of pace judgement and failed to finish. Four years on in Tokyo Matthews was a convincing winner, finishing ahead of Dieter Linder of East Germany and the Russian Leonid Spirin, who had won the Olympic title in 1960

and was to win a second gold medal in 1968 after Matthews had retired.

Matthews, who was an electrician at Hams Hall Power Station, near Sutton Coldfield, was the only British Olympic champion in Tokyo who was not honoured with an MBE at the end of the year. A campaign from within the sport to rectify this finally succeeded in 1978 and Matthews was appointed an MBE 14 years after his Olympic victory.

Merriman, *Frederick*

Born: 18 May 1873, Campden, Gloucestershire   Died: 27 June 1940, Gloucestershire

GOLD: 1908 (TUG-OF-WAR)

Fred Merriman was a member of the City of London Police team which won the Tug-of-War event at the 1908 Olympics.

Mills, *Edwin Archer*

Born: 17 May 1878, Stretton Bushville, Warwickshire   Died: 12 November 1946, Ashby-de-la-Zouche, Leicestershire

GOLD: 1908 (TUG-OF-WAR)   1920 (TUG-OF-WAR)   SILVER: 1912 (TUG-OF-WAR)

Edwin Mills was some three months past his 42nd birthday when he won his second Olympic gold medal in 1920. He was one of three City of London policemen who won medals in the Tug-of-War at three successive Olympic Games.

O'Connor, *Peter*

Born: 18 October 1874, Ashtown, Wicklow, Ireland   Died: 9 November 1957, Upton, Newton, Waterford, Ireland

GOLD: 1906 (TRIPLE JUMP)   SILVER: 1906 (LONG JUMP)

In August 1900, Peter O'Connor set his first world long jump record, and in a phenomenal 1901 season he improved his record no less than four times. He also bettered the old record on five other occasions, although these marks were not recognised because of various irregularities. The highlight of the season was a jump of 24ft 11¾in (7.61m) off a board runway at Ball's Bridge, Dublin, on 5 August, which was subsequently recognised as the first official IAAF record. It remained on the books for 20 years and was not beaten as an Irish All-Comers record until 1968.

In the long jump at the 1906 Olympics O'Connor had trouble with his run-up, which resulted in a fierce dispute with the judges. They repeatedly called him for 'no-jumping' and he finished in second place with a mark more than one foot below his best. Frustrated by this result, O'Connor turned to his secondary event, the triple jump, in search of a gold medal. On paper his fellow-Irishman Con Leahy, the newly-crowned high jump champion and an excellent all-round jumper, was the favourite, but things went well for O'Connor and he finally won an Olympic gold medal.

O'Connor retired at the end of the 1906 season and concentrated on his solicitor's practice, but he maintained a keen interest in the sport and was one of the judges at the 1932 Olympic Games in Los Angeles. He was also a spectator at the 1936 Games and press interviews at the time revealed that his style of jumping was remarkably similiar to that of Jesse Owens, the winner at the Berlin Olympics.

Ovett, *Stephen Michael James*

Born: 9 October 1955, Brighton, Sussex

GOLD: 1980 (800 METRES)   SILVER: 1980 (1500 METRES)

After winning the 1973 European Junior 800 metres title when he was only 17 years old, Steve Ovett was in the forefront of world middle-distance running for more than a decade. He took part in three Olympic Games (1976–84) and although he won the Olympic 800 metres title in 1980, he was probably at his best over the 1500 metres/1 mile distance. In 1980, after setting two world records at 1500 metres and bettering Seb Coe's world 1 mile record, Ovett was a firm favourite for the Olympic 1500 metres title but his run of 45 successive victories over the distance, which stretched back to May 1977, was broken when he finished third in Moscow. In 1981 he bettered the world 1 mile record for a second time and 1983 saw him achieve his third world record at 1500 metres. Between 1977 and 1983 he set 12 UK records at distances ranging from 800 to 2000 metres.

Apart from his record breaking feats, Steve Ovett was a brilliant competitor and built an outstanding record in major championships. At 800 metres he won the European Junior title in 1973, the European Cup in 1975 and the Olympic gold medal in 1980. Over 1500 metres Ovett won at the European Cup in 1977, the World Cup in 1977 and 1981, and the European Championships in 1978. Proof of his amazing versatility at the very highest level came when he won the 5000 metres at the 1986 Commonwealth Games.

He was always able to produce a devasting finishing burst off a fast pace,

and this talent made him one of the finest middle-distance runners in the history of the sport. When Ovett and Seb Coe were at their peak, no other country could match Britain's strength in the middle-distance events, and both athletes rendered a great service to British sport.

Apart from his defeat in the 1980 Olympic 1500 metres final, Ovett suffered a major disappointment at the 1984 Olympics when, because of bronchial problems, he was not at his best and after finishing last in the 800 metres final he was forced to drop out of the 1500 metres final. After failing to qualify for the 1990 Commonwealth Games team, he gradually dropped out of big-time athletics and spent more time developing his career as a television commentator.

Steve Ovett, Olympic champion at 800 metres in 1980

Rampling, *Godfrey Lionel*

Born: 14 May 1909, Greenwich, London

GOLD: 1936 (4 × 400 METRES RELAY)   SILVER: 1932 (4 × 400 METRES RELAY)

Although he was eliminated in the semi-finals of the individual 400 metres at both the 1932 and 1936 Olympics, Godfrey Rampling won a relay medal in both Los Angeles and Berlin. An officer in the Royal Artillery, he won the AAA 440 yards title in 1931 and then made his mark on the international scene in the England v Germany match in Cologne later in the season, when after running 47.0 sec in the 4 × 400 metres relay, he covered the 400 metres stage of the medley relay in 46.7 sec.

The following season saw him win a silver medal in the relay at the Los Angeles Olympics when the British team set a European record of 3 min 11.6 sec behind the USA. In 1934, Rampling had his second win at the AAA Championships and then took the British Empire title with a British record of 48.0 sec.

Although he was in fine form at the 1936 Games, he narrowly missed making the final of the individual 400 metres; but he made amends for this disappointment with a marvellous run in the relay. Running the second leg, Rampling took over the baton 12 metres behind the leader, but with a 46.7 sec run he handed over with a three-metre advantage and Britain went on to take the gold medals in 3 min 9.0 sec. In doing so, as in 1932, they set a European record. Rampling retired from the Army as a lieutenant colonel and was, for a time, the secretary of a golf club. His daughter, Charlotte, is a famous film actress.

Rimmer, *John Thomas*

Born: 27 April 1878, Ormskirk, Lancashire   Died: 6 June 1962, Liverpool, Lancashire

GOLD: 1900 (4000 METRES STEEPLECHASE; 5000 METRES – TEAM)

As the runners in the steeplechase at the 1900 Olympics had to contend with 'stone fences, a water jump, hurdles and other obstacles', Great Britain was well served by the cross-country experience of her representatives.

There were two steeplechase events in Paris, the 2500 metres event being held first with the race over 4000 metres scheduled for the following day. Unlike most of the leading contenders, John Rimmer did not start in the shorter event and went to the post for the 4000 metres race fresher than the majority of the field. The British trio of Rimmer, Bennett and Robinson came home virtually together but it was Rimmer who caught the judges' eye and was awarded first place.

Rimmer, a Liverpool policeman who began his athletic career with Sefton Harriers before joining Southport Harriers, later won a second gold medal in the 5000 metres team race in which he himself finished second. He was second in the AAA 10 miles for three successive years from 1899 and his only win at these championships came in 1901 when he won the 4 miles.

Roberts, *William*

Born: 5 April 1912, Lancashire

GOLD: 1936 (4 × 400 METRES RELAY)

After finishing second to Godfrey Rampling in the 440 yards at the 1934 British Empire Games, Bill Roberts of Salford AC took over as Europe's leading quarter-miler in 1935, winning the AAA title and all three international match events.

Roberts achieved the best performance of his career when he ran 46.8 sec in the 400 metres at the 1936 Berlin Olympics, finishing in fourth place only one metre behind the winner. In the relay final, Roberts' estimated 46.4 sec was the fastest of all the stages and made a major contribution to Britain's victory. In post-Olympic meetings, Roberts beat the American Olympic 400 metres champion Archie Williams over the first leg of the 4 × 440 yards relay in the British Empire v USA match, and five days later he met the Olympic 800 metres champion Johnny Woodruff over 400 metres in Oslo. Woodruff set a career best of 46.8 sec and Roberts, in second place with 47.1 sec, had only ever run faster in the Berlin final.

Roberts won the AAA title in 1937 and was the British Empire champion in 1938. Although he did not compete in 1939, he made a successful comeback after the war. In 1946, he finished second to the Jamaican Arthur Wint at the AAA Championships, then won the international against France, and closed the season with a silver medal in the relay and fifth place in the individual 400 metres at the European Championships in Oslo. After a quiet 1947 season, Roberts, in third place, was the first Briton home at the 1948 AAA Championships and was elected captain of the British team for the Olympic Games.

But the successes of Berlin were not to be repeated. The 36-year-old Roberts was eliminated in the second round of the individual 400 metres and despite a fine leg in the relay heats he narrowly failed to take Britain through to the final. Roberts finally retired at the end of the season and concentrated on his work with the family furniture business.

Robertson, *Arthur James*

Born: 19 April 1879, Sheffield, Yorkshire   Died: 18 April 1957, Peterborough, Cambridgeshire

GOLD: 1908 (3 MILES – TEAM)   SILVER: 1908 (3200 METRES STEEPLECHASE)

Arthur Robertson, the son of a Glasgow doctor who reached the closing stages of the English Amateur Golf Championship in 1885, was educated at Kelvinside Academy, Glasgow, before moving to King's School, Peterborough, as a 14-year-old. At both schools he was a brilliant all-round sportsman, and the school 1 mile record he set at King's in 1894 remained unbeaten for many years. On leaving school, Robertson concentrated on cycling and it was not until he was 25 that he began to take athletics seriously. Representing Peterborough AC, he finished fifth in the 1906 AAA 1 mile and at the end of the season transferred to Birchfield Harrriers. In 1907 he took part in four events at the AAA Championships, with second place in the steeplechase being his best performance.

In March 1908, Robertson won the English and the International cross-country titles, while second place in the AAA 4 miles in July earned him a place in the Olympic team. At the Games, he won a gold medal in the 3 miles team race, in which he individually finished second, a silver medal in the steeplechase and was fifth in the 5 miles. He closed the Olympic season with a highly successful tour of Scandinavia, and on 13 September, running on a banked concrete cycle track in Stockholm, he set a world record of 15 min 1.2 sec for 5000 metres. The following day, he failed by only 83 yards to better Walter George's world 1 hour record.

In 1909, Robertson finished second in both the 1 mile and the 4 miles at the AAA Championships and his final race came at the Glasgow Rangers Sports when he was only one second outside Alf Shrubb's British record for 1½ miles. At the age of 30, after a track and cross-country career lasting only four years, he returned to cycling. Both his brothers were well-known cyclists and his youngest brother, DC 'Dabbs' Robertson, competed in the 1908 Olympic Games. Arthur owned a sports shop in Peterborough for many years and the business was later taken over by his son.

Robinson, *Sidney J*

GOLD: 1900 (5000 METRES – TEAM)   SILVER: 1900 (2500 METRES STEEPLECHASE)
BRONZE: 1900 (4000 METRES STEEPLECHASE)

Although Sidney Robinson won a full set of medals at the 1900 Olympics, his silver and bronze in the two steeplechase events probably represented greater achievements than his gold medal in the 5000 metres team race, in which he only finished sixth individually in a field of ten.

Robinson, who represented the Northampton Cycling & Athletic Club, won the AAA steeplechase four times and was twice the champion at 10 miles. He was also the National cross-country champion in 1897 and 1898, and in the latter year he led England home against France in the match which was the forerunner of the International Cross-Country Championship.

Russell, *Arthur*

Born: 1886

GOLD: 1908 (3200 METRES STEEPLECHASE)

Arthur Russell, of Thomson-Houston AC and Walsall H & AC, won the AAA steeplechase in 1904, 1905 and 1906; but at the 1908 Championships he lost narrowly to Reg Noakes of Sparkhill Harriers. Noakes was unable to compete at the 1908 Olympics, so Russell took over as the first-string of the 11 British competitors in the steeplechase. He confirmed his position as one of the favourites by winning the fastest of the six heats and in the final he ran a well-judged race to beat his team-mate, Arthur Robertson, by two metres.

Arthur Russell beats team-mate Arthur Robertson for the 3200 metres steeplechase title in 1908.

Sewell, *John*

Born: 23 April 1882, Halfmorton, Scotland   Died: 18 July 1947, Cambridge, Cambridgeshire

GOLD: 1920 (TUG-OF-WAR)   SILVER: 1912 (TUG-OF-WAR)

After winning a silver medal in 1912, John Sewell went on to win a gold medal in 1920. Like a number of his colleagues on the City of London Police Tug-of-War team, Sewell was also an accomplished wrestler. He was the British heavyweight champion in the Cumberland & Westmoreland style for four successive years from 1907 to 1910.

Shepherd, *John James*

Born: 2 June 1884, Bicknor, Gloucestershire   Died: 9 July 1954, Aston, Herefordshire

GOLD: 1908 (TUG-OF-WAR)   1920 (TUG-OF-WAR)   SILVER: 1912 (TUG-OF-WAR)

John Shepherd was one of the three City of London policemen to win three Olympic medals in the Tug-of-War event. His 26-year career with the police was interrupted by war service with the Military Police in France. After the war he won the British Cumberland & Westmoreland style heavyweight wrestling title in 1922 and 1923. He was also said to be a champion javelin-thrower, although there is no record of any performances to verify this claim.

Stiff, *Harry Joseph*

Born: 23 October 1881, Sudbury, Suffolk   Died: 17 April 1939, Finchingfield, Essex

GOLD: 1920 (TUG-OF-WAR)

Although aged 38, Harry Stiff was a newcomer to the City of London Police Tug-of-War team which won the gold medals at the 1920 Olympics.

Thompson, *Donald James*

Born: 20 January 1933, Hillingdon, Middlesex

GOLD: 1960 (50 KILOMETRES WALK)

Don Thompson of the Metropolitan Walking Club took up race walking in 1951, and 1955 saw the first of eight successive wins in the London to Brighton walk. In 1956 he began another great series of victories with the first of his seven successive National 50km titles. The big disappointment of the 1956 season for Thompson, though, was his failure to finish in the Olympic 50km after collapsing when approaching the stadium.

No athlete prepared more assiduously than the diminutive Don Thompson for the 1960 Olympics. With the aid of heaters and steam kettles he exercised in a sealed bathroom at his home in conditions which he felt simulated the heat and humidity he could expect in Rome. This unique training method paid off as he won the gold medal with a new Olympic record of 4 hr 25 min 30 sec. Among those he defeated were all the post-war Olympic 50km walking champions: John Ljunggren (Sweden, 1948), Guiseppe Dordoni (Italy, 1952) and Norman Read (New Zealand, 1956).

Thompson took part in his third Olympics in 1964 and finished 10th. His best performance in three European Championships was his third place in 1962, but it was fitting that he chose the 1968 London to Brighton for his final race. He had a magnificent record in the classic road race, having won the event nine times and set a course record in 1957.

Thirty years after winning his Olympic gold medal, Thompson came out of retirement at the age of 57 and finished in second place in the 1990 RWA National 100 mile championship.

Thompson, *Francis Morgan 'Daley'*

Born: 30 July 1958, Notting Hill, London

GOLD: 1980 (DECATHLON)   1984 (DECATHLON)

With four world records, two Olympic gold medals, three Commonwealth titles, and wins in the World and European Championships, Daley Thompson is, without doubt, the greatest decathlete the world has ever seen.

The second son of a Nigerian father and Scottish mother, Daley showed a remarkable aptitude for sport while at boarding school in Sussex. Initially he was a member of Haywards Heath Harriers but when he returned to London in 1975 he joined the Essex Beagles club. Later that year he won the first two decathlon competitions he entered, while in 1976 he won the AAA title and was 18th at the Montreal Olympic Games. The following year, he won the European Junior title and in 1978 came the first of his three Commonwealth titles.

In 1979, he failed to finish in his only decathlon of the year but won the long jump at the UK Championships. He then opened the 1980 Olympic season with a world decathlon record of 8648 points at Gotzis, Austria, in May, and followed this with a comfortable win at the Moscow Olympics. After a quiet 1981 season he was in devastating form in 1982; back at Gotsiz in May, he raised the world record to 8730 points and then in September, at the European Championships in Athens, he took the record up to 8774 points. The following month in Brisbane, Thompson took his second Commonwealth title.

In 1983 Daley was crowned the all-round king at the World Championships and became the first decathlete to hold the European, World and Olympic titles simultaneously. He spent much of the summer of 1984 in California preparing for the defence of his Olympic title, with Jurgen Hingsen, the West German who had taken over from Thompson as the world record holder, expected to be a major threat. Thompson took the lead in the first event and was never headed throughout the competition, although it seemed that, by easing off in the 1500 metres he had missed recapturing the world record by just one point. When the photo-finish pictures were examined, however, it was found that Thompson should have been credited with one more point in the 110 metres hurdles so he had, in fact, equalled Hingsen's record. Then when the new scoring tables were introduced, Thompson became the sole record holder once more with a re-calculated score of 8847 points.

Daley Thompson, gold medallist in 1980 and 1984, and only the second man in history successfully to defend an Olympic decathlon title.

After his Olympic success, Thompson won his third Commonwealth title in 1986 but after that he never quite recaptured the superlative form of earlier years. In 1987 he suffered his first decathlon defeat for nine years when he finished ninth in the World Championships, and at his third Olympics in Seoul in 1988 he finished fourth. He made the Commonwealth Games team for the fourth time in 1990 but was forced to withdraw because of injury.

Apart from his four world records and numerous victories in major championships, Daley Thompson set three world junior records and bettered the UK and Commonwealth record no less than ten times. As befits such a talented all-round athlete, Thompson produced some fine individual performances in the events which go to make up the decathlon; he was the AAA long jump champion in 1977 and was the lead-off man for the sprint relay team at the 1984 Olympics.

Note: The points scores given above have been re-calculated according to the current scoring tables which were introduced on 1 April 1985.

Thorne, *Ernest Arthur*

Born: 7 June 1887, Wandsworth, London   Died: 18 November 1968, Taplow, Buckinghamshire

GOLD: 1920 (TUG-OF-WAR)

Ernest Thorne was a 33-year-old member of the City of London Police team which won the Tug-of-War event on the last occasion it was staged at the Olympics.

Tysoe, *Alfred Edward*

Born: 21 March 1874, Skerton, Nr Lancaster, Lancashire   Died: 26 October 1901, Blackpool, Lancashire

GOLD: 1900 (800 METRES & TEAM 5000 METRES)

Alfred Tysoe, a Lancashire farm worker, achieved his first championship successes in 1896 when he won the Northern Counties 1000 yards and 1 mile titles. The following year he established a national reputation by winning the AAA 1 mile and 10 miles championships, and in 1898 he was a member of the Salford Harriers team which won the National cross-country team championship. In view of his obvious talent as a distance runner, it came as a surprise when Tysoe turned to the shorter distances but the decision was soon justified. He won the AAA 880 yards title in 1899 and retained the title in 1900 in 1 min 57.8 sec, which topped the world rankings that year. One week after his AAA victory Tysoe won the Olympic 800 metres title in Paris in a slow 2 min 1.2 sec, and he later won a gold medal in the 5000 metres team race in which he himself finished seventh. After his disappointing time in the 800 metres Tysoe was anxious to give the French a better indication of his true abilities, and he entered for the handicap events which concluded the Games. Although he was eliminated after finishing only fifth in his heat in the 800 metres handicap race, his time of 1 min 57.8 sec, off scratch, was a new French All-Comers record.

Tysoe concluded the 1900 season by defeating the new Olympic 1500 metres champion, Charles Bennett of Finchley Harriers, in a challenge match over 1320 yards. Tragically, this was to be the last race of his career. Early in 1901 he contracted pleurisy and died later that year at his father's home at the age of 27.

Voigt, *Emil Robert*

Born: December 1882, Manchester, Lancashire   Died: 16 October 1973, Auckland, New Zealand

GOLD: 1908 (5 MILES)

Born in England of German parentage, Emil Voigt retained for Great Britain the Olympic 5 miles title which Henry Hawtrey had won in 1906. By virtue of his win in the AAA 4 miles ten days earlier, Voigt was one of the favourites for the 1908 Olympic title; his main opposition came from John Svanberg of Sweden, the world record holder at 5000 metres, and Charles Hefferon, the versatile holder of the South African 1 mile record, who was to finish second in the marathon later in the Games. Voigt soon disposed of this foreign challenge and won the Olympic title with 70 yards to spare over fellow Mancunian Eddie Owen. Voigt later claimed that his victory was mainly due to his being vegetarian.

Emil Voigt retained his AAA 4 miles title in 1909, and after winning the 1 mile in 1910 he retired from competition. In 1911 he sailed for Australia, where he became one of the pioneers of radio, setting up his own broadcasting station specialising in wrestling commentaries,

and he served for 12 years as President of the Australian Federation of Broadcasting Stations. In 1948 Voigt moved to New Zealand, where he continued with his various business interests until his death at the age of 90.

Wells, *Allan Wipper*
Born: 3 May 1952, Edinburgh, Scotland
GOLD: 1980 (100 METRES)   SILVER: 1980 (200 METRES)

Allan Wells began his athletic career by winning the 1970 Scottish Junior triple jump title and in 1972 he cleared a respectable 7.32m (24ft ¼in) in the long jump. But after seeing the Jamaican Don Quarrie win both sprints at the 1970 Commonwealth Games in Edinburgh, Wells decided to try the sprints himself, though it was not until 1976 that he first achieved a legal clocking of better than 11.0 sec for the 100 metres.

Although he won the AAA Indoor 60 metres title in 1977, his outdoor season was relatively undistinguished. The following year, however, saw him establish himself as a world-class sprinter. His powerful physique and sprinting skills were developed by his coach Wilson Young, a former professional sprinter, although Young was unable to convince Wells of the merit of using starting blocks.

In July 1978, Wells equalled Peter Radford's 20-year-old UK 100 metres record of 10.29 sec and six days later he brought the record down to 10.15 sec. The following month he showed magnificent form at the Commonwealth Games in Edmonton; in the 200 metres he set a UK record of 20.61 sec in the heats before running a wind-assisted 20.12 sec to win the final, while he won a second gold medal in the relay and a silver medal in the 100 metres.

In 1979, Wells twice improved the UK

200 metres record and claimed a major scalp when he defeated the Italian Pietro Mennea at the European Cup final in Turin. Due to an alteration in IAAF rules, Wells was obliged to use starting blocks at the Moscow Olympics but he soon showed that he had adapted to the change by setting a UK record of 10.11 sec in the heats of the 100 metres. He went on to win a desperately close final – both he and the pre-race favourite, Silvio Leonard of

Alan Wells at Los Angeles in 1984. Four years earlier, at 28, he had become the oldest-ever winner of the Olympic 100 metres title.

Cuba, were given the same electronic time of 10.25 sec but it was Wells, at the age of 28, who became the oldest ever winner of the Olympic 100 metres title. He failed by the narrowest of margins to win the 200 metres and his time of 20.21 sec behind Mennea was a UK record. He claimed a third UK record as a member of the relay team which finished in fourth place. Although Wells had other successes ahead of him, his times in Moscow were to prove the fastest of his career without the benefit of wind assistance.

With wins in the IAAF 'Golden Sprints', the World Cup and the European Cup in 1981, Wells confirmed his position at the top of world sprinting but his early form in 1982 was disappointing. However, in October at the Commonwealth Games in Brisbane he won the 100 metres and shared the 200 metres title with Mike McFarlane.

In 1984, at 32, he made the Olympic team for a second time and although he was eliminated in the semi-finals of the 100 metres he was a member of the relay team which did well to reach the final.

The UK records of Wells, who was married to the international sprinter Margot Wilkie, remained unbeaten for a number of years and even today, some ten years later, very few British sprinters have recorded better times.

Whitlock, *Hector Harold*
Born: 16 December 1903, Hendon, Middlesex   Died: 27 December 1985, Wicklewood, Norfolk
GOLD: 1936 (50 KILOMETRES WALK)

After finishing second in the RWA 50km championship in 1931, Harold Whitlock won the title in 1933. He was champion again in 1935 and with victories in each of the next four years up to the outbreak of war, he won a total of six championships.

Whitlock traded wins with Tommy Green, the 1932 Olympic champion, in many of the classic road races of the thirties but as he was ten years Green's junior, Whitlock inevitably got the upper hand as the years passed. In 1934 he won the first of four successive London to Brighton races and in 1935 he became the

first man to complete the course in under eight hours. His winning time of 4 hr 30 min 38 sec in the 1936 RWA 50km championship ultimately proved to be the fastest of his career and established him as one of the favourites for the Olympic title.

Like the other British walkers in Berlin, Whitlock suffered from a severe bout of sickness during the race but he overcame the handicap and retained the Olympic title for Britain by a comfortable margin. Two years later he completed a magnificent double by winning the 1938 European title in Paris. In the immediate

Harold Whitlock wins the 50 kilometres walk in 1936.

post-war years he only competed intermittently, but his younger brother Rex upheld the family tradition with his selection for the 1948 Olympics. In 1952, Harold made a serious comeback and after finishing third in the RWA 50km he made a second Olympic appearance in Helsinki, aged 48 years 218 days; he still holds the record of being Britain's oldest ever international athlete. In Helsinki he finished 11th, a creditable performance in a field of 31, but brother Rex did even better, finishing fourth.

Harold Whitlock, a tall stylish walker who was a member of the Metropolitan Walking Club, worked as a motor mechanic and as he had a special aptitude for tuning racing cars he was often called upon to assist with record attempts at the old Brooklands circuit. A highly respected coach and judge in his later years, he officiated at the 1960 Olympics in Rome when his star pupil, Don Thompson, won the gold medal. In 1966, Whitlock was awarded the MBE for his services to the sport.

Wolff, *Frederick Ferdinand*

Born: 13 October 1910, Hong Kong   Died: 26 January 1988, Marylebone, London

GOLD: 1936 (4 × 400 METRES RELAY)

After winning his first race at the Kowloon Cricket Club, Hong Kong, in 1919, Freddie Wolff went away to school in England where he attended Beaumont College. On leaving school in 1929 he joined the London Athletic Club and narrowly failed to win selection for the 1932 Olympics in Los Angeles. He reached the final of the AAA 220 yards that year and achieved the fastest 400 metres time of his career when he ran 48.6 sec in Paris.

In 1933 Wolff won his only AAA 440 yards title and later in the season was the winner in the international match against France. His next major international test came in the 1600 metres relay at the 1936 Olympics when he ran the first leg for the British team which won the gold medals with a new European record of 3 min 9.0 sec. Although he handed over the baton in fourth place at the end of his leg, he had just managed to keep within striking distance of the strong American team and Rampling, Roberts and Brown eventually recorded a comfortable victory.

After an international tour of Scandanavia in 1937, Wolff retired and devoted himself to the family business. He served in the war as a captain in the Oxford & Bucks Light Infantry and then went on to head his grandfather's firm of commodity brokers. In 1970 he served as Chairman of the London Metal Exchange and in 1975 he was awarded the CBE for his services to invisible exports. On his retirement from business, the *Financial Times* described him as 'the best-known metal trader in the world' but Wolff always said that his Olympic gold medal was one piece of metal that he would never trade.

The bonhomous Freddie Wolff died on the day that a reception was held at Buckingham Palace for all surviving British Olympic medallists but the British Olympic Association had earlier delivered his commemorative award to his bedside at the London Clinic.

The three athletes listed below were non-scoring members of winning teams in 1900 and 1908. By today's reckoning they would certainly be considered as gold medallists:

Hallows, *Norman Frederic*

Born: 29 December 1886, Doncaster, Yorkshire   Died: 16 October 1968, Marlborough, Wiltshire

GOLD: 1908 (3 MILES – TEAM)   BRONZE: 1908 (1500 METRES)

Norman Hallows took the bronze medal behind the American Mel Sheppard and Harold Wilson in the 1500 metres at the 1908 Games and he was also a talented performer over longer distances. Earlier in the year, he had won the 3 mile event for the third successive time in the Oxford v Cambridge match and in the 3 mile team event at the Olympics he finished in seventh place and was a non-scoring member of the winning team. In his fourth appearance in the University match, in 1909, Hallows ran in the 1 mile and finished second to Philip Baker of Cambridge.

After leaving Felsted School, he first attended Keble College, Oxford, and then became a science scholar at Leeds University. He completed his education by studying medicine at St Thomas' Hospital. He was with the Red Cross in the Balkan Wars of 1912–13, then served in World War I as a Captain in the RAMC in France. In 1919 he was appointed as the resident Medical Officer to Marlborough College. Under the pseudonym 'Duplex' he wrote, together with Ian Bradley, a number of books on light engineering.

Rowley, *Stanley Rupert*

Born: 11 September 1876, Young, New South Wales, Australia
Died: 1 April 1924, Manly, New South Wales, Australia

GOLD: 1900 (5000 METRES – TEAM)   BRONZE: 1900 (60 METRES, 100 METRES & 200 METRES)

Stan Rowley was an outstanding schoolboy sprinter at Sydney Boys' High School, and as a 19-year-old he finished second in the 100 yards at the 1895 Australian Championships and won the title the following year. In 1897 and 1899 he won both sprints at the Australasian Championships, a bi-annual meeting which brought together the best athletes from Australia and New Zealand; at the second meeting, at Brisbane in November 1899, he equalled the Australian 100 yards record of 9.9 sec and set a new Australasian record of 22.2 sec for 220 yards.

Although the Australian authorities decided not to send a team to the 1900 Paris Olympics, sufficient funds were raised by private subscription to enable Rowley to go to Europe. Taking five months leave from his job as a stock-keeper, he arrived in London in June and after reaching the final of the AAA 100 yards, the English Association agreed to pay his expenses to Paris. At the Olympics, he finished third in each of the three sprints. Medals were not awarded at the 1900 Games and Rowley was presented with a carriage clock, a ladies' purse and a silver paper knife. He then became involved in the charade that was the 5000 metres team race.

The French officials insisted that although only four runners were to count in the scoring, teams must consist of five runners, each of whom must complete the race. With Tysoe, Bennett, Rimmer and Robinson available, Britain's victory seemed assured if only they could find a fifth runner. Apparently the three British marathon runners were not available; the Anglo-Indian sprinter Norman Pritchard

was asked to make up the team but declined because of injury; and the French officials ruled out the Canadian winner of the steeplechase, George Orton; but they accepted the entry of Stan Rowley. Why an Australian sprinter but not a Canadian distance runner, who might have performed well in the race, was acceptable to the French authorities seems to be a decision that would not bear close scrutiny. When the event finally started, Rowley jogged the first lap, then started walking and the officials,

recognizing the absurdity of the situation, permitted him to retire.

Rowley finally arrived back in Sydney in October and announced his retirement. After a brief return to racing in 1905, he served as honorary treasurer of the Australian AAU from 1908 to 1924. As a young man, he was an active rugby footballer and in his later years a keen golfer and cricketer, being honoured with membership of the exclusive cricket club, I Zingari.

Wilson, *Harold Allan*
Born: 22 January 1885, Horncastle, Lincolnshire   Died: 1916
GOLD: 1908 (3 MILES – TEAM)   SILVER: 1908 (1500 METRES)

After setting a 'world record' of 3 min 59.8 sec at 1500 metres in the 1908 British Olympic trials, Harold Wilson won the AAA 1 mile title in 4 min 20.2 sec, which topped the world rankings for the year. He could not quite repeat his earlier form

in the Olympic 1500 metres final and took the silver medal two metres behind the American Mel Sheppard.

In the 3 miles team event he finished fifth individually and for a man who was running well beyond his usual distance it

was an excellent performance to beat all but John Eisele (USA) of the foreign entrants. In 1909 Wilson turned professional and met with a certain amount of success in Canada and South Africa.

Track & Field
WOMEN

Packer, *Ann Elizabeth*   (Later Mrs RI Brightwell)
Born: 8 March 1942, Moulsford, Berkshire
GOLD: 1964 (800 METRES)   SILVER: 1964 (400 METRES)

Ann Packer of Reading AC, the winner of the 800 metres at the 1964 Tokyo Olympics, was one of the most versatile British athletes. In 1959 she won the English Schools 100 yards title, while the following year she was the WAAA long jump champion and made her international debut against Italy in that event. In 1962, she was a finalist in the 200 metres at the European Championships and the 80 metres hurdles at the Commonwealth Games. When she turned her attention to the 400 metres in 1963, she ran a world class 53.6 sec in only her fourth race at the distance.

For the Tokyo Olympics, Packer decided to concentrate on the 400 metres but she added a second string to her bow by trying the 800 metres early in 1964. In the Olympic 400 metres, although setting

Ann Packer, winner of the 800 metres in 1964, with her fiancee Robbie Brightwell who was a silver medallist in the 1600 metres relay.

a European record of 52.0 sec, she had to settle for the silver medal behind the Australian Betty Cuthbert, but then caused one of the major upsets of the Games in the 800 metres. She went to Tokyo with no experience of international 800 metres running and the Olympic heat was only her sixth race at the distance at any level. The eighth and final 800 metres race of her career was the 1964 Olympic final and with a devastating attack down the home straight, she broke the tape five metres clear in a new Olympic and European record of 2 min 1.1 sec.

Packer retired from the sport after the Tokyo Olympics at the age of 22, and she later married Robbie Brightwell, the silver medallist in the 1600 metres relay. Both were awarded the MBE in the 1969 New Year's Honours list.

Peters, *Mary Elizabeth*
Born: 6 July 1939, Halewood, Lancashire
GOLD: 1972 (PENTATHLON)

In the 45th pentathlon of her career, the veteran Mary Peters of Spartan Ladies AC achieved the ultimate athletic success by

winning an Olympic title with a new world record.

The English-born Peters spent much

of her life in Ireland and her first pentathlon competition was at Ballymena in 1955. In the 17 years leading up to her

Olympic triumph, she won seven WAAA pentathlon titles as well as the gold medal at the Commonwealth Games in 1970, and finished fourth in the 1964 Olympics and ninth in 1968. She also won the WAAA shot put title twice and was the Commonwealth Games champion in 1970. After the 1970 Commonwealth Games in Edinburgh, she took a rest from competition and devoted 1971 to intensive training, guided by her coach Buster McShane.

Her form early in 1972 indicated that despite her age she would be a strong contender for the Olympic title. After the opening event (100 metres hurdles) in Munich the 33-year-old Peters was in second place, just six points behind the leader. She moved into the lead after the second event (shot put) and at the end of the first day she held a lead of 301 points. The West German Heidi Rosendahl, in front of her home crowd, made a superb effort on the second day and made up 291 points on Peters, but she still finished a tantalising 10 points behind the ecstatic British winner. The last event was the 200 metres, with the two contenders for the gold medal drawn in the same heat. Rosendahl came home ahead of Peters, her overall score of 4791 points giving her the world record for a fraction over one second. Precisely 1.2 seconds after Rosendahl had completed the race, and the competition, Peters reached the 200 metres finishing line and with a total of 4801 points the world record passed to her.

Mary Peters, who was awarded the MBE in 1973 and the CBE in 1990, competed for two more years and in her fifth appearance at the Commonwealth Games in 1974 she successfully defended her pentathlon title. After retirement she remained active in sports-related civic affairs and fund-raising in Belfast, and was the team manager for many women's international athletic teams.

Mary Peters, winner of the 1972 pentathlon with a new world record.

Rand, *Mary Denise* (née Bignall; later Twomey)

Born: 10 February 1940, Wells, Somerset

GOLD: 1964 (LONG JUMP)   SILVER: 1964 (PENTATHLON)   BRONZE: 1964 (4 × 100 METRES RELAY)

After finishing second in the English Schools long jump in 1955, Mary Bignall accepted a sports scholarship to Millfield School, where she developed her precocious talents. In 1957, as a 17-year-old schoolgirl, she set an English record in her first ever pentathlon competition and later in the season made her international debut as a high jumper.

In 1958, after leaving Millfield, she joined the London Olympiades AC and finished second in the long jump at the Commonwealth Games. In the pentathlon at the European Championships, although finishing no higher than seventh, she posted a new British record of 4466 points. In 1959 she became the first British woman long jumper to clear 20 feet, with a new British record of 20ft 4in (6.20m), and improved her pentathlon record to 4679 points.

In May 1960 Bignall added another inch to her British long jump record and a gold medal at the Rome Olympics in August seemed a distinct possibility. Hopes were raised further when she led the qualifiers in Rome at 6.33m (20ft 9¼in) but things went drastically wrong in the final. She ran through the pit on her first two attempts and a half-hearted last jump left her back in ninth place with a performance more than a foot behind her qualifying jump. Although she finished fourth in the 80 metres hurdles, the Rome Olympics were a stunning disappointment.

Fortunately she had the character to put this setback behind her and produced some superlative performances during the four years she had to wait before getting a second chance of Olympic honours. After the Rome Games she married the Olympic oarsman Sidney Rand, and only four months after the birth of their daughter, Mary was winning bronze medals in the long jump and the relay at the 1962 European Championships. In 1963 she twice improved both her British long jump and pentathlon records and after bettering each record again in the summer of 1964, she went to Tokyo in October to try again for Olympic gold.

As in Rome four years earlier, Mary Rand – as she now was – led the qualifiers; but this time there were no mistakes in the final. With her first jump she set a new Olympic and British record, improving on this with her fourth jump, and on her fifth she virtually put the gold medal beyond the reach of her rivals with a new world record of 6.76m (22ft 2¼in). To crown this wonderful performance, she won a silver medal in the pentathlon and completed her set of Olympic medals with a bronze in

1964 long jump champion Mary Rand. The first British woman to win an Olympic field event.

the relay.

She carried on competing for the next three seasons, winning the Commonwealth long jump title in 1966, but injury prevented her from making the Olympic team for a third time in 1968 and

she announced her retirement.

Her marriage to Sidney Rand ended in divorce and in 1969 she married the 1968 Olympic decathlon champion Bill Twomey, but this marriage was also subsequently dissolved.

Sanderson, *Theresa Ione*
Born: 14 March 1956, St Elizabeth, Jamaica
GOLD: 1984 (JAVELIN)

A few months after Tessa Sanderson was born, her father went to England in search of work. When her mother joined him a year later, Tessa stayed in Jamaica where she was raised by her grandmother. In the spring of 1965, however, the nine-year-old Tessa was reunited with her parents, although her joy was tempered by the unattractive contrast between her tropical island home and the bleak industrial Midlands where Tessa's parents had settled.

After some promising performances in schools competitions, Tessa Sanderson joined Wolverhampton & Bilston AC where, in addition to her obvious potential as a javelin thrower, she showed great promise as a pentathlete. In 1975 she won the first of her eight British javelin titles and the following year she improved the UK record three times before finishing tenth at the Montreal Olympic Games. In 1977, Tessa improved her personal best in the javelin by exactly 10 metres and moved into second place on the all-time list; she then confirmed her position in

Tessa Sanderson celebrates her gold medal in the javelin in 1984.

1978 by taking the Commonwealth title and finishing second at the European Championships. Her ambitions received a severe setback when she failed to qualify for the final at the 1980 Moscow Olympics, but four years later she took the gold medal in Los Angeles to become the first British woman to win a throwing event at the Olympics.

Although injury had prevented her from competing in the European and Commonwealth meets in 1982, she did win the Commonwealth title in 1986. But at the 1988 Olympics she was again handicapped by injury and did not qualify for the final. Nevertheless, she gained the distinction of becoming one of only six British women to have competed at four Olympic Games.

After winning her third Commonwealth gold in 1990, she won her eighth WAAA javelin title and earned a place on the team for the European Championships. Surprisingly, this was the first time she had competed in the European Championships since winning a silver medal in 1978, but in Split in 1990 she finished back in 12th place.

During her career, Tessa Sanderson set ten UK javelin records, of which five were also Commonwealth bests, and in 1981 she twice posted new UK and Commonwealth records for the heptathlon. As retirement approached, she began a career as a television commentator and presenter.

Water Polo

Bentham, *Isaac*
Born: 26 October 1886, Wigan, Lancashire
GOLD: 1912

Isaac Bentham, a forward from Wigan, and Arthur Hill were the only members of Britain's 1912 water polo team whose Olympic success was restricted to one gold medal. All the other team members won a second gold, either in 1908 or 1920.

Bugbee, *Charles*
Born: 29 August 1887, West Ham, London   Died: 18 October 1959, Edgware, Middlesex
GOLD: 1912 & 1920

After winning two gold medals, Charles Bugbee, a City of London policeman, made a third Olympic appearance in 1924 when Britain lost to Hungary in the first round after three periods of extra time.

Coe, *Thomas*

Born: 1880

GOLD: 1900

Tom Coe was a member of the Manchester Osborne Club which represented Great Britain at the 1900 Olympic Games.

Cornet, *George Thomson*

Born: 15 July 1877, Inverness, Scotland   Died: 22 November 1952, Scotland

GOLD: 1908 & 1912

George Cornet of the Inverness SC was the oldest member of the winning British team at both the 1908 and 1912 Olympics. He played 17 times as a back for Scotland between 1897 and 1912, and his working life was spent as an employee of the Highland Railway.

Dean, *William Henry*

Born: 6 February 1887, Manchester, Lancashire   Died: 2 May 1949, Withington, Lancashire

GOLD: 1920

Billy Dean first began to take swimming seriously at the age of seven and when he was only ten he won the Royal Humane Society's medallion. He began his water polo career playing for Manchester Swan and Salford, and won his first cap for England when still a teenager. In 1909, when his family moved to Hyde, Dean became one of the stars of the Hyde Seal club which dominated English water polo at the time, playing at right-forward. He formed a prolific goalscoring partnership with George Wilkinson which made a major contribution to the club's success, as Hyde Seal won the international championship of France three times, the English championship nine times and were the Northern champions for 21 successive years. Dean played 18 times for England and captained the team on six occasions.

He was also an excellent soccer player and was on the books of Manchester United as a goalkeeper for two seasons. He developed a successful business in Hyde and at the time of his death he was the managing director of the electrical engineering firm, Dean & Noble.

DERBYSHIRE, John Henry – see Swimming section for biography.

Forsyth, *Charles Eric*

Born: 10 January 1885, Manchester, Lancashire   Died: 24 February 1951, Manchester, Lancashire

GOLD: 1908

In addition to winning an Olympic gold medal for water polo, Charles Forsyth of Salford SC was also a champion swimmer. In 1904 he beat the rising star, Henry Taylor, for the ASA 220 yards freestyle title and later in the season he won the ASA 500 yards freestyle championship.

Hill, *Arthur Edwin*

Born: 9 January 1888, Birmingham, Warwickshire

GOLD: 1912

Centre-half Arthur Hill of Aston SC and Isaac Bentham of Wigan were the only members of Britain's 1912 water polo team who won only one Olympic gold medal. All the other team members won a second gold, either in 1908 or 1920.

Jones, *Christopher*

Born: 23 June 1886, Pontypridd, Glamorgan, Wales   Died: 18 December 1937, Penarth, Glamorgan, Wales

GOLD: 1920

Chris Jones was a member of the Weston-super-Mare team which won the English water polo championship three times. He won his first international cap against Ireland in 1904 and was a fixture as full-back on the Welsh team for many years.

Jones was also an excellent rugby player, appearing regularly for Penarth from 1910 until 1915 when he joined the Army and served with the Royal Engineers and the Hampshire Regiment. After the war he retired from rugby, but carried on playing water polo and won an Olympic gold medal in 1920. He built a successful business in South Wales and was the senior partner in Christopher Jones & Co., a major firm of coal exporters.

Kemp, *Peter*

Born: 1878

GOLD: 1900   BRONZE: 1900 (200 METRES OBSTACLE)

On the same day that he won a gold medal for water polo at the 1900 Olympics, Peter Kemp of Manchester Osborne SC entered for the obstacle race held in the River Seine. In this highly unusual event, competitors had to climb over a pole then scramble over one row of boats before finally swimming under another. Some sources indicate that the competitors swam through barrells instead of over and under the boats, but whatever the hazards may have been, Kemp finished third and was the best placed of the British competitors. He also swam in the 200 metres freestyle at the Olympics, but was unplaced.

Lister, *William Houghton*

Born: 1882

GOLD: 1900

Eighteen-year-old William Lister of Manchester Osborne SC is the youngest of the 20 Britons who have won an Olympic gold medal for water polo.

Nevinson, *George Wilfred*

Born: 3 October 1882, Wigan, Lancashire   Died: 13 March 1963, Lancaster, Lancashire

GOLD: 1908

After winning a gold medal in 1908, George Nevinson had to decline an invitation to compete in the 1912 Games due to a leg injury. For the major part of his playing career he was a member of Salford SC, but he moved to Lancaster in 1913 when he obtained a job as joiner with the local Corporation. Nevinson was twice married and had seven daughters and three sons.

Peacock, *William*

Born: 6 December 1891, Poplar, London   Died: 14 December 1948, Sawtrey, Huntingdonshire

GOLD: 1920

In addition to winning a gold medal in 1920, Bill Peacock of Paisley SC was also a reserve on the Olympic water polo team in 1912 and 1924. In the 1920 Olympic final he scored Britain's first goal in their 3-2 win over Belgium.

Purcell, *Noel Mary*

Born: 14 November 1891, Ireland   Died: 31 January 1962, Dun Laoghire, Ireland

GOLD: 1920

Great Britain originally selected seven Englishmen for the 1920 water polo tournament in Antwerp, where they were seeking their third successive Olympic victory. But at the final trial at Stockport the 'Rest', a side from Ireland, Scotland and Wales, defeated the English team 6-0 and the selectors were forced to make some hasty changes. Of the newcomers, the most interesting character was Noel Purcell, a 28-year-old solicitor.

Purcell was educated at Belvedere College and Trinity College, Dublin. After being commissioned into the Royal Leinster Regiment he was wounded in action while serving in France. He was the half-mile swimming champion of Ireland both before and after the war and in 1913 he was the Irish champion and an international at roller skating. He won his first Irish cap for water polo in 1910 and was a regular member of the Irish team for

the next 18 years. When Ireland first competed as a separate nation at the 1924 Olympics, Purcell captained the side. He was again selected as team captain for the 1928 Games but was unable to accept the invitation because of the demands of his growing legal practice.

Despite these successes, Noel Purcell will be best remembered by the Irish sporting public for his contribution to rugby football. He played for the Barbarians before the war and as captain of Lansdowne RFC he played for Ireland in

all four of their international matches in the 1920–21 season. He later became a referee, but by the time he was chosen for the international panel he had put on some weight and was a trifle slow around the field – after the 1927 Calcutta Cup match, *The Times* was moved to comment, 'NM Purcell from Ireland refereed casually and from a great distance.' Not surprisingly, he soon gave up refereeing but he maintained his interest in the sport and in 1938 he was appointed an Irish international selector.

Radmilovic, *Paul*

Born: 5 March 1886, Cardiff, Glamorgan, Wales   Died: 29 September 1968, Weston-super-Mare, Somerset

GOLD: 1908, 1912 & 1920 (WATER POLO)   1908 (4 × 200 METRES FREESTYLE RELAY)

Welsh-born of a Greek father and an Irish mother, Paul Radmilovic competed for Britain in the Olympic Games a record six times and captained the water polo team four times. Possibly his finest moment in an outstanding Olympic water polo career came when he scored the winning goal against Belgium three minutes from time in the 1920 final. He made his Olympic debut in 1906 when he reached the final of

both the 100 metres and 400 metres freestyle and his final appearance was as a 42-year-old in 1928 as a member of the water polo team.

'Raddy' spent most of his life in Weston-super-Mare where he represented the local club both at swimming and water polo. Although he won nine ASA freestyle titles and his international swimming career lasted an incredible 30 years, it was as a water polo

player that he received recognition and in 1967 he became the first Briton to be inducted into the Swimming Hall of Fame in Florida. He was also a scratch golfer and a talented soccer player and he was, for many years, the licensee of the Imperial Hotel in Weston-super-Mare. After his death, his son took over the license and continued to display his father's impressive collection of trophies.

Robertson, *Arthur G*

Born: 1879

GOLD: 1900

Arthur Roberston was a member of the Manchester Osborne SC which represented Great Britain at the 1900 Olympic Games.

Robinson, *Eric*

Born: 1878

GOLD: 1900

Eric Robinson was a member of the Manchester Osborne SC which represented Great Britain at the 1900 Olympic Games.

Smith, *Charles Sydney*

Born: 26 January 1879, Worsley Mosnes, Pemberton, Lancashire   Died: 6 April 1951, Southport, Lancashire

GOLD: 1908, 1912 & 1920

Charles Smith of Salford SC captained the winning British water polo team at the 1908 Olympics and after joining Southport SC he won two more gold medals in 1912 and 1920. At the time of winning his third

gold in Antwerp in 1920, Smith was 41 years and 270 days old and is the oldest water polo gold medallist in Olympic history. He made a fourth Olympic appearance in 1924 at the age of 45, was

England's goal-keeper for 25 years from 1902 to 1926, and in recognition of his talents he was inducted into the Swimming Hall of Fame in Florida.

Thould, *Thomas Henry*

Born: 11 January 1886, Axbridge, Somerset   Died: 15 June 1971, Weston-super-Mare, Somerset

GOLD: 1908 & 1912

Apart from war service with the Royal Engineers in France and Palestine, Tom Thould spent his life in Weston-super-Mare where he worked as a clerk for the Gas Company for 35 years. He played at half-back, and with Paul Radmilovic he formed the backbone of the local club's water polo team which won the national championship in 1906 and 1907. Thould also won numerous Somerset swimming titles.

Wilkinson, *George*

Born: 3 March 1879, Gorton, Manchester, Lancashire   Died: 7 August 1946, Hyde, Cheshire

GOLD: 1900, 1908 & 1912

George Wilkinson, a prolific goalscorer with a variety of shots, is generally recognised as the world's first great water polo player. In 1899 he was only playing in the Division III of the Manchester League, but the following year he was recruited by the famous Manchester Osborne club and they included him in their team for the Paris Olympics without even giving him a trial.

After being on the winning Manchester team for the 1901 ASA championships, Wilkinson moved to Hyde Seal SC in 1902. He captained the Hyde team for 22 years, leading them to nine ASA titles and a victory over Brussels in the 'World Championship' at Paris in 1904. Wilkinson won three Olympic gold medals, captained the winning team at the 1912 Olympics and was a reserve for the 1920 and 1924 Olympic teams. He won a total of 24 caps for England between 1900 and 1922, captaining the team on four occasions.

Wilkinson had been an enthusiastic swimmer since boyhood and as a 17-year-old he finished third in the 1896 500 yards world championship race when, although he was beaten by Jack Tyers and Rob Derbyshire, he succeeded in pushing the redoubtable Jack Jarvis back into fourth place. Although he never won an ASA title, Wilkinson often placed well at the championships, finishing second in the 1000 yards in 1898 and the 220 yards in 1901. Like a number of notable sportsman of the time, be became a publican and was the landlord at the Wheatsheaf Hotel in Hyde for many years.

Weightlifting

Elliot, *Launceston*

Born: 9 June 1874, India   Died: 8 August 1930, Melbourne, Australia

GOLD: 1896 (ONE-HANDED LIFT)   SILVER: 1806 (TWO-HANDED LIFT)

Britain's first Olympic champion, Launceston Elliot was born in India to Charles Elliot and his third wife Ann. He spent part of his early childhood in Australia and it was only when his father, a kinsman of the Earls of Minto, gave up his post as a magistrate in India in 1887 and returned to farm in Essex that young Launceston saw England for the first time. He soon showed a keen interest in weightlifting and in 1891 at the age of 16, by which time he was already a pupil of the great Eugen Sandow, he entered for the first British weightlifting championship and made a creditable showing in a contest won by Lawrence Levy. In 1894 he won the British title and in 1896 he went to Athens for the first Modern Olympic Games.

Elliot was often described as one of the most handsome men of his generation and he certainly appealed to the Greeks. The Official Report of the 1906 Games noted: 'This young man attracted universal admiration by his uncommon beauty. He was of impressive stature, tall, well-proportioned, his hair and complexion of surprising fairness.' Clearly the Englishman created something of a stir in Athens and one paper carried the report that 'His handsome figure procured for him an offer of marriage from a highly-placed lady admirer.' Elliot was evidently not distracted by the publicity – he won the one-handed lift and his second place in the two-handed rested on a disputed decision. He raised the same weight as the winner, Viggo Jensen of Denmark, but as Elliot moved one of his feet during the lift, the Dane was awarded first prize on the basis of having a 'superior style'. In Athens, Elliot also ran in the 100 metres, took part in the rope-climbing event and was fourth in the Greco-Roman heavyweight wrestling.

In 1899 he literally went from strength to strength and set four new British records at the amateur championships. Around 1905, he turned professional and put on a Music Hall act with a partner named Montague Spencer. The two strongmen performed amid scenery representing the Roman arena and, bedecked in the garb of gladiators, they engaged in a mock contest during which they used the cestus, trident, net and other weapons of the arena. At the end of the show Elliot gave exhibitions of strength, the favourite of which was to support across his shoulders a long metal pole from which, at each end, was suspended a bicycle and rider. With this load Elliot would start revolving, slowly at first, but finally at such a speed that the 'riders' would be swung into a horizontal position.

Despite being offered the hand of a 'highly-placed lady' in Athens, Elliot married Emelia Holder, the daughter of a Kentish vicar, in 1897. In 1923 they settled in Australia, the scene of Launceston Elliot's early childhood, and he became an honoured member of a group of old-time athletes. In 1930 he failed to recover from an operation for cancer of the spine and is buried in the Fawker Cemetry in Melbourne.

Wrestling

Bacon, *Stanley Vivian*

Born: 13 August 1885, Camberwell, London   Died: 13 October 1952, Streatham, London

GOLD: 1908 (MIDDLEWEIGHT FREESTYLE)

Stanley Bacon was the eldest and most successful of five brothers who were in the top-flight of British wrestling for more than a decade. Between them, the Bacon brothers won almost 30 British championships, with Stanley winning 15 titles.

To reach the middleweight freestyle final at the 1908 Games, Stanley Bacon defeated three British wrestlers and then met a fourth Briton, George de Relwyskow, in the final. The two were very evenly matched but Bacon won the first two bouts on points, after the expiration of the fifteen-minute time limit,

Stanley Bacon (left) and George de Relwyskow in the 1908 middleweight final.

and the scheduled third bout was not contested. He also competed in the Greco-Roman middleweight event in 1908

but lost in the first round and in 1912, when there were no freestyle events, he again suffered an early defeat in the Greco-Roman style competition. At the 1920 Olympics, his third, he returned to the freestyle events but he was by now 35 years old and lost his first bout.

Bacon was a civil servant and an enthusiastic supporter of their sports club. He was the Civil Service diving and middleweight boxing champion and played rugby for their first XV for ten years. He was held in high regard in wrestling circles and was a judge at the 1928 Olympic Games.

O'Kelly, *George Cornelius*

Born: 29 October 1886, Gloun, Co. Cork, Ireland   Died: 3 November 1947, Stockport, Cheshire

GOLD: 1908 (HEAVYWEIGHT FREESTYLE)

Con O'Kelly left his native Ireland in 1903 to join the Hull Fire Brigade and it was while serving on Humberside that he took up wrestling. By 1907 he had won the British heavyweight title and went on to win an Olympic gold medal.

At the 1908 Olympics, O'Kelly overcame some tough opposition before meeting Jacob Gundersen in the final. The

Norwegian-born Gundersen was representing his native country at the Olympics, although he had been living in New York for nine years and was the reigning American champion. At 33, Gundersen was conceding 11 years to O'Kelly but he enjoyed a massive physical advantage and it took O'Kelly more than 13 minutes to pin his opponent in the first bout. O'Kelly won the second bout rather

more easily to take the Olympic title.

In the early 1920s O'Kelly emigrated to America, but he soon returned to become a farmer in Ireland before moving to England where he subsequently died. His son Cornelius Jr represented Britain as a heavyweight boxer at the 1924 Olympics and later fought as a professional before becoming a priest.

de Relwyskow, *George Frederick William*

Born: 18 June 1887, Kensington, London   Died: 9 November 1942, Leeds, Yorkshire

GOLD: 1908 (LIGHTWEIGHT FREESTYLE)   SILVER: 1908 (MIDDLEWEIGHT FREESTYLE)

George de Relwyskow of Hammersmith won the British lightweight and middleweight titles in 1907 and 1908 and contested both events at the 1908 Olympics. After losing to Stanley Bacon in the middleweight final, de Relwyskow had no difficulty in winning the gold medal in the lightweight division where he

defeated the novice William Wood, who had only taken up the sport six months previously. De Relwyskow had celebrated his 21st birthday the previous month and held the record of being the youngest winner of an Olympic gold medal for wrestling until 1976 when the 20-year-old Russian Suren Nalbandyan won the

Greco-Roman lightweight title.

De Relwyskow, who was coach to the 1924 British Olympic team, eventually settled in Yorkshire and was a builder and decorator in Leeds, where he was also a part-time masseur to various sporting clubs.

Yachting
MEN

Aspin, *John Symington*

Born: 31 March 1877, Glasgow, Scotland   Died: 19 February 1960, Partick, Glasgow, Scotland

GOLD: 1908 (12 METRES)

John Aspin, a wealthy varnish manufacturer, was a member of all the leading yacht clubs on the Clyde. In 1908 he joined the crew raised by Thomas Glen-Coats at the Royal Clyde Yacht Club to sail *Hera* to victory in the 12 metres class at the Olympics.

Bellville, *Miles Aubrey*

Born: 28 April 1909, Leicester, Leicestershire   Died: 27 October 1980, Bromyard, Herefordsire

GOLD: 1936 (6 METRES)

Miles Bellville was educated at Malvern and Jesus College, Cambridge, where his prowess as an oarsman led to him being elected a member of the Leander Club. A member of the Royal Corinthian Yacht Club and the Royal Ocean Racing Club, in 1934 he crewed on the *Endeavour* when Tommy Sopwith challenged for the America's Cup. At the 1936 Olympic Games he was one of a crew of five who all sailed at Burnham, and won gold medals in the 6 metres class aboard *Lalage*. As a Major in the Royal Marine Commandos, Bellville won a Military Cross in 1942 in the attack on the Vichy French base at Diego Suares in Madagascar, and the following year he was awarded the MBE. A gentleman farmer, he served as Sheriff of Hereford from 1966 to 1969.

Bingley, *SS Norman*

GOLD: 1908 (7 METRES)

Norman Bingley was a member of the Royal Victoria Yacht Club at Cowes and crewed aboard Charles Rivett-Carnac's *Heroine* in the 7 metres class at the 1908 Olympic Games. The only other entrant withdrew and their yacht – from the club which hosted the Olympic regatta – won the title on a sail-over.

Boardman, *Christopher Alan*

Born: 11 June 1903, Norwich, Norfolk   Died: 29 September 1987, Aylsham, Norfolk

GOLD: 1936 (6 METRES)

After attending the Royal Naval College, Dartmouth, and Trinity College, Cambridge, Chris Boardman joined the family firm of Colman's Mustard in his home town of Norwich. An appointment to the Board of Directors allowed him ample time for sailing and after captaining Cambridge against Oxford he became a member of many leading clubs, including the Royal Yacht Squadron. Boardman was the assistant helmsman aboard the *Endeavour* in Tommy Sopwith's challenge for the America's Cup in 1934 and he took a keen interest in the project for the restoration of the *Endeavour* in 1986.

At the 1936 Olympics he was the helmsman of *Lalage* which won the 6 metres class in Kiel. After war service as the commander of a corvette on Atlantic convoy duty, he resumed his business interests in Norfolk. His younger brother Humphrey was also an Olympian, rowing in the double sculls at the 1928 Olympic Games as well as winning two gold medals at the 1930 Empire Games.

Bond, *David John Were*

Born: 27 March 1922, Falmouth, Cornwall

GOLD: 1948 (SWALLOW)

With the experienced Stewart Morris as helmsman and David Bond as crew, Britain's entry, *Firefly*, won the Swallow class event on the only occasion it was included in the Olympic yachting programme.

Bond himself was educated at Harrow and served as an aircraftsman in the RAF in the war, after which he worked for the British Aircraft Corporation. He later became a yacht builder in Cornwall.

Buchanan, *John*

Born: 1 January 1884, Rhu, Scotland   Died: 17 November 1943, Rhu, Scotland

GOLD: 1908 (12 METRES)

Like all the crew members aboard Thomas Glen-Coats' *Hera* in the 12 metres class at the 1908 Olympics, John Buchanan was a member of the Royal Clyde Yacht Club. He was a farmer and an enthusiastic sailor for many years who in 1936 won the Tarbert Cup sailing his 8 metres boat, *Falcon*.

Bunten, *James Clark*

Born: 28 March 1875, Glasgow, Scotland   Died: 3 June 1935, Glasgow, Scotland

GOLD: 1908 (12 METRES)

James Bunten, a mechanical engineer, was a member of the Royal Clyde Yacht Club and crewed aboard Thomas Glen-Coats' *Hera* which won the 12 metres class at the 1908 Olympics.

Campbell, *Charles Ralph*   (Later Sir CR Campbell, Bt.)

Born: 14 December 1881, Torquay, Devon   Died: 19 April 1948, Bembridge, Isle of Wight

GOLD: 1908 (8 METRES)

Charles Campbell's father emigrated to New Zealand in 1874 to become a sheep farmer, but the Olympic gold medallist was born in England and educated at Eton. At the 1908 Olympics, he sailed aboard Blair Cochrane's *Cobweb* and, like the other crew members, lived on the Isle of Wight and was a member of the Royal Victoria Yacht Club and the Royal Yacht Squadron.

During the war, Campbell served in the Life Guards and the Royal Tank Corps and was on the personal staff of General Sir Alex Godley, the officer commanding the New Zealand Expeditionary Force. As his elder brother had been killed in action in 1915, Charles succeeded to the Baronetcy on the death of his father in 1919.

Cochrane, *Blair Onslow*

Born: 11 September 1853, Darlington, Co. Durham   Died: 7 December 1928, Bembridge, Isle of Wight

GOLD: 1908 (8 METRES)

Blair Cochrane's entry in the 8 metres class at the 1908 Olympics was something of a family affair. Both he and crew member John Rhodes were married to daughters of Sir Richard Sutton, Bt., while Sir Richard's son Henry was also a crew member.

The 54-year-old Cochrane entered *Cobweb* from the Royal Victoria Yacht Club, which assisted with the organization of the Olympic Regatta at Cowes. As chairman of the club committee, Cochrane was not only involved in the racing but also in the administration of the Olympic programme.

He was the Rear Commodore of the Royal Victoria Yacht Club from 1909 to 1913 and after war service as a captain in the Royal Horse Artillery he was awarded the OBE in 1919. He lived on the Isle of Wight for many years and served as a Deputy Sheriff of Hampshire.

Coleman, *Robert Henry Schofield*

Born: 1888   Died: 1 January 1960, Brentwood, Essex

GOLD: 1920 (7 METRES)

The 7 metres class was only on the Olympic yachting programme in 1908 and 1920 and Great Britain won the event on both occasions. Robert Coleman was a crew member in 1920 aboard Cyril Wright's entry, *Ancora*, from the Royal Burnham Yacht Club.

Crichton, *Charles William Harry*

Born: 7 July 1872, Colchester, Essex   Died: 8 November 1958, Borthwnog, Merionithshire, Wales

GOLD: 1908 (6 METRES)

Charles Crichton and Gilbert Laws acted as crew to owner and helmsman Tom McMeekin aboard *Dormy* which won the 6 metres class at the 1908 Olympics.

Crichton was a member of the Royal Cruising and Royal Southern Yacht Clubs and while on military service in India he sailed with the Royal Bombay Yacht Club. During the war, Major Crichton served with the 10th Hussars and two days after being awarded the DSO in 1915 he was promoted to Lt Colonel.

Educated at Radley, Crichton could claim a notable aristocratic pedigree. His paternal grandfather was the Earl of Erne and the Earl of Northrook his maternal grandfather. He was the son of Colonel The Hon. GL Crichton and in 1912 he married Dorothy, the daughter of the Hon. Eustace Dawnay.

Currie, *Lorne Campbell*

Born: 25 April 1871   Died: 21 June 1926, Le Havre, France

GOLD: 1900 (OPEN CLASS & 0.5–1 TON CLASS, RACE I)

Lorne Currie was the owner of *Scotia*, which took part in two events in the 1900 Olympic regatta at Meulan on the River Seine. After winning the Open class, *Scotia* won Race I of the 0.5–1 ton class but in Race II she finished only fourth. Currie served as a Captain in the Royal Army Service Corps during the war.

Davies, *Christopher*

Born: 29 June 1946

GOLD: 1972 (FLYING DUTCHMAN)

Chris Davies, a contracts officer from Hampshire, crewed for the 1968 Olympic champion Rodney Pattisson aboard *Superdoso* in the Flying Dutchman class at the 1972 Games. After winning four of the first six races, Pattisson and Davies did not even start in the final race as they were already assured of the gold medals.

Dixon, *Richard Travers*

Born: 20 November 1865, Sydney, Australia   Died: 14 November 1949, Mylor, Cornwall

GOLD: 1908 (7 METRES)

Richard Dixon was born in Australia, where his father was a well-known railway engineer, and came to England as a child. He was educated at Harrow and the Royal Military Academy, Woolwich, before being commissioned into the Royal Engineers in 1885. He retired from the Army in 1897 but rejoined the Colours for the First World War.

Dixon started yacht racing in 1895 and in a career lasting more than 50 years he won over 1000 races, plus an Olympic gold medal in 1908 as a crew member of Charles Rivett-Carnac's *Heroine* which won the 7 metres class unopposed. A member of the Royal Southampton Yacht Club and all the other Solent clubs, he made a notable contribution to the development of the sport as a founder member of the Yacht Racing Association, serving on the council from 1900 to 1938, and also as a member of the original committee of the Royal Ocean Racing Club.

Downes, *Arthur Drummond*

Born: 23 February 1883, Kelvinside, Partick, Scotland   Died: 12 September 1956, Helensburgh, Strathclyde, Scotland

GOLD: 1908 (12 METRES)

Dr Arthur Downes was a member of the Royal Clyde Yacht Club and crewed aboard Thomas Glen-Coats' entry *Hera* which won the 12 metres class at the 1908 Olympics. Two weeks before winning his Olympic gold medal, Downes had qualified as a doctor at Glasgow University and after spending five years at Kelvinside he practiced at Helensburgh for more than 40 years. He was the youngest of five sons of a wealthy Glasgow paper manufacturer; his elder brother Henry also crewed aboard *Hera*.

Downes, *John Henry*

Born: 18 October 1870, Glasgow, Scotland   Died: 1 January 1943, Hunters Quay, Dunoon, Scotland

GOLD: 1908 (12 METRES)

Henry Downes was the mate and his younger brother Arthur a crew member aboard *Hera* which won the 12 metres class at the 1908 Olympics. Henry was an electrical engineer and a member of the leading Scottish clubs including the Royal Clyde Yacht Club and the Royal Western Yacht Club.

Dunlop, *David*

GOLD: 1908 (12 METRES)

David Dunlop was one of a large family who were well-known in yachting circles. He was a member of the Royal Clyde Yacht Club and crewed aboard *Hera* which won the 12 metres class at the 1908 Olympics.

Exshaw, *William Edgard*

Born: 15 February 1866, Arcachon, France   Died: 16 March 1927, Valencia, Spain

GOLD: 1900 (2–3 TON CLASS, RACE I AND II)

William Exshaw's yacht *Olle* was the winner of both races in the 2–3 ton class at the 1900 Olympics. In Race I, *Olle* actually finished second to the French entry *Favorite*, but was declared the winner on adjusted time. In Race II, though, *Olle* finished ahead of *Favorite* to take the line honours.

Exshaw lived at Arcachon in the Bordeaux region of France, where he looked after the interests of the family firm of brandy producers. He was a prominent figure in local society and was Master of the Arcachon otter hounds from 1888 to 1903. Despite having his roots in France he maintained regular contact with Britain, keeping an estate at Glen Cannich in Inverness and serving for a time as a lieutenant in the Duke of Wellington's Regiment.

He added to his already considerable fortune when he married the daughter of Sir Sandford Fleming, one of the pioneers of the Canadian Pacific Railway. He died aboard the *Elmina*, one of the many yachts he owned, when cruising in the Mediterranean.

Glen-Coats, *Thomas Coats Glen*   (Later Sir TCG Glen-Coats, Bt.)

Born: 5 May 1878, Paisley, Scotland   Died: 7 March 1954, Paisley, Scotland

GOLD: 1908 (12 METRES)

There were no foreign entries for the 12 metres class at the 1908 Olympics but the event did have a certain international flavour as Charles McIver's *Mouchette* was crewed exclusively by Englishmen from Merseyside and the crew of Thomas Glen-Coats' *Hera* were all Scotsmen from the Royal Clyde Yacht Club. Rather than take both boats all the way to Cowes, where the rest of the Olympic races were held, it was agreed to hold the 12 metres class races on the Clyde and thus it became the only Olympic event ever to be held in Scotland. The local entry, *Hera*, won the first two races of a three-race series and the third race was not contested.

Thomas Glen-Coats was the eldest of four sons of Sir Thomas Glen-Coats, Bt. and succeeded to the Baronetcy on the death of his father in 1922. Educated at Eton and Merton College, Oxford, he enjoyed a life of leisure and played no part in the hugely prosperous family business, J & P Coats Ltd, the spinning merchants. In 1935, at the age of 57, Sir Thomas married Louise Hugon (formerly Mrs JC Newman) of Paris and as there was no issue to the marriage, the Baronetcy died with Sir Thomas in 1954.

Gretton, *John, MP*   (Later Lord Gretton of Stapleford, PC, CBE, DL, JP, MP)

Born: 1 September 1867, Burton-on-Trent, Staffordshire   Died: 2 June 1947, Melton Mowbray, Leicestershire

GOLD: 1900 (OPEN CLASS & 0.5–1 TON CLASS, RACE I)

Substantial family brewing interests gave Old Harrovian John Gretton the financial means to devote his time to sailing and politics, and he was eminently successful at both. He was a Member of the House from 1895 to 1943 and although other gold medallists have subsequently become Members of Parliament he is the only person to have won an Olympic title while actually serving as an MP.

In 1900 Gretton, who was a member of the Royal Yacht Squadron, married the daughter of Lord Ventry. He was awarded the CBE in 1919, became a Privy Councillor in 1926 and in 1944 was created the 1st Baron Gretton of Stapleford.

Harmer, *Russell Thomas*

Born: 5 November 1896, Cambridge, Cambridgeshire   Died: 31 October 1940, Rackheath, Norfolk

GOLD: 1936 (6 METRES)

Russell Harmer attended Uppingham and the RMA, Woolwich, before being commissioned into the Royal Signals in 1915. After being wounded in action, he was demobilised with the rank of Captain and then joined the family wholesale clothing business, eventually succeeding his father, Sir Sidney Harmer, as managing director.

Harmer was a member of the Royal Corinthian Yacht Club and was one of the four club members who sailed *Lalage* to victory at the 1936 Olympics. He was also a member of the Royal Norfolk & Suffolk Yacht Club. In addition to his sailing interests he was an active member of the Norwich & Norfolk Aero Club.

Laws, *Gilbert Umfreville*

Born: 6 January 1870, Tynemouth, Northumberland   Died: 3 December 1918, Newchurch, Isle of Wight

GOLD: 1908 (6 METRES)

Tom McMeekin, owner of the winning boat *Dormy* in the 6 metres class at the 1908 Olympics, nominated Gilbert Laws as helmsman while McMeekin was joined by Major Charles Crichton as crew. As Laws was the designer of *Dormy*, his intimate knowledge of its capabilities played a significant part in the British victory.

The son of a ship broker, Laws went to Burnham-on-Crouch in 1893 and started the Burnham Boat Building Company with JA Youl. The venture proved a great success and was soon established as one of the leading boatbuilding and design firms in the country. Laws subsequently bought out his partner and became managing director of the company.

During the war, he was commissioned into the RNVR and served in the Mediterranean, but his health broke down early in 1918 and he died later in the year in a nursing home for officers on the Isle of Wight.

Leaf, *Charles Symonds*

Born: 13 November 1895, Marylebone, London   Died: 19 February 1947, Reading, Berkshire

GOLD: 1936 (6 METRES)

Charles Leaf was the owner of *Lalage* which won the 6 metres class at the 1936 Olympic Games. Leaf was educated at Harrow and Trinity College, Cambridge, where he was a contemporary of Chris Boardman who skippered *Lalage* at the Olympics. In 1922, Leaf captained Cambridge in their match against Oxford. He later became a member of many of the leading yacht clubs, including the Royal Corinthian at Burnham which he chose as base for the successful challenge for Olympic honours in 1936.

Leaf enjoyed private means and was a distinguished amateur archaeologist; he wrote numerous papers on the subject and donated the majority of his finds to the Fitzwilliam Museum, Cambridge. In 1917 he married Catherine Blanche, the fourth daughter of Lord Shuttleworth, and they maintained fine homes in London and Suffolk.

In the First World War, Leaf served as a Lieutenant in The Buffs and in World War II he was initially with the RAF Balloon Command before becoming a Lieutenant in the Royal Marines at the age of 47.

MacDonald-Smith, *Iain Somerled*

Born: 3 July 1945

GOLD: 1968 (FLYING DUTCHMAN)

Iain MacDonald-Smith first teamed-up with Rodney Pattisson in 1967, when they finished second in the British championships. With Pattisson as helmsman and MacDonald-Smith as crew, it proved to be a highly successful partnership and together they won three World, two European and three British titles.

At the 1968 Olympics, they entered the ultra-modern *Superdocious* and won the gold medals with the most overwhelming victory ever achieved in any class in the history of Olympic yachting.

Iain MacDonald-Smith, who was educated at Marlborough and Selwyn College, Cambridge, before becoming a solicitor, was only a reserve for the 1972 Olympics but he competed again in 1976, finishing 13th in the Soling Class.

McIntyre, *Michael*

Born: 29 June 1956, Glasgow, Scotland

GOLD: 1988 (STAR)

Mike McIntyre first competed in the Olympics in 1984 and finished seventh in the Finn Class. On his second Olympic appearance in 1988 he partnered Bryn Vaile in the Star class and after a desperately close contest they won the gold medals.

In Seoul, Vaile and McIntyre needed to win the final race and the Americans Mark Reynolds and Hal Haenel had to finish in worse than sixth place if the

British pair were to win the title. Vaile and McIntyre succeeded in winning the race and as the Americans were forced to retire with a broken mast the gold medals went to Britain.

McIntyre, a sales manager who lives at Salisbury, was the British champion in the Finn class in 1980, 1981 and 1984 and is a member of the Helensburgh Sailing Club and the Bosham Sailing Club.

Mike McIntyre and Bryn Vaile, winners of the Star Class in 1988.

Mackenzie, *John*

Born: Greenock, Scotland

GOLD: 1908 (12 METRES)

During a sailing career that lasted fully 50 years, John McKenzie won more than 250 prizes. He was a member of many of the leading Scottish clubs, including the Royal Clyde Yacht Club, and crewed aboard Thomas Glen-Coats' *Hera* in the 12 metres class at the 1908 Olympics.

McMeekin, *Thomas D*

GOLD: 1908 (6 METRES)

Tom McMeekin was the owner of *Dormy* which won the 6 metres class at the 1908 Olympic Games. He nominated the designer of the boat, Gilbert Laws, as helmsman and chose to act as crew together with Charles Crichton.

McMeekin did much of his sailing from the Itchenor Club.

Maddison, *WJ*

GOLD: 1920 (7 METRES)

Maddison was a member of the Royal Burnham Yacht Club and crewed for Cyril Wright aboard *Ancora* in the 7 metres class at the 1920 Olympics.

Martin, *Albert*

GOLD: 1908 (12 METRES)

Albert Martin was a member of the Royal Clyde Yacht Club and crewed aboard Thomas Glen-Coats' *Hera* at the 1908 Olympics.

Martin, *Leonard Jack*

Born: 24 November 1901, Wandsworth, London

GOLD: 1936 (6 METRES)

Like his fellow Olympic gold medallists, Chris Boardman and Miles Bellville, Leonard Martin was a member of Tommy Sopwith's crew when the *Endeavour* challenged for the America's Cup in 1934.

Martin served in the RNR from 1917 to 1919 and after the war he entered the family business as a wholesale tobacconist.

He was a member of the Royal Burnham Yacht Club and the Royal Ocean Racing Club.

Maudslay, *Algernon*

Born: 10 January 1873, Tetbury, Gloucestershire   Died: 2 March 1948, Winchester, Hampshire

GOLD: 1900 (OPEN CLASS & 0.5–1 TON CLASS, RACE I)

The name of Algernon Maudslay does not appear in any other Olympic reference book but research has shown that he was definitely the helmsman aboard *Scotia* at the 1900 Olympics.

Maudslay, who was educated privately, was a prominent yachtsman of the time and a member of the Royal Thames Yacht Club, the Royal London Yacht Club and the Royal Yacht Squadron. He also served as Hon. Treasurer of the Yacht Racing Association from 1927 until his death.

Much of his life was devoted to British and International Red Cross and Relief Organizations and in 1919 he was awarded the CBE for his work with the War Refugees Committee.

Morris, *Stewart Harold, OBE*

Born: 25 May 1909, Bromley, Kent

GOLD: 1948 (SWALLOW CLASS)

Stewart Morris began sailing as a small boy and when he went up to Trinity College, Cambridge, from Charterhouse he was in the University team against Oxford for three years.

Morris was a reserve for the 1936 Olympic team but in 1948 he used his vast experience to take the Olympic title in the Swallow class with David Bond as his partner. In 1952 he was again an alternate on the Olympic team. He scored his first victory in the Prince of Wales Cup in 1932, with his record 12th and last win coming 33 years later, and claimed countless other victories in major events, including wins in the European championships. He was also the British champion in both the Swallow and Firefly classes.

Stewart Morris is a member of many yachting clubs, including the Royal Yacht Squadron. In 1944 he was awarded the OBE for his part in the Normandy landings while serving as a Commander in the RNVR.

Osborn, *John*

Born: 8 September 1945

GOLD: 1976 (TORNADO CLASS)

As reigning world champions, and with five major international victories earlier in the season, John Osborn and his brother-in-law Reg White were the overwhelming favourites in the Tornado class at the 1976 Olympics. With White as helmsman and Osborn as crew, they won four of the first six races and did not need to compete in the seventh and final race in order to claim their gold medals. Both Osborn and White were awarded the MBE in the 1977 New Year's Honours List.

Pattisson, *Rodney Stuart*

Born: 5 August 1943, Campbelltown, Scotland

GOLD: 1968 (FLYING DUTCHMAN) 1972 (FLYING DUTCHMAN) SILVER: 1976 (FLYING DUTCHMAN)

Rodney Pattisson stands alone as Britain's most successful Olympic yachtsman. On each of his three Olympic appearances he sailed with a different crew but won a medal on each occasion.

Pattisson's first major success came in 1960 when as a 17-year-old he won the world cadet title, with his brother John crewing. In 1968 he won the world and European titles before going on to win an Olympic gold medal with Iain MacDonald-Smith. A second gold followed in 1972 with Chris Davies as his partner and in 1976 Pattisson took the silver medal with Julian Brooke-Houghton. He was awarded the MBE for his Olympic successes.

Rodney Pattisson (right) and Iain McDonald-Smith (left) were the winners of the Flying Dutchman class in 1968. Pattisson won a second gold in 1972 and a silver in 1976.

After his first Olympic victory Pattisson resigned his commission in the Navy and joined a boat building firm in Dorset, which allowed him more time for training than his naval duties had permitted. He consolidated his position as the world's leading helmsman in the Flying Dutchman class and was the world and European champion from 1968 to 1972.

Pattisson built his success on meticulous attention to detail and a dedication to physical fitness; he came close to making the Olympic team for a fourth time in 1984 in his favourite Flying Dutchman class. Despite his domination of this class, Rodney Pattisson was a versatile sailor and in 1983 was co-skipper of *Victory*, Peter de Savary's entry for the America's Cup.

Quentin, *Cecil*

Born: 1852   Died: 29 October 1926, Ramsgate, Kent

GOLD: 1900 (OVER 20 TONS)

Only four of the 14 entries started in the Over 20 tons class at the 1900 Olympics and British yachts occupied the first two places. Selwin Calverley's 153-tonner *Brynhild* took the line honours but Cecil Quentin's 96-ton *Cicely* won on time adjustment.

As a friend and one-time business partner of Cecil Rhodes, Cecil Quentin was, in his early days, one of the country's most prominent financiers and as a yachtsman his most notable achievement was to captain *Cicely* to three successive victories over the German Emperor's yacht, *Meteor III*. On his retirement from the financial world, Quentin settled in Ramsgate where he was a leading member of the Royal Temple Yacht Club.

Rhodes, *John Edward*

Born: 13 February 1870, Twyford, Berkshire   Died: 6 February 1947, Ryde, Isle of Wight

GOLD: 1908 (8 METRES)

On leaving Winchester College, John Rhodes was commissioned into the Royal Berkshire Regiment but after two years he transferred to the King's Royal Rifle Corps. He fought in the Boer War before being sent to India and Ceylon to take charge of prisoners of war. On his return to Britain he resigned from the Army but remained on the reserve with the 60th Rifles and he later took over command of

Princess Beatrice's Isle of Wight Rifles which he led in the early stages of the Gallipoli campaign. As a result of ill-health he was invalided home where he became a member of the organisation controlling food distribution for the Channel Islands and the Isle of Wight.

In 1897 Rhodes married Beatrice, the eighth daughter of Sir Richard Sutton, Bt., and among his fellow crew members aboard *Cobweb*, which won the 8 metres

class at the 1908 Olympics, were his brothers-in-law Henry Sutton and Blair Cochrane.

Rhodes served as Commodore of the Bembridge Sailing Club and was a member of the Royal Victoria Yacht Club, the Solent Yacht Club, Lymington Yacht Club and the Island Sailing Club which he had joined in 1892 when he was first posted to the Isle of Wight as a subaltern.

Rivett-Carnac, *Charles James*

Born: 18 February 1853, Berhampur, India   Died: 9 September 1935, Jersey, Channel Isles

GOLD: 1908 (7 METRES)

Charles Rivett-Carnac came from a family which had prospered in India for generations. Indeed, the family were so well known that in *The Tomb of his Ancestors* Rudyard Kipling wrote, 'If there were but a single loaf of bread in all India, it would be divided equally between the Plowdens, the Trevors, the Beadons and the Rivett-Carnacs.'

After schooling at Rugby, Charles returned to India to join the Civil Service

but he left the ICS in 1897 and was appointed Accountant General to Burma. The following year, his services were placed at the disposal of the King of Siam by the British Government and for seven years he was the Financial Adviser to the Siamese Government. On his return to England in 1905, he continued to serve Siam as their Agent in Europe.

His first wife, a daughter of Colonel JH Ogilvie of the Indian Army, died in 1905,

and he later married Frances Greenstock. At the 1908 Olympics, Charles was the owner and helmsman of *Heroine* which was the only entry in the 7 metres class, and with his wife as one of the crew members the Rivett-Carnacs became the first husband and wife in Olympic history to win gold medals.

Charles Rivett-Carnac is the oldest Briton, at 55, to have won an Olympic gold medal for yachting.

Sutton, *Henry Cecil*

Born: 26 September 1868   Died: 24 May 1936, Beenham, Berkshire

GOLD: 1908 (8 METRES)

Henry Sutton was the fourth son of Sir Richard Sutton, Bt., who challenged for the America's Cup in 1885. He was

educated at Radley and, like his father, was a member of the Royal Yacht Squadron and served as Commodore of the Royal Victoria Yacht Club. At the 1908

Olympics, Henry sailed aboard *Cobweb* which was owned by his brother-in-law Blair Cochrane.

Tait, *Thomas Gerald*

Born: 7 November 1866, Campelltown, Scotland   Died: 19 December 1938, Glasgow, Scotland

GOLD: 1908 (12 METRES)

Gerald Tait was a member of the Royal Clyde Yacht Club and won his Olympic gold medal as a crew member aboard

Hera, the Club's entry in the 12 metres class at the 1908 Olympics. He was a partner in the family firm of solicitors in

Girvan and held office as Clerk to the Lord Lieutenant of Ayrshire.

Taylor, *J Howard*

GOLD: 1900 (3–10 TON CLASS, RACE II)

In 1900, Howard Taylor had enjoyed a fine season in the Mediterranean with *Bona Fide*, winning 16 races in 25 starts. He missed the first race of the 3–10 ton class

in the 1900 Olympic regatta as he was delayed obtaining clearance by French Customs, but he arrived at Meulan in time for the second race which he duly won by a margin of more than five minutes.

While in France, Taylor sold *Bona Fide* to an Italian and the winning Olympic yacht returned to southern waters.

Vaile, *Philip Bryn*

Born: 16 August 1956, Enfield, Middlesex

GOLD: 1988 (STAR)

Bryn Vaile of the Royal Lymington Yacht Club partnered Mike McIntyre in the Star class at the 1988 Olympics. After managing no better than seventh place in the 4th, 5th and 6th races, they not only needed to win the seventh and final race but the American leaders would have to finish in worse than 6th place if Vaile and McIntyre were to win the gold medals. Unfortunately for the Americans, they broke a mast and were unable to complete the race and the British pair duly won the gold medals.

White, *Reginald J*

Born: 28 October 1935, Brightlingsea, Essex

GOLD: 1976 (TORNADO CLASS)

Winning four of the first six races, Reg White did not need to start in the seventh race to clinch the first Olympic title for the Tornado class. Helmsman White had his brother-in-law John Osborn as his crew and the family Olympic tradition was continued in 1984 when Reg's son Robert was the helmsman for Britain's entry in the Tornado class. Reg himself was the reserve helmsman.

A boatbuilder from Brightlingsea, Reg White was the world champion in the Hornet class in 1964 and the Tornado class in 1976 and 1980. He was awarded the MBE in the 1977 New Year's Honours List.

Wood, *Arthur Nicholas Lindsay* (Later Sir ANL Wood, Bt.)

Born: 29 March 1875, Chester-le-Street, Co. Durham   Died: 1 June 1939, St Andrews, Fife, Scotland

GOLD: 1908 (8 METRES)

Arthur Wood won his Olympic gold medal in 1908 as a crew member aboard Blair Cochrane's *Hera* in the 8 metres class.

Wood was educated at Eton and succeeded his father, the first Baronet, in 1920. He served in the Northumberland Artillery and was Sheriff of County Durham in 1933. He died in Scotland while on holiday from his home at Chester-le-Street.

Wright, *Cyril Macey*

Born: 17 September 1885, Hampstead, London   Died: 27 June 1960, Bournemouth, Hampshire

GOLD: 1920 (7 METRES)

Cyril Wright and his father-in-law Percy Machin were the co-owners of *Ancora* which won the 7 metres class at the 1920 Olympics. Machin did not take part in the Olympic regatta at Ostend and it was with Wright as helmsman that *Ancora* sailed against the Norwegian boat *Fornebo*, which was the only other entry. The Norwegians won the first race but the British entry from the Royal Burnham Yacht Club won the next two races to take the gold medals.

One of the crew members aboard *Ancora* was Cyril's wife Dorothy whom he had married while on leave from the RNVR at Christmas in 1917. When he gave up his practice as a Naval Architect in London Cyril retired with Dorothy to Poole in Dorset.

1900 Yachting

Although it is known that the placings in the 10–20 ton class at Le Havre in 1900 were decided on aggregate points over a 3-race series, there is no evidence that a similar overall result was declared for the smaller classes sailed earlier at Meulan. There were two races in five of the six classes at Meulan and not only were the races in the same class sometimes held over different distances, separate prizes of different values were awarded for each race within the same class.

In view of these differing conditions, and as no overall winners were officially declared, I have considered each race at Meulan to be a separate Olympic event and have referred to them as Race I and Race II.

Reports on many aspects of the 1900 Yachting events are inconclusive and the identity of the crew members aboard the British entry 'Scotia' in the 0.5–1 ton class and the Open class has never been positively settled. The records of the British Olympic Association give the crew as Linton Hope, Lorne Currie and John Gretton, but it has been established that Linton Hope was actually in England at the time of the Olympic races and his name only appears in the Olympic records as he was the designer of the 'Scotia'. Similarly, the names of Lorne Currie and John Gretton are probably only listed as the owners of 'Scotia' but as it is possible that they sailed their own boat at Meulan, they have been listed as Olympic champions, although the participation of Lorne Currie, in particular, is in doubt. The one crew member whose participation has definitely been established is Algernon Maudslay, whose name does not appear in any Olympic records, but from contemporary press reports it is clear that he was the helmsman of 'Scotia'.

Yachting
WOMEN

Rivett-Carnac, *Frances Clytie* (née Greenstock)
Born: 1875   Died: 1 January 1962, Hampstead, London

GOLD: 1908 (7 METRES)

Frances, the daughter of Canon Greenstock, was the second wife of Charles Rivett-Carnac and when she crewed aboard her husband's *Heroine* in the 7 metres class at the 1908 Olympics they became the first married couple to win Olympic gold medals.

Wright, *Dorothy Winifred* (née Machin)
Born: 19 August 1889, West Ham, Essex

GOLD: 1920 (7 METRES)

Dorothy Wright was the only woman to compete in the Olympic yachting events in 1920. She won her Olympic gold medal as a member of the crew aboard *Ancora* which was jointly owned by her husband and her father.

British Olympic Champions

Biographies

Winter Games

Bobsleigh

Dixon, *Hon. Thomas Robin Valerian*

Born: 21 April 1935, Ireland

GOLD: 1964 (TWO-MAN BOBSLEIGH)

As Britain does not have a single bobsleigh run, the victory of Robin Dixon and Tony Nash in the two-man bobsleigh in 1964 has been compared with a competitor from a country without a pool winning a gold medal for swimming.

Dixon and Nash had been well advised in their preparation by Tony Brooks and in 1963 they finished third in the World Championship which was held over the Olympic course at Igls, near Innsbruck, Austria. At the 1964 Olympics, the British pair were lying second to the Canadians after the opening run but moved into first position on the second run. They then lost the lead to the Italians before a

The Hon. Robin Dixon (left) and Tony Nash (right) after winning the gold medals in the two-man bob in 1964.

magnificent fourth and final run gave them victory by the margin of 12/100ths of a second.

The 1964 World Championship went with the Olympic title and with Nash as driver and Dixon as brakeman they retained their world title at St Moritz in 1965. Although they failed to retain their Olympic title in 1968, they finished a commendable fifth at Alpe d'Huez, France.

Dixon, the heir of Lord Glentoran, was educated at Eton and was awarded the MBE in recognition of his Olympic success.

Nash, *Anthony James Dillon*

Born: 18 March 1936, Amersham, Buckinghamshire

GOLD: 1964 (TWO-MAN BOBSLEIGH)

Tony Nash, a director of the family engineering firm, was one of the key figures in the technical developments behind the resurgence of British bobsledding in the 1960s. He was also a brilliant driver and with Robin Dixon as his brakeman they won the Olympic title in 1964 and the world title in 1964 and 1965.

Nash and Dixon were such an outstanding partnership that their names are seldom mentioned separately and 25 years later no British pair has come close to matching their achievements. Both were awarded the MBE to mark their Olympic victory.

Figure Skating

MEN

Cousins, *Robin John*

Born: 17 August 1957, Bristol, Gloucestershire

GOLD: 1980

After finishing tenth at the 1976 Olympics, Robin Cousins won a bronze medal at the 1978 World Championships and improved to take second place in 1979. Then at the 1980 Olympics at Lake Placid he retained for Britain the title that John Curry had won in 1976. Cousins, a student from Bristol, gave a superb display of free skating at Lake Placid to edge ahead of Jan Hoffman of East Germany, though Hoffman later turned the tables on Cousins at the World Championships.

Cousins came from a sporting family and his father was at one time goalkeeper for Millwall. In 1989 Robin was appointed head of the coaching staff at Ice Castle International, a new advanced training centre in the San Bernardino Mountains of Southern California.

Curry, *John Anthony*

Born: 9 September 1949, Birmingham, Warwickshire

GOLD: 1976

John Curry first took up skating at the age of 12 under the guidance of Ken Vickers at the Summerhill Road rink in Birmingham, But in 1965 he left for London to learn from Arnold Gerschwiler and later Alison Smith at Richmond. After winning his first British junior championship in 1967, he won the senior title in 1970. Steadily improving performances in the world and European championships and 11th place in the 1972 Olympics led to invaluable sponsorship being provided by Ed Moseler, an American millionaire. Moseler's support gave Curry freedom from financial worries, coaching by the renowned Carlo Fassi and superb training facilities at Denver, Colorado.

These new-found advantages paid handsome dividends and in 1975 Curry was second in the European and third in the World Championships. In 1976 he opened his Olympic season by taking the European title at Innsbruck and then gave one of the greatest performances in skating history to take the Olympic gold medal. Graceful, athletic and with a perfectly co-ordinated programme, he completely outclassed the rest of the world's finest skaters. Curry quickly confirmed his position by winning the World Championship at Gothenburg and

then turned professional – as the holder of the European, World and Olympic titles he was able to negotiate a highly lucrative contract. He brought a magnificent ice show to London but never forsook his ambition to be an actor. Although he appeared regularly in provincial productions, he never made it to Broadway or the West End.

Curry, who was awarded the OBE in 1976, was undoubtedly one of the major influences in popularising the sport in Britain and, remembering his early struggles to finance his own training, he was a generous supporter of the National Skating Association.

The only two British men ever to win gold medals in figure skating. John Curry (right) was the winner in 1976 and Robin Cousins (left) succeeded him as Olympic champion in 1980.

Dean, *Christopher Colin*
Born: 27 July 1958, Nottingham, Nottinghamshire
GOLD: 1984 (ICE DANCE)

Christopher Dean, a Nottingham policeman, began his competitive ice dancing career with Sandra Elson as his partner and together they won the British junior title in 1974. The following year, Dean teamed up with Jayne Torvill and they won their first British championship three years later. In 1980 they finished fifth at the Olympic Games and in 1981 established themselves as performers of the highest class by winning the European and world championships. After successfully defending both titles in 1982, the pair were forced to withdraw from the 1983 European Championships because of

injury but they won the world title for the third successive year.

The performance of Torvill and Dean at the 1984 Olympics in Sarajevo will go down in history as one of the greatest sporting performances of all time. Their brilliant interpretation of Ravel's *Bolero* drew a '6.0' for artistic impression from each of the nine judges and their total of twelve 'sixes' for the entire competition broke all previous records. Four weeks later, in Ottawa, they even managed to better their Olympic score with a total of thirteen 'sixes' to take their fourth world title.

Their style of ice dancing enchanted audiences throughout the world and their memorable performance at Sarajevo has made Torvill and Dean one of the legends of Olympic history. Like most modern ice skating champions they turned professional and appeared in a highly successful ice show.

In 1990 Jayne Torvill married and Christopher Dean became engaged to the French-Canadian Isabelle Duchesnay, the world second ranked ice dancer, and with these marital commitments the pairing of the greatest ice dancers in history drew to a close.

Figure Skating
WOMEN

Altwegg, *Jeannette Eleanor* (Later Mrs M Wirz)
Born: 8 September 1930, India
GOLD: 1952   BRONZE: 1948

Although born in India, Jeannette Altwegg was raised and educated in Lancashire where her Swiss father worked for the Liverpool Cotton Exchange. Herman Altwegg became a naturalised British subject but returned to Switzerland in 1946 when the Cotton Exchange was nationalised.

Jeannette first began ice skating when she was eight years old but she was also an excellent lawn tennis player – in 1947 she was runner-up in the junior championships at Wimbledon. But after winning the British figure skating title and

finishing fifth in the World Championships in 1947, she gave up tennis to concentrate exclusively on skating. A bronze medal in the Olympics and fourth and fifth places respectively in the European and world championships in 1948 were an indication that she was making satisfactory progress towards her goal of being the best skater in the world.

In the years leading up to the 1952 Olympics, progress was maintained and each season saw Altwegg improve on the previous year's results. In 1949, she finished third in both the European and

world championships; in 1950 she improved to finish second in both championships and in 1951 she won the European title in Zurich and the world crown in Milan.

In Olympic year, Altwegg retained her European title in Vienna three weeks before the Games and she went to Oslo in 1952 as the reigning world and European champion. There she established a substantial lead in the compulsory figures and although she was only fourth in the free skating, her early advantage was sufficient to give her a narrow victory over

Tenley Albright of America, who was to succeed her as Olympic champion in 1956.

Immediately after the Olympics, Jeannette Altwegg retired and did not defend her world title the following month. Although she was offered vast sums to turn professional she preferred to take up a teaching post at a children's orphanage in Switzerland. She remained with the Pestalozzi Children's Village for a year, and after being awarded the CBE in 1953 Jeannette married Marc Wirz, a Swiss engineer who was the brother of her husband. The following year Madge and friend Susy Wirz, the Swiss skating champion. Marc and Jeannette divorced in 1973 but there were four children from the marriage and in 1983 their daughter Cristina became the world curling champion at Moose Jaw, Canada.

Syers, *Florence Madeline* (née Cave)

Born: 1882   Died: 9 September 1917, St George's Hill, Weybridge, Surrey

GOLD: 1908 (SINGLES)   BRONZE: 1908 (PAIRS)

Florence Madeline Cave, known to her friends as 'Madge', was one of 15 children of Edward Jarvis Cave, a gentleman of independent means. Like many young girls in her position she joined fashionable London Society at the Prince's Skating Rink in Knightsbridge, but unlike most of her contemporaries Madge took her skating seriously and it was through the sport that she met her future husband, Edgar Syers. Syers, who was 19 years her senior, wielded a considerable influence on Madge Cave's development as a skater. He encouraged her to forsake the outdated 'English' style, with its minimal body movement, and adopt the free and flowing 'International' style of skating. Madge Cave soon became the world's leading woman skater.

She won the first British pairs competition in 1899 with her future husband. The following year Madge and Edgar Syers were married and soon afterwards they finished second in one of the first international pairs competitions in Berlin.

Although the newly married couple were a formidable combination in pairs competitions, it was in individual events that Madge Syers really shone. As there was no rule prohibiting women from competing, she created a sensation by entering the World Championships in 1902 where – even more sensationally – she finished second to the great Ulrich Salchow of Sweden. The authorities immediately barred women from the championships but in 1905 the ban was rescinded and the following year a separate ladies' event was introduced at the world championships. Madge easily won this event in 1906 and 1907, but it was not until 1920 that these events were retroactively recognised as official world championships. She also won the first British singles championship in 1903, finishing ahead of Horatio Torrome, and in 1904 she defeated her husband to retain the title.

With this record, Madge Syers was a clear favourite for the 1908 Olympic women's singles and with all five judges placing her a clear first in both the compulsory figures and the free skating, she was an undisputed winner of the gold medal. She also won a bronze medal partnering her husband in the pairs event.

After the 1908 Olympics, Madge Syers, who was also a prize winning swimmer and equestrienne, retired because of ill health and she died at the early age of 35.

Torvill, *Jayne* (Later Mrs P Christensen)

Born: 7 October 1957, Nottingham, Nottinghamshire

GOLD: 1984 (ICE DANCING)

At the 1983 world championships in Helsinki, ice dance history was made when all nine judges gave Jayne Torvill and Christopher Dean a perfect '6.0' for artistic impression with their interpretation of *Barnum*. Although other triumphs were ahead, it was perhaps this performance that first set Torvill and Dean apart from the rest of the world's ice dancers and raised them to the status of a sporting legend.

Jayne Torvill, a clerk in a Nottingham insurance office, won both a British junior and senior championship with Michael Hutchison as her partner, but in 1975 she teamed up with Christopher Dean and together they developed the most memorable partnership in the history of the sport.

They won their first British title in 1978 and although they finished no higher than 11th at that year's World Championships in Canada, a fortuitous meeting in Ottawa with the inspirational teacher Betty Calloway was a vital factor in the successes that were to come. Torvill and Dean improved to eighth place at the 1979 World Championships, then finished fourth in 1980 and took fifth place at the Lake Placid Olympics. In 1981 they won both the European and world championships and defended both titles in 1982. They were forced to withdraw from the 1983 European Championships because of injury but won the world title for the third succesive year and went to the 1984 Olympics in Sarejovo as clear favourites.

Jayne Torvill and Christopher Dean, winners of the first Olympic ice dance title in 1984.

With a brilliant interpretation of Ravel's *Bolero*, they matched their performance at the 1983 World Championships by drawing 'sixes' for artistic impression from all nine judges, and their total of twelve 'sixes' for the entire competition broke all previous records. Four weeks later, in Ottawa, they won their fourth successive world title and with a total of thirteen 'sixes' they bettered the record they had set at the Olympics.

Torvill and Dean then turned professional but the enchanting performances of their amateur days will always be remembered, not only by the cogniscenti but also by the millions of television viewers who, while probably not having any special interest in sport, could not fail to recognise the superlative talents of this couple from Nottingham.

In September 1990, Jayne married Phil Christensen, a technician with the Phil Collins road show, and as Christopher Dean had announced his engagement the most memorable partnership in the history of ice dancing gradually drew to a close.

Ice Hockey

Archer, *Alexander*

Born: 1 May 1910, West Ham, Essex

GOLD: 1936

'Sandy' Archer left England for Canada at the age of three and learned his hockey in Winnipeg, where he was twice a Manitoba All-stars selection. He was one of a group of 14 players, which included fellow-Olympian Jimmy Foster, who returned to play in England in the 1930s without first obtaining clearance from the Canadian authorities. The inclusion of Archer and Foster in the 1936 British Olympic team drew strong protests from the Canadians but the objection was eventually withdrawn and Sandy Archer of Wembley Lions played on the right-wing in all seven Olympic matches.

Archer subsequently played in the British team which won the European Championships in 1937 and 1938. His playing career was ended by injury in 1945 and he then coached at Wembley, Nottingham and Murrayfield before being appointed general manager of Murrayfield Ice Rink in 1952.

Borland, *James Andrew*

Born: 25 March 1911, Manchester, Lancashire

GOLD: 1936

While with the Grosvenor House Canadians, Jimmy Borland was selected for the British team for the 1934 World Championships. He missed the 1935 season but in Olympic year he was captain of Brighton Tigers and was in the line-up for five of Britain's seven matches at Garmisch-Partenkirchen.

An electrician by trade, Borland was a keen all-round sportsman and excelled at golf, swimming and baseball.

Brenchley, *Edgar*

Born: 10 February 1912, London   Died: 1975, Canada

GOLD: 1936

Like most of the 1936 British Olympic team, 'Chirp' Brenchley left England for Canada at a very early age. He began playing hockey with the Niagara Falls team but in 1935 returned to England and enjoyed a successful career with Richmond Hawks and Harringay Greyhounds. At the 1936 Olympics, Brenchley played in every match and scored a total of four goals in the tournament, including the only goal in Britain's victory over Sweden in the opening game and the vital winning goal against Canada.

He eventually returned to Canada where he coached and then acted as scout for the Washington Capitols.

Chappell, *James*

Born: 25 March 1914, Huddersfield, Yorkshire   Died: April 1973, Florida, USA

GOLD: 1936

At the age of ten, Jimmy Chappell was taken to Canada by his parents and started playing hockey with the Oshawa Collegians in 1930. After three years, he joined Whitley and was a member of the team which won the intermediate championship of Ontario in 1935. He also played cricket for the Canadian national team before his return to England, where he was signed up by Earl's Court Rangers.

At the 1936 Olympics, Chappell played in all the matches except the one against Japan and was subsequently a member of the team which won the European Championship in 1937 and 1938. At the outbreak of war Chappell was playing for Dunfermline, but he later joined the Army and took part in the D-Day landings. When the game was revived on a national scale after the war he joined Brighton Tigers and was one of three 1936 gold medallists who also played for the 1948 Olympic side.

Coward, *John*

Born: 28 October 1910

GOLD: 1936

After missing the opening match against Sweden, Johnny 'Red' Coward of Richmond Hawks played at left-wing in the remaining six matches at the 1936 Olympics. He was also a member of the British team at the 1937 World Championships. When his hockey career in Britain ended, Coward settled in Canada.

Dailley, *Gordon Debenham*

Born: 24 July 1911, Winnipeg, Manitoba, Canada   Died: 3 May 1989, Cambridge, Ontario, Canada

GOLD: 1936

After Gordon Dailley had graduated from the University of Manitoba, he went from Winnipeg to Montreal on a cattle train and then worked his way on to a cattle boat to England, where he was appointed a representative of the Kaufman Rubber Co. in 1932.

Dailley was one of the founders of the Grosvenor House Canadians, who won the English championship in the year they were formed. He represented Great

Britain at the 1934 world and European championships and played in defence in all seven matches at the 1936 Olympic Games. He was subsequently a member of the British team which won the European Championships in 1937 and 1938. After helping to form the Grosvenor House Canadians, Dailley joined Wembley Lions, and he also played for Wembley Canadians and Wembley Monarchs.

Following a tour of duty with the

Canadian forces in Europe during World War II, Dailley served with the United Nations peacekeeping force in Korea. He was promoted to Colonel in 1955 and posted to Yugoslavia as Canada's military attaché. After his retirement from the Army in 1964, Colonel Dailley played a prominent role in civic affairs in Ontario and founded the first major Wild Life Park in Canada, which is still operated as a successful business by his son.

Davey, *John Gerald*

Born: 5 September 1914, Barking, Essex

GOLD: 1936

London-born Gerry Davey went to Canada as a boy and learned his hockey in Port Arthur, Ontario, before returning to England as a teenager in 1931. A London newspaper assisted him in joining the Prince's Club and this was the beginning of a long and distinguished career in British hockey. He won his first international honours when only 16 and went on to win more than 100

international caps.

At the 1936 Olympics, Davey was Britain's top scorer with a total of seven goals, including a hat-trick against Czechoslovakia. Most importantly, he scored after only 20 seconds in the crucial semi-final match against Canada. He later featured prominently in Britain's victories at the European Championships in 1937 and 1938.

After his initial introduction to the Prince's Club, Davey subsequently played for Queen's Club, Streatham and Wembley Lions; he also played and coached for Falkirk in the Scottish League. He made a second Olympic appearance in 1948 and then refereed for several years in the English National League.

Erhardt, *Carl Alfred*

Born: 15 February 1897, Beckenham, Kent   Died: 3 May 1988, Esher, Surrey

GOLD: 1936

Great Britain won the 1936 Olympic ice hockey tournament on the day after Carl Erhardt's 39th birthday and he is the oldest player in Olympic history to have won a gold medal for ice hockey.

Erhardt learned the game at school in Switzerland, Austria and Germany, and on his return to England he joined the Prince's Club when it was revived in 1926.

He later played for Streatham and captained the British team which finished third at the 1935 World Championships. He was also captain of the 1936 Olympic team, playing in six of the seven matches.

After his retirement, Erhardt wrote a book on the sport and coached the 1948 Olympic team. He was a referee at the 1950 World Championships in London

and served as a committee member of the governing body for many years, before being elected a life vice-president of the British Ice Hockey Association.

As well as being a director of an engineering company, Erhardt was also a founder and the first president of the British Water Ski Federation.

Foster, *James*

Born: 13 September 1905, Glasgow, Scotland

GOLD: 1936

Jimmy Foster went to Canada as a child and learned his hockey in Winnipeg, where he developed into the world's outstanding amateur goalkeeper and was judged to have few, if any, equals in the professional game. While with Moncton Hawks he missed only one of the 220 games they played and when they won the Allan Cup in 1931 and 1932 he became the

first goalkeeper to register two straight shut-outs in Allan Cup finals. Foster once held the Canadian record of playing for 417 minutes without having a score against him and he enhanced his considerable reputation at the 1936 Olympics by conceding only three goals in seven matches.

At the time of the Games, Foster, like

Sandy Archer, was under suspension by the Canadian authorities as he had not obtained clearance before coming to England to play for Richmond Hawks. He later played for Harringay Greyhounds before returning to Canada with Glace Bay Miners and Quebec Aces. As he had once thought of entering the Church, Foster was nicknamed 'The Parson'.

Kilpatrick, *John*

Born: 7 July 1917, Bootle, Lancashire

GOLD: 1936

Jack Kilpatrick of Wembley Lions is the youngest Briton, at 18, to have won an Olympic gold medal at the Winter Games. At the 1936 Olympics he played on the left-wing in the opening match against Sweden but was replaced by Johnny Coward for the remaining six matches.

Stinchcombe, *Archibald*

Born: 17 November 1912, Cudworth, nr. Barnsley, Yorkshire

GOLD: 1936

Archie Stinchcombe went to Canada when he was six months old and later played hockey at all levels in Ontario. After playing with Mic-Macs, the Ontario Hockey Association champions, Stinchcombe returned to England to join Streatham and after only a few weeks in the English League he was chosen for the 1936 Olympic team.

At the Olympics, Stinchcombe played in six of the seven matches and was later a member of the British team which won the European title in 1937 and 1938. Despite losing the sight of one eye in a hockey accident as a child, he enjoyed a long and successful playing career. After leaving Streatham he played for Nottingham Panthers and Wembley Lions and captained the British team at the 1948 Olympics before closing his career as a coach at Nottingham.

During the war, Stinchcombe worked in bomber construction and later entered the engineering business.

Wyman, *James Robert*

Born: 27 April 1909, West Ham, Essex

GOLD: 1936

As a speed skater, Bob Wyman was a British champion and record holder and he used his speed to good advantage when he turned to hockey. He played in the English League for Richmond Hawks, Harringay Greyhounds and Streatham, and in the first post-war season he was with Wembley Lions.

Wyman, who was one of only two members of the 1936 Olympic team who learned the game in England, only played in the game against Japan at the Olympics before joining the BBC radio commentary team which brought listeners news of Britain's memorable victory at Garmisch-Partenkirchen.

Wyman worked in the motor trade in London and during the war he served as a Lt Commander in the Royal Navy.

The British ice hockey team who were surprise winners in 1936.

The March Past of the British team at the 1908 Games.

British Olympic Competitors

Full Listing

Summer Games

Listed here is every British competitor
who has actually taken part in the Olympic Games. Reserves and
those who were obliged to withdraw from the
team after selection are not listed.

Summer Games

Archery
MEN

Archery for men was on the Olympic programme in 1900, 1904, 1908 and 1920. At these early editions of the Games, Great Britain competed only in 1908. Archery was restored as an Olympic sport in 1972 and Britain has competed on every occasion since then. In 1988 a team event was introduced.

F = Double FITA Round   Y = York Round   Tm = Team event
50m = 50 metres Continental Round*

COMPETITOR	DATE OF BIRTH-DEATH	YEAR	EVENT/S
Backhouse, *Robert Ormston*	1854–10.4.1940	1908	Y/50m
Bagnall-Oakeley, *RH*	—	1908	Y/50m
Bishop, *Ronald Proctor*	30.5.1931	1972	F
Blenkarne, *Mark*	7.10.1957	1980	F
Bridges, *John Henry*	26.3.1852–12.2.1925	1908	Y/50m
Brooks-King, *Reginald*	1861–19.9.1938	1908	Y
Coates, *Charles Hutton*	4.5.1857–15.2.1922	1908	Y
Cornewall, *Geoffrey*	7.5.1869	1908	Y/50m
Dod, *William*	18.7.1867–8.10.1954	1908	Y
Gillam, *Peter*	2.1.1956	1984	F
Hallard, *Steven*	22.2.1965	1984	F
		1988	F/Tm
Heathcote, *Robert Webster*	28.12.1864	1908	Y/50m
James. *HV*	—	1908	Y
Keene, *Charles John Perry*	1864–29.11.1926	1908	Y
Keyworth, *John Bunyan*	9.5.1859–24.2.1954	1908	Y/50m
Littlefair, *Stewart*	9.7.1946	1976	F
Matthews, *Roy Derek*	10.9.1926	1972	F
Nesham, *Hugh Percy*	1877–26.6.1923	1908	Y
Penrose, *John*	5.5.1850–21.4.1932	1908	Y
Pink, *David Anthony*	31.12.1939	1976	F
Pownall, *Capel George Pell*	1869–8.2.1933	1908	Y/50m
Priestman, *Richard*	16.7.1955	1984	F
		1988	F/Tm
Robinson, *T*	—	1908	Y
Savory, *Dennis*	13.6.1943	1980	F
Snelling, *John*	8.3.1946	1972	F
Stopford, *John Thomas Sarsfield*	—	1908	Y/50m
Watson, *Leroy*	6.7.1965	1988	F/Tm

* The only official British entrant in the 50m Continental Round in 1908 was JB Keyworth. The other British competitors listed above took part as guests but had RO Backhouse been an official competitor he would have been placed second.

Archery
WOMEN

Archery was an Olympic sport for women in 1904 and 1908 with Great Britain only competing on the latter occasion. It was again included in the women's programme in 1972, since when Great Britain has been regularly represented. A team event was introduced in 1988.

F = Double FITA Round   N = National Round   Tm = Team event

COMPETITOR	DATE OF BIRTH-DEATH	YEAR	EVENT/S
Appleyard, *Gertrude*	1865–9.6.1917	1908	N
Armitage, *Mrs SH*	—	1908	N
Babington, *Mrs SC*	—	1908	N
Boddam Whetham, *Mrs*	—	1908	N
Cadman, *Christine*	—	1908	N
Conway, *Christine*	16.1.1944	1976	F
Day, *Doris E Hermitage*	1878	1908	N

COMPETITOR	DATE OF BIRTH-DEATH	YEAR	EVENT/S
Dod, *Charlotte*	24.9.1871–27.6.1960	1908	N
Edwards, *Pauline Mary*	23.4.1949	1972	F
		1988	F/Tm
Evans, *Lynn Avril*	5.8.1948	1972	F
Fenwick, *Rachael Dorothy Mary*	25.10.1935	1976	F
Franks, *Joanne*	1.10.1967	1988	F/Tm
Goodall, *Angela*	29.8.1961	1984	F
Harris, *Christine*	14.1.1956	1980	F
Hill-Lowe, *Beatrice Geraldine*	—	1908	N
Honnywill, *Mrs GW*	—	1908	N
Hyde, *Martina Esther*	1866–17.5.1937	1908	N
Leonard, *Mrs E*	—	1908	N
Mudge, *KG*	—	1908	N
Newall, *Sybil Fenton 'Queenie'*	17.10.1854–24.6.1929	1908	N
Nott Bower, *Mrs E*	—	1908	N
Patterson, *Gillian*	26.9.1963	1980	F
Priestly-Foster, *Mrs*	—	1908	N
Robertson, *Mrs N*	—	1908	N
Robinson, *Eileen*	6.3.1951	1984	F
Rushton, *Mrs*	—	1908	N
Sutton, *Cheryl*	23.9.1946	1988	F/Tm
Sykes, *Carol*	11.12.1941	1972	F
Thackwell, *Albertine Anne*	1862–22.9.1944	1908	N
Vance, *J*	—	1908	N
Wadworth, *Jessie Ellen*	1864–8.7.1936	1908	N
Wadworth, *Miss*	—	1908	N
Weedon, *Margaret Kate*	1854–19.10.1930	1908	N
Willcox, *Susan*	6.4.1954	1984	F
Williams, *Hilda*	—	1908	N
Wilson, *Lillian Sarah*	1864–1.3.1909	1908	N
Wood, *Ina*	—	1908	N

The legendary Lottie Dod, Wimbledon champion at the age of 15, English Ladies' Golf champion and Olympic archery silver medallist in 1908.

Lady archers change ends in 1908. The stadium flags indicate the difficult windy conditions encountered by the competitors.

The Whittall Family

Olympic history was made in the 1906 soccer tournament when the entire forward line of an international team entered by Smyrna (now Izmir) of Turkey consisted of members of one family: Albert, Edward and Godfrey Whittall were the sons of Edward Whittall, and Donald and Harold were their first cousins, being the sons of Richard Easton Whittall, Edward's brother.

Richard Whittall sent both his sons to Rugby School – Donald later attended New College, Oxford, while Harold qualified as a doctor at University College Hospital but died of pneumonia in Smyrna in 1909. Of Edward's three sons it is known that Albert attended Uppingham School and it seems likely that Edward and Godfrey were also educated in England.

The Whittall family have a fascinating background. They were the most influential British family in the Levant and established a trading and shipping business in Smyrna back in Elizabethan times. The international nature of their prosperous business led to many contacts throughout Europe and the family were related by marriage to Tsar Peter the Great.

Association Football

With the exception of 1896 and 1932, Association Football has been included at every Olympic Games.

In 1900, Great Britain were represented by Upton Park FC and in 1908, although designated as a United Kingdom team, all the players were from English clubs. At the time, England were the only home country who were members of FIFA. In 1910, Ireland, Scotland and Wales joined FIFA but the 1912 Olympic team was again drawn exclusively from English clubs.

Because of a dispute with FIFA, Britain did not compete in 1924 and 1928. In 1956 qualifying matches were held for the first time and Britain only competed in Melbourne after a number of teams had withdrawn for political reasons. Great Britain survived the qualifying round in 1960 but failed to make the finals in 1964, 1968 and 1972. From 1976 onwards they did not enter the Olympic competition as by then the governing bodies of the four home countries had dispensed with the separate definition of amateurs.

Players who competed in the pre-Olympic qualifying rounds from 1960–1972 are not listed.

COMPETITOR	DATE OF BIRTH-DEATH	YEAR EVENT/S
Aitken, *Al*	—	1948
Amor, *William G*	6.11.1919	1948
Atkinson, *George*	—	1920
Bailey, *Horace Peter*	3.7.1881–1.8.1960	1908
Barridge, *JE*	—	1900
Bennett, *Edward*	22.8.1925	1952
Berry, *Arthur*	3.1.1888–15.3.1953	1908
		1912
Boyd, *J. Alan*	—	1948
Brebner, *Ronald Gilchrist*	23.9.1881–11.11.1914	1912
Bromilow, *George Joseph*	4.12.1931	1956
Brown, *Leslie*	27.11.1936	1960
Brown, *Robert Henry*	2.5.1940	1960
Buckenham, *Claude Percival*	16.1.1876–23.2.1937	1900
Bunyan, *MT*	—	1920
Burn, *Thomas Christopher*	29.11.1888–25.9.1916	1912
Carmichael, *Andrew ME*	—	1948
Chalk, *Alfred Ernest*	27.11.1874	1900
Chapman, *Frederick William*	10.5.1883–7.9.1951	1908
Clements, *Bertram Arthur*	1.12.1913	1936
Corbett, *Walter Samuel*	26.11.1880–c1955	1908
Crawford, *James*	21.5.1904–5.1976	1936
Devine, *John H*	1.12.1935	1960
Dines, *Joseph*	12.4.1886–27.9.1918	1912
Dodds, *John McDonald*	10.1.1907	1936
Dodkins, *Herbert Edward*	20.12.1929	1956
Donovan, *Frank J*	21.2.1919	1948
Edelston, *Maurice*	27.4.1918	1936
Farrer, *Leslie Thomas*	22.12.1922	1956
Finch, *Lester Charles*	26.8.1909	1936
Forde, *Hugh*	31.1.1936	1960
Fright, *Eric G*	—	1948
Fuller, *Charles Edward*	25.5.1919	1952
Fulton, *Robert Patrick*	6.11.1906	1936
Gardiner, *John*	23.12.1911	1936

COMPETITOR	DATE OF BIRTH-DEATH	YEAR EVENT/S
Gosling, *William Sullivan*	19.7.1869–2.10.1952	1900
Greenwood, *Michael M*	9.4.1935	1960
Hanney, *Edward Terrance*	19.1.1889	1912
Harbidge, *Charles William*	15.7.1891	1920
Hardisty, *John Roderick Elliott*	1.12.1921–31.10.1986	1948
		1952
		1956
Hardman, *Harold Payne*	4.4.1882–9.6.1965	1908
Haslam, *A*	—	1900
Hasty, *Patrick J*	17.3.1932	1960
Hawkes, *Robert Murray*	18.10.1880–12.9.1945	1908
Hegan, *Kenneth Edward*	24.1.1901–3.3.1989	1920
Hill, *Hadyn Henry Clifford*	4.7.1913	1936
Hoare, *Gordon Rahere*	18.4.1884–27.10.1973	1912
Holmes, *Guy Gorham*	1.12.1905	1936
Holt, *David Duff*	3.1.1936	1960
Hopper, *Thomas*	—	1948
Howard, *Terence T*	13.9.1937	1960
Hunt, *Kenneth Reginald Gunnery*	24.2.1884–28.4.1949	1908
		1920
Jones, *JH*	—	1900
Joy, *Bernard*	29.10.1911–18.7.1984	1936
Kelleher, *Denis*	—	1948
Kippax, *Frederick Peter*	17.7.1922	1948
Knight, *Arthur Egerton*	7.9.1887–10.3.1956	1912
		1920
Kyle, *Joseph Reid*	16.10.1913	1936
Laybourne, *John Sylvester*	26.5.1927	1956
Lee, *Eric G*	18.9.1922	1948
Lewin, *Derek James*	18.5.1930	1956
Lewis, *James Leonard*	26.6.1927	1952
		1956
		1960
Lindsay, *Hugh M*	23.8.1938	1960
Littlewort, *Henry Charles*	7.7.1882–21.11.1934	1912
McAlinden, *Kevin*	—	1948
McBain, *Douglas M*	—	1948
McColl, *James*	—	1948
McIlvenney, *Harold J*	5.10.1922	1948
McKinven, *Ronald*	8.1.1936	1960
McWhirter, *Douglas*	13.8.1886–14.10.1966	1912
Manning, *GT*	—	1948
Mitchell, *James Frederick*	11.11.1897–30.5.1975	1920
Neale, *CR*	—	1948
Neil, *W*	—	1960
Nicholas, *Frederick William Herbert*	25.7.1893–20.10.1962	1920
Nicholas, *J*	—	1900
Noble, *Alfred William Thomas*	18.9.1924	1952
Payne, *JE*	—	1920
Pettit, *Daniel Eric Arthur*	19.2.1915	1936
Pinner, *Michael John*	16.2.1934	1960
Prince, *HM*	—	1920
Prince, *Stanley Terence*	24.1.1927	1956
Purnell, *Clyde Honeysett*	14.5.1877–14.8.1934	1908
Quash, *William Francis Patterson*	27.12.1868	1900
Rawlings, *JW*	—	1948
Riley, *Frederick*	9.1.1912	1936

COMPETITOR	DATE OF BIRTH-DEATH	YEAR EVENT/S
Robb, *George*	1.6.1926	1952
Saunders, *Derek William*	6.1.1928	1952
Sharpe, *Ivor Gordon*	15.6.1889 – 9.2.1968	1912
Sharratt, *Harry*	16.12.1929	1956
Shearer, *Edgar Donald Reid*	6.6.1909	1936
Simpson, *Ronald Campbell*	11.10.1930	1948
Slater, *William John*	29.4.1927	1952
Sleap, *Roy W*	5.9.1940	1960
Sloley, *Richard*	20.8.1891	1920
Smith, *Herbert*	22.11.1879 – 6.1.1951	1908
Spackman, *FG*	—	1900
Stamper, *Harold*	6.10.1889	1912
Stapley, *Henry*	29.4.1883 – 29.4.1937	1908
Stewart, *Thomas*	1926	1952
Stoker, *Donald*	30.12.1922	1956
Stratton, *Leslie Eugene*	1925	1952
Sutcliffe, *John*	27.6.1913	1936
Thompson, *Thomas W*	9.3.1938	1960
* Thornton, *Eric*	—	1900
Topp, *Lawrence Robert*	11.11.1923	1952
		1956
Turner, *RR*	—	1900
Twissell, *Charles Herbert*	16.12.1932	1956
Walden, *Harold Adrian*	10.10.1889 – 2.12.1955	1912
● Whittal, *Albert James*	6.1879 – 8.1957	1906
● Whittal, *Donald*	25.2.1881 – 1959	1906
(Also see Rowing)		
● Whittal, *Edward Sidney*	–1947	1906
● Whittal, *Godfrey*	1882 – 1957	1906
● Whittal, *Harold Frederick*	16.1.1880 – 1909	1906
Woodward, *Vivian John*	3.6.1879 – 31.1.1954	1908
		1912
Wright, *Edward Gordon Dundas*	3.10.1884 – 5.6.1947	1912
Zealey, *James Edward*	7.3.1868	1900

* In 1900, E Thornton played for the Belgian Students team which finished in third place.
● In 1906, five members of the Whittal family played for the Smyrna team which finished in second place.

Basketball

Basketball was introduced as an Olympic sport in 1936. Great Britain competed only in 1948.

COMPETITOR	DATE OF BIRTH-DEATH
Cole, *Frank*	—
Davies, *Trevor C*	—
Eke, *Alex F*	—
Finlay, *Malcolm*	—
Hunt, *Colin L*	—
Legg, *Douglas C*	—
Legg, *Ronald H*	—
McMeekan, *Stanley*	—
McMeekan, *Sydney*	—
Norris, *Robert H*	—
Price, *Lionel*	—
Weston, *Harry L*	—
Weston, *Stanley B*	—

Boxing

Boxing was not on the Olympic programme in 1896, 1900 and 1906 or in 1912 when the sport was illegal in Sweden.

Apart from 1904, Great Britain has been represented on each occasion that boxing events have been held.

B = Bantamweight   Fe = Featherweight   Fl = flyweight
H = Heavyweight   L = Lightweight   LF = Light-flyweight
LH = Light-heavyweight   LM = Light-middleweight
LW = Light-welterweight   M = Middleweight
SH = Super-heavyweight   W = Welterweight

COMPETITOR	DATE OF BIRTH-DEATH	YEAR	EVENT/S
Adams, *E*	—	1908	Fe
Adams, *Frederick Thomas*	—	1920	Fe
Addison, *Roy*	17.2.1939	1960	M
Akinwonde, *Henry*	12.10.1965	1988	H
Anderson, *David*	23.12.1965	1988	Fe
Barber, *Albert Oliver*	1902	1924	B
Barnes, *Albert Richard*	2.7.1913	1936	B
Basham, *Joseph J*	—	1924	W
Beavis, *Arthur Henry*	1905	1924	Fe
Blake, *Eric John*	30.8.1946	1968	LM
Bowling, *Daniel*	—	1920	B
Brander, *Peter*	1928	1948	Fe
Brewer, *Harold*	—	1908	H
Brown, *Hugh*	2.2.1894	1920	LH
Carpenter, *Henry F*	1926	1948	Fl
Carter, *Michael*	17.6.1949	1968	B
Cater, *James*	–17.4.1947	1920	Fe
Cheshire, *John William*	11.9.1947	1968	Fe
Childs, *William*	—	1908	M
Clifton, *AJ*	1897	1924	H
Clinton, *Patrick*	4.4.1964	1984	Fl
Cole, *Neville*	19.6.1952	1972	L
Condon, *John*	28.2.1889 – 21.2.1919	1908	B
Cooper, *Henry William*	3.5.1934	1952	LH
Cooper, *Ronald D*	1929	1948	L
Courtis, *John*	22.8.1902	1924	LH
Cowdell, *Patrick*	18.8.1953	1976	B
Cuthbertson, *William*	1902	1920	Fl
Davies, *Robert*	10.12.1949	1976	LM
Dees, *William J*	—	1908	M
Deveney, *Michael*	14.12.1965	1988	B
Dickson, *Alex*	7.10.1962	1984	L
Dingley, *H*	1903	1924	Fe
Douglas, *John William Henry Taylor*	3.9.1882 – 19.12.1930	1908	M
Douglas, *Roderick*	20.20.1964	1984	LM
Dove, *Frank Sydney*	3.9.1897	1920	H
Dower, *David William 'Dai'*	20.6.1933	1952	Fl
Dunn, *HT*	—	1928	W
Dunne, *James*	14.5.1941	1964	L
Elliot, *Mark*	2.2.1966	1988	LW
Elliott, *John*	1901 – 25.6.1944	1924	M
Epton, *Mark*	22.10.1965	1988	LF
Evans, *Ralph*	20.12.1953	1972	LF
Evans, *Sydney Charles H*	1881 – 8.1.1927	1908	H
Fearman, *EA*	—	1908	L
Fee, *Patrick*	—	1908	L
Finnegan, *Christopher Martin*	5.6.1944	1968	M
Fisher, *William*	14.3.1940	1960	LM
Foster, *Bernard*	28.9.1931	1952	LM
Franks, *Harold*	—	1920	LH
Frost, *Joseph Michael*	14.7.1960	1980	W
Gardner, *Jack Leonard*	6.11.1929 – 11.11.1978	1948	H
Gargano, *Nicholas*	1.11.1934	1956	W
Garland, *John*	2.1911	1928	B
Gilbody, *George*	1.1.1955	1980	L
Gilbody, *Raymond*	23.3.1960	1980	B
Gilmour, *James*	—	1920	L
Gooding, *Terence*	15.4.1931	1952	M
Goyder, *Joseph William*	—	1928	H
Grace, *Frederick*	29.2.1884 – 23.7.1964	1908	L
		1920	L

COMPETITOR	DATE OF BIRTH-DEATH	YEAR	EVENT/S
Griffin, *Thomas James*	25.1.1913	1936	LH
Griffiths, *David*	26.11.1963	1984	LW
Gunn, *Richard Kenneth*	16.2.1871–23.6.1961	1908	Fe
Hanlon, *Peter Joseph*	13.4.1959	1980	Fe
Hearn, *Edgar William*	3.4.1929	1952	H
Holmes, *Harold*	—	1908	L
Hope, *Maurice*	6.12.1951	1972	W
Hughes, *Michael*	13.6.1962	1984	W
Hyland, *John*	20.11.1963	1984	W
Ireland, *Alexander*	1901	1920	W
Ireton, *Albert*	15.5.1879–4.1.1947	1908	H
(Also see *Track & Field*)			
Jackson, *Alfred*	—	1928	LH
Jessup, *G*	—	1908	L
Johnson, *HH*	—	1908	L
Jones, *Colin*	21.3.1959	1976	W
Kane, *Charles*	2.7.1968	1988	L
Kaylor, *Mark Ian*	11.5.1961	1980	M
Kelsey, *Robert J*	8.12.1938	1960	LW
Knight, *William*	26.7.1951	1972	M
Lee, *Daniel*	5.1.1940	1960	Fl
Lewis, *Percival J*	31.12.1928	1952	Fe
Lloyd, *J*	—	1908	Fe
Lloyd, *James*	5.7.1939	1960	W
Lundgren, *Philip H*	2.1.1940	1960	Fe
Lyon, *John Patrick*	9.3.1962	1984	LF
		1988	Fl
McCleave, *David Edward*	24.12.1911–19.5.1988	1932	W
McCluskey, *John*	23.1.1944	1964	Fl
McCormack, *John*	9.1.1935	1956	LM
McGonigle, *John*	14.9.1944	1968	Fl
McGurk, *Frank*	—	1908	B
McKenzie, *Clinton*	15.9.1955	1976	LW
McKenzie, *George*	1901–4.1941	1920	B
McKenzie, *James*	1903	1924	Fl
McTaggart, *Richard*	15.10.1935	1956	L
		1960	L
		1964	LW
Magri, *Charles*	20.7.1956	1976	Fl
Mallin, *Frederick Glanville*	4.3.1902–1987	1928	M
Mallin, *Henry William*	1.6.1892–8.11.1969	1920	M
		1924	M
Maloney, *John Patrick*	30.5.1932	1952	W
Minter, *Alan*	17.8.1951	1972	LM
Mitchell, *Harold James*	5.1.1898–8.2.1983	1924	LH
Mittee, *Sylvester*	29.10.1956	1976	L
Mizler, *Hyman*	22.1.1913–22.3.1990	1932	L
Morris, *Charles W*	—	1908	Fe
Moughton, *Graham*	2.12.1948	1972	LW
Murdoch, *A*	—	1908	M
Myrams, *I*	—	1908	H
Nicholls, *Thomas G*	12.10.1931	1952	B
		1956	Fe
Odwell, *David*	20.11.1952	1976	M
O'Hanrahan, *Patrick*	1895	1924	W
O'Kelly, *Cornelius*	1907–8.9.1968	1924	H
Oldman, *Albert Leonard*	18.11.1883	1908	H
Osborne, *F*	—	1908	L
O'Sullivan, *Maurice*	4.12.1952	1972	Fl
Ould, *John*	19.5.1940	1960	LH
Pack, *Walter Seaforth*	30.12.1914	1936	W
Packer, *Brian*	2.3.1944	1964	B
Pardoe, *Thomas*	4.1911	1932	Fl
Parks, *Frank*	–3.1945	1908	H
Perry, *Frederick Mostyn*	—	1928	Fe
Perry, *H*	—	1908	B
Philo, *W*	—	1908	M
Profitt, *Thomas*	13.7.1927	1948	B
Rawson, *Ronald Rawson*	17.6.1892–30.3.1952	1920	H
Reardon, *Frederick Albert*	1931	1952	L
Redrup, *Ronald*	30.5.1935	1956	M
Reilly, *Owen*	21.1.1937	1956	B
Ringer, *Thomas*	1883–1969	1908	Fe
Robinson, *William*	20.2.1936	1964	LM
Roddin, *Hugh*	—	1908	Fe
Russell, *Alfred*	25.1.1915	1936	Fl
Schumacher, *Brian*	14.5.1960	1984	M
Scott, *Donald E*	23.7.1928	1948	LH
Shacklady, *Maximilian Baldwin*	31.12.1918–6.3.1986	1948	W
Shorter, *GR*	—	1924	L
Shrimpton, *Richard Thomas*	29.1.1910	1936	M
Simpson, *Frederick John*	18.6.1916	1936	L
Smith, *Ronald Anthony*	15.10.1944	1964	Fe
Spiller, *M Frederick*	22.2.1885	1908	L
Spinks, *Terence George*	28.2.1938	1956	Fl
Stack, *William Joseph*	30.9.1936	1964	M
Stracey, *John Henry*	22.9.1950	1968	L
Straugh, *Andrew McDonald*	11.5.1961	1980	LH
Stuart, *Vincent Anthony*	28.12.1907	1936	H
Tarrant, *Leslie M*	1903–5.1970	1924	B
Taylor, *Cuthbert*	11.12.1909–12.1977	1928	Fl
Taylor, *Francis J*	2.9.1942	1960	B
Taylor, *Kevin*	10.8.1963	1984	Fe
Taylor, *William*	14.9.1952	1972	Fe
Thomas, *Henry*	1889	1908	B
Thomas, *David John*	29.8.1937–12.10.1980	1960	H
Tottoh, *Alan*	21.10.1944	1968	W
Treadway, *John William*	24.6.1914	1936	Fe
Turpin, *George*	10.1.1952	1972	B
Varley, *Michael Andrew*	30.11.1939	1964	W
Virtue, *Frederick Walker*	—	1920	Fl
Wallace, *Keith*	29.3.1961	1980	Fl
Waller, *Terence Leslie*	9.3.1946	1968	LW
Warnes, *Ruben Charles*	1875–16.1.1961	1908	M
Warwick, *Ernest*	1904	1924	Fl
Waterman, *Peter*	8.12.1934–15.1.1986	1952	LW
Webb, *William*	1882	1908	B
Webster, *Frederick*	19.6.1909–7.1970	1928	L
Wells, *Matthew*	14.12.1886–8.7.1953	1908	L
Wells, *Robert*	15.5.1961	1984	SH
Wells, *William*	7.9.1936	1968	H
Whitbread, *Frederick William*	—	1920	W
White, *Edward*	—	1920	M
White, *W*	—	1924	L
Willis, *Anthony*	17.6.1960	1980	LW
Wilshire, *Nicholas Colin*	3.11.1961	1980	LM
Wilson, *Anthony Everall*	15.4.1961	1984	LH
Woodhall, *Richard*	17.4.1968	1988	LM
Wright, *John A*	1929	1948	M
Young, *Douglas*	12.12.1961	1984	H

Canoeing & Kayaking

MEN

A canoe race was held at the 1906 Games and demonstration events were held in 1924 before the sports became official Olympic events in 1936. Great Britain has been represented on each occasion that the sports have been on the official programme. Unless otherwise indicated, events were held over a distance of 1000 metres.

C1 = Canadian singles   C1S = Canadian singles (Slalom)
C2 = Canadian pairs   C2S = Canadian pairs (Slalom)
F1 = Folding kayak singles   F2 = Folding kayak pairs
K1 = Kayak singles   K1S = Kayak singles (Slalom)
K2 = Kayak pairs   K4 = Kayak fours
KR = 4 × 500 m kayak singles relay

COMPETITOR	DATE OF BIRTH-DEATH	YEAR	EVENT/S
Alan-Williams, *Anthony Kenneth*	13.1.1964	1976	K4
Allen, *David*	1944	1972	C2S
Avery, *Robin*	4.12.1948	1972	K2/K4
Ayres, *Anthony*	5.5.1961	1988	K4
Ballard, *Christopher Neil*	10.10.1958	1980	K2/K2 (500m)

COMPETITOR	DATE OF BIRTH-DEATH	YEAR	EVENT/S
Blick, *Raymond Charles*	27.5.1930	1956	K2/K2 (10K)
		1960	KR
Bourne, *Grayson H*	30.5.1959	1980	K1 (500m)
		1984	K4
		1988	K2 (500m)
Brearly, *Alex R*	8.12.1913	1936	F2 (10k)
Brown, *Stephen James*	9.5.1956	1976	K2
		1980	K4
Bullivant, *Brian Milton*	10.2.1927	1956	K2/K2 (10k)
Burgess, *Reuben*	30.9.1966	1988	K4
Canham, *Christopher*	3.8.1962	1984	K2
Calverley, *Raymond*	3.4.1951	1972	K1S
Collier, *Adrian*	1.11.1965	1988	K4
Colyer, *Geoffrey John*	18.5.1931	1952	K1/K1 (10k)
Court, *John*	8.3.1943	1972	C2S
Cronk, *Edward G*	5.6.1936	1960	KR
Dinsdale, *Geoffrey*	24.7.1942	1972	C1S
Dobson, *NW*	—	1948	K1
Dudderidge, *John Webster*	24.8.1906	1936	F2 (10k)
Edwards, *Alan*	21.10.1943	1968	K4
Glavin, *John Patrick*	16.2.1944	1968	K1
Goodwin, *John Stuart*	19.6.1943	1972	C2S
Hancock, *Steven*	25.6.1957	1980	K4
Harris, *John B*	28.5.1938	1960	K2
Haynes, *Brian Robert*	16.8.1951	1976	K4
Henderson, *JL*	—	1948	K2
Jackson, *Stephen*	18.9.1956	1984	K1
Jamieson, *Eric*	11.8.1960	1984	C2 (500m)
		1988	C1 (500m); C1
Lawler, *Ivan*	19.11.1966	1988	K1/K2 (500m)
Lawler, *Peter Sidney*	25.4.1941	1964	K4
		1968	K2
		1976	K4
Lawton, *George Wilfrid*	9.2.1911	1936	F1 (10k)
Lowery, *Robert Johnson*	22.5.1957	1900	KR
		1964	K4
		1972	K1S
MacLeod, *John Arthur Torquil Gordon*	31.3.1947		
Maidment, *HE*	—	1948	C1
Marchand, *Gerald Denys*	24.4.1921	1952	C1/C1 (10k)
Mason, *Norman Andrew*	23.7.1952	1976	K2
Mean, *Michael Donald*	18.2.1947	1968	K4
Mitchell, *David Arthur*	5.2.1943	1972	K1S
Oliver, *John Laurence*	12.1.1943	1968	K4
		1972	K1/K4
		1976	K4
Osborne, *Rowan*	17.9.1946	1972	C1S
Palmer, *Glenn Ivor*	17.3.1945	1964	K4
Palmer, *Graham Charles*	1922	1952	K2 (10k)
Parker, *Raymond Leslie*	1919	1952	K2(10k)
Parnham, *Douglas Robert*	23.7.1951	1972	K2/K4
		1976	K1/K1 (500m)
		1980	K1/K4
Pratt, *Basil D*	26.6.1938	1960	K2
Prout, *Francis Spencer Trouchet*	1921	1952	K2
Prout, *Roland Grandpienne*	1020	1952	K2
Raciborski, *Jan*	23.7.1961	1984	K2
		1988	K4
Reichenstein, *William*	7.12.1947	1976	C1
		1980	C1/C1 (500m)
Rhodes, *Ronald*	31.10.1937 – 12.1.1962	1960	K1/KR
Robson, *Neil*	30.12.1957	1980	K2/K2 (500m)

COMPETITOR	DATE OF BIRTH-DEATH	YEAR	EVENT/S
Sherriff, *Andrew*	2.4.1957	1984	K2 (500m)/K4
		1988	K2
Simmons, *AWJ*	—	1948	K2
Smith, *Kevin*	22.3.1961	1984	K4
		1988	K2
Symons, *J*	—	1948	C2
Train, *Andrew*	21.9.1963	1984	C2 (500m)/C2
		1988	C2 (500m)/C2
Train, *Stephen*	23.2.1962	1984	C2 (500m)/C2
		1988	C2 (500m)/C2
Upson, *David*	19.3.1962	1984	K1 (500m)
Van Zwananberg, *H*	—	1948	C2
West, *Jeremy*	29.4.1961	1984	K2 (500m)/K4
		1988	K1 (500)
Whitby, *Mark*	29.1.1950	1968	K2
Williams, *Alan John*	21.4.1954	1976	K4
		1980	K4
Williams, *Lindsay*	22.4.1946	1972	C2S
Wilson, *Alastair Carmichael*	20.8.1939	1964	K1/K4
		1968	K4

Canoeing & Kayaking
WOMEN

Women compete only in the kayak events at the Olympics. Great Britain has been represented on every occasion since women's events were introduced in 1948. All events are contested over a distance of 500 metres.

K1 = Kayak singles   K1S = Kayak singles (Slalom)
K2 = Kayak pairs   K4 = Kayak fours

COMPETITOR	DATE OF BIRTH-DEATH	YEAR	EVENT/S
Ascot, *Shirley Ann*	10.12.1930	1952	K1
Brown, *Victoria*	14.1.1950	1972	K1S
Burnett, *Sheila*	4.7.1949	1976	K1
Dallaway, *Andrea*	14.10.1970	1988	K4
Dawson, *Angela*	14.1.1968	1988	K4
Goodman, *Heather Blanche*	30.3.1935	1972	K1S
Goodwin, *Pauline Mary Joan*	25.6.1946	1972	K1S
		1976	K2
Jackson, *Sylvia Margaret*	12.6.1945	1968	K1
Lawler, *Janine*	16.8.1965	1984	K4
		1988	K2/K4
Mean, *Barbara Ann*	5.1.1950	1968	K2
Moody, *Patricia Josephine*	13.11.1914	1956	K1
Oliver, *Lesley Jean*	31.8.1948	1968	K2
Peacock, *Hilary Jean*	8.12.1951	1976	K2
Perrett, *Amanda Lucy*	30.11.1960	1980	K1
		1984	K2/K4
Perrett, *Suzannah*	30.9.1967	1988	K1/K4
Renshaw, *Pamela Ann*	2.3.1951	1972	K2
Richards, *Joyce*	—	1948	K1
Rouse, *Jane*	23.4.1946	1972	K1
Sharman, *Elizabeth St Clare*	8.8.1957	1988	K2
Smither, *Lesley*	12.3.1958	1980	K2
		1984	K1/K2/K4
Tucker, *Marianne*	23.10.1937	1960	K1
		1964	K1
Watson, *Deborah*	30.5.1964	1984	K4
Wetherall, *Frances Mary*	3.2.1952	1980	K2
Woodehouse, *Helen*	6.5.1953	1972	K2

1900 Team Games

In 1900, a large number of the sporting and quasi-sporting events which were affiliated with the Paris Exposition claimed Olympic status, but whether they should, in retrospect, be considered as Olympic events has generally been decided by agreement among historians rather than by official definition.

For example, the American Report of the 1900 Games, prepared by AG Spalding, devotes almost a whole page to the Fire-Extinguishing Competition which was won by Kansas City and 'it's famous engine and hook and ladder company No.1'. Clearly, such an event did not merit Olympic status but other more traditional sports such as association and rugby football and cricket, despite having only a loose association with the Exposition, are now considered to have been of Olympic calibre.

A British team competed in each of these three sports, all of which took place at the municipal Velodrome de Vincennes. The first team event on the protracted Olympic programme was the two-day cricket match at the end of August when Britain were represented by 'The Devon & Somerset Wanderers Cricket Club', who were on a three-match tour of the Paris area. Their opponents were the best cricketers in France drawn from member clubs of the Union des Societies Francais de Sports Athletiques, the team being made up mainly of English residents of France. The visitors, who were based on the Castle Cary club in Somerset, won by 158 runs. Devon & Somerset Wanderers scored 117 and 145 for 5 dec, with the USFSA scoring 28 and 76.

One month later, Upton Park FC were the British representatives in the association football tournament and although they did not play against Belgium, they were awarded first place after a 4—0 victory over France. It should be noted that the Upton Park FC which played in 1900 was not the same club as the one which was well-known as a founder member of the Football Association. The original Upton Park club had been disbanded in 1887 but in 1890 the name was taken up again by Belmont FC which had been formed in 1883 and it was the former Belmont club who competed in the 1900 Olympic tournament.

The third British team to take part in the 1900 Olympics was the rugby football XV known as Moseley Wanderers. Consisting mainly of players from the Birmingham area, they lost 27-8 to the French selection but in the circumstances the British team played remarkably well. Many of the players had been engaged in club matches in the Midlands the previous day and after catching the night ferry across the Channel the team only arrived in Paris at 6 o'clock on the morning of the match, a bare three hours before the kick-off. The visitors' efforts were appreciated by a crowd of more than 6000, which was the largest attendance at any event at the 1900 Olympics.

Cricket

The only time that cricket has been included in the Olympic Games was in 1900. In a two-day 12-a-side match, Great Britain were represented by 'Devon & Somerset County Wanderers'.

COMPETITOR	DATE OF BIRTH-DEATH
Beachcroft, *CBK*	—
Birkett, *Arthur Ernest Burrington*	25.10.1875–1.4.1941
Bowerman, *Alfred James*	22.11.1873–1959
Buckley, *George John*	1876
Burchell, *Francis Romulus*	25.9.1873–6.7.1947
Christian, *Frederick William*	1877–13.5.1941
Corner, *Harry Richard*	9.7.1874–7.6.1938
Cuming, *Frederick William*	27.5.1875–22.3.1942
Donne, *William Stephens*	2.4.1876–24.3.1934
Powlesland, *Alfred James*	1875–25.2.1941
Symes, *John*	1879
Toller, *Montagu Henry*	2.1871–5.8.1948

Cycling

MEN

Cycling is one of the few sports to have been included at every Olympic Games. Great Britain has competed on each occasion with the exception of 1904 and possibly 1900. Some sources indicate that two British cyclists competed in 1900 but there is no substantial evidence to support this.

In 1912, despite protests from the French, Great Britain were surprisingly permitted to enter three separate teams. The members of these teams have been identified by the appropriate initials, i.e. (E)ngland, (I)reland and (S)cotland. The Olympic cycling programme has varied considerably with numerous changes to the events and the distances over which these events were held.

The code below lists events according to type; for example, all match sprints are listed identically, regardless of the distance over which the races were held.

Until 1960 there was only one road race and aggregate performances in the individual race were used to determine the placings in the team event. In 1960 a separate team road race, the 100km time trial, was introduced.

In 1906 the heats of the 5km event were held over 2000m and the heats of the 20km were held over a distance of 10km.

IP = 4km individual pursuit   MS = Match sprint
PR = Points race   RR = Road race — Individual and team prior to 1960
RRi = Road race — Individual (From 1960 onwards)
RRt = Road race — Team (From 1960 onwards)   T = Tandem match sprint
TP = 4km team pursuit   TT = Individual time trial

660 yards, 5km, 20km, 50km & 100km indicate track events held over these distances.

COMPETITOR	DATE OF BIRTH-DEATH	YEAR	EVENT/S
Addy, *Robert Charles*	24.1.1941	1964	RRt
Alden, *Cyril Albert*	1884	1920	T/TP/
			50km
		1924	50km
Alexander, *Edward*	10.8.1964	1988	MS
Alsop, *Ian Clunies*	14.6.1943	1968	TP

COMPETITOR	DATE OF BIRTH-DEATH	YEAR	EVENT/S
Anderson, *GC*	—	1908	660
Bailey, *Sydney Frederick*	1886	1908	100km
Bailey, *William James*	6.4.1888–1971	1908	660/MS/5km
Banbury, *Ian*	27.11.1957	1976	TP
Bannister, *Alan*	3.11.1922	1948	T
		1952	T
Barnard, *John Lewis*	25.2.1886–22.5.1977	1908	T
Barnett, *Reginald Albert*	15.10.1945	1968	MS
Bartlett, *Charles Henry*	6.2.1885–30.11.1968	1908	100km
Barry, *Mark*	13.5.1964	1984	MS/TT
Barton, *Karl Edward James*	17.7.1937	1960	MS/TT
		1964	MS/TT
Bateman, *Philip*	8.9.1962	1988	RRt
Battell, *F*	—	1896	RR
Bayton, *Philip*	18.9.1950	1972	RRi/RRt
Bell, *Mark*	21.6.1960	1984	RRi
Bennett, *Michael John*	8.6.1949	1972	TT/TP
		1976	TP
Bent, *Stephen*	9.4.1961	1984	IP/TP
Bettison, *John*	10.12.1940	1968	RRt
Bevan, *Alick*	27.3.1915	1936	RR
Bilsland, *William Law*	9.11.1945	1968	RRi
Binch, *Lloyd*	28.8.1931	1960	MS
Bishop, *JH*	—	1908	100km
Boardman, *Christopher*	26.8.1968	1988	TP
Bone, *John Gavin*	17.9.1914	1936	RR
Bouffler, *Herbert Clifford*	1881	1906	MS/TT/5km/20km
		1908	20km
Bradley, *William*	30.3.1933	1960	RRi/RRt
Brittain, *Arthur Stanley*	4.10.1931	1956	RR
Brooks, *Colin*	—	1908	T/20km
Brotherton, *Peter Frederick*	4.2.1931	1956	T
Bull, *Trevor Geoffrey*	28.12.1944	1964	TP
Burgess, *Donald Christopher*	8.2.1933	1952	TP
		1956	TP
Butler, *Stanley Meredith*	—	1932	RR
Calvert, *AE*	—	1908	5km
Carbutt, *Paul*	4.7.1950	1976	RRt
Cavenagh, *GE*	—	1924	TP
Chambers, *Ernest Henry*	7.4.1907	1928	T
		1932	MS/T
		1936	T
Chambers, *Stanley*	—	1932	T
Church, *Christopher Charles*	4.10.1940	1964	T
Clark, *CV*	—	1908	5k
Clements, *Ernest Albert*	1922	1948	RR
Clewarth, *John*	15.1.1948	1972	RRi/RRt
Cooke, *Geoffrey*	26.7.1944	1972	MS/T
Corsar, *George*	7.2.1881	1912	RR(S)
Coull, *Robert*	28.8.1966	1988	TP
Cowley, *Michael Joseph*	8.11.1941	1964	RRi/RRt
Cozens, *Sidney Turner*	1908	1928	MS
Croker, *Robin*	10.5.1954	1976	TP
Cromack, *Roy*	18.2.1940	1968	RRt
Crowther, *Herbert*	1882–1916	1906	MS/TT/5km/20km
		1908	MS
Crutchlow, *Ernest*	6.11.1948	1972	MS
Curran, *Paul*	15.1.1961	1984	PR/TP
		1988	RRi
Danson, *Alan*	25.1.1933	1956	TTtm
Davey, *Charles Frederick*	27.8.1886	1912	RR(E)
Denny, *AJ*	—	1908	660/20km
Denny, *Charles A*	—	1908	100k
Downs, *Robert*	27.7.1954	1980	RRt
Doyle, *Anthony*	19.5.1958	1980	TP
Doyle, *Bernhard Joseph*	9.4.1888	1912	RR(I)
Draper, *J*	—	1906	20km/RR
Edwards, *Philip*	3.9.1949	1972	RRi/RRt
Elliott, *Malcolm*	1.7.1961	1980	TP
Fretwell, *Desmond*	13.7.1955	1980	RRt
Flynn, *Daniel*	—	1908	660/MS/5km/20km

COMPETITOR	DATE OF BIRTH-DEATH	YEAR	EVENT/S
Fuller, *HE*	1902	1924	MS
Gadd, *Trevor J*	18.4.1952	1976	MS
Gambrill, *Michael John*	23.8.1935	1956	TP
		1960	TP
Gayler, *Herbert Henry*	3.12.1881	1912	RR(E)
Geddes, *John Reuben*	13.8.1936	1956	TP
Geldard, *Robert Alan*	16.4.1927	1948	TP
Genders, *WH*	—	1920	RR
Gibbon, *Arthur William John*	1884	1912	RR(E)
Godwin, *Thomas Charles*	5.11.1920	1948	TT/TP
Gornall, *Mark*	25.10.1961	1988	RRi
Griffiths, *AJ*	30.11.1881	1912	RR(S)
Griffiths, *Philip W*	18.3.1949	1976	RRi/RRt
Grubb, *Frederick Henry*	27.5.1887–6.3.1949	1912	RR(E)
Guy, *Francis*	1885	1912	RR(I)
Habberfield, *Frederick Henry*	1895	1924	T
Hallam, *Ian*	24.11.1948	1968	IP/TP
		1972	IP/TP
		1976	IP/TP
Hamlin, *Frederick G*	—	1908	T/20km
Hammond, *William Robert*	1.7.1886	1912	RR(E)
Handley, *David*	3.2.1932	1960	T
Harris, *Reginald Hargreaves*	1.3.1920	1948	MS/T

Silver medallist Reg Harris (right) in the 1948 1000 metres sprint final. Mario Ghella of Italy (left) took the title in two straight races.

COMPETITOR	DATE OF BIRTH-DEATH	YEAR	EVENT/S
Harrison, *Derek John*	5.3.1944	1964	RRi/RRt
Harrison, *Keith John*	28.3.1933	1956	MS
Harvell, *William Gladstone*	25.9.1907–13.3.1985	1932	TT/TP/RR
Harvey, *Thomas*	1888	1920	50km
		1924	T
Hayton, *M. Dudley*	22.4.1953	1976	RRi/RRt
Herety, *John*	8.3.1958	1980	RRi
Hicks, *Raymond*	3.3.1917	1936	MS/TT
Higgins, *Francis Cecil*	29.1.1882–19.4.1948	1912	RR(E)
Hill, *Charles*	15.8.1886	1912	RR(S)
Hill, *Harold Heaton*	8.5.1916	1936	TP
Hinds, *James F*	6.6.1937	1960	RRi/RRt
Hoban, *Neil*	4.2.1966	1988	RRi
Hoban, *P Barry*	5.2.1940	1960	TP
Holland, *Charles*	20.9.1908	1932	TP/RR
		1936	RR
Holmes, *William*	14.1.1936	1956	RR
		1960	RRi/RRt
Hunter, *Samuel George Ridley*	21.8.1895–5.7.1976	1924	RR
Ingman, *William Leslie*	17.8.1927	1952	RR
Isaacs, *Walter HT*	—	1908	T
Jackson, *Alan Wharmby*	19.11.1933	1956	RR
Jackson, *Harold Kenneth*	26.5.1941	1964	TP
		1968	TP
Johnson, *Ernest Alfred*	18.11.1912	1932	TP
		1936	TP
Johnson, *Horace Thomas 'Tiny'*	1889–12.8.1966	1908	T
		1920	MS/TP/50km
Johnson, *Victor Louis*	10.5.1883–23.6.1951	1908	660/MS
Jolly, *Brian*	1.3.1946	1968	RRi
Jolly, *R*	—	1908	T/100km
Jones, *Benjamin*	1882	1908	660/MS/TP/5km/20km

An Early Incident

One of the very earliest Olympic 'incidents' involved a British Olympic cyclist. In 1896 F Battell, a servant at the British Embassy in Athens, entered for the road race but a number of British residents sought to have him barred from the race. They reasoned that because of his occupation he could not possibly be a gentleman and that it therefore followed that he could not claim to be an amateur. However, the last word went to Battell. He was one of three competitors to complete the 87km course and no doubt the prize he recevied for placing third was later proudly displayed in the butler's pantry at the Embassy.

COMPETITOR	DATE OF BIRTH-DEATH	YEAR	EVENT/S	COMPETITOR	DATE OF BIRTH-DEATH	YEAR	EVENT/S
Jones, *Stanley Lawrence*	24.3.1888	1912	RR(E)	Payne, *Ernest*	23.12.1884–10.9.1961	1908	660/MS/TP/5km
Jones, *Stephen*	4.12.1957	1980	RRt	Peacock, *Cyril Francis*	1929	1952	MS
Keeble, *Ronald James*	14.1.1946	1968	TP	Pett, *William James*	25.8.1873–27.12.1954	1906	20km/RR
		1972	TP			1908	100km
Keeping, *F*	—	1896	12-hour	Piercy, *EC*	—	1908	T
Kerridge, *EJ*		1928	TT	Pilcher, *EC*	1893	1924	RR
King, *Charles Thomas*	12.6.1911	1936	TP	Porter, *Hugh William*	27.1.1940	1964	IP
Kingsbury, *Clarence Brickwood*	3.11.1882–4.3.1949	1908	660/MS/TP/5km/20km	Poulter, *Steven*	3.12.1954	1984	RRt
				Pryor, *H*	—	1924	TP
Kirk, *John William*	20.11.1890	1912	RR(E)	Reynolds, *Harold Thomas*	12.10.1935	1956	RR
Laidlaw, *Thomas A Kenneth*	—	1960	RRi/RRt	Reynolds, *Keith*	25.12.1963	1984	RRt
Lance, *Thomas Glasson*	14.6.1891–29.2.1976	1920	MS/T	Ricketts, *David Edward*	—	1948	TP
Lauterwasser, *John Jacob*	19.6.1904	1928	RR	Robertson, *DC*	—	1908	20km/100km
Lavery, *J*	—	1908	660/MS/5km				
Lee, *HH*	1887	1920	T	Robinson, *Brian*	3.11.1930	1952	RR
		1924	TP	Robinson, *Desmond*	1927	1952	RR
Lewis, *Colin*	27.7.1941	1964	RRi/RRt	Rollinson, *David*	11.1.1947	1968	RRi
Lillestone, *Simon*	13.2.1969	1988	TP	Rowe, *David John*	2.3.1944	1972	T
Lloyd, *David*	12.10.1949	1972	RRi/RRt	Rushen, *Arthur*	—	1906	MS/TT/T/5km/20km
Lodge, *Harold*	23.9.1967	1988	RRt				
Lower, *W*	—	1908	20km			1908	T
Luckwell, *Benjamin*	30.3.1966	1988	RRt	Ryan, *Harry Edgar*	21.11.1893–14.4.1961	1920	MS/T
McClean, *Joseph P*	30.7.1935	1960	TP	Sanders, *Peter*	19.3.1961	1984	RRi/RRt
McCoy, *Charles*	14.12.1937	1960	TP	Sandy, *Brian*	24.11.1932	1964	TP
McKaig, *G*	—	1908	T	Scott, *CS Ian*	—	1948	RR
McKellow, *Donald Arthur*	1925	1952	TT	Sibbitt, *John Ephraim*	4.3.1895	1928	T
McKeown, *Brendon*	18.3.1944	1968	TT			1936	T
Magee, *W*	—	1908	660/MS/5km	Simpson, *Thomas*	30.11.1937–13.7.1967	1956	TP
Maitland, *Robert John*	31.3.1924	1948	RR	Smith, *Peter David*	1.5.1944	1968	RRt
Marsh, *David Broadhead Robertson*	28.12.1894	1920	RR	Southall, *Frank William*	1904–5.4.1964	1928	RR
		1924	RR			1932	TP/RR
		1928	RR	Southall, *M George*	—	1928	TP
Marshall, *C*	—	1980	RRi	Spencer, *David*	3.12.1964	1988	RRt
Martin, *Neil*	1.4.1960	1984	RRi	Stevenson, *DM*	17.1.1882	1912	RR(S)
Matthews, *Thomas John*	16.8.1884–20.10.1969	1906	MS/TT/T/5km/20km	Stevenson, *James*	1.2.1887	1912	RR(S)
		1908	MS/T	Stewart, *William George*	1883	1920	T/TP/50km
Medhurst, *Paul A*	12.12.1953	1976	TT			1924	TP
Mecredy, *Ralph JR*	12.7.1888	1912	RR(I)	Stokes, *Arthur Joseph*	13.11.1875	1912	RR(E)
Meredith, *Leon Lewis*	2.2.1882–27.1.1930	1908	TP/T/20km/100km	Stretton, *Ronald Charles*	13.2.1930	1952	TP
		1912	RR(E)	Sturgess, *Colin*	15.12.1968	1988	IP
		1920	RR	Summers, *GF*	—	1908	660/MS
				Sword, *Glen*	10.11.1967	1988	TP
				Thomas, *Gordon W*	—	1948	RR
				Thompson, *Eric Gordon*	—	1956	T
Merlin, *Ernest Alfred*	5.9.1886	1912	RR(E)			1960	T
Messer, *William Alfred*	8.7.1915	1936	RR	Thompson, *Robert*	28.4.1884	1912	RR(S)
Middleton, *John Kenneth*	21.6.1906	1928	RR	Timmis, *Adrian*	20.6.1964	1984	TP
Miller, *John*	27.2.1882	1912	RR(S)	Tinsley, *Terence*	6.7.1957	1980	MS/TT
Mills, *Ernest Victor*	10.4.1913	1936	TP	Vines, *Graham Joseph*	1930	1952	RR
Mitchell, *Glen*	11.5.1958	1980	TP	Walker, *John*	23.12.1888	1912	RR(I)
Moore, *William*	2.4.1947	1972	TP	Walker, *Michael*	31.8.1886	1912	RR(I)
Moss, *Charles*	6.3.1882	1912	RR(E)	Wallace, *Shaun*	20.11.1961	1984	IP/PR
Mussen, *Harry*	—	1908	100km	Walsh, *Matthew*	4.7.1887	1912	RR(I)
Newberry, *George Albert*	6.6.1917	1952	TP	Waters, *Wilfrid*	—	1948	TP
Newell, *E*	—	1920	RR	Watson, *Edward John*	1.4.1947	1968	RRt
Newton, *Alan*	19.3.1931	1952	TP	Waugh, *Joseph A*	28.7.1952	1976	RRi
Nickson, *Francis William*	30.1.1953	1976	RRi/RRt			1980	RRt
Noble, *Mark*	23.5.1963	1984	TP	Webster, *Darryl*	7.5.1962	1984	RRi/RRt
Noon, *David R*	—	1908	100km	West, *Leslie George*	11.11.1943	1968	RRi
Norman, *J*	—	1908	T/100km	West, *Terence Henry*	19.9.1939	1964	RRi
Ormston *WA*	—	1920	T	White, *Albert*	1889–1965	1920	MS/TP
Owen, *G*	1893	1924	MS	Whitfield, *Roger Cyril*	29.12.1944	1964	TT/TP
				Williams, *Jeffrey*	18.8.1958	1980	RRi

COMPETITOR	DATE OF BIRTH-DEATH	YEAR	EVENT/S
Willis, *AE*	—	1906	1000/5km/20km
Wilson, *A*	1902	1924	RR
Wilson, *John*	17.11.1876 – 24.11.1957	1912	RR(S)
Wilson, *Leslie*	1926	1952	T
Wyld, *Frederick Henry*	5.6.1900 – 5.4.1976	1924	50km
		1928	TP
Wyld, *Leonard Arthur*	1906	1928	TP
Wyld, *Percy*	1908	1928	TP
Yates, *Sean*	11.5.1960	1980	IP/TP

Cycling
WOMEN

A cycling event for women was first included in the Olympics in 1984 when an individual road race was held. In 1988 a Match Sprint event was added to the women's programme.

COMPETITOR	DATE OF BIRTH-DEATH	YEAR	EVENT/S
Blower, *Maria*	21.8.1964	1984	RRi
		1988	RRi
Brambani, *Lisa*	18.8.1967	1988	RRi
Gornall, *Linda*	21.3.1964	1984	RRi
Hodge, *Sally*	31.5.1966	1988	RRi
Jones, *Louise*	8.6.1963	1988	MS
Sharp, *Muriel*	2.5.1953	1984	RRi
Swinnerton, *Catherine*	12.5.1958	1984	RRi

Diving
MEN

Diving was included in the Olympics for the first time in 1904. Great Britain were not represented in 1904 or 1932

HD = Highboard-Platform   PHD = Plain high diving (1924 only)
SD = Springboard

COMPETITOR	DATE OF BIRTH-DEATH	YEAR	EVENT/S
Aldous, *H James H*	—	1908	HD
Arbon, *Jeffrey*	17.11.1967	1988	HD
Baker, *John David*	4.1.1951	1972	SD
Baskerville, *Robin*	6.4.1950	1968	HD
Beckett, *AJ*	—	1908	SD
Brown, *Martyn*	21.6.1953	1976	HD
		1980	HD
Bull, *WJ*	—	1908	SD
Burne, *William Godfrey Thomas*	—	1928	HD
Candler, *John*	13.12.1939	1960	HD
		1964	SD
Cane, *GF*	—	1908	HD
Cann, *Raymond Eric*	13.12.1937	1956	HD/SD
Carter, *Frank*	27.10.1942	1968	SD
Clarke, *Gordon Melville*	—	1906	HD
Clarke, *Harold*	1888	1908	SD
		1920	HD
		1924	PHD
Collin, *Keith Roper*	18.1.1937	1960	SD
Collins, *FJ*	—	1908	HD
Crank, *Harry*	1885	1908	SD
Cross, *CA*	—	1908	SD
Dickin, *Albert Edward*	1901	1920	HD
(Also see *Swimming*)		1924	PHD
DuffICY, *Frank Sean*	11.6.1953	1972	HD
Elliott, *Peter John Henry*	14.6.1930	1948	SD
		1952	SD
Errington, *FE*	—	1908	SD
Gill, *Andrew Michael*	19.6.1948	1972	HD

COMPETITOR	DATE OF BIRTH-DEATH	YEAR	EVENT/S
Goodworth, *Harold*	—	1908	HD
Harrington, *T*	—	1908	HD
Heatly, *Peter*	9.6.1924	1948	HD/SD
		1952	HD/SD
Hoare, *WG*	—	1908	HD/SD
Hodges, *Frederick George*	8.5.1921	1936	SD
Johnson, *Charles*	—	1948	SD
Kitcher, *Anthony William*	18.3.1941	1964	HD
Knight, *Albert Reginald*	1900	1924	HD/PHD
		1928	HD
MacDonald, *Eric M*	—	1924	HD/SD
Marchant, *Louis Walter George*	5.7.1916	1948	HD
Mather, *Thomas J*	—	1928	HD
Matveieff, *Gregory*	25.10.1901 – 15.8.1965	1924	SD
Mercer, *SC*	—	1928	SD
Morgan, *Robert*	27.3.1967	1988	HD/SD
Morris, *Graham*	28.3.1964	1988	SD
Phelps, *Brian Eric*	21.4.1944	1960	HD
		1964	HD
Pott, *Herbert Ernest*	15.1.1883	1908	SD
		1912	SD
Priestly, *David*	9.2.1946	1968	HD
Simpson, *Trevor*	17.3.1951	1976	HD
Smyrk, *Harold Nelson*	1889	1906	HD
		1908	SD
Snode, *Christopher*	23.3.1959	1976	SD
		1980	HD/SD
		1984	HD/SD
Squires, *Peter John*	23.5.1936	1960	SD
Stanton, *Nigel*	10.11.1964	1984	SD
Tarsey, *Peter David*	5.8.1937	1956	HD/SD
Taylor, *AJB*	—	1908	SD
Tomalin, *Charles Douglas*	20.8.1914	1936	HD
Turner, *Anthony Abraham*	1933	1952	HD/SD
Walls, *Christopher Stephen*	3.8.1952	1972	SD
Walmsley, *Ernest*	—	1920	SD
Walsh, *Roy*	6.9.1936	1956	HD/SD
Ward, *Gordon Frank*	31.7.1920	1948	HD
Webb, *WE*	—	1908	HD
Wetheridge, *Brian Albert*	13.1.1953	1972	HD/SD
Wood, *William Ralph*	9.6.1946	1964	HD
Yvon, *George*	15.2.1887	1912	HD

Diving
WOMEN

Diving events for women were introduced into the Olympics in 1912. Great Britain has been represented on every occasion except for 1932.

COMPETITOR	DATE OF BIRTH-DEATH	YEAR	EVENT/S
Armstrong, *Beatrice Eileen*	11.1.1894 – 12.3.1981	1920	HD
		1924	HD
Bisbrown, *Lettice Margaret Everton*	8.6.1919	1948	HD
Bishop, *Naomi*	19.8.1967	1988	SD
Child, *Edna Lilian*	10.10.1922	1948	SD
Childs, *Alison*	13.12.1962	1984	SD
Cramp, *Frances Caroline*	27.6.1947	1964	HD
Cuthbert, *Kay Rebecca*	6.2.1925	1948	SD
Drake, *Alison Jean*	26.12.1952	1972	SD
		1980	SD
Drew, *Dorothy Ann*	2.11.1934	1952	SD
Ferris, *Elizabeth Anne Esther*	19.11.1940	1960	SD
Fraser, *Lindsey*	24.1.1958	1980	HD
		1984	HD
Gilbert, *Jean*	1.12.1919	1936	HD
Grimes, *D*	—	1928	HD
Harris, *Esme G*	—	1948	SD
Haswell, *Mandi*	1.10.1949	1968	HD
Hider, *Maire A*	—	1948	HD
Hudson, *Amelia*	1903	1924	SD
Jay, *Deborah*	24.10.1961	1980	SD

COMPETITOR	DATE OF BIRTH-DEATH	YEAR	EVENT/S
Koppell, *Helen Mary*	15.6.1955	1972	HD/SD
		1976	SD
Larsen, *Katinka*	9.11.1907	1936	SD
Le Rossingol, *K*	—	1928	HD
Lloyd-Chandos, *Valerie Pauline*	24.5.1933	1952	HD
Long, *Phyllis Ann*	6.7.1936	1952	HD/SD
		1956	HD/SD
		1960	HD/SD
Luscombe, *Gladys Mary*	13.11.1908	1924	SD
Moulton, *Madge*	15.6.1917	1936	HD
Newman, *Denise St Aubyn*	—	1948	HD
Newman, *Joy Ernestine*	17.11.1945	1964	HD
Newman, *Verrall Maude*	21.1.1897	1924	HD
O'Bryen, *Cicely*	1899	1924	SD
Roscoe, *Carolyn*	2.8.1966	1984	HD
		1988	HD/SD
Rowlatt, *Katherine*	14.5.1948	1968	SD
Saunders, *Marion*	1.6.1960	1980	HD
Slade, *Betty Joyce*	18.6.1921	1936	SD
Spencer, *Diana May*	1934	1952	HD
Thomas, *Norma*	13.6.1940	1960	HD
Welsh, *Charmain Isobel*	17.5.1937	1952	SD
		1956	HD/SD
White, *Isobel Mary*	1.9.1894 – 7.7.1972	1912	HD
		1920	HD
		1924	HD
		1928	HD
Williams, *Beverly Ann Maria*	5.1.1957	1972	HD

Equestrian

MEN

After the inclusion of a limited programme in 1900, equestrian events became a regular part of the Olympic programme in 1912. Great Britain made its Olympic debut in 1912 and has competed at each subsequent Games with the exception of 1920, 1928, 1932 and 1980.

Three-Day Event: Team scores have always been decided by the performances of riders in the individual event. Hence, all those riders listed competed in both the individual and the team event.

Show Jumping: From 1924 to 1956 and also in 1964 there was no seperate individual competition and team scores were decided by the results of performances in the individual competition. Consequently, the competitors in those years took part in both the individual and team competitions.

In 1912, 1920 (when GB did not compete), 1960 and from 1968 onwards separate individual and team competitions were held.

Dressage: An individual event was first held in 1912 and a team event was introduced in 1928. Both individual and team events have been held regularly since their introduction with the exception of 1960 when no team scores were calculated. From 1928 to 1968 team scores were calculated by aggregating scores from the individual event but from 1972 onwards only the leading competitors from the team event have qualified to enter the separate individual competition. Britain first competed in the individual event in 1956 and in the team event in 1972.

3 = Three-day event–Team & Individual   DR = Dressage-Individual
DRt = Dressage-Team   SJ = Show Jumping-Individual
SJt = Show Jumping-Team

COMPETITOR	DATE OF BIRTH-DEATH	YEAR	EVENT/S
Allhusen, *Derek Swithen*	9.1.1914	1968	3
Arthur, *John Norman Stewart*	6.3.1931	1960	3
Barker, *Charles David*	22.9.1935	1960	SJt
Barker, *David Boston*	12.4.1943	1964	SJ/SJt

COMPETITOR	DATE OF BIRTH-DEATH	YEAR	EVENT/S
Bartle, *Christopher*	19.2.1952	1984	DR/DRt
Bolton, *Lyndon*	—	1948	3
Borwick, *Peter Malise*	21.11.1913 – 23.12.1983	1948	3
Bowden-Smith, *Philip Ernest*	27.3.1891 – 28.4.1964	1924	3/SJ/SJt
Brooke, *Geoffrey Francis Heremon*	14.6.1884 – 26.6.1966	1924	SJ/SJt
Broome, *David McPherson*	1.3.1940	1960	SJ/SJt
		1964	SJ/SJt
		1968	SJ/SJt
		1972	SJ/SJt
		1988	SJ/SJt
Brunker, *Capel Howard Molyneux*	19.12.1898 – 25.6.1988	1924	SJ/SJt
		1936	SJ/SJt
Bullen, *Michael Fitzherbert Symes*	20.5.1937	1960	3
		1964	3
Carr, *Arthur*	26.7.1910 – 11.9.1986	1948	SJ/SJt
Carr, *William Greenwood*	10.3.1901 – 27.1.1982	1936	SJ/SJt
Fanshawe, *Richard Gennys*	22.6.1906	1936	3
Fernyhough, *Rowland*	9.7.1954	1976	SJt
Fletcher, *Graham*	9.1.1951	1976	SJ/SJt
de Fonblanque, *Edward Barrington*	29.5.1895	1924	3
Grubb, *Timothy*	30.5.1954	1984	SJ/SJt
Hervey, *Keith Wilson*	3.11.1898 – 22.2.1973	1924	3/SJ/SJt
Hill, *Albert Edwin*	7.2.1927	1952	3
		1956	3
		1960	3
Hindley, *John Reginald*	1914	1952	3
Howard-Vyse, *Edward Dacre*	27.11.1905	1936	3
Jones, *Reuben Samuel*	19.10.1932 – 3.1.1990	1964	3
		1968	3
Kenna, *Paul Alyoysius*	16.8.1862 – 30.8.1915	1912	3/SJ
Lawrence, *Bryan Turner Tom*	9.11.1873 – 6.6.1949	1912	3
Llewellyn, *Henry Morton*	18.7.1911	1948	SJ/SJt
		1952	SJ/SJt
Meade, *Richard John Hannay*	4.12.1938	1964	3
		1968	3
		1972	3
		1976	3
Nash, *ER see Radcliffe-Nash*			
Nicoll, *Henry Morrison Vere*	17.4.1908	1948	SJ/SJt
Phillips, *Mark Anthony Peter*	22.9.1948	1972	3
		1988	3
Pyrah, *Malcolm*	26.8.1941	1988	SJt
Radcliffe-Nash, *Edward*	9.6.1888	1912	3
Robeson, *Peter David*	21.10.1928	1956	SJ/SJt
		1964	SJ/SJt
		1976	SJ/SJt
Rook, *Arthur Laurence*	26.5.1921 – 30.9.1989	1952	3
		1956	3
Saywell, *Michael John*	27.8.1942	1972	SJ/SJt
Scott, *Alec Brassey Johnathan*	16.10.1906	1936	3
Scott, *Herbert Stuart Lauriston*	29.12.1885 – 3.6.1966	1912	3/SJ
Skelton, *Nick*	30.12.1957	1988	SJ/SJt
Smith, *Robert Harvey*	29.12.1938	1968	SJ/SJt
		1972	SJt
Smith, *Steven*	22.10.1962	1984	SJt
Stark, *Ian David*	22.2.1954	1984	3
		1988	3
Stewart, *Douglas Norman*	24.6.1913	1948	3
		1952	SJ/SJt
Talbot-Ponsonby, *John Arthur*	10.3.1907 – 29.12.1969	1936	SJ/SJt
Templer, *James Robert*	8.1.1936	1964	3
Thomas, *Hugh*	29.2.1948	1976	3
Tod, *Alec Frederick*	2.5.1898	1924	3
Turi, *Joseph*	18.11.1956	1988	SJ/SJt
Weldon, *Francis William Charles*	2.8.1913	1956	3
		1960	3
Whitaker, *John*	5.8.1955	1984	SJ/SJt
Whitaker, *Michael*	17.3.1960	1984	SJ/SJt
White, *Wilfred Harry*	30.3.1904	1952	SJ/SJt
		1956	SJ/SJt

Equestrian
WOMEN

Women were not permitted to compete in Olympic equestrian events prior to 1952. A British equestrienne first took part in 1956 and, apart from the boycott in 1980, British women riders have competed at every subsequent Olympics.

COMPETITOR	DATE OF BIRTH-DEATH	YEAR	EVENT/S
Bartle-Wilson, *Jane*	14.2.1951	1984	DRt
Bullen, *Jane Mary Elizabeth*	7.1.1948	1968	3
Clapham, *Diana*	8.6.1957	1984	3
Coakes, *Marion Janice*	6.6.1947	1968	SJ/SJt
Gordon-Watson, *Mary Diana*	3.4.1948	1972	3
Gardiner, *Patricia*	16.8.1935	1988	DRt
Green, *LJ* see Prior-Palmer			
Hall, *Johanna Sybille*	24.5.1934	1960	DR
		1964	DR
		1968	DR/DRt
Hammond, *Barbara*	26.7.1943	1988	DRt
Holgate, *Virginia*	1.2.1955	1984	3
(As Leng in 1988)		1988	3
Johnsey, *Deborah*	3.7.1957	1976	SJ/SJt
Johnstone, *Hilda Lorna*	4.9.1902–18.5.1990	1956	DR
		1968	DR/DRt
		1972	DR/DRt
Lawrence, *Domini Margaret*	8.5.1928	1968	DR/DRt
		1972	DRt
Leng, *V* see Holgate			
Loriston-Clarke, *Ann Jennifer Francis*	22.1.1943	1972	DRt
		1976	DRt
		1984	DRt
		1988	DR/DRt
Mason, *Diana*	29.4.1933	1976	DRt
		1988	DRt
Moore, *Ann Elizabeth*	20.8.1950	1972	SJ/SJt
Parker, *Bridget M*	5.1.1939	1972	3
HRH Princess Anne	15.8.1950	1976	3
Prior-Palmer, *Lucinda Jane*	7.11.1953	1976	3
(As Green in 1984)		1984	3
Smythe, *Patricia Rosemary*	22.11.1928	1956	SJ/SJt
		1960	SJ/SJt
Straker, *Karen*	17.9.1964	1988	3
Whitmore, *Sarah*	9.8.1931	1976	DRt
Williams, *Brenda*	9.6.1895–8.1966	1956	DR
		1960	DR
Wofford, *Dawn*	23.5.1936	1960	SJ

In 1956 show jumper Pat Smythe became the first British equestrienne to win an Olympic medal.

Fencing
MEN

Fencing events have been held at every Olympic Games. Great Britain first competed in 1906 and has been represented at every Games since then.

E = Epee F = Foil S = Sabre t = Team event

COMPETITOR	DATE OF BIRTH-DEATH	YEAR	EVENT/S
Acfield, *David Laurence*	24.7.1947	1968	St
		1972	St
Alexander, *Gordon Reuben*	1888–24.4.1917	1912	E/F
Alexander, *Michael O'Donel Bjarne*	19.6.1936	1960	Et
Amberg, *Michael J*	25.4.1926	1960	S/St
Ames, *Gerald R*	1880	1912	E
Amphlett, *Edgar Montague*	1.9.1867–9.1.1931	1908	E/Et
		1912	E/Et/F
Anderson, *Robert James Gilbert*	1922	1952	S/St
Badman, *RA*	—	1908	S
Bartlett, *Anthony*	4.8.1955	1988	Ft
Bartlett, *Henry David Hardington*	18.3.1912–13.9.1989	1936	F/Ft
Beatly, *W Maurice*	1923	1952	S/St
Beaumont, *Charles Louis de*	5.5.1902–6.7.1972	1936	E/Et
		1948	E/Et
		1952	Et
Beevers, *Martin*	11.6.1946	1976	Et
Beddard, *Terrance Elliott*	30.10.1901	1936	Et
		1948	Et
Bell, *Nicholas Julian*	5.9.1950	1976	Ft
		1984	F/Ft
Belson, *Timothy*	25.4.1951	1976	E/Et
Biscoe, *Charles Henry*	1875–22.12.1948	1924	E/Et
		1928	E/Et
Blake, *John Percy*	1874	1908	E
		1912	E/Et
		1920	E/Et
Bourne, *Edward Owen*	30.9.1948	1968	Et
		1972	E/Et
		1076	E/Et
Brekin, *John Michael*	16.5.1946	1968	F/Ft
		1972	F/Ft
Brook, *Ralph Ellis (Robin)*	19.6.1908	1936	S/St
		1948	S/St
Brookfield, *Edward Williams Hamilton*	1880	1908	S/St
		1912	S/St
		1920	S/St
		1924	St
		1928	S/St
Bruniges, *Robert John*	3.7.1956	1976	F/Ft
		1980	Et/F/Ft
		1984	F/Ft
Burt, *GM*	—	1920	E/Et
		1924	Et
Butterworth, *Harry Robert*	—	1912	S/St
Campbell, *Ronald Bruce*	14.9.1878–7.3.1963	1920	E/S/St
Campbell-Gray, *Hon Ian Douglas*	14.7.1901	1936	E/Et
Cawthorne, *Derrick*	24.4.1931	1960	Ft
		1964	Ft
Chalke, *AP*	—	1908	S
Chalmers, *Ralph*	13.1.1891	1908	E
Childs, *Bertie S*	20.10.1894	1928	E/Et
		1936	Et
Cohen, *Richard*	9.5.1947	1972	S/St
		1976	S/St
		1984	S/St
Cooke, *Harold*	29.5.1907	1948	Ft
		1952	Ft
Cooke, *Stenson*	5.10.1874–19.11.1942	1912	E/F
Cooperman, *Arnold Ralph*	16.11.1927	1956	Ft/S/St
		1960	F/Ft/S/St
		1964	Ft/S/St

COMPETITOR	DATE OF BIRTH-DEATH	YEAR	EVENT/S
Corble, *Archibald Harrison*	1883	1912	S/St
		1924	S/St
		1928	St
Craig, *Archibald Douglas E*	1887	1924	Et
		1948	Et
Craig, *Rodney*	30.4.1945	1968	S/St
		1972	St
Crawshay, *Richard Oakes*	1881	1912	S
Dalglish, *Robin Campsie*	1880	1920	E/S/St
		1924	S/St
Daniell, *C Leaf*	—	1908	E/Et
Davids, *H*	—	1908	E
Davis, *Jonathan*	4.11.1960	1988	Ft
Davson, *Percival May*	30.9.1887–5.12.1959	1908	E
		1912	E/Et/F
Deanfield, *John Eric*	28.4.1952	1972	S/St
		1976	S/St
Desborough, *Lord William Henry Grenfell*	30.10.1885–11.1.1945	1906	Et
Dexter, *Douglas*	1889	1936	E/Et
Doyne, *Philip Geoffrey*	31.10.1886–22.1.1959	1920	F/Ft
		1924	F/Ft
		1928	Et
Drury, *DD*	—	1912	E/Et
Everitt, *Arthur Francis Graham*	27.8.1872	1912	E/Et
Fagan, *Arthur William*	10.12.1890	1912	F
Fildes, *Frederic Luke Val*	13.6.1879–22.4.1970	1908	E
Forrest, *HA*	—	1928	St
Frater, *R*	—	1924	E/Et
Godfree, *Douglas William* (Also see *Modern Pentathlon*)	16.10.1881–5.8.1929	1908	S
		1912	S/St
Gordon, *Sir Cosmo Edmund Duff, Bt*	22.7.1862–20.4.1931	1906	Et
Gosbee, *William*	20.5.1961	1984	F/Ft
		1988	F/Ft
Grimmett, *Geoffrey Richard*	20.12.1950	1976	Ft
Grose-Hodge, *Christopher Dorrien Moresby*	6.3.1924	1952	Et
Haig, *Cecil Henry*	16.3.1862	1908	E/Et
Halsted, *Nicholas*	24.10.1942	1968	E/Et/Ft
Hammersly, *Christopher Ralph*	1889	1936	Ft
Hammond, *W*	1872	1920	St
		1924	St
Harper, *Pierre*	2.3.1957	1980	F/Ft
		1984	F/Ft
		1988	F/Ft
Harrison, *Raymond Alan*	4.8.1929	1952	Et
		1960	Et
Harry, *Guy Lionel Greville*	19.12.1894	1928	S/St
		1936	S/St
Hett, *Geoffrey Vyvyan Arundell Seccombe*	5.3.1909	1936	Ft
Holt, *Martin Drummond Vesey*	13.1.1881–2.11.1956	1908	E/Et
		1912	E/Et
		1920	E/Et
		1924	E/Et
		1928	E/Et
		1956	E/Et/Ft/S/St
		1960	E/Et/F/Ft
		1964	E/Et/F/Ft/St
		1968	E/Et/F/Ft
		1972	Et
		1976	Et/S
Howard, *Michael John Peter*	24.12.1928	1956	E/Et
		1960	Et
		1964	Et/St
Howard de Walden, *Lord*	9.5.1889–5.11.1946	1906	F
Hudson, *Edward*	26.3.1946	1976	Et
Huntingdon, *Herbert Francis Searanche*	15.1.1898–1969	1920	S/St
Jacobs, *Peter*	26.11.1938	1964	E/Et
		1968	Et
James, *H Evan*	—	1908	S/St
		1920	F/Ft
James, *J Evan*	—	1928	Ft
Jay, *Allan Louis Neville*	30.6.1931	1952	E/Et/Ft
		1956	E/Et/F/Ft/St
		1960	E/Et/F/Ft
		1964	E/Et/F/Ft
		1968	Ft
Jeffreys, *Robin Edmund*	—	1928	St
Johnson, *William Ralph*	3.6.1948	1968	E/Et
		1972	E/Et
		1976	E/Et
		1984	Et
Keene, *Alfred Valentine*	—	1908	S
		1912	St
		1988	E
Kernohan, *Hugh*	2.7.1958	1988	E
Kershaw, *Cecil Ashworth*	3.2.1895–1.11.1972	1920	F/Ft/S/St
		1924	S/St
Leckie, *Alexander Mallace*	25.5.1938	1960	S/St
		1964	F/Ft/S/St
		1968	S/St
Leith, *Lockhart*	—	1908	S
Llewellyn, *John Patrick*	7.8.1957	1980	E/Et
		1984	E/Et
		1988	E
Lloyd, *John Emrys*	8.9.1908	1932	F
		1936	F/Ft/St
		1948	F/Ft/St
		1952	Ft/St
McCready, *Michael David*	23.3.1913	1948	Et
McKenzie, *Donald*	3.8.1960	1988	F/Ft
McKenzie, *R Angus*	13.3.1936	1960	Ft
Mallett, *Neal Pelham*	30.9.1957	1980	Et/F/Ft
		1984	Et
Marsh, *William Walter*	29.3.1877–12.2.1959	1908	S/St
		1912	S/St
		1920	St
		1924	St
Martin, *Alfred Ridley*	9.5.1881–6.5.1970	1912	S/St
		1920	S/St
Martineau, *Sydney*	6.1.1863	1908	E/Et
		1912	E/Et/F
Mather, *Peter*	9.9.1953	1976	S/St
Montgomerie, *Robert Cecil Lindsay*	15.2.1880–24.8.1939	1908	E/Et
		1912	E/Et/F
		1920	E/Et/F/Ft
		1924	Et/F/Ft
		1928	F/Ft
Moore, *GJC*	—	1948	St
Murray, *AC*	—	1908	S/St
Newton Robinson, *Charles Edmund*	14.10.1853–21.4.1913	1906	ET
Notley, *C Barry*	1879	1908	S
		1920	E/Et
		1924	Et
		1928	S/St

William Hoskyns, one of only two Britons to have taken part in six Olympic Games.

COMPETITOR	DATE OF BIRTH-DEATH	YEAR	EVENT/S
Oldcorn, *Richard*	21.2.1938	1964	S/St
		1968	S/St
		1972	S/St
Parfitt, *Ronald*	1913	1948	E/Et
		1952	E/Et
Paul, *Barry Christopher*	10.5.1948	1972	F/Ft
		1976	F/Ft
Paul, *Graham René*	15.5.1947	1968	F/Ft
		1972	E/Et/F/Ft
		1976	F/Ft
Paul, *Raymond Rudolf Valentine*	21.11.1927	1952	F/Ft
		1956	F/Ft/St
Paul, *Ronald René Charles*	20.1.1921	1948	F/Ft
		1952	E/Et/F/Ft
		1956	Et/F/Ft
		1960	Ft
Paul, *Steven*	28.9.1954	1980	E/Et/Ft
		1984	E/Et
Pearce, *A Denison*	8.4.1896	1928	F/Ft
		1936	F/Ft
Pelling, *Albert Edward*	1903	1936	Et
		1948	E/Et
Pelling, *John Albert*	25.5.1936	1960	E/Et
		1964	Et
Pilbrow, *Arthur Gordon*	18.5.1902	1936	St
		1948	S/St
Porebski, *Olgierd Boleslaw Richard*	6.9.1922	1952	S/St
		1956	S/St
Power, *Anthony*	13.5.1945	1976	Ft
Seccombe-Hett, *GVA see* Hett			
Seligman, *Edgar Isaac*	14.4.1867–27.9.1958	1906	E/Et/F
		1908	E/Et
		1912	E/Et/F
		1920	Et/F/Ft
		1924	F/Ft/S
Sherriff, *Frederick George*	8.3.1899–31.1.1943	1924	F/Ft
		1928	Ft
Simey, *Cyril Stillingfleet Aylmer*	–18.9.1952	1928	Ft
Single, *Ian*	7.4.1947	1972	Ft
Slade, *Mark Gainsford*	2.8.1958	1980	S
		1988	S
Smith, *AR*	—	1948	F/Ft
Stanbury, *Johnathan*	8.3.1951	1984	E/Et
Startin, *EC*	—	1920	S/St
Strauss, *Michael G*	16.5.1929	1960	St
Stringer, *DD*	—	1960	St
Syson, *Alfred Edward*	—	1912	St
Tredgold, *Roger Francis*	23.10.1911–24.12.1975	1936	Ft/St
		1948	S/St
		1952	St
Trinder, *Oliver Geoffrey*	1907	1936	S/St
Turquet, *Pierre Maurice*	—	1948	Ft
Vander Byl, *Charles Fennelly*	5.4.1874	1912	Et/St
Wand-Tetley, *Thomas Harrison*	26.2.1898–4.2.1956	1920	F
(Also see *Modern Pentathlon*)		1928	F/Ft
Wendon, *Ulrich Luke*	17.4.1926	1948	Ft
		1952	F/Ft/St
		1956	St
Willoughby, *Richard Moffatt Perowne*	6.9.1870–15.2.1954	1920	E/F/Ft
		1924	Ft
Wilson, *CA*	—	1908	S/St
Zarno, *John*	27.9.1950	1984	St

Fencing
WOMEN

Fencing for women was introduced into the Olympics in 1924 and has been on the programme regularly since then. Great Britain has competed on every occasion. Women compete only in the foil at the Olympics and a team event was introduced in 1960.

COMPETITOR	DATE OF BIRTH-DEATH	YEAR	EVENT/S
Agar, *Wendy Caroline*	2.7.1953	1976	F/Ft
Arbuthnot, *Elizabeth Carnegy*	4.12.1916	1936	F
		1948	F
Bailey, *Jeannette A*	9.4.1931	1960	Ft
Bain, *Judith Margaret*	11.10.1944	1968	F/Ft
Bewley-Cathie, *Janet Clouston*	15.2.1940	1964	F/Ft
(As Wardell-Yerburgh in 1968 & 1972)		1968	F/Ft
		1972	F/Ft
Brannon, *Ann*	10.10.1958	1980	F
		1988	Ft
Buller, *Patricia Moray*	1929	1952	F
Butler, *Maude Margaret*	—	1928	F
		1932	F
Cawthorne, *Hilary Fredericke*	31.12.1951	1976	Ft
		1980	Ft
Daniell, *Gladys*	1884	1924	F
		1928	F
Davies, *Eva Nancy*	—	1968	Ft
Davies, *Gladys Muriel*	1893	1924	F
Davis, *Julia Marion*	25.2.1941	1968	Ft
Freeman, *Muriel B*	1897	1924	F
		1928	F
Glen Haig, *Mary Alison*	18.7.1918	1948	F
		1952	F
		1956	F
		1960	F/Ft
Grant, *Wendy*	2.7.1953	1980	F
Green, *Susan*	26.6.1950	1968	F/Ft
		1972	F/Ft
		1976	Ft
Guinness, *Heather Seymour 'Judy'*	14.8.1910	1932	F
(As Penn-Hughes in 1936)		1936	F
Halsted, *C see* Henley			
Henley, *Clare*	18.8.1948	1972	F/Ft
(As Halsted in 1976)		1976	F/Ft
Littlejohns, *Sally Anne*	20.8.1948	1972	Ft
McIntosh, *Fiona*	24.6.1960	1984	F
		1988	F/Ft
Martin, *Linda Ann*	12.6.1954	1980	Ft
		1984	F/Ft
		1988	F/Ft
Minton, *Gytte*	—	1948	F
Netherway, *Shirley A*	19.5.1937	1960	Ft
		1964	F/Ft
Offredy, *Thoresa Mary*	4.5.1930	1964	Ft
Penn-Hughes, *HS see* Guinness			
Sheen, *Gillian Mary*	21.8.1928	1952	F
		1956	F
		1960	F/Ft
Stafford, *ME*	—	1960	F
Strachan, *Linda*	18.10.1961	1988	Ft
Thurley, *Elizabeth*	6.1.1959	1984	F/Ft
		1988	F/Ft
Walker, *Alice B*	—	1924	F
Wardell-Yerburgh, *JC see* Bewley-Cathie			
Watts-Tobin, *Mary Ann Elizabeth Blake*	21.12.1939	1964	F/Ft
Wrigglesworth, *Susan Jane*	16.9.1954	1972	Ft
		1976	F/Ft
		1980	F/Ft

Olympic Golf

Golf was an Olympic sport in 1900 and 1904 and Great Britain was only represented on the first occasion, when at the Compiegne Golf Club, Paris, the British players were Walter Rutherford of Jedbergh GC, David Robertson and William Dove, both of Northwood GC, and George Thorne of Weston-super-Mare GC.

Rutherford finished second, one stroke behind the American Charles Sands, and in third place was the versatile David Robertson, who in addition to his Olympic medal was capped for Scotland at rugby and golf and won a Cambridge blue for rugby, golf and hockey.

Both individual and team competitions were scheduled for the 1908 Games, with rounds to be played at the Royal St George's and Prince's Clubs at Sandwich and the Cinque Ports Club at Deal, but some correspondence between the British Olympic Council and the Royal & Ancient Golf Club was mislaid and the events were never held. Unfortunately, the news of the cancellation did not reach the Canadian George Lyon, who had won at St Louis in 1904 and had come to England to defend his Olympic title. Lyon was offered the gold medal by default but he declined.

Golf

Golf was an Olympic sport in 1900 and 1904 and Great Britain competed only in 1900, in the 36-hole individual stroke play competition. A golf tournament for women was also held in 1900 but there were no British competitors.

COMPETITOR	DATE OF BIRTH-DEATH
Dove, *William Bathurst*	17.4.1872 – 14.8.1944
Robertson, *David Donaldson*	21.3.1869 – 13.9.1937
Rutherford, *Walter*	—
Thorne, *George*	—

Gymnastics

MEN

Gymnastic competitions, in various forms, have been held at every Olympic Games since 1896. Great Britain has been represented on each occasion, with the exception of 1904, 1932 and 1936.

Some sources indicate that eight British gymnasts competed in 1900 but the names of only two (Broabeck & Connor) have been positively verified.

COMPETITOR	DATE OF BIRTH-DEATH	YEAR EVENT/S
Andrew, *S*	—	1920
Arnold, *Edward Randall*	20.11.1949	1972
Aspinall, *E*	—	1908
Bailey, *G*	—	1908
Baker, *PA*	—	1908
Barrett, *WF*	—	1908
Bartlett, *Terence*	2.12.1963	1984
		1988
Bauscher, *O*	—	1906
		1908
Benyon, *Richard*	30.6.1964	1984
Betts, *Albert Edward*	8.2.1888	1912
		1920
Bonney, *R*	—	1908
Booth, *Michael*	20.1.1946	1968
Broabeck	—	1900
Brown, *H*	1904	1924
Buffin, *Kenneth F*	1.11.1923	1948
		1952
		1960
Catley, *JH*	—	1908
Clay, *M*	—	1908
Clough, *E*	—	1908
Cocksedge, *AE*	—	1920
Cook, *J*	—	1908
Connor, *—*	—	1900
Cooper, *RS*	–3.1918	1906
(Also see *Swimming*)		
Cotterell, *J*	—	1908
		1920

COMPETITOR	DATE OF BIRTH-DEATH	YEAR EVENT/S
Cowhig, *William*	5.4.1887	1912
		1920
Cowy, *W*	—	1908
Cronin, *W*	—	1928
Cross, *Sydney*	5.1.1891	1912
		1920
Cullen, *GC*	—	1908
Davis, *Jeffrey*	31.3.1954	1976
Dawswell, *HS*	—	1920
Denby, *F*	—	1908
Dick, *FB*	—	1908
Dickason, *Harold*	16.4.1890	1912
Dingley, *JE*	—	1920
Domville, *S*	—	1908
		1920
Doncaster, *HW*	—	1920
Drury, *Herbert James*	5.1.1883 – 11.7.1936	1908
		1912
Dyson, *E*	—	1908
Edgecombe, *RE*	—	1920
Edwards, *W*	—	1920
Elliot, *Launceston*	9.6.1874 – 8.8.1930	1896
(Also see *Track & Field,*		
Weightlifting & Wrestling)		
Fergus, *W*	—	1908
Finchett, *Henry John*	1900	1920
		1924
		1928
Fitt, *W*	—	1908
Flaherty, *Jack*	—	1948
Ford, *A*	—	1908
Franklin, *Bernard Wallis*	10.11.1889	1912
		1920
Gill, *H*	—	1908
Gradley, *Richard*	6.3.1932	1960
Graham, *J*	—	1908
Hanley, *R*	—	1908
Hanson, *Leonard*	1887	1908
		1912
Harcourt, *Graham*	16.4.1934	1952
Harley, *AS*	—	1908
Harris, *J*	—	1920
Hawkins, *AE*	—	1908
Hawkins, *FW*	1897	1924
Hoare, *WO*	—	1908
Hodges, *A*	—	1908
Hodgetts, *Samuel*	28.10.1887	1908
		1912
		1920
Hopkins, *G*	—	1948
Hopkins, *T*	1903	1924
Horridge, *JA*	—	1908
Humphreys, *S*	1904	1924
		1928
Huskinson, *HJ*	—	1908
Jones, *JW*	—	1908
Justice, *E*	—	1908
Keighly, *NJ*	—	1908

COMPETITOR	DATE OF BIRTH-DEATH	YEAR EVENT/S
Langley, *Keith*	3.6.1961	1980
		1984
Laycock, *R*	—	1908
Leigh, *E*	1896	1924
Leigh, *Stanley*	1902	1920
		1924
Luck, *Charles James*	19.11.1886	1912
McGaw, *R*	—	1908
MacKune, *William*	6.8.1882	1912
McLean, *Ronald Gordon*	26.3.1881	1912
		1920
McPhail, *J*	—	1908
Manning, *W*	—	1908
Masters, *G*	—	1920
May, *P*	—	1948
Meade, *G*	—	1908
Merrifield, *WG*	—	1908
Messenger, *Alfred William*	4.12.1887	1912
Morris, *Andrew*	30.11.1961	1984
		1988
Morris, *O*	—	1920
Mulhall, *John William*	18.8.1938	1960
		1964
Neale, *Ian G*	11.8.1954	1976
Ness, *EP*	—	1920
Norgrave, *William*	15.4.1947	1972
Oberholzer, *Henry Arthur*	12.4.1893	1912
Oldaker, *CJ*	—	1908
Page, *AE*	—	1920
Pancott, *John Edward*	1.4.1933	1960
		1964
Parkinson, *TB*	—	1928
Parrott, *G*	—	1908
Parsons, *E*	—	1908
Pepper, *Edward Ernest*	12.11.1879	1912
Pinner, *AO*	—	1920
Potts, *Edward William*	12.7.1881	1908
		1912
Potts, *Reginald Hubert*	3.1.1892	1912
Pugh, *F.*	—	1920
Raynes, *GC*	—	1928
Richardson, *EF*	—	1908
Robertson, *J*	—	1908
Ross, *George James*	1.12.1887	1908
		1912
Scott, *D*	—	1908
Simmons, *Charles*	24.12.1885	1912
Simpson, *JF*	—	1908
Skeeles, *WR*	—	1908
Smith, *CH*	—	1908
Southern, *Arthur George Heron*	26.3.1883	1912
Speight, *J*	—	1908
Spencer, *A*	1897	1924
Starling, *O Peter C*	15.8.1925	1952
		1960
Stell, *H*	—	1908
Stuart, *Wray 'Nik'*	20.7.1927	1956
		1960
Suderman, *CV*	—	1908
Taylor, *HW*	—	1920
Titt, *William*	8.2.1881	1908
		1912
Turner, *Frank Conway*	5.11.1922	1948
		1952
		1956
Tysal, *S Walter*	—	1908
Van Hoof, *Edmund*	22.8.1956	1984
Vice, *I*	—	1948
Vigurs, *Charles Alfred*	11.7.1888–3.1917	1908
		1912
Wales, *A*	—	1948
Walker, *JA*	—	1920
Walker, *Samuel John*	5.10.1883	1912
Walters, *JA*	—	1908

COMPETITOR	DATE OF BIRTH-DEATH	YEAR EVENT/S
Walton, *E*	—	1908
		1928
Warren, *EW*	—	1928
Waterman, *H*	—	1908
Watkins, *EA*	—	1908
Watters, *W*	—	1908
Weedon, *G George*	1920	1948
		1952
Whitaker, *John T*	9.4.1886	1908
		1912
Whitehead, *F*	—	1908
Whitford, *Arthur John*	2.7.1908	1928
Whitford, *John A*	1924	1952
Wild, *Stanley*	19.2.1944	1968
		1972
Wilson, *Thomas*	17.8.1953	1976
		1980
Winch, *Barry*	17.4.1958	1980
		1984
Zandell, *RH*	—	1920

Gymnastics

WOMEN

Gymnastics for women was introduced into the Olympics in 1928. It was not on the programme in 1932 but was reinstated in 1936 and has been held regularly since then. Great Britain has been represented on every occasion.

In 1928, 1936 and 1948 there was only a team competition but from 1952 onwards separate individual and team competitions have been held.

COMPETITOR	DATE OF BIRTH-DEATH	YEAR EVENT/S
Airey, *Joan W*	—	1948
Alred, *Barbara*	31.10.1953	1972
Bell, *CM* see Hanson		
Bell, *Margaret Ann*	23.2.1945	1968
Black, *Lisa*	3.6.1967	1988
Blake, *Doris*	2.11.1911	1936
Broadbent, *Annie*	—	1928
Carter, *Marjorie*	10.5.1934	1960
Cheeseborough, *Susan*	9.9.1959	1976
		1980
Crowe, *Brenda*	31.7.1913	1936
Dando, *Suzanne*	3.7.1961	1980
Davies, *Cissie*	1.12.1932	1948
		1952
Davies, *Natalie*	1.12.1966	1984
Desmond, *Lucy*	17.4.1889	1928
Evans, *PB*	—	1948
Goddard, *Denise Elizabeth*	20.4.1945	1964
Gross, *Edna*	12.12.1910	1936
Hanson, *Clarice M*	23.3.1911	1936
(As Bell in 1948)		1948
Hargate, *Karen*	14.10.1972	1988
Harrison, *Amanda*	6.6.1965	1984
Hartley, *Margaret B*	—	1928
Heaton, *Mary*	24.2.1911	1936
Hey, *Dorothy*	—	1948
		1952
Hirst, *Irene*	11.7.1930	1948
		1952
Hirst, *Mary Patricia*	18.11.1918	1948
		1952
		1956
Hopkins, *Pamela Jean*	18.9.1953	1972
Hutchinson, *Pamela Ruth*	7.12.1953	1972
Jagger, *Amy C*	—	1928
Jones, *Denise*	11.12.1962	1980
Judd, *Isabel MR 'Queenie'*	—	1928
Kelly, *Mary*	30.5.1907	1936
Kennedy, *Karen*	4.12.1966	1988

COMPETITOR	DATE OF BIRTH-DEATH	YEAR EVENT/S
Kite, *Jessie T*	—	1928
Larner, *Sally*	1.3.1969	1984
Leavy, *Jacqueline*	21.4.1965	1984
Lennox, *Avril Johnston Clegg*	26.4.1956	1972
		1976
Lewis, *Gwynedd*	28.12.1934	1952
Lingard, *GM*	—	1960
Moreman, *Marjorie*	—	1928
Morgan, *Margaret*	29.12.1929	1952
Mugridge, *Yvonne*	27.4.1953	1972
Mullins, *Valerie*	1935	1952
Neale, *Margaret R*	22.8.1931	1960
Parkinson, *Ann*	30.12.1954	1972
Perks, *Patricia J*	1.5.1940	1960
Pickles, *Edith Carrie*	—	1928
Pollard, *Gillian*	21.7.1935	1960
Prestidge, *Mary*	18.12.1948	1968
Price, *Hayley*	14.3.1966	1984
Priest, *Lorraine*	5.6.1966	1984
Raistrick, *Marjorie*	1934	1952
Rennard, *Audrey*	—	1948
Ridgewell, *Lilian*	19.10.1912	1936
Rutherford, *M Kathleen*	29.3.1944	1964
Seymour, *Ethel*	1881–13.11.1963	1928
Slater, *Barbara*	10.5.1959	1976
Smith, *Ada*	—	1928
Smith, *Dorothy*	—	1948
Smith, *Hilda*	—	1928
Summers, *Dorothy M*	29.9.1941	1960
Thomas, *Margaret*	1931	1952
Wharton, *Marion*	16.7.1908	1936
Willett, *Elaine*	8.1.1956	1972
Williams, *Kathleen*	16.2.1964	1984
Woods, *Doris*	—	1928
Young, *Lisa*	3.1.1966	1984

Hockey

MEN

Hockey has been played at every Olympics since 1908, with the exception of 1912. In 1908, four separate teams from the home countries competed and the players have been identified by the appropriate initial: i.e. (E)ngland, (I)reland, (S)cotland and (W)ales. A team from England again competed in 1920 and a British team next took part in 1948 when a combined team from Great Britain competed.

From 1948 onwards, Great Britain entered each tournament but were eliminated in the qualifying round in 1976 and 1984 and in 1980 they chose to boycott the Moscow Games. A boycott also influenced Britain's participation in the 1984 Games when, after failing to qualify, they were eventually called on to play in the finals following the withdrawal of the Soviet Union for political reasons.

Players in the pre-Olympic qualifying rounds have not been listed.

COMPETITOR	DATE OF BIRTH-DEATH	YEAR EVENT/S
Adlard, *Robert E*	—	1948
Ahmad, *Sheikh Mahmood*	25.6.1942	1972
Allman-Smith, *Edward Percival*	—	1908(I)
Archer, *David Douglas*	16.4.1928	1956
Atkin, *Charles Sydney*	26.2.1889–9.5.1958	1920
Austen, *Patrick B*	18.3.1933	1960
Baillon, *Louis Charles*	5.8.1881–2.9.1965	1908(E)
Barber, *Paul Jason*	21.5.1955	1984
		1988
Barham, *Jeremy Gavin*	27.2.1941	1968
Batchelor, *Stephen James*	22.6.1961	1984
		1988
Bell, *John H*	26.2.1933	1960
Bennett, *John Hadfield*	11.8.1885–27.5.1973	1920
Bhaura, *Kulbir Singh*	15.10.1955	1984
		1988

COMPETITOR	DATE OF BIRTH-DEATH	YEAR EVENT/S
Borrett, *Norman Francis*	1.10.1917	1948
Brodie, *David LS*	—	1948
Brown, *Henry Joseph*	—	1908(I)
Burt, *Alexander Baird*	9.4.1884	1908(S)
Burt, *John*	—	1908(S)
Cadman, *John Frank*	27.3.1934	1964
Cahill, *Harold Alexander*	9.6.1930	1960
		1964
		1968
Campbell, *Walter Islay Hamilton*	14.10.1886	1908(I)
Carnill, *Denys John*	11.3.1926	1952
		1956
		1960
Carr, *Gerald Duncan*	13.6.1938	1968
Cassels, *Harold Kennedy*	4.11.1898–23.1.1975	1920
Cattrall, *Robert L*	1957	1984
Christenson, *Basil*	9.7.1938	1968
Clift, *Robert John*	1.8.1962	1988
Cockett, *John Ashley*	27.12.1927	1952
		1956
Connah, *F*	1895	1908(W)
Conroy, *John Valentine*	27.11.1928–9.11.1985	1952
		1956
Cooke, *Harold Douglas*	—	1920
Corby, *Michael Wells*	18.2.1940	1964
		1972
Cotton, *Bernard James*	30.6.1948	1972
Crockford, *Eric Bertram*	13.10.1888–17.1.1958	1920
Croft, *Peter D*	7.7.1933	1960
Crowe, *Michael John Brook*	14.8.1942	1972
Crummack, *Reginald William*	16.2.1887–25.10.1966	1920
Cutter, *Geoffrey Michael*	1.10.1934	1956
		1964
Dadds, *Graham Bassett*	16.3.1911	1952
Dale, *Colin Henry*	29.6.1931	1956
Davies, *Ronald*	1915–24.10.1989	1948
Davis, *Francis Howard Vincent*	24.9.1932	1956
		1960
		1964
Day, *Derek Malcolm*	29.11.1927	1952
Deegan, *James Frederick Alexander*	6.11.1933	1964
		1968
Dennistoun, *Andrew G*	—	1908(S)
Dodds, *Richard David Allan*	23.2.1959	1984
		1988
Donald, *Charles Buchan*	22.7.1939	1968
Doughty, *Michael Owen Harry*	29.4.1932	1956
Duthie, *James Livingstone*	27.10.1957	1984
Eagan, *Dennis Michael Royal*	13.8.1926	1952
Ekins, *Anthony Howard*	4.1.1944	1968
		1972
Evans, *Graham John*	3.5.1945	1972
Evans, *Llewellyn*	–16.12.1963	1908(W)
Faulkner, *David Andrew Vincent*	10.9.1963	1988
Fishwick, *Paul Darrell*	24.8.1936	1964
Fletcher, *Robin Anthony*	30.5.1922	1952
Flood, *Roger Newton*	15.8.1939	1968
Forster, *Neil Millward*	29.5.1927	1956
Foulkes, *Charles Howard*	1.12.1875–6.5.1969	1908(S)
Fraser, *Hew Thomson*	—	1908(S)
Freeman, *Harry Scott*	7.2.1876–5.10.1968	1908(E)
French, *John Colin*	26.7.1946	1972
Garcia, *Russell Simon*	20.6.1970	1988
Graham, *William Ernest*	1874	1908(I)
Green, *Eric Hubert*	28.8.1878–23.12.1972	1908(E)
Gregg, *Richard George Stanley*	—	1908(I)
Gregg, *Terence Adrian*	23.11.1950	1972
Griffiths, *William S*	—	1948
Grimley, *Martyn Andrew*	24.1.1963	1988
Harper-Orr, *James*	18.10.1878	1908(S)
Haslam, *Harry Eustace*	7.2.1883–7.2.1955	1920
Hay, *Dennis*	5.10.1940	1972
Hindle, *John A*	20.11.1934	1960
		1964
Holmes, *EPC*	—	1908(I)
Hughes, *Norman*	30.9.1952	1984

COMPETITOR	DATE OF BIRTH-DEATH	YEAR EVENT/S
Johnson, *Steven Henry*	26.1.1929	1956
Jones, *Charles Ian McMillan*	10.11.1934	1960
		1964
Judge, *Harold David*	19.1.1936	1964
Kennedy, *Robert L*	—	1908(I)
Kerly, *Sean Robin*	29.1.1960	1984
		1988
Kirkwood, *James W*	12.2.1962	1988
Laing, *Iain*	—	1908(S)
Land, *John James*	17.7.1938	1964
Langhorne, *Christopher John*	18.9.1940	1964
		1972
Law, *AA*	—	1908(W)
Lawson, *Timothy Maben*	24.11.1940	1968
Leighton, *Arthur Francis*	6.3.1889–15.6.1939	1920
Leman, *Richard Alexander*	13.7.1959	1984
		1988
Lindsay, *F Robin*	11.1.1914	1948
Lindsay, *William LC*	—	1948
Livingstone, *W Neil*	4.6.1938	1960
Logan, *Gerald*	29.12.1879	1908(E)
Lyne, *R*	—	1908(W)
McBryan, *John Crawford William*	22.7.1892–14.7.1983	1920
McConnell, *Willam DR*	19.4.1956	1984
McGrath, *George F*	—	1920
Marcon, *Charles Sholto Wyndham*	31.3.1890–17.11.1959	1920
Marsh, *Peter Richard James*	12.5.1951	1972
Martin, *Stephen A*	13.4.1959	1984
		1988
Mayes, *Stuart David*	6.3.1937	1960
Midgley, *Roger Keith*	23.11.1924	1952
Miller, *Derek Robert*	14.2.1936	1960
		1964
Morris, *James Stewart Millner*	7.12.1940	1968
Mills, *Peter Aubrey*	25.8.1945	1972
Murphy, *Henry Lawson*	12.12.1883	1908(I)
Neill, *John Whitley*	15.5.1934	1960
		1964
		1968
Neilson, *Hugh EB*	—	1908(S)
Noble, *Alan H*	—	1908(E)
Norris, *Richard Owen Alfred*	10.12.1931	1952
Nugent, *Neil Algernon D*	6.12.1936	1952
Nunn, *Anthony Stuart*	24.5.1927	1952
Oliver, *Richard Michael*	25.9.1944	1968
		1972
Orchardson, *William GJ*	—	1908(S)
Page, *Alan Graham*	28.5.1937	1964
Page, *Edgar Wells*	31.12.1884–12.5.1956	1908(E)
Pallott, *WJ*	—	1908(W)
Pappin, *Veryan Guy Henry*	19.5.1958	1984
		1988
Peake, *John Morris*	26.8.1924	1948
Peterson *Walter E*	—	1908(I)
Phillips, *Frederick Gordon*	13.3.1884	1908(W)
Potter, *Johnathan Nicholas Mark*	19.11.1963	1984
		1988
Power, *CF*	—	1908(I)
Precious, *Mark*	29.8.1956	1984
Pridmore, *Reginald George*	29.4.1886–13.3.1918	1908(E)
Read, *Malcolm Trevor Fitzwalter*	8.3.1941	1968
Rees, *Percy Montague*	27.9.1883–12.6.1970	1908(E)
Reynolds, *Frank O*	21.8.1917	1948
Richards, *EWG*	—	1908(W)
Robinson, *Anthony John Backhouse*	22.7.1925–24.7.1982	1952
		1956
Robinson, *Frank L*	—	1908(I)
Robinson, *John Yate*	6.8.1885–23.8.1916	1908(E)
Saldanha, *Ninnian Rui*	21.10.1947	1972
Saunders-Griffiths, *Christopher John D*	10.1.1929	1960
Savage, *David Austin*	15.2.1940	1972
Scott, *Frederick Hugh*	29.11.1932	1956
		1960
Scott-Freeman, *H see Freeman*		
Shephard, *CW*	—	1908(W)

COMPETITOR	DATE OF BIRTH-DEATH	YEAR EVENT/S
Sherwani, *Imran Ahmed Khan*	9.4.1962	1988
Shoveller, *Stanley Howard*	2.9.1881–24.2.1959	1908(E)
		1920
Sime, *George B*	—	1948
Sinclair, *Keith*	26.6.1945	1968
		1972
Smith, *William Faulder*	14.11.1886–3.3.1937	1920
Stevenson, *Norman Lang*	—	1908(S)
Strover, *John Anthony*	2.2.1931	1956
Sutton, *Roger Macklin*	20.12.1936	1964
Svehlik, *Paul Joseph Thomas*	15.4.1947	1972
Taylor, *Ian Charles Boucher*	24.9.1954	1984
		1988
Taylor, *Ian David*	18.4.1938	1960
Taylor, *John Paskin*	18.3.1928	1952
Thomas, *David Frederick Colman*	27.6.1927	1956
Trentham, *Andrew Bruce*	21.12.1946	1968
Turnbull, *W Bruce*	4.11.1880	1908(W)
Turnbull, *PB*	—	1908(W)
Veit, *David Michael*	21.10.1938	1964
Walford, *Michael Moore*	27.11.1915	1948
Walker, *Hugh Stewart*	—	1908(S)
Westcott, *David Guy*	14.5.1957	1984
Whalley, *Colin James Campbell*	8.3.1941	1968
White, *William Neil*	2.5.1920–1990	1948
Wilkinson *Cyril Theodore Anstruther*	4.10.1884–16.12.1970	1920
Williams, *James Ralph*	28.7.1878	1908(W)
Wilman, *David*	19.12.1934	1964
		1968
Wilson, *Peter James*	9.8.1942	1968
Wood, *Harvey Jesse*	10.4.1885	1908(E)

There are various different versions of the composition of the England teams for their two Olympic matches in 1920. *The Times* reported that for the match against Belgium CH Campbell, HK Cassells and JCW McBryan replaced CS Atkin, HD Cooke and GF McGrath who had played in the opening match against Denmark. However, the Belgian newspaper, *Le Matin*, reported an unchanged team for both matches, the players being: Haslam, Bennett, Atkin, Wilkinson, Crockford, Cooke, Leighton, Marcon, Shoveller, McGrath and Smith.

Although CH Campbell is mentioned by *The Times* he does not appear in the team photograph and it seems unlikely that he went to Antwerp. Campbell has not, therefore, been listed as a competitor but as both HK Cassells and JCW McBryan appear in the team photograph it has been assumed that they played in one of the two matches and have been listed above.

Hockey

WOMEN

Women's hockey was introduced into the Olympics in 1980. Britain did not qualify in 1984 and first took part in the finals in 1988.

COMPETITOR	DATE OF BIRTH-DEATH
Atkins, *Jillian*	30.5.1963
Banks, *Wendy*	27.2.1960
Brewer, *Caroline*	21.12.1962
Brown, *Gillian*	26.2.1965
Brow, *Karen*	9.1.1963
Cook, *Julie*	8.3.1954
Dixon, *Victoria*	5.8.1959
Fraser, *Wendy*	23.4.1963
Hambly, *Barbara*	12.3.1958
Jordan, *Caroline*	2.8.1964
McBride, *Violet*	16.10.1954
Macleod, *Moira*	16.10.1957
Nevill, *Mary*	12.3.1961
Parker, *Kate*	9.9.1963
Ramsey, *Alison*	16.4.1959
Sixsmith, *Jane*	5.9.1967

Judo

Judo first became an Olympic sport in 1964 and although it was not included at the 1968 Games it has been held regularly since 1972. Great Britain has been represented on every occasion.

B = Bantamweight   F = Featherweight   H = Heavyweight
HH = Half-heavyweight   HL = Half-lightweight
HM = Half-middleweight   L = Lightweight
LH = Light-heavyweight   LM = Light-middleweight
M = Middleweight   O = Open/Unlimited   W = Welterweight
XL = Extra lightweight

COMPETITOR	DATE OF BIRTH-DEATH	YEAR	EVENT/S
Adams, *Adrian Neil*	27.9.1958	1980	L
		1984	HM
		1988	HM
Adshead, *Mark*	4.4.1963	1988	HL
Alexander, *Constantine*	8.4.1950	1976	L
Bowles, *Christopher*	19.9.1957	1980	LM
Brown *Kerrith*	11.7.1962	1984	L
		1988	ML
Chittenden, *Mark*	12.7.1956	1980	L
Donnelly, *Peter*	3.12.1951	1980	M
Eckersley, *Neil*	5.4.1964	1984	XL
		1988	XL
Gawthorp, *Stephen*	4.7.1958	1984	HL
Gordon, *Elvis*	23.6.1958	1984	H
		1988	H
Hoare, *Sydney Reginald*	18.7.1939	1964	M
Holliday, *John*	10.11.1960	1980	B
Jacks, *Brian Albert Thomas*	5.10.1946	1964	L
		1972	M
		1976	M
Kokotaylo, *Nicholas*	9.3.1955	1984	HH
Mapp, *Arthur*	6.11.1953	1980	P
Morrison, *Vacinuff*	19.5.1952	1976	LM
Mullen, *Edward*	22.6.1949	1972	L
Neenan, *Raymond*	7.9.1952	1980	F
Parisi, *Angelo*	1.1.1953	1972	O
(Also competed for France in 1980 & 1984)			
Petherbridge, *David Alan*	9.10.1927	1964	U
Radburn, *Paul*	23.5.1955	1980	H
		1984	O
Remfry, *Keith*	17.11.1947	1972	H
		1976	H/O
Starbrook, *David Colin*	9.8.1945	1972	LH
		1976	LH
Stewart, *Dennis*	12.5.1960	1988	HH
Sullivan, *Robert*	18.6.1949	1972	W
Sweeney, *Anthony John*	20.5.1938	1964	H
White, *Densign*	21.12.1961	1984	M
		1988	M

Lacrosse

Lacrosse was an official Olympic sport only in 1908 although it was held as a demonstration event in 1928, 1932 and 1948.

COMPETITOR	DATE OF BIRTH-DEATH	YEAR EVENT/S
Alexander, *Gustav Bernard*	20.9.1881	1908
Buckland, *George Frederick*	13.4.1884–4.1937	1908
Dutton, *EO*	—	1908
Hayes, *SN*	—	1908
Johnson, *Wilfrid Alexander*	15.10.1885–21.6.1960	1908
Jones, *Edward Percy*	1880–17.11.1951	1908
Martin, *RGW*	—	1908
Mason, *G*	—	1908
Parker-Smith, *J*	—	1908
Ramsey, *HW*	—	1908
Scott, *Charles Hubert*	1883–7.11.1954	1908
Whitley, *Norman Henry Pownall*	29.6.1883–12.4.1957	1908

The British lacrosse team which won the silver medals in 1908. Back row, left to right: A Norris (Referee), RG Martin, J Parker Smith, GH Buckland, E Dutton, G Alexander. Middle: CH Scott, ET Jones, HW Ramsey (captain), G Mason, NHP Whitley. Front: S Hayes, WA Johnson.

Lawn Tennis
MEN

Lawn Tennis was held at every Olympic Games from 1896 to 1924 and was re-introduced as an Olympic sport in 1988 by which time the word 'Lawn' had been dropped and the game was universally known simply as 'Tennis'. Great Britain were not represented in 1904 and 1906 or in the outdoor events in 1912 which coincided with the Wimbledon championships.

Indoor events were held in 1908 and 1912.

S = Singles   D = Doubles   MC = Mixed Doubles   (I) = Indoor event

COMPETITOR	DATE OF BIRTH-DEATH	YEAR	EVENT/S
Barrett, *Herbert Roper*	24.11.1873–27.7.1943	1908	D(I)
		1912	S(I)/D(I)/MD(I)
Bates, *Michael Jeremy*	12.9.1962	1988	S/D
Beamish, *Alfred Ernest*	6.8.1879–28.2.1944	1912	S(I)/D(I)
		1920	S/D/MD
Boland, *John Mary Pius*	16.9.1870–17.3.1958	1896	S/D
Caridia, *George Aristedes*	20.2.1869	1908	S/S(I)/D(I)
		1912	S(I)/D(I)
Castle, *Andrew*	15.11.1963	1988	S/D
Cazalet, *Clement Haughton Langston*	16.7.1869–25.3.1950	1908	D
Crawley, *Walter Cecil*	29.3.1880	1908	S/D
Dixon, *Charles Percy*	7.2.1873–29.4.1939	1908	S/D
		1912	S(I)/D(I)/MD(I)
Doherty, *Hugh Laurence*	8.10.1875–21.8.1919	1900	S/D/MD

COMPETITOR	DATE OF BIRTH-DEATH	YEAR	EVENT/S
Doherty, *Reginald Frank*	14.10.1872–29.12.1910	1900	S/D/MD
		1908	D
Eaves, *Wilberforce Vaughan*	10.12.1867–12.2.1920	1908	S/S(I)/D(I)
Escombe, *Lionel Hunter*	1875–15.10.1914	1908	S(I)/D(I)
Gilbert, *John Brian*	17.7.1887–28.6.1974	1924	S/MD
Godfree, *Leslie Allison*	27.4.1885–17.11.1971	1924	D/MD
Gore, *Arthur William (Wentworth)*	2.1.1868–1.12.1928	1908	S(I)/D(I)
Charles		1912	D(I)
Hillyard, *George Whiteside*	6.2.1864–24.3.1943	1908	D/D(I)
Kingscote, *Algernon Robert*	3.12.1888–21.12.1964	1924	S/D
Fitzhardinge			
Lippman, *A*	—	1900	S
Lowe, *Arthur Holden*	29.1.1886–22.10.1958	1912	S(I)/D(I)
Lowe, *Francis Gordon*	21.6.1884–17.5.1972	1912	S(I)/D(I)
		1920	S/D/MD
Mahoney, *Harold Segerson*	13.2.1867–27.6.1905	1900	S/D/MD
Marshall, *F*	—	1896	D
Marshall, *George*	—	1896	S/D
(Also see *Track & Field*)			
Mavrogordato, *Theodore Michel*	31.7.1883–29.8.1941	1912	S(I)/D(I)/
			MD(I)
Norris, *ABJ*	—	1900	S/D
Parke, *James Cecil*	26.7.1881–27.2.1946	1908	S/D
Powell, *Kenneth*	8.4.1885–18.2.1915	1908	S/D
(Also see *Track & Field*)			
Ritchie, *Major Josiah George*	18.10.1870–28.2.1955	1908	S/D/S(I)/
			D(I)
Robertson, *George Stuart*	25.5.1872–29.1.1967	1896	S/D
(Also see *Track & Field*)			
Simond, *George Mieville*	23.1.1867	1908	D(I)
Turnbull, *Oswald Graham Noel*	23.12.1890–17.12.1970	1920	S/D/MD
Warden, *Archibald Adam*	11.5.1869–17.10.1943	1900	S/D/MD
Wheatley, *John David Patrick*	1.1.1899–5.12.1967	1924	S/D
Woosnam, *Maxwell*	6.9.1892–14.7.1965	1920	S/D/MD
		1924	S/D

Lawn Tennis
WOMEN

In 1900, lawn tennis became the first sport in which women competed at the Olympic Games and thereafter the women's programme ran parallel to that of the men. British women did not compete in 1904 and 1906 or in the outdoor events in 1912

COMPETITOR	DATE OF BIRTH-DEATH	YEAR	EVENT/S
Aitchison, *Francis Helen*	1881	1912	S(I)/
			MD(I)
Beamish, *Winifred Geraldine*	23.6.1885–10.5.1972	1920	S/D/MD
Boothby, *Penelope Dora Harvey*	2.8.1881–22.2.1970	1908	S/S(I)
Coles, *Mildred*	—	1908	S(I)
Colyer, *Evelyn Lucy*	16.8.1902–4.11.1930	1924	D
Cooper *Charlotte Reinagle*	22.9.1870–10.10.1966	1900	S/MD
Covell, *Phyllis Lindrea*	22.5.1895–28.10.1982	1924	S/D/MD
Eastlake-Smith, *Gladys Shirley*	14.8.1883–18.9.1941	1908	S(I)
Gomer, *Sara*	13.5.1964	1988	S/D
Greene, *Alice Nora G*	1879	1908	S/S(I)
Hannam, *Edith Margaret*	28.11.1878–16.1.1951	1912	S(I)/
			MD(I)
Holman, *Edith Dorothy*	18.7.1883	1920	S/D/MD
Lambert Chambers, *Dorothea*	3.9.1878–7.1.1960	1908	S
Katharine			
McKane, *Kathleen*	7.5.1896	1920	S/D/MD
		1924	S/D/MD
McNair, *Winifred Margaret*	9.8.1877–28.3.1954	1920	D/MD
Morton, *Agnes Mary 'Agatha'*	6.3.1872–5.4.1952	1908	S
Parton, *Mabel Bramwell*	22.7.1881	1912	S(I)/
			MD(I)
Pinckney, *Violet M*	—	1908	S(I)
Satterthwaite, *Phyllis Helen*	26.1.1889–20.1.1962	1924	S
Shepherd-Barron, *Dorothy Cunliffe*	24.11.1897–20.2.1953	1924	S/D

COMPETITOR	DATE OF BIRTH-DEATH	YEAR	EVENT/S
Winch, *Ruth Joan*	—	1908	S
Wood, *Clare*	8.3.1968	1988	S/D

Modern Pentathlon

The Modern Pentathlon was introduced into the Olympic programme in 1912 and has been held regularly since that date. In 1952 a team event was introduced with the performances of the competitors being combined to decide the team scores. Hence, since 1952 all pentathletes have competed in both the individual and the team event. Great Britain has been represented on every occasion.

COMPETITOR	DATE OF BIRTH-DEATH	YEAR	EVENT/S
Barlow, *Vernon William*	5.11.1909	1932	
Barton, *Frederick Bertram*	19.6.1900	1924	
Boustead, *John Edmund Hugh*	14.4.1895–3.4.1980	1920	
Brooke, *Geoffrey AG*	—	1948	
Brookhouse, *Graham*	19.6.1962	1988	
Clarke, *Edward George Herris*	—	1920	
Clarke, *Nigel*	25.3.1956	1980	
Clilverd, *Ralph Egerton*	30.7.1887	1912	
Cobley, *Donald*	17.10.1928	1956	
		1960	
Durant, *Hugh*	23.2.1887	1912	
(Also see *Shooting*)			
East, *Lancelot Crofts*	22.5.1908	1928	
Finnis, *Fortescue Benjamin*	8.7.1937	1964	
Fox, *Jeremy Robert*	19.9.1941	1964	
		1968	
		1972	
		1976	
Gedge, *EG*	—	1920	
Godfree, *Douglas William*	16.10.1881–5.8.1929	1912	
(Also see *Fencing*)			
Goodwin, *Alfred Allan*	16.12.1902	1928	
Hart, *Peter*	20.8.1960	1988	
Harvey, *Patrick John*	28.11.1935	1960	
Hewitt, *John Alfred*	6.1.1925	1952	
Hudson, *Thomas*	15.12.1935	1956	
Horrocks, *Brian Gwynne*	7.9.1895–4.1.1985	1924	
Jack, *Archibald Frank Maclean*	21.7.1903	1936	
Legard, *Charles Percy Digby*	17.6.1906	1932	
(Also see *Nordic Skiing*)		1936	
Lillywhite, *Barry*	4.5.1946	1968	
		1972	
Little, *Peter Clince*	26.12.1933	1960	
Lumsdaine, *Leon Sydney*	31.1.1923	1952	
Lumsden, *Jack Michael G*	—	1948	
MacDougall, *Jeffrey A*	16.9.1911	1932	
		1936	
Mahoney, *Dominic JM*	26.4.1964	1988	
Martin, *AC*	—	1948	
Mumford, *Micheal*	16.12.1955	1984	
Nightingale, *Robert Daniel*	21.5.1954	1976	
		1980	
Norman, *George Richard*	17.6.1927	1956	
Parker, *Adrian Philip*	2.3.1951	1976	
Percy, *Jervis Joscelyn*	21.7.1928	1952	
Phelps, *Richard Lawson*	19.4.1961	1984	
		1988	
Phelps, *Robert*	22.7.1939	1964	
		1968	
Sowerby, *Stephen*	14.3.1955	1984	
Turquand-Young, *David*	1904	1924	
		1928	
Vokins, *George Louis*	3.8.1896	1924	
Wand-Tetley, *Thomas Harrison*	26.2.1890–4.2.1956	1920	
(Also see *Fencing*)			
Whiteside, *Peter*	23.6.1952	1980	

Motor Boating

MEN

Motor Boating was an Olympic sport in 1908 only.

B = Class 'B'   C = Class 'C'   O = Open class   (G) = Gyrinus
(Q) = Quicksilver   (S) = Seadog   (W) = Wolesley Siddeley

COMPETITOR	DATE OF BIRTH-DEATH	YEAR EVENT/S
Atkinson, *GH*	—	1908 O(W)
Clowes, *Winchester St George*	4.10.1879	1908 O(W)
Field-Richards, *John Charles*	10.5.1878–18.4.1959	1908 O(G)
Gorham, *John Marshall*	1853–12.1.1929	1908 B(Q)
Laycock, *Joseph Frederick*	12.6.1867–5.11.1952	1908 O(W)
Redwood, *Bernard Boverton*	21.11.1874–28.9.1911	1908 B/C(G)
Thornycroft, *Isaac Thomas*	22.11.1881–6.6.1955	1908 B/C(G)
Westminster, *Duke of*	19.3.1879–19.7.1953	1908 O(W)
Wright, *Warwick*	—	1908 C(S)
Wynn Weston, *TD*	—	1908 C(S)

In the second race of the Open class, GH Atkinson replaced JF Laycock as a crew member on the Duke of Westminster's boat.

Motor Boating

WOMEN

COMPETITOR	DATE OF BIRTH-DEATH	YEAR EVENTS
Gorham, *Mrs JM*		1908 B(Q)

Polo

Polo was an Olympic event in 1900, 1908, 1920, 1924 and 1936 and Great Britain competed in every tournament.

Britain entered two teams in 1900 and three teams in 1908; these have been identified as follows:

1900	1 = Foxhunters (Hurlingham)
	2 = Wanderers (Rugby)
1908	3 = Hurlingham
	4 = Ireland
	5 = Roehampton

COMPETITOR	DATE OF BIRTH-DEATH	YEAR EVENT/S
Barrett, *Frederick Whitfield*	20.6.1875–7.11.1949	1920 1924
Beresford, *Hon John George*	10.6.1847–8.2.1925	1900(1)
Bingham, *Hon John Dennis Yelverton*	11.8.1880–28.12.1940	1924
Buckmaster, *Walter Selby*	16.10.1872–30.10.1942	1900(2) 1908(3)
Daly, *Denis St George*	5.9.1862–16.4.1942	1900 (1)
Dawnay, *David*	10.7.1903	1936
Fowler, *Bryan John*	18.8.1898	1936
Freake, *Frederick Charles Maitland*	7.3.1876–12.12.1950	1900(2) 1908(3)
* Gill, *Frederick Agnew*	5.1873–4.6.1938	1900
Guest, *Rt Hon Frederick Edward*	14.6.1875–28.4.1937	1924
Guinness, *Humphrey Patrick*	24.3.1902–10.2.1986	1936
Hinde, *William Robert Norris*	25.6.1900	1936
Jones, *Walter John Henry*	4.6.1866–14.4.1932	1908(3)
Keene, *Foxhall Parker*	18.12.1967–25.9.1941	1900(1)
Lloyd, *John Hardress*	14.8.1874–28.2.1952	1908(4)
Lockett, *Vivian Noverre*	18.7.1880–31.5.1962	1920
McCann, *John Paul*	—	1908(4)
McCreery, *Walter Adolphe*	—	1900(2)
Mackey, *Frank Jay*	—	1908(5)
Madre, *Count Joe de*	—	1908(2)
Melvill, *Teignmoth Philip*	13.2.1877–12.12.1951	1920

COMPETITOR	DATE OF BIRTH-DEATH	YEAR EVENT/S
Miller, *Charles Darley*	23.10.1868–22.12.1951	1908(5)
Miller, *George Arthur*	6.12.1867–21.2.1935	1908(5)
Nickalls, *Patteson Wormesley*	23.1.1876–10.9.1946	1908(5)
O'Reilly, *Percy Philip*	27.7.1870–2.7.1942	1908(4)
Rawlinson, *Alfred*	17.1.1867–1.6.1934	1900(1)
Rotherham, *Auston Morgan*	11.6.1876–24.2.1947	1908(4)
Wilson, *Herbert Haydon*	14.2.1875–11.4.1917	1908(5)
Wise, *Percival Kinnear*	17.4.1885–7.16.1938	1924
Wodehouse, *Lord John*	11.11.1883–16.4.1941	1908(3) 1920

* In 1900, the Englishman FA Gill played for the French team, Bagatelle. FP Keene and FJ Mackey, who played on the winning Foxhunters team in 1900 were Americans.

The Wanderers team in 1900 included the American, WA McCreery, and the Spaniard, Count J de Madre.

Rackets

Rackets was an Olympic sport only in 1908 when all seven competitors were British and each won a medal.

D = Doubles   S = Singles

COMPETITOR	DATE OF BIRTH-DEATH	YEAR EVENT/S
Astor, *John Jacob*	20.5.1886–19.7.1971	1908 S/D
Brougham, *Henry*	8.7.1888–18.2.1923	1908 S
Browning, *Cecil*	29.1.1883–23.3.1953	1908 S/D
Bury, *Edmund William*	4.11.1884–4.12.1915	1908 D
Leaf, *Henry Meredith*	18.10.1862–23.4.1931	1908 S/D
Noel, *Evan Baillie* (Also see *Real Tennis*)	23.1.1879–22.12.1928	1908 S/D
Pennell, *Vane Hungerford* (Also see *Real Tennis*)	16.8.1876–17.6.1938	1908 S/D

Real Tennis

Real Tennis [Jeu de Paume] was an Olympic sport only in 1908. The singles competition drew an entry of eleven players of whom nine were British and two were Americans.

COMPETITOR	DATE OF BIRTH-DEATH	YEAR EVENT/S
Biedermann (later Best), *Edwin Anthony*	5.7.1877	1908
Cazalet, *William Marshall*	8.7.1865–22.10.1932	1908
Lytton, *Hon Neville Stephen*	6.2.1879–9.2.1951	1908
Miles, *Eustace Hamilton*	22.9.1868–20.6.1948	1908
Noel, *Evan Baillie* (Also see *Rackets*)	23.1.1879–22.12.1928	1908
Page, *Arthur*	9.3.1876–1.9.1958	1908
Palmer, *Arthur Nottage*	14.9.1886–27.11.1973	1908
Pennell, *Vane Hungerford* (Also see *Rackets*)	16.8.1876–17.6.1938	1908
Tatham, *Charles Edmund*	5.8.1864–27.2.1925	1908

Appearance Records

The record number of Olympic appearances for Great Britain is 6 by Paul Radmilovic (Swimming & Water Polo) and Bill Hoskyns (Fencing). The women's record of four appearances is shared by six competitors: Isobel White (Diving), Jennifer Loriston-Clarke (Equestrian), Mary Glen-Haig (Fencing), Phylis Harding (Swimming), Dorothy Odam-Tyler (Track & Field) and Tessa Sanderson (Track & Field).

At the Winter Games, Jeremy Palmer-Tomkinson (Alpine Skiing & Luge) and Denys Lloyd (Bobsleigh) share the record with four

appearances and the women's record of three appearances is shared by Davina Galica (Alpine Skiing), Gina Hawthorn (Alpine Skiing) and Ethel Muckelt (Figure Skating).

The record for the longest Olympic career of a British competitor is 32 years and is held by Enoch Jenkins who competed in the clay pigeon shooting events in 1920, 1924 and 1952. This record was threatened by Tom Thornycroft who came close to a career span of 44 years. He won two gold medals for motor boating in 1908 and went to Helsinki in 1952 as

a reserve on the yachting team. Had Thornycroft actually competed in 1952 he would have been able to claim the record for the longest Olympic career by a competitor of any country.

Durward Knowles competed as a yachtsman for Great Britain in 1948 and represented the Bahamas at the the next six Games (1952–72) and again in 1988, a total span of 40 years.

The longest career span by a British woman is 20 years by Dorothy Odam-Tyler who competed in the high jump from 1936 to 1956.

Rowing

MEN

Except for 1896 and 1904, rowing events have been held at every Olympic Games and British oarsmen have competed on each occasion.

In 1908 and 1912, Britain entered two crews for certain events and they have been identified as follows:

1908	Coxless Pairs(I)	Leander Club
	Coxless Pairs(II)	Leander Club
	Coxless Fours(I)	Magdalen College, Oxford
	Coxless Fours(II)	Leander Club
	Eights(I)	Leander Club
	Eights(II)	Cambridge University
1912	Eights(I)	Leander Club
	Eights(II)	New College, Oxford

Other abbreviations used are:

SS = Single Sculls   DS = Double Sculls   2 = Coxless Pairs
2w = Coxed Pairs   4 = Coxless Fours   4w = Coxed Fours
8 = Eights   QS = Quadruple Sculls

COMPETITOR	DATE OF BIRTH-DEATH	YEAR	EVENT/S
Almand, *Alan*	19.3.1943	1972	4w
Almond, *Harry Hudson*	10.4.1928	1952	4
Ashe, *St George*	23.5.1871	1900	SS
Askwith, *Thomas Garrett*	24.5.1911	1932	8
		1936	8
Ayling, *Richard J*	1.6.1952	1976	4
Badcock, *John Charles*	17.1.1903–29.5.1976	1928	8
		1932	4
Baillieu, *Christopher Latham*	12.12.1949	1976	DS
		1980	DS
Bare, *Reginald George*	14.6.1900	1924	8
Barker, *Harold Ross*	12.4.1886	1908	4(II)
Barnsley, *HL*	1905	1924	4w
Barrett, *Alan John*	1912	1936	4
Barry, *William Louis*	16.10.1940	1964	4
Barton, *Christopher Bertram Ronald*	21.11.1927	1948	8
Bate, *Richard Charles Ian*	22.10.1938	1960	8
Bayles, *Andrew Alan*	4.10.1946	1968	8
Beamont, *GW*	—	1928	4w
Beattie, *John M*	9.4.1957	1980	4
		1984	2
		1988	8
Beaumont, *Peter*	2.1.1965	1928	4
Beesly, *Richard*	27.7.1907–28.3.1965	1928	4
Beresford, *Jack Jr*	1.1.1899–3.12.1977	1920	SS
		1924	SS
		1928	8
		1932	4
		1936	DS

COMPETITOR	DATE OF BIRTH-DEATH	YEAR	EVENT/S
Beresford, *John Michael*	23.3.1934	1960	4
Beresford, *Julius*	29.6.1868–29.9.1959	1912	4w
Berrisford, *JN Simon*	29.12.1963	1988	4
Bevan, *Edward Vaughan*	3.11.1907–23.2.1988	1928	4
Bircher, *Ernest Augustus Paul*	11.11.1928	1948	8
Birkmyre, *Nicholas John*	21.2.1937	1960	DS
Bishop, *Thomas JA*	8.4.1947	1976	QS
Blackstaffe, *Henry Thomas*	28.7.1868–22.8.1951	1908	SS
Bland, *John L*	23.8.1958	1984	4
Boardman, *Humphrey Colman*	26.7.1904	1928	DS
Bourne, *Robert Croft*	15.7.1888–7.8.1938	1912	8(II)
Bovington, *VJ*	1903	1924	4w
Boyle, *Richard Frederick Robert Pochin*	10.10.1888–6.2.1953	1908	8(II)
Brandt, *Peter Augustus*	2.7.1931	1952	DS
Bristow, *Thomas Richard Martin*	15.11.1913	1936	4
Buckingham, *Mark AH*	10.11.1964	1988	4
Bucknall, *Henry Cresswell*	4.7.1885–1.1.1962	1908	8(I)
Budgett, *Richard Gordon McBride*	20.3.1959	1984	4w
Burdekin, *Beaufort*	27.12.1891–15.5.1963	1912	8(II)
Burfitt, *Nicholas*	17.12.1966	1988	8
Burgess, *Edgar Richard*	23.9.1891–23.4.1852	1912	8(I)
Burn, *John Southerden*	25.6.1884–28.8.1958	1908	8(II)
Burnell, *Charles Desborough*	13.1.1876–3.10.1969	1908	8(I)
Burnell, *Richard Desborough*	26.7.1917	1948	8
Burnford, *David Wrayford*	6.1.1915–10.6.1984	1936	2
Bushnell, *Bertie Thomas*	7.5.1909	1948	DS
Butcher, *Anthony Sidney Fairbank*	1.6.1926	1948	4
Cadbury, *George Adrian Hayhurst*	15.4.1929	1952	4
Callender, *David Norman*	25.7.1930	1952	4
Campbell, *John Alan*	13.4.1899–20.2.1939	1920	8
Carmichael, *Malcolm James*	8.9.1955	1980	2
Carr, *Geoffrey*	22.1.1886	1912	4w
Carter, *Bruce Leonard Andrew*	14.6.1943	1968	4
Carver, *Oswald Armitage*	2.2.1887–7.6.1915	1908	8(II)
Chandler, *Edward Charles*	1902	1924	8
Cherry, *John Conrad Hazlehurst*	7.9.1914–1.2.1943	1936	8
Chester, *John Richard*	25.10.1935	1960	8
Christie, *Alastair Neil*	11.1.1953	1976	2
		1980	2w
Christie, *Thomas Hildred*	—	1948	4
Clack, *Nicholas Barry Menzies*	17.8.1930	1952	8
Clack, *Richard James Scott*	15.7.1950	1972	4
		1976	8
		1980	DS
Clay, *John Henry*	20.3.1955	1976	2
		1980	2
Clift, *David Adam*	3.1.1962	1984	8
		1988	4w
Clift, *Marcus Jonathon*	25.8.1964	1984	4
Clive, *Lewis*	8.9.1910–2.8.1938	1932	2
Collet, *Theodore David Anthony*	19.10.1901–26.4.1984	1928	SS
Collins, *Robert Anthony*	1924	1948	4w
Cooke, *Arnold Vivian*	13.4.1941	1964	DS

COMPETITOR	DATE OF BIRTH-DEATH	YEAR	EVENT/S
Cooper, Graham Vaughan	14.3.1941	1960	8
Cooper, Matthew Michael Kenneth	17.4.1948	1968	8
		1972	2
Couchman, John Malcolm	1913	1936	8
Cree, Thomas Scott	1.5.1915	1936	2
Crooks, Timothy John	12.5.1949	1972	DS
		1976	8
Cross, Martin P	19.7.1957	1980	4
		1984	4w
		1988	4w
Crosse, Simon C	—	1960	4w
Croucher, Bernard Cecil D	1901	1924	4w
Crowden, James Gee Pascoe	14.11.1927	1952	4
Cudmore, Collier Robert	13.6.1885–16.5.1971	1908	4(I)
Davidge, Christopher Guy Vere	5.11.1929	1952	2
		1956	8
		1960	4
Davis, Carl Michael	24.6.1940	1960	8
Dearlove, Jack G	—	1948	8
Debenham, HC	1903	1924	8
De Giles, Peter Anthony	8.4.1927	1952	4w
Delafield, Patrick Geoffrey Robert	14.4.1946	1972	DS
Delahooke, Michael Garwood	24.9.1935	1956	8
Dillon, Terence G	8.5.1964	1988	8
Duckworth, John Noel	25.12.1912–24.11.1980	1936	8
Dulley, Hugh William McPherson	11.7.1903–1941	1924	8
Dwan, Kenneth Victor	6.7.1948	1968	SS
		1972	SS
Earl, Sebastian	2.1.1900–14.8.1983	1920	8
Edwards, Hugh Robert Arthur	17.11.1906–21.12.1972	1932	2/4
Eley, Charles Ryves Maxwell	16.9.1902–15.1.1983	1924	4
Elliott, Ian Lea	11.1.1938	1960	8
Ellison, Adrian C	11.9.1958	1984	4w
Etherington-Smith, Raymond Broadley	11.4.1877–19.4.1913	1908	8(I)
Fairbairn, George Eric	18.8.1888–20.6.1915	1908	2(II)
Fairbairn, Stephen Ian	14.4.1896	1924	8
Farquharson, Stewart	27.4.1940	1960	2w
		1964	2
Fenning, John Reginald Keith	23.6.1885–3.1.1955	1908	2(I)/4(II)
Filleul, Philip Rowland	15.7.1885	1908	4(I)
Fishlock, Richard Laurence Seymour	17.8.1936	1960	8
Fisk, Graham Chudleigh	5.2.1928	1952	4w
Fison, William Guy	25.10.1890–6.12.1964	1912	8(II)
Fleming, Philip	15.8.1889–13.10.1971	1912	8(I)
Fox, Thomas Anthony	27.7.1928	1952	SS
		1956	SS
Garrett, John L	6.1.1963	1984	4
		1988	4w
Garton, Arthur Stanley	31.3.1889–20.10.1960	1912	8(I)
Genziani, Adrian N	6.5.1962	1984	2w
George, Rowland David	15.1.1905	1932	4
Gillan, James Angus	11.10.1885–23.4.1981	1908	4(I)
		1912	8(I)
Gillespie, Thomas Cunningham	14.12.1892–10.10.1914	1912	8(II)
Gladstone, Albert Charles	28.10.1886–2.3.1967	1908	8(I)
Godwin, JS	—	1924	8
Goldsmith, Henry Mills	22.7.1885–9.5.1915	1908	8(II)
Gollan, Donald Herbert Louis	19.1.1896	1928	8
Guest, Laurence	3.1.1936	1952	4w
Guye, Denis	—	1928	DS
Haig-Thomas, David	1.12.1908–6.6.1944	1932	8
Hamilton, James Hamish	15.11.1900–24.5.1988	1928	8
Hart, Michael John	24.10.1951	1972	2w
		1976	DS
		1984	8
		1988	8
Hassan, Salih H	26.12.1962	1976	QS
Hayter, Mark	24.10.1949	1948	4w
Healey, John Alexander Dick	25.10.1927	1952	8
Hinde, John Frederick Keeling	3.10.1928	1956	8
		1984	4w
		1988	2/2w
Holmes, Andrew John	15.10.1959	1912	8(I)
Horsfall, Ewart Douglas	24.5.1892–1.2.1974	1920	8

COMPETITOR	DATE OF BIRTH-DEATH	YEAR	EVENT/S
Inns, Alan Frederick	28.8.1945	1972	2w
		1984	2w
Ives, Harold R	—	1928	4w
Jackson, Peter Herbert	1913	1936	4
James, HB	—	1948	2w
James, John Jesse	21.9.1937	1964	4
James, Walter Ernest Christopher	18.1.1896–17.6.1982	1920	8
Jefferies, Simon H	11.7.1955	1988	8
Jennens, David Michael	8.4.1929	1952	8
Jerwood, Frank Harold	29.11.1885–17.7.1971	1908	8(II)
Johnstone, Banner Carruthers	11.11.1882–20.6.1964	1908	8(I)
Johnstone, Robin Talbot	6.8.1901–20.2.1976	1920	8
Jones, John Stephen Major	22.4.1930	1952	4
Justice, Andrew	19.1.1951	1976	QS
		1980	8
Justicz, George C	27.2.1931	1960	DS
Kelly, Frederick Septimus	29.5.1881–13.11.1916	1908	8(I)
Keron, Neil A	24.3.1953	1976	8
Killick, Gordon Cecil	1899–10.10.1962	1924	2
		1928	8
Kingsford, Annesley Douglas	30.7.1912	1936	8
Kingsford, Desmond Glover	24.7.1914–8.1944	1936	8
Kinnear, William Duthie	3.12.1880–5.3.1974	1912	SS
Kirby, Alister Graham	14.4.1886–29.3.1917	1912	8(I)
Kirk, Timothy	19.5.1945	1968	8
Kirkpatrick, Peter Crichton	1916	1948	4
Kitching, Harold Edward	31.8.1885–18.8.1980	1908	8(II)
Knapp, Peter George	27.10.1949	1968	8
Knight, K Richard	18.5.1928	1960	4w
Knight, Martin	17.10.1957	1984	4
Lander, John Gerard Heath	7.9.1907–12.1941	1928	4
Lane, Harold M	—	1928	8
Lang, William J	18.3.1956	1984	2w
Lapage, Michael Clement	15.11.1923	1948	8
Laurie, William George Ranald Mundell	4.5.1915	1936	8
		1948	2
Leckie, William Joseph Hannay	25.8.1928	1948	4w
Lee Nicholson, James David	31.11.1938	1964	2
Lester, Kenneth AJ	1937	1960	2w
Lester, Richard C	24.3.1949	1976	8
Lindsay, Alexander Thomas	18.12.1936	1960	8
Littlejohn, Charles William Berry	4.1.1889–8.1960	1912	8(II)
Lloyd, Charles Brian Murray	11.3.1927	1948	8
		1952	8
Logan, Bruce	2.3.1886	1912	4w
Long, AF	1900	1924	8
Lonnon, McAllister Pender	20.4.1916	1936	8
Lucas, Richard Saville Clement	27.7.1886–29.5.1968	1920	8
Luxton, Lewis	12.9.1910	1932	8
McCarthy, Jeremiah Thomas	20.7.1941	1972	2
McCowen, Donald Henry Ewan	26.2.1908	1932	8
McCulloch, Alexander	25.10.1887–5.9.1951	1908	SS
McDougal, Duncan	14.3.1959	1980	8
		1984	8
McGowan, Malcolm R	24.10.1955	1980	8
		1984	8
Mackinnon, Duncan	29.9.1887–9.10.1917	1908	4(I)
Macklin, David Drury	1.9.1928	1952	8
Maclagan, Gilchrist Stanley	5.10.1879–25.4.1915	1908	8(I)
MacLeod, Alastair Leoid	2.11.1924	1952	8
MacLeod, James	25.7.1953	1976	2
		1980	2w
MacMillan, John Roderick Alexander	3.5.1930	1952	DS
Macmillan, Roderick Alan Fitzjohn	2.5.1928	1952	4w
Macnabb, James Alexander	26.12.1901–6.4.1990	1924	4w
McNuff, Ian T	10.3.1957	1980	8
Mahoney, Christopher John	2.1.1959	1980	8
		1984	8
Marshall, Clive L	1.1.1939	1960	2
Mason, Hugh Walter	7.12.1915	1936	8
Mason, William Graham	20.8.1950	1972	4
		1976	4
Massara, Rooney William John	22.1.1943	1972	4w
Masser, Kenneth Alfred	29.4.1943	1956	8
Massey, Paul Mackintosh Orgill	12.3.1926	1948	8
		1952	4w

COMPETITOR	DATE OF BIRTH-DEATH	YEAR	EVENT/S
Matheson, *Hugh Patrick*	16.4.1949	1972	4w
		1976	8
		1980	SS
Maxey, *John*	19.7.1958	1988	4w
Maxwell, *David Lindsay*	8.4.1951	1972	2w
		1976	8
Mellows, *Alfred Paul*	1922	1948	8
Meyrick, *David John Charlton*	2.12.1926	1948	8
Monk, *TS*	1904	1924	4w
Morphy, *HL*	1902	1924	8
Morrison, *Robert Erskine*	26.3.1903 – 19.2.1980	1924	4
Moynihan, *Colin Berkeley*	13.9.1955	1980	8
		1984	8
Mulkerrins, *Peter R*	5.9.1964	1988	4
Mullard, *John Kenneth*	6.3.1945	1968	8
Nicholson, *Richard J*	22.11.1937	1960	2
Nickalls, *Guy*	13.11.1866 – 8.7.1935	1908	8(I)
Nickalls, *Guy Oliver*	4.4.1889 – 26.4.1974	1920	8
		1928	8
Nisbet, *Robert Archibald*	23.11.1900 – 13.9.1986	1928	2
O'Brien, *Terence Noel*	23.12.1906 – 19.12.1982	1928	2
Obholzer, *Anton*	29.6.1968	1988	8
Parker, *Sir William Lorenzo, Bt*	9.1.1889 – 27.10.1971	1912	8(II)
Payne, *Kenneth Martin*	8.9.1912 – 24.4.1988	1932	8
Peel, *Stephen*	29.12.1965	1988	4
Pierce, *Christopher Thomas*	21.12.1942	1972	4w
Pitman, *Frederick Archibald Hugo*	1.6.1892 – 25.7.1963	1912	8(II)
Porter, *Colin F*	11.10.1930	1960	4
Potter, *LG*	—	1928	4w
Powell, *Eric Walter*	6.5.1886 – 17.8.1933	1908	8(II)
Pritchard, *John Martin*	30.11.1957	1980	8
		1984	8
Purssell, *Anthony John Richard*	5.7.1926	1948	4w
Rand, *Sidney Charles*	17.8.1934	1956	DS
		1960	SS
Rand, *William Henry*	29.12.1935	1956	DS
Rankine, *Gordon A*	30.5.1954	1980	4w
Ranking, *John Maurice*	3.7.1910	1932	8
Redgrave, *Stephen G*	23.3.1962	1984	4w
		1988	2/2w
Reeves, *Jeffrey R*	15.1.1936	1960	2w
Rew, *Charles Harry*	1898 – 3.10.1972	1924	8
Reynolds, *Peter John*	26.8.1937	1960	8
Richardson, *Guy Colquhoun*	8.9.1921 – 27.10.1965	1948	8
Rickett, *Harold Robert Norman*	20.7.1909 – 31.1.1969	1932	8
Roberts, *Clive G*	19.3.1958	1984	8
Roberts, *John*	22.12.1953	1980	4w
Robertson, *Leonard David*	10.10.1950	1972	4
		1976	8
		1980	4w
Rosslyn-Smith, *TH*	—	1960	4w
Rought, *Charles Gardner*	16.10.1884 – 31.1.1918	1912	4w
Rowe, *Anthony Duncan*	4.8.1924	1948	SS
Rushmere, *HW*	—	1948	4
Russell, *John Alastair Legh*	1.6.1933	1956	8
Russell, *John Michael*	3.8.1935	1960	4w
		1964	4
Sambell, *William Austin Tyers*	29.10.1910 – 27.3.1974	1932	8
Sanders, *Terence Robert Beaumont*	2.6.1901 – 6.4.1985	1924	4
Sanderson, *Ronald Harcourt*	11.12.1876 – 17.4.1918	1908	8(I)
Scott, *MB*	—	1948	2w
Sergell, *Charles John Scott*	12.5.1911 – 21.5.1980	1932	8
Seymour, *Colin*	27.10.1953	1980	4w
Sharpley, *Roger Fielding Anthony*	17.5.1929	1952	8
Shaw, *Donald William*	3.2.1939	1960	8
Shove, *Ralph Samuel*	31.5.1889 – 2.2.1966	1920	8
Smallbone, *Frederick John*	22.1.1948	1972	4
		1976	8
Somers-Smith, *John Robert*	15.12.1887 – 1.7.1916	1908	4(I)
Southgate, *CT*	1895	1924	2
Southwood, *Leslie Frank*	18.1.1906 – 7.2.1986	1932	SS
		1936	DS
Stanhope, *Richard*	27.4.1957	1980	8
		1984	2
		1988	8

COMPETITOR	DATE OF BIRTH-DEATH	YEAR	EVENT/S
Starkey, *OB*	—	1928	4w
Stewart, *Gavin B*	27.4.1957	1988	8
Stuart, *Douglas Cecil Rees*	1.3.1885	1908	8(II)
Sturge, *David Philip*	5.6.1948	1976	2
Sturrock, *John Duncan*	20.3.1915	1936	4
Sulley, *Arthur Lindsay*	8.11.1908	1928	4w/8
Swann, *Sidney Ernest*	24.6.1890 – 19.9.1976	1912	8(I)
		1920	8
Sweeney, *Patrick John*	12.8.1952	1972	4w
		1976	8
		1988	2w
Thomas, *Hugh Vaughan*	12.6.1964	1988	4w
Thomas, *Peter Leslie*	16.4.1945	1968	8
Thomson, *Gordon Lindsay*	27.3.1884 – 8.7.1953	1908	2(I)/4(II)
Tilbury, *John W*	4.1.1931	1960	4w
Townend, *JH*	1903	1924	4w
Townsend, *David GH*	28.8.1955	1976	4
		1980	4
Tozer, *Simon George Douglas*	24.12.1933	1956	8
Turner, *Stephen*	17.9.1964	1988	8
Verdon, *Philip*	22.2.1886 – 18.6.1960	1908	2(II)
Vernon, *Karl*	19.6.1880	1912	4w
Vigurs, *John PC*	21.3.1930	1960	4
Walker, *DS*	—	1948	2w
Walker, *John Drummond*	4.1.1891	1912	8(II)
Wardell-Yerburgh, *Hugh Arthur*	11.1.1938 – 28.1.1970	1964	4
Warren, *Humphrey Lloyd*	15.5.1910 – 14.7.1978	1936	SS
Warriner, *Michael Henry*	3.12.1905 – 7.4.1986	1928	4
Watson, *Alan Richard*	9.7.1929	1956	8
Webb, *David A*	21.4.1943	1976	2w
		1980	2w
Webb, *Peter James*	2.10.1940	1964	DS
Wells, *Henry Bensley*	12.1.1891 – 4.7.1967	1912	8(I)
Welsh, *Ian William*	10.3.1933	1956	8
West, *Harold E*	—	1928	8
Wheadon, *Richard Anthony*	31.1.1933	1956	8
* Whittall, *Donald*	25.2.1881 – 1959	1906	4w
(Also see *Association Football*)			
Whitwell, *Allan*	5.5.1954	1976	QS
		1980	8
		1984	8
Wiggin, *A Charles D*	8.1.1950	1980	2
Wiggins, *Arthur Frederick Reginald*	4.12.1891	1912	8(II)
Williams, *Edward Gordon*	20.7.1888 – 12.8.1915	1908	8(II)
Wilson, *John Hyrne Tucker*	17.9.1914	1948	2
Windham, *William Ashe Dymoke*	2.4.1926	1952	8
Woodward, *William Winslow*	14.10.1920 – 18.1.1987	1948	4w
Worlidge, *Edward John*	3.12.1928	1952	8
Wormwald, *Leslie Graham*	19.8.1890 – 10.7.1965	1912	8(I)
Wright, *Patrick John*	20.5.1945	1968	8
Yallop, *John C*	24.10.1949	1976	8
Yarrow, *Robin Deighton*	8.2.1946	1968	8

* In 1906, D Whittal rowed in a crew from Smyrna in the coxed fours.

Rowing

WOMEN

Great Britain has been represented at every Games since rowing for women was introduced as an Olympic sport in 1976.

COMPETITOR	DATE OF BIRTH-DEATH	YEAR	EVENT/S
Andreae, *Sally*	16.9.1960	1988	DS
Ayling, *Astrid*	9.12.1951	1980	DS
Bailey, *Susan*	15.2.1961	1984	8
Ball, *Kathryn*	8.6.1963	1984	4w
Bird, *Pauline*	31.7.1957	1976	4w
Bishop, *Diana*	28.9.1947	1976	4w
Bloomfield, *Sally*	3.6.1956	1984	DS

Rugby Internationals

Of the 19 British Olympians who have represented their countries at rugby in the International Championship, only six actually competed in the Olympic rugby tournaments. The other thirteen took part in a variety of Olympic sports and the full list of Olympian rugby internationals is:

ENGLAND: *Fencing*: CA Kershaw *Modern Pentathlon*: D Turquand-Young *Rackets*: H Brougham *Rugby Football*: AJL Darby, J Davey, EJ Jackett, B Solomon, TG Wedge and AJ Wilson *Track & Field*: JA Gregory and CB Holmes *Yachting*: J Baxter
IRELAND: *Lawn Tennis*: JC Parke *Water Polo*: NM Purcell

SCOTLAND: *Golf*: DD Robertson *Track & Field*: EH Liddell, RH Lindsay-Watson and CEWC Mackintosh. Additionally, ECK Douglas (Track & Field) played in a wartime international in 1942.
WALES: *Track & Field*: KJ Jones

COMPETITOR	DATE OF BIRTH-DEATH	YEAR	EVENT/S
Bonner, *Alison*	27.6.1962	1988	2
Boyes, *Nicola Vivien*	16.12.1954	1980	8
Brown, *Sue*	29.6.1958	1980	4w
Buckley, *Bridget*	25.6.1955	1980	4w
Callaway, *Ann*	8.3.1960	1984	8
Clark, *Linda*	1.11.1949	1976	2
		1980	8
Clugston, *Rosemary*	15.2.1954	1980	8
Gross, *Janet*	23.8.1954	1980	8
Forbes, *Alexa*	2.4.1961	1984	8
Genchi, *Jean*	25.9.1956	1984	4w
Gill, *Alison*	23.8.1966	1988	DS
Gough, *Joanne*	17.11.1964	1988	4w
Grose, *Katherine*	7.2.1959	1988	4w
Grove, *Clare*	24.11.1953	1976	4w
Hanscombe, *Susan*	21.9.1956	1980	DS
Hart, *Pauline*	31.7.1957	1980	4w
Hodges, *Gillian*	13.8.1957	1980	8
		1984	8
Holmes, *Belinda*	8.2.1962	1984	8
Holroyd, *Kathryn*	5.6.1963	1984	8
Hunter-Jones, *Sarah Louise*	1.2.1959	1984	8
Janson, *Pauline*	26.11.1957	1980	8
Johnstone, *Fiona*	3.12.1966	1988	4w
Jones, *Beverly Ann*	25.11.1956	1980	8
McNicol, *Katherine*	19.7.1961	1984	8
Millar, *Teresa*	22.9.1956	1984	4w
Mitchell, *Beryl*	26.6.1950	1976	2
		1980	SS
		1984	SS
Norrish, *Alison*	19.12.1968	1988	4w
Paton, *Elizabeth*	8.11.1952	1980	8
Ray, *Nonie Jane*	3.10.1958	1984	DS
Smith, *Susan*	1.6.1965	1988	4w
Sweet, *Penelope*	16.10.1957	1980	8
Talbot, *Kathryn*	17.8.1961	1984	4w
Thomas, *Kim*	10.10.1967	1988	2
Toch, *Joanna*	13.10.1961	1980	8
		1984	4w
Webb, *Gillian*	12.1.1956	1979	4w
Wright, *Pauline*	2.12.1954	1976	4w
		1980	8

Rugby Football

Rugby was an Olympic sport in 1900, 1908, 1920 and 1924 and a British team played on the first two occasions. In 1900 a team known as Moseley Wanderers, which was made up mainly of players from Midland clubs, played against France and in 1908 the County champions, Cornwall, played against the Australian touring team.

COMPETITOR	DATE OF BIRTH-DEATH	YEAR	EVENT/S
Baylis, *FC*	—	1900	
Birtles, *J Henry*	—	1900	
Cantion, *J*	—	1900	
Darby, *Arthur John Lovett*	9.1.1876–15.1.1960	1900	
Davey, *James*	25.12.1880–18.10.1951	1908	
Dean, *LF*	—	1908	
Deykin, *CP*	—	1900	
Hood, *L*	—	1900	
Jackett, *Edward John*	4.7.1882–1935	1908	
Jackett, *Richard*		1908	
Jones, *EJ*	—	1908	
Jose, *JT*	—	1908	
Lawrey, *A*	—	1908	
Logan, *ML*	—	1900	
Loveitt, *HA*	—	1900	
Marshall, *CR*	27.1.1880	1908	
Nicol, *HS*	—	1900	
Smith, *V*	—	1900	
Solomon, *Bert*	8.3.1885–30.6.1961	1908	
Solomon, *JC 'Barney'*	—	1908	
Talbott, *MW*	—	1900	
Tregurtha, *Nicholas Jacobs*	1884–14.5.1964	1908	
Trevaskis, *J*	—	1908	
Wallis, *JG*	—	1900	
Wedge, *Thomas Grenfell*	1881–11.12.1964	1908	
Whittindale, *Claud*	1881–10.2.1907	1900	
Whittindale, *K*	1883–9.4.1915	1900	
Wilcocks, *A*	—	1908	
Wilson, *Arthur James*	29.12.1886–1.7.1917	1908	
Wilson, *FH*	—	1900	

Family Firsts

Husband & wife: Charles and Frances Rivett-Carnac in the 6 metres yachting event in 1908. They were also the first married couple from any nation to win gold medals.
Brothers: Hugh and Reginald Doherty who both won gold medals in the 1900 lawn tennis tournament.
Twin brothers: Noel and Godfrey Chavasse who both competed in the 400 metres track event in 1908.
Sisters: Sheena and Vora Mackintosh who both competed in the Alpine skiing events in 1952. The first British sisters to compete in the Summer

Games were Jane Bullen and Jennifer Loriston-Clarke (née Bullen) who took part in the equestrian events in 1968 and 1972–88 respectively.
Twin sisters: Ann and Janet Osgerby who both took part in the butterfly swimming events in 1980.
Brother & sister: Willy and Charlotte 'Lottie' Dod who won gold and silver medals respectively in the 1908 archery competitions.
Father & son: In 1920 Jack Beresford and Guy Oliver Nickalls took part in the rowing events and their fathers

were both Olympic oarsmen. Julius Beresford won a silver medal in 1912 and Guy Nickalls Snr won a gold medal in 1908.
Father & daughter: Frederick Dix, who competed as a speed skater in 1924 and 1928, and his daughter Janet Dix who took part in the 1932 Games as a figure skater.
Mother & daughter: Mrs Jessie Wadworth and her daughter were both archery competitors in 1908. There is no example in British Olympic history of a mother & son competing in the Games.

Shooting

MEN

Shooting events have been held at every Olympic Games except for those of 1904 and 1928. Great Britain was not represented in 1900, 1932 and 1936 or in 1980 when the British shooting team chose to boycott the Moscow Games.

The Olympic programme has varied widely, especially in the early years, and in the following table of abbreviations only sufficient information is given to identify an event. In certain cases, the name given to an event may differ slightly from that given on the official programme. The method used below does, however, permit an orderly grouping of events.

AP = Air Pistol   AR = Air Rifle
CP = Clay Pigeon – Trap   CS = Clay Pigeon – Skeet
DP = Duelling Pistol   FP = Free Pistol   FR = Free Rifle
MP = Military Pistol   MP (1873) = Military Pistol – 1873 type
MR = Military Rifle   RD = Running Deer   RF = Rapid Fire Pistol
RG = Running Game or Wild Boar   SB = Small Bore
SP = Sporting Pistol   a = any position   d = disappearing target
ds = double shot   k = kneeling   m = moving target   p = prone
ss = single shot   s = standing   t = team event   3 = positions

Great Britain entered two teams in the 1908 Clay Pigeon team event and they have been identified as 'A' and 'B' teams.

COMPETITOR	DATE OF BIRTH-DEATH	YEAR	EVENT/S
Allan, *Alister Millar*	28.1.1944	1968	SBp
		1976	SBp
		1984	SBp/SB3
		1988	AR/SB3
Amoore, *Edward J*	—	1908	SBa/SBd/
			SBm/SBt
Antal, *Laslo Charles*	10.4.1936	1976	FP
Anthony, *John Rosyln*	4.12.1932	1972	WB
		1976	WB
Artis, *William John*	1884	1924	SBp
Bailey, *Brian Walford*	20.8.1932	1972	CP
Barlow, *Jocelyn Arthur*	26.8.1901	1948	FR
		1952	FR
Barnes, *George*	—	1908	SBa
Barnett, *Richard Whieldon*	6.12.1863–17.10.1930	1908	MR
Bashford, *J*	—	1908	RDds/FP
Bentley, *Paul*	7.2.1946	1984	CS
Black, *Alfred William*	17.11.1856	1912	CP
Blood, *Maurice*	1870–31.3.1940	1908	FR3/MR/
			RDss/
			RDds
Boden, *Peter*	18.9.1947	1976	CP
		1984	CP
Bonnett, *Alec*	8.9.1922	1968	CS
Bostock, *J*	—	1908	FR3t
Bounton, *Charles Edward*	1881	1924	RF
Bracegirdle, *Frederick William*	1885	1924	SBp
Braithwaite, *John Robert*	28.9.1925	1964	CP
		1968	CP
Bray, *Alan Herbert*	19.6.1929	1964	RF
Breton, *Adrian*	4.10.1962	1988	RF
Brown, *RH*	—	1908	FR3t
Burr, *Henry George*	21.3.1872	1912	MRa/MRt
Burt, *Harold*	6.5.1876	1912	SBp/SBd
Butt, *John Hurst*	30.10.1852	1908	CP/
			CPt(B)
		1912	CP/CPt
Caldwell, *T*	—	1908	MR
Capper, *Ingram Ord*	17.11.1907	1952	RD
Carnell, *Arthur Ashton*	21.3.1862–11.9.1940	1908	SBa
Carter, *Ronald George*	11.7.1938	1972	CP
Chandler, *John*	—	1948	SBp
Chaney, *HE*	—	1908	FR3
Chapman, *David*	30.10.1963	1984	RG
Chivers, *Anthony James*	30.11.1936	1964	FP
Churcher, *CW*	—	1908	FR3

COMPETITOR	DATE OF BIRTH-DEATH	YEAR	EVENT/S
Churchill, *John Robert*	21.2.1939	1972	SB3
Clark, *Anthony John*	17.6.1924	1960	RF
		1964	RF
		1968	RF
		1972	RF
Clift, *John George Nielson*	1877	1924	SBp
Coles, *Geoffrey Horsman*	13.3.1871–27.1.1916	1908	FP/FPt
Cooke, *John Patrick*	17.3.1939	1972	RF
		1976	RF
		1984	RF
Cooper, *Frederick*	31.5.1910	1956	FP/RF
Cooper, *Malcolm Douglas*	20.12.1947	1972	SB3/FR
		1976	SB3
		1984	SB3/AR
		1988	SBp/SB3/
			AR
Cowan, *James Henry*	28.9.1856–7.8.1943	1908	RDss/
			RDds
Cranmer, *Steffan Borries Ozrik*	8.5.1934	1952	SB3/SBp
		1956	FR/SB3/
			SBp
		1960	SB3
Creasey, *HP*	—	1908	CP/
			CPt(B)
Croft, *Peter*	4.7.1950	1984	CP
Cullum, *Harry*	29.8.1929	1964	FP
		1972	FP
Dagger, *Barry Edward*	19.5.1937	1976	SB3
		1984	AR
Davies. *Robert MF*	10.12.1876	1912	MRa/MR3
Douglas, *Henry Percy*	1.11.1876–4.11.1939	1924	FR3
Durant, *Hugh*	23.2.1877	1912	FP/FPt/
(Also see *Modern Pentathlon*)			RFt
Easte, *P*	—	1908	CP/
			CPt(A)
Ellicot, *W*	—	1908	FP/FPt/
			RDss/
			RDds/
			RDt
		1920	CPt
Faunthorpe, *John Champion*	30.5.1871–1.12.1929	1924	RDss/
			RDsst
Fear, *Ernest Edward*	5.10.1903	1956	CP
Fleming, *John Francis*	26.8.1881–9.1.1965	1908	SBd/SBm
Fremantle, *Hon. Thomas Francis*	5.2.1862–19.7.1956	1908	MR
Fulton, *Arthur George*	16.9.1877–26.1.1972	1908	MRt
		1912	MR3/
			MRa/MRt
Gallie, *John K*	—	1948	FP
Gilbert, *Victor Henry*	27.5.1905–6.12.1978	1948	SBp
Girling, *Brian Edward*	14.5.1938	1976	RF
Godwin, *William B*	8.8.1912	1960	SBp
Goodwin, *John Morris*	14.3.1859	1912	CP
Gough, *John McKinley*	25.9.1929	1976	WB
Granet, *GEA*	—	1948	FP
Grantham, *Eric Arthur*	7.9.1913	1968	CP
Greenfield, *Anthony Horace*	11.12.1931	1976	SBp
Griffiths, *David James*	31.3.1874	1912	SBp/SBd
Griffiths, *PH*	1892	1924	RF
Grosvenor, *William Percy*	18.7.1869	1912	CP/CPt
		1920	CPt
		1924	CPt
Guy, *Ronald Frederick Bowden*	3.11.1912	1952	FP
Hall, *John*	12.11.1906	1964	SBp
Harman, *Kenneth*	—	1988	CS
Harvey, *Graham*	28.5.1944	1984	RF
Hassal, *Robert Seymour*	24.2.1929	1960	RF
		1968	RF
Hawkins, *HI*	—	1908	SBa/SBd/
			SBm
Hawkins, *R*	—	1908	FR3/FRt
Hebditch, *Anthony Brian*	15.7.1948	1976	CS
Hopkinson, *Frederick William*	1.3.1922	1956	SB3/SBp
Hopton, *John Dutton (né Hunt)*	30.12.1858–1.6.1934	1908	MR

COMPETITOR	DATE OF BIRTH-DEATH	YEAR	EVENT/S
Humby, *Harold Robinson*	8.4.1879–23.2.1923	1908	SBa/SBd/
			SBt
		1912	CP/CPt
		1920	CPt
Huthart, *Victor Brett*	16.12.1924	1960	CP
Hutton, *R*	—	1908	CP/
			CPt(B)
Hyde, *Charles John*	29.11.1904	1952	SB3/SBp
Jackson, *Alexander Townsend*	—	1908	FR3
Jenkins, *Enoch*	6.11.1892–4.1.1984	1920	CP
		1924	CP/CPt
		1952	CP
Jones, *Malcolm*	27.12.1914	1976	CP
Jones, *George AJ*	—	1948	SBp
Jones, *Peter H*	3.9.1879	1908	FP
		1912	FP
Kemp, *Francis William*	—	1912	SBp/SBd
Kempster, *Albert Joseph*	23.8.1875	1908	RDss/
			RDds
		1912	FP/FPt/
			RFt
Knott, *John CJ*	—	1948	FR
Kynoch, *John Marriott*	19.3.1933	1972	WB
Lane-Joynt, *WR*	—	1908	RDss/
			RDds/
			RDt/FP
Larsen, *Herbert Victor*	1894	1924	CPt
Lawrence, *Philip*	17.3.1945	1972	SBp
Leatherdale, *Paul*	21.9.1958	1988	FP/AP
Le Fevre, *JN*	—	1908	FP
Lessimore, *Edward John*	20.1.1881–7.3.1960	1912	SBp/SBd/
			SBpt
Lewis, *DE*	1879	1924	SBp
LLoyd, *Langford Newnan*	28.12.1873–20.4.1956	1912	MR3
Loader, *Marcus Peter Croot*	5.11.1943	1968	FP
Lucas, *Charles*	18.7.1886	1952	CP
Lynch-Staunton, *Henry George*	5.11.1873–15.11.1941	1908	FP/FPt
Mackie, *CH*	1885	1924	RF
McClure, *William*	20.5.1883	1912	FP/RF/
			MR3
Mackworth-Praed, *Cyril Winthrop*	21.9.1891–30.6.1974	1924	RDss/
			RDds/
			RDt/CPt
		1952	RD
Marchant, *Peter VL*	—	1948	FP
Marsden, *WB*	—	1908	SBm
Martin, *Alexander Elsdon*	21.1.1895	1924	FR
Martin, *JE*	—	1908	FRt
Maslen-Jones, *RG*	—	1948	FR
Matthews, *MK*	—	1908	SBa/SBd/
			SBm/SBt
Maunder, *Alexander*	3.2.1861–2.2.1932	1908	CP/
			CPt(A)
		1912	CP/CPt
Meggison, *Michael*	31.10.1949	1984	RG
Merlin, *Gerald Eustace*	3.8.1884–1945	1906	MR(200m)/
			FR3/MP/
			MP(1873)/
			FP(20m)/
			FP(25)/
			FP(50m)/
			DP(20m)/
			DP(25m)/
			CPss/CPds
		1908	CP

COMPETITOR	DATE OF BIRTH-DEATH	YEAR	EVENT/S
Merlin, *Sidney Louis Walter*	26.4.1856–1952	1896	RF
		1906	MR(200m)/
			MR(300m)/
			FR3/
			FRs&k/
			MP(20m)/
			MP(1873)/
			FP(20m)/
			FP(25m)/
			FP(50m)/
			DP(20m)/
			DP(25m)/
			CPss/CPds
Millner, *Joshua Kearney*	1849–16.11.1931	1908	MR/
			RDss/
			RDds
Milne, *JL*	—	1908	SBa/SBd/
			SBm
Milne, *William*	23.3.1852	1908	SBa/SBd/
			SBm
		1912	SBp/SBd/
			SBdt
Morgan, *Thomas Peter*	2.9.1927	1964	SBp
Moore, *FW*	—	1908	CP/
			CPt(A)
Morris, *WB*	—	1908	CP/
			CPt(B)
Munday, *H*	—	1908	FP
Murray, *Robert Cook*	18.2.1870	1912	SBp/
			SBpt/
Neal, *GR*	1894	1924	CPt
Neame, *Philip*	12.12.1888–28.4.1978	1924	RDdst
Neville, *Joseph Martin*	6.1.1944	1972	CP
		1976	CS
Newitt, *Edward JD*	—	1908	SBd/SBm
Newton, *WJ*	—	1908	FP
Nix, *Charles George Ashburton*	—	1908	RDss/
			RDds/
			RDsst
Northcote, *TV*	1895	1924	FR3
O'Leary, *John J*	1880	1924	CP/CPt/
			Rdsst
Ommundsen, *Harcourt*	23.11.1878–1915	1908	MR3/MRt
		1912	MRa/MRt
Padgett, *WG*	—	1908	MRt
Palin, *John Charlton*	16.7.1934	1968	SBp
		1972	SBp
Palmer, *Charles*	18.8.1869	1908	CP,
			CPt(A)
		1912	CP/CPt
		1920	CPt
Parnell, *Edward Louis*	21.6.1875	1912	MRa/
			MR3/MRt
Pearson, *John Joseph*	1926	1952	FR
Peel, *Ian*	18.1.1958	1988	CP
Pepé, *Joseph*	5.3.1881	1912	SBp/
			SBpt/
			SBd/SBdt
Perry, *Herbert Spencer*	23.1.1894–20.7.1966	1924	RDds/
			RDdst
Pike, *JF*	—	1908	CP/
			CPt(A)
Pimm, *William Edwin*	10.12.1864	1908	SBa/SBd/
			SBm/SBt
		1912	SBp/
			SBpt/
			SBd/SBdt
Pinchard, *George Ernest*	17.6.1871	1912	CP
Plater, *Phillip Edward*	—	1908	SBd/SBm
		1912	MRa/MR3
Pocock, *Ernest Edward*	—	1920	CPt
Postans, *JM*	—	1908	CPt(A)
Poulter, *Horatio Orlando*	29.10.1877	1912	FP/FPt/
			RFt
Raddall, *TW*	—	1908	FR3t

The Plater Incident

Olympic history is full of hard luck stories but few can match the misfortune suffered by British marksman Philip Plater in the individual small-bore event in 1908.

The conditions of the competition permitted twelve entries from each country but as the entry forms for George Barnes, the nominee of the Twenty Two Club, went astray, Philip Plater was named as the twelfth British entry in his place. Shortly afterwards, the entry form for George Barnes arrived and as the USA had been granted an extension to the closing date for entries, a similiar facility was given to Great Britain and Barnes' entry was duly accepted. This meant, of course, that Britain had 13 official entries instead of the permitted 12 but greater confusion was to follow.

When the competition got underway, the British team officials lost count of the number of British marksmen who had shot in the competition. Thinking that only eleven men had already fired, Plater was called on although there was only half an hour to spare before the time limit for the competition expired. Plater ran to the firing-point and in varying light, a gusty wind and fine drizzle, he moved from mat to mat and fired his 80 rounds in less than 30 minutes. In his 40 rounds from 50 yards Plater fell only five points short of the maximum possible and at 100 yards he dropped only four points. His total of 391 points was a new world record and in the initial results list issued by the National Rifle Association Philip Plater was shown as the winner of the competition and the Olympic champion.

It then transpired that the British team officials had made a major error and at the time Plater shot, the permitted number of twelve British marksmen had already taken part. It took some days to decide whether the score of Plater or that of Barnes should be erased from the records and eventually George Barnes was declared the official British entrant. In October, Philip Plater was presented with a special gold medal and a record diploma by the British Olympic Council, but his amazing feat of marksmanship remains unrecorded in the official Olympic records.

COMPETITOR	DATE OF BIRTH-DEATH	YEAR	EVENT/S
Ranken, *Thomas 'Ted'*	18.5.1875–27.4.1950	1908	MR/
			RDss/
			RDds/
			RDt/
		1924	RDss/
			RDds
Reid, *James*	8.3.1875	1912	MRa/MRt
Richardson, *Philip Wigham*	26.1.1865–23.11.1953	1908	FRt
		1912	MRa/MR3
Robinson, *Derek J*	31.7.1931	1960	SB3
Robinson, *Geoffrey*	15.10.1947	1984	FP
Rogers, *Alexander Elliott*	14.4.1867	1908	FR/RDss/
			RDds
		1924	RDss
Sedgewick, *John*	12.8.1873	1912	MRa/MR3
Sellars, *John Christopher*	—	1908	MR
Sephton, *Colin John*	10.7.1945	1968	CS
		1972	CS
Sexton, *Charles Henry*	15.9.1906	1968	FP
Skilton, *Edward*	26.9.1863	1912	MRa/MRt
Skinner, *Arthur D*	24.5.1919	1960	SBp
Skinner, *GH*	—	1908	CPt(B)
Somers, *John Percy*	12.7.1874	1912	MRa/MR3
Spencer, *Arthur*	21.5.1947	1984	FP
Steele, *Henry Albert*	10.9.1911	1948	RF
		1952	RF
		1956	RF/FP
Stewart, *Charles Edward*	1881	1912	FP/FPt/
			RFt
Styles, *William Kensett*	11.10.1874	1908	SBd/SBm
		1912	SBp/SBd/
			SBdt
Sullivan *Michael*	6.12.1942	1984	SBp
Swire, *Henry Louis Victor*	28.4.1901–9.7.1964	1948	RF
		1952	RF
Sykes, *Wallace*	25.10.1942	1984	CS
Taylor, *AE*	—	1908	SBa
Tickell, *Edward James*	9.2.1861–4.1.1942	1912	FP
Tomlinson, *John J*	20.10.1933	1960	FP
Varley, *Fleetwood Ernest*	12.7.1862	1908	MRt
		1912	MRa/MR3
Wallingford, *Jesse Alfred*	—	1908	FR3/
			FR3t/FP/
			FPt/
Warner, *Jack*	—	1908	SBa
Wheater, *Joseph*	6.10.1918	1956	CP
		1960	CP
		1964	CP

COMPETITOR	DATE OF BIRTH-DEATH	YEAR	EVENT/S
Whitaker, *George*	25.8.1864	1908	CP/
			CPt(B)
		1912	CP/CPt
		1920	CP/CPt
White, *William Benjamin*	1912	1952	FP
Whitehead, *PK*	—	1908	FR
Whitty, *Allen*	5.5.1867–22.7.1949	1924	RDds/
			RDt
Wilde, *AW*	—	1908	SBa/SBd/
			SBm
Willott, *Charles Courtie*	2.10.1904–13.6.1973	1948	RF
Wirgman, *Charles Wynn*	—	1908	FP
Wyatt, *Iles Frank*	2.12.1946	1972	FP

J Wheater (1956–64) changed his name to Nother but subsequently reverted to Wheater.

Shooting

WOMEN

Prior to 1984, shooting, yachting and the equestrian events were the only Olympic sports in which women competed on equal terms with men. In 1984 separate shooting events for women were introduced.

AP = Air pistol   AR = Air rifle
SB3 = Small bore rifle, 3 positions   SP = Sport pistol

COMPETITOR	DATE OF BIRTH-DEATH	YEAR	EVENT/S
Bartlett, *Carol*	19.10.1948	1984	SP
Bennett, *Adrienne*	1.6.1949	1984	SP
Cooper, *Sarah*	23.3.1949	1984	AR/SB3
		1988	AR/SB3
Daw, *Irene*	13.2.1941	1984	AR/SB3
Thomas, *Margaret*	25.11.1953	1988	AP/SP

Swimming

MEN

Swimming has been on the programme at every Olympic Games and Great Britain has, with the exception of 1896 and 1904, been represented on each occasion.

For some British competitors at the 1900 Games, it has not been possible to verify the events in which they actually competed. These instances have been noted in the following manner: ***

Where no letters follow the distance this indicates a freestyle event. For other styles the following abbreviations have been used:

Bf = Butterfly   Bk = Backstroke   Bs = Breaststroke
IM = Individual medley   MR = Medley relay   R = Relay (freestyle)

COMPETITOR	DATE OF BIRTH-DEATH	YEAR	EVENT/S
Abraham, *Gary*	8.1.1959	1976	100Bk
		1980	100Bk/
			100Bf/
			400MR
Annison, *Harold Edward*	1895	1920	100/400/
(Also see *Water Polo*)			1500/
			800R
		1924	400/1500/
			800R
Astbury, *Andrew*	29.11.1960	1980	400/1500/
			800R
		1984	200/400/
			800R
Atkinson, *Carlyle*	—	1912	200Bs
Bailey, *Michael*	14.2.1948	1972	200/800R
Baillee, *Charles Kennett*	31.7.1902	1924	100
Barnes, *Brian*	2.3.1934	1952	200BS
Battersby, *Thomas Sydney*	18.11.1887	1908	400/1500
		1912	400/1500/
			800R
Besford, *John Charles Preston*	30.1.1911	1928	100Bk
		1936	100Bk
Binfield, *Gary Michael*	13.3.1966	1988	200Bk/
			400MR
Black, *Ian Macintosh*	27.6.1941	1960	400/
			400MR/
			800R
Bland, *Donald*	27.3.1931	1948	1500
Blatherwick, *Sam*	16.10.1888–2.1.1975	1908	400/1500
Blyth, *Ian*	11.10.1942	1960	200Bf
Botham, *Frank Royston*	19.4.1923	1948	400, 800R
		1952	800R
Boyd, *Kevin Thomas*	23.6.1966	1988	400/1500/
			800R
Brew, *Paul*	20.11.1965	1988	400IM
Brew, *Robin*	28.6.1962	1984	200IM
Brinkley, *Brian*	28.12.1953	1972	100/200/
			400/1500/
			200Bf/
			800R
		1976	200/400/
			200Bf/
			400MR/
			800R
Brockway, *William John*	8.10.1928	1948	100Bk
		1952	100Bk
		1956	100Bk
Brooks, *Norman Standish*	11.3.1910	1928	100
Broughton, *Jonathan*	1.7.1969	1988	800R
Burns, *Kevin Robert*	19.9.1955	1976	100
Burns, *Ronald Stuart*	10.4.1933	1952	400/800R
Burrell, *Richard*	22.3.1959	1984	400R/
			400MR
Campbell, *A*	—	1900	***
Campbell, *Douglas*	30.9.1960	1980	100Bk/
			200Bk/
			800R

COMPETITOR	DATE OF BIRTH-DEATH	YEAR	EVENT/S
Campbell, *Iain*	21.4.1965	1984	100Bs/
			200Bs
Campion, *Richard*	11.3.1941	1960	400/1500/
			800R
Carter, *James Hill*	12.2.1957	1972	1500
		1976	100Bk/
			200Bk/
			400IM/
			400MR
		1980	200Bk
Clarke, *Stanley Richard*	31.7.1938	1960	100/
			400MR
Cleworth, *John Duncan*	20.4.1957	1976	400IM
Cochran, *Neil*	12.4.1965	1984	200Bk/
			200IM/
			800R
		1988	100Bf/
			100Bk/
			200IM
Collins, *Ian*	22.11.1962	1984	100Bf/
			100Bk
Cooper, *RS*	–3.1918	1906	Mile
(Also see *Gymnastics*)			
Courtman, *Percy*	14.5.1888–1915	1908	200Bs
		1912	200Bs/
			400Bs
Crawshaw, *Robert Arnold*	6.3.1869–14.9.1952	1900	200/
			200Bk
Cunningham, *Colin*	15.9.1954	1972	100Bk/
			200Bk/
			400MR/
			800R
Davey, *John Philip*	29.12.1964	1988	200Bk/
			200IM/
			400IM
Davies, *A*	—	1908	200Bs
Davies, *John Goldup*	—	1948	200Bs
Day, *John Anthony*	14.4.1965	1988	400/1500
Derbyshire, *John Henry*	29.11.1878–30.7.1938	1900	***
(Also see *Water Polo*)		1906	100/400/
			1000yR
		1908	100/800R
		1912	100
Dexter, *Neil Edward*	29.4.1955	1972	400/1500
Dickin, *Albert Edward*	1901	1920	100
(Also see *Diving*)		1924	100/800R
		1928	800R
Dickson, *John*	1900	1920	100
Dockrell, *GS*	—	1908	100
Dove, *Frederick*	27.9.1917	1936	100
Downie, *Gordon Hunter*	3.3.1955	1976	200/400/
			800R
Dunne, *David Michael*	30.11.1955	1976	800R
Easter, *Paul Robert*	14.5.1963	1984	100/200/
			400R/
			800R
Edwards, *C Wilfred*	1890	1908	100
Edwards, *Martin*	21.9.1955	1972	100Bf
Ffrench-Williams, *Martyn Yanto*	12.10.1914	1932	100/800R
		1936	100/800R
Fibbens, *Michael Wenham*	31.5.1968	1988	50/400R
Flint, *Reginald*	16.7.1903	1924	200Bs
		1928	200Bs
Foster, *Mark Andrew*	12.5.1970	1988	50/400R/
			400MR
Foster, *William*	10.7.1890–17.12.1963	1908	400/1500/
			800R
		1912	400/1500/
			800R
Francis, *William*	23.2.1911	1928	100Bk
		1932	100Bk
Gabrielson, *Romund*	22.7.1917	1936	100/800R
Gillingham, *Nicholas*	22.1.1967	1988	200Bs
Gooday, *SH*	—	1908	200Bs
Goodhew, *Duncan Alexander*	27.5.1957	1976	100Bs

COMPETITOR	DATE OF BIRTH-DEATH	YEAR	EVENT/S
		1980	100Bs/ 200Bs/ 400MR
Gough, *AJ*	—	1900	***
Gray, *Simon*	29.4.1959	1980	400/1500/ 400IM
Green, *Michael*	15.11.1963	1988	200
Hale, *Jack Irwin*	8.6.1922	1948	400/1500/ 800R
Haller, *David Joseph Geroge*	27.1.1945	1964	100
Haresnape, *Herbert Nickall*	2.7.1880–1968	1908	100Bk
		1912	100Bk
Harper, *Neil John*	21.2.1965	1984	100Bk/ 200Bk, 400MR
		1988	100Bk/ 400MR
Harrop, *Trevor James*	—	1948	100
Hassell, *RH*	—	1908	1500
Hatfield, *John Gatenby* (Also see *Water Polo*)	15.8.1893–30.3.1965	1912	400/1500/ 800R
		1920	400/1500
		1924	400/1500
		1928	400
Haynes, *WH*	—	1908	400
Head, *Peter Michael*	18.2.1935	1952	400
Hembrow, *David*	2.6.1947	1968	400R
Henry, *William*	28.6.1859	1900	4000/200 obstacle
		1906	1000yR
Hewitt, *Gordon Davison*	20.3.1958	1976	200Bf
Hodgson, *Nicholas Stephen*	26.11.1964	1984	200Bf
		1988	200Bf
Holman, *Frederick*	3.1885–23.1.1913	1908	200Bs
Holt, *John David*	27.5.1922	1948	800R
Holt, *Thomas Patrick*	21.10.1923	1948	400
Howe, *Paul Tony*	8.1.1968	1984	400/800R
		1988	200/800R
Hubble, *Philip*	19.7.1960	1980	100Bf/ 200Bf/ 800R
		1984	200Bf
Innocent, *George*	13.5.1885–4.4.1957	1908	100
		1912	200Bs/ 400Bs
Iredale, *Richard Norman*	2.2.1957	1976	100Bf
Jackson, *John Neil*	6.3.1946	1968	100Bk/ 100Bf/ 400MR
Jameson, *Andrew David*	19.2.1965	1984	100Bf/ 400MR
		1988	100/400R/ 100Bf/ 400MR
Jarvis, *Anthony A*	3.3.1946	1968	100/200/ 400R/ 800R
Jarvis, *John Arthur*	24.2.1872–9.5.1933	1900	1000/4000
		1906	400/Mile/ 1000yR
		1908	1500
Jenkins, *Brian*	20.6.1943	1964	200Bf/ 400MR
Johnson, *Nigel Robert*	14.7.1953	1972	200BS
Jones, *Roderick Stephen Gerard*	2.12.1944	1968	100Bk
Jones, *Timothy Duncan*	16.1.1967	1988	200Bf
Jones, —	—	1900	4000
Kemp, *Peter* (Also see *Water Polo*)	1878	1900	4000/200 obstacle
Kendall, *Patrick Hume*	1928	1948	100
Kendrew, *Peter*	25.4.1940	1964	400R
Kinnear, *Albert David*	24.10.1923	1948	100Bk
Lassam *Rex Goodson*	13.7.1896–14.1.1983	1920	200Bs/ 400Bs
Lee, *Kevin*	3.3.1961	1980	200/800R

COMPETITOR	DATE OF BIRTH-DEATH	YEAR	EVENT/S
Lee, *Roland*	30.7.1964	1984	400R
		1988	100/400R/ 800R/ 400MR
Leigh, *David William*	22.12.1956	1976	100Bs/ 200Bs
Leivers, *Robert Hanford*	27.12.1914–28.8.1964	1932	400/800R
		1936	400/1500/ 800R
Lerpiniere, *Peter*	3.2.1957	1976	200Bk
Lewis, *Colin*	1882	1908	100Bk
Lord, *Robert Thomas*	6.5.1945	1964	100/400/ 400R/ 800R
Lowe, *David*	28.2.1960	1980	100Bf/ 400MR
		1984	100/400R/ 400MR
McClatchey, *Alan*	16.9.1956	1976	200/400/ 400IM/ 800R
McDowall, *John*	1902	1924	100Bk
McGregor, *Robert Bilsland*	3.4.1944	1964	100/400R/ 800R/ 400MR
		1968	100/400R/ 800R/ 400MR
McKecknie, *Neil John*	28.4.1939	1956	400/800R
Maher, *Sean Lyndon*	12.5.1954	1972	100Bf/ 200Bf
		1976	200Bf
Marshall, *Paul*	28.4.1961	1980	100Bk/ 400MR
Martin-Dye, *John*	21.5.1940	1960	800R
		1964	400/400R/ 800R
Maw, *Edward*	15.6.1902	1924	200Bs
Middleton, *Jack Evan*	28.4.1917	1936	100Bk
Mills, *John Maurice*	28.3.1953	1972	200/ 100Bf/ 200Bf/ 800R/ 400MR
		1976	100Bf/ 400MR
Milton, *Hamilton Pirie Matt*	22.3.1938	1960	800R
Moist, *Lewis*	1881–14.4.1940	1908	1500
Moorhouse, *Adrian David*	24.5.1964	1984	100Bs/ 200Bs/ 400MR
		1988	100Bs/ 200Bs/ 400MR
Morris, *Peter*	30.11.1961	1980	200Bf
Naisby, *Paul Charles*	18.7.1955	1972	100Bs
		1976	200Bs
Naylor, *FH*	—	1908	200Bs
Nicholson, *Neil*	19.1.1945	1964	200Bs/ 400MR
O'Connell, *Malcolm Gregory*	19.3.1955	1972	100Bs/ 200Bs/ 400MR
O'Donnell, *William*	30.6.1942	1960	100
Park, *John Reginald*	21.2.1957	1976	100Bf
Parker, *David Geoffrey*	18.2.1959	1976	1500
Parker, *Ernest*	14.11.1895	1920	100Bk/ 200Bs
Parrack, *James Guy*	10.3.1976	1988	100Bs
Parvin, *S*	—	1908	100Bk
Pearson, *William*	1917	1936	400
Peter, *Edward Percival* (Also see *Water Polo*)	28.3.1902	1920	400/1500/ 800R
		1924	400/800R
		1928	800R

163

The Hollywood Connection

The daughters of two British Olympians became famous film actresses. The father of Jean Simmons competed as a gymnast in 1912 and Charlotte Rampling's father won a gold medal in the 1600 metres relay in 1936. Additionally, Rex Harrison's son Noel competed at the 1952 and 1956 Winter Olympics.

The 1936 figure skater Belita Jepson-Turner appeared in a number of films with skating themes under the name Belita and while a number of other British Olympians have played cameo roles, none have become well-know for their acting abilities. One Olympian who might have succeeded in this field was the 1936 figure skater Jack Dunn. In 1938 he went to Hollywood to play the lead in a film of the life of Rudolph Valentino but before shooting had begun, Dunn died of a rare disease at the age of 21.

COMPETITOR	DATE OF BIRTH-DEATH	YEAR	EVENT/S
Poulter, *Stephen*	19.2.1961	1980	200Bf/400IM
		1984	400IM
Prime, *Barry Edward*	15.7.1954	1972	200IM/400IM
Pycock, *Alfred Harold*	1900	1924	100
Radmilovic, *Paul* (Also see *Water Polo*)	5.3.1886–29.9.1968	1906	100/400/Mile
		1908	100/400/1500/800R
		1912	100
Rawlinson, *Austin*	7.11.1902	1924	100Bk
Richards, *Michael*	13.9.1950	1972	100Bk
Rigby, *Hadyn*	18.12.1936	1956	100Bk
		1960	100Bk
Roberts, *John Stuart*	22.10.1951	1968	100Bs/200Bs
Roberts, *Roger P*	12.10.1948	1968	100Bs/200Bs/400MR
Roberts, *Ronald Nathan*	11.12.1922	1952	100
		1956	100/800R
Robertson, *George G*	—	1920	200Bs/400Bs
Robinson, *William Walker*	23.6.1870	1908	200Bs
Romain, *Royston Isaac*	27.7.1918	1948	200Bs
Rowlinson, *Gerard*	15.8.1941	1960	200Bs
Rushton, *Clive*	27.10.1947	1972	100Bk
Sandon, *Frank*	3.6.1890–29.5.1979	1912	100Bk
Savage, *Leslie*	1897	1920	100/800R
Seaward, *E*	—	1908	100Bk
Service, *John Burgess*	1930	1948	200Bs
Sharp, *AT*	—	1908	400
Smith, *Hugh*	1910	1928	200Bs
Smith, *Trevor Martin*	10.1.1958	1976	100
		1980	100/200/800R/400MR
Sparkes, *Paul William*	3.8.1960	1976	1500
Sreenan, *Robert Christie*	7.5.1934	1952	1500
		1960	1500
Stacey, *David*	22.1.1965	1984	1500
Stapleton, *F*	1880	1900	200/200 obstacle
Stedman, *Ronald Edwin*	3.6.1927	1948	100
Stoney, *William S*	9.5.1898	1920	200Bs
		1924	200Bs
Summers, *Thomas Philip*	3.1.1924	1948	100Bk
Sutton, *Reginald James Cushing* (Also see *Water Polo*)	10.5.1909	1928	100/800R
		1932	100/800R
Sykes, *Graham*	20.7.1937	1956	100Bk
		1960	100Bk/400MR
Symonds, *Graham Henry*	21.3.1937	1956	200Bf
Taylor, *Henry*	17.3.1885–28.2.1951	1906	400/Mile/1000yR

COMPETITOR	DATE OF BIRTH-DEATH	YEAR	EVENT/S
		1908	400/1500/800R
		1912	400/1500/800R
		1920	400/1500/800R
Taylor, *John Philip*	6.4.1904	1924	1500
Taylor, *John Robert*	25.1.1884–22.10.1913	1908	400/100Bk
Taylor, *Mark*	24.9.1960	1980	100/800R/400MR
Terrell, *Raymond James*	5.5.1953	1968	200IM/400IM/800R
Thomson, *John S*	18.2.1903	1924	800R
Thurley, *John Philip*	12.12.1947	1964	400/1500/800R
		1968	100Bf/200Bf/800R
Thwaites, *Geoffrey Richard*	25.4.1947	1964	200Bk/400MR
Turner, *Michael*	16.6.1948	1968	100/400R
Tyldesley, *A*	—	1908	100
Unwin, *Frederick A*	1888	1908	100Bk
Wainwright, *Norman*	4.7.1914	1932	400
		1936	400/1500/800R
		1948	800R
Walkden, *Christopher Charles*	18.4.1938	1956	200Bs
		1960	400MR
Wardrop, *John Caldwell*	26.5.1932	1948	1500
		1952	100/400/800R
		1956	400/800R
Wardrop, *Robert*	26.5.1932	1952	100Bk
Watts, *Arthur G*	1911	1928	400
Webster, *George Henry*	31.7.1875	1912	100Bk
		1920	100Bk
Welsh, *Thomas Douglas*	20.4.1933	1952	100/800R
Whiteside, *Joseph*	4.8.1906	1928	800R
		1932	100/800R
Wilkie, *David Andrew*	8.3.1954	1972	100Bs/200Bs/200IM/400MR
		1976	100Bs/200Bs/400MR
Williams, *Kenneth*	17.2.1937	1956	100/800R
Willis, *S*	—	1908	100Bk
Willmott, *Stuart*	4.6.1964	1984	1500/400IM
Windeatt, *Malcolm Barrie*	5.4.1952	1972	100/400MR
Winter, *HC*	—	1900	***

COMPETITOR	DATE OF BIRTH-DEATH	YEAR	EVENT/S
Woodroffe, *Martin John*	8.9.1950	1968	100Bf/
			200Bf/
			200IM/
			400IM/
			400MR
Worthington, *James*	3.1902	1924	100Bk

Swimming
WOMEN

Swimming for women was introduced into the Olympic programme in 1912 and Great Britain has been represented on every occasion.

Where no letters follow the distance this indicates a freestyle event. For other styles the following abbreviations have been used:

Bf = Butterfly   Bk = Backstroke   Bs = Breaststroke
IM = Individual medley   MR = Medley relay
R = Relay (freestyle)   SS = Synchronised swimming-solo
SSd = Synchronised swimming-duet

COMPETITOR	DATE OF BIRTH-DEATH	YEAR	EVENT/S
Adams, *Anne Wilma*	30.1.1960	1976	400IM
Admans, *Jane*	21.6.1959	1980	100Bk
Alexander, *Jane Elizabeth*	13.12.1958	1976	100Bf/
			200Bf
Allardice, *Lesley*	8.7.1957	1972	100/200/
			400R/
			400MR
Amos, *Linda*	22.6.1946	1964	100
Ashton, *Diana Elizabeth*	26.9.1955	1972	100Bk/
			200Bk
Atkin, *Tracey Anne*	14.8.1971	1988	800/
			400IM
Atkinson, *Joanne Louise*	4.3.1959	1976	100Bf/
			200Bf
Auton, *Margaret M*	9.2.1951	1968	100Bf/
			200Bf/
			400MR
Bairstow, *Pamela*	15.4.1954	1972	200Bk/
			400MR
Barker, *Florence*	1908	1924	100/400R
Barnard, *Susan*	18.1.1961	1976	200/400
Barnwell, *Angela Mary*	11.1.1936	1952	100/400R
Beasley, *Joy Wendy*	25.7.1962	1976	100Bk/
			200Bk/
			400MR
		1980	100Bk
Beavan, *Patricia Catherine*	27.5.1951	1972	200Bs
Bewley, *Helen*	14.5.1968	1988	200Bf
Birkenhead, *Lillian*	19.1.1905–3.1979	1920	100
Botham, *Jean Annabel*	12.2.1935	1952	100/400R
Bowman, *Sandra*	10.4.1967	1984	100Bs
Boyle, *Helen L*	1907	1924	100Bk
Bradshaw, *Ann Patricia Mary*	25.3.1957	1976	200/
			400IM/
			400R
Brown, *Jacqueline Elizabeth*	6.6.1953	1968	100Bk/
			200Bk
		1972	100Bk
Brown, *Moira Catherine*	20.11.1952	1972	200Bf
Brownsdon, *Susannah*	16.10.1965	1980	100Bs
		1984	200Bs
		1988	100Bs/
			200Bs/
			400IM/
			400MR
Burnham, *Helen Blanche Mary*	10.5.1956	1976	100Bs
Burrell, *Wendy*	16.5.1952	1968	100Bk/
			200Bk/
			400MR
Caplin, *Jean M*	12.1930	1948	200Bs

COMPETITOR	DATE OF BIRTH-DEATH	YEAR	EVENT/S
Carson, *Gladys Helena*	1903	1924	200Bs
Church, *Elizabeth Mabel*	11.3.1930	1948	200Bs
Clayton, *Sheila*	19.7.1951	1968	400
Cooper, *Margaret Joyce*	18.4.1909	1928	100/
			100Bk/
			400R
		1932	100/400/
			100Bk/
			400R
Cooper, *Susan*	24.6.1963	1980	100Bf
Cotterill, *Mary Anne*	16.10.1945	1964	100Bf/
			400MR
Coull, *Joanna*	4.12.1973	1988	400R/
			400MR
Cripps, *Annabelle*	16.2.1968	1984	200/800/
			400R
		1988	50/100/
			100Bf/
			400R
Croft, *June Alexandra*	17.6.1963	1980	100/400/
			400R/
			400MR
		1984	100/200/
			400/400R/
			400MR
		1988	100/200/
			400/400R
Curwen, *Daisy*	6.12.1889	1912	100
Davies, *Elizabeth Valerie*	29.6.1912	1932	100/
			100Bk/
			400R
Davies, *Sharron*	1.11.1962	1976	100Bk
		1980	400/
			400IM/
			400R
Davison, *Sally*	1.12.1950	1968	200/400
Donnelly, *Linda*	21.10.1969	1988	400R
Edmondson, *Susan Stewart*	21.2.1956	1972	100/200/
			400/400R
		1976	100/200/
			400/400R
Edwards, *Margaret*	28.3.1939	1956	100Bk
Ellery, *Vera Patricia*	10.8.1926	1948	100Bk
Enfield, *Jacqueline Ida*	19.9.1947	1964	200Bs
Ewart, *Fearne*	20.11.1936	1956	100/400R
Fibbens, *Nicola*	29.4.1964	1984	100/
			100Bf/
			400R/
			400MR
Fletcher, *Jennie*	19.3.1890–1968	1912	100/400R
Foot, *Caroline Joy*	14.3.1965	1988	100Bf/
			400MR
Frampton, *Lorna*	2.4.1920	1936	100Bk
Frank, *Helen*	1.1.1971	1988	200Bs
Gegan, *Judith Ann*	10.11.1944	1964	100Bf
Gibbs, *Dora E*	—	1928	200Bs
Gibson, *Catherine*	25.3.1931	1948	400/
			100Bk/
			400R
Gilbert, *Irene*	22.1.1903	1924	200Bs
Gilfillan, *Ruth*	6.3.1967	1988	200/400
Girvan, *Margaret Therese*	2.10.1932–1979	1956	400/400R
Gomm, *Margaret Olive*	27.3.1921	1936	200Bs
Goodwin, *Lian Elizabeth*	29.4.1968	1988	SSd
Gordon, *Helen Orr*	10.5.1934	1948	200Bs
(As McKay in 1956)		1952	200Bs
		1956	200Bs
Gore, *Debra*	16.7.1967	1984	400R
Gosden, *Christine Loraine*	16.9.1939	1956	200Bs
		1960	200Bs
Grant, *Zilpha*	29.7.1919	1936	100/400R
Gray, *Elaine Dorothy*	29.5.1958	1976	100/400R
Green, *June Margaret*	18.1.1959	1972	400/800
Grinham, *Judith Brenda*	5.3.1939	1956	100Bk/
			400R

COMPETITOR	DATE OF BIRTH-DEATH	YEAR	EVENT/S
Hamblen, *Mabel*	1905–18.4.1955	1928	200Bs
Hancock, *Audrey Morris*	28.2.1919	1936	100Bk
Hardcastle, *Sarah*	9.4.1969	1984	400/800/400IM
Harding, *Phylis May*	15.12.1907	1924	100Bk
		1928	100Bk
		1932	100Bk
		1936	100Bk
Harris, *Christine Robertson Stuart*	24.6.1942	1960	400R
Harris, *Dianne Adrienne*	14.8.1948	1968	100Bs/200Bs
		1972	100Bs
Harris, *Valerie Gladys*	5.12.1935	1952	100Bs
Harrison, *Dorothy Elizabeth*	16.3.1950	1968	100Bs/200Bs/400MR
		1972	100Bs/400MR
Hill, *Deborah*	21.6.1960	1976	400R/400MR
Hill, *Jean Cameron*	15.7.1964	1984	100Bs/400MR
		1988	200IM
Hinton, *Margery*	25.6.1915	1928	200Bs
		1932	200Bs
		1936	100
Hogben, *Frances*	16.10.1937	1956	100/400R
Hohmann, *MM see* Kelly			
Holmyard, *Caroline*	17.12.1961	1984	SS/SSd
Hoyle, *Julie*	27.3.1939	1956	100Bk
Hughes, *Edna Tildesley*	1.8.1916	1932	100/400R
		1936	400R
Jackson, *Alexandra Elizabeth*	10.6.1952	1968	100/200/400R/400MR
James, *Amanda Elizabeth*	25.10.1960	1976	100Bk
James, *Hilda May*	1904	1920	300/400R
Jameson, *Helen*	25.9.1963	1980	100Bk/200Bk/400MR
Jarvis, *Christine Anne*	21.12.1949	1972	100Bs/200Bs
		1976	100Bs/200Bs
Jeans, *Constance Mabel*	23.8.1899	1920	100/300/400R
		1924	100/400/400R
Jeavons, *Jean Anne*	22.5.1956	1972	100Bf/200Bf/400MR
Jeffrey, *Margaret*	23.1.1920	1936	400/400R
Jenner, *Sue Pamela*	26.3.1960	1976	100Bf/400MR
Johnson, *Pamela*	25.9.1948	1964	400IM
Jones, *Susan Mary*	19.9.1954	1972	800
Keen, *Sandra*	13.8.1947	1964	100/400R
Kellock, *Fiona J*	26.10.1948	1968	100/400R
Kelly, *Margaret Mary*	22.9.1956	1976	100Bs/200Bs/400MR
(As Hohmann in 1988)		1980	100Bs/200Bs/400MR
		1988	100Bs
Kerswell, *Sarah*	6.8.1965	1980	400IM
King, *Ellen Elizabeth*	16.1.1909	1924	100Bk
		1928	100Bk/400R
Kingston, *Vera*	4.2.1917	1936	200Bs
Langford, *Mary*	23.11.1894	1912	100
Lewis, *Sylvia Anne*	23.12.1941	1960	100Bk/400MR
		1964	100Bk
Linton, *Phyllis Margaret*	9.6.1929	1952	400R
Long, *Elizabeth Carole*	10.6.1947	1964	100/400R/400MR
Long, *Zara Letitia*	6.11.1970	1984	200IM
		1988	200IM
Lonsbrough, *Anita*	10.8.1941	1960	200Bs/400MR
		1964	400IM
Lovatt, *Kaye*	13.4.1964	1980	400R
Ludgrove, *Linda Kay*	8.9.1947	1964	100Bk/400MR
McDowell, *Jean H*	22.9.1908	1928	100
McDowell, *Margaret Gibson*	10.1.1936	1952	100Bk
McKay, *HO see* Gordon			
McKenzie, *Grace*	8.7.1903	1920	100/400R
		1924	400R
Mayne, *Edith*	29.9.1905–5.1953	1928	400
Mellor, *Karen Marie*	6.5.1969	1988	800
Mitchell, *Stella Marian Minter*	21.7.1947	1964	200Bs/400MR
Molesworth, *Doris M*	1902	1924	400
Moore, *Isabella*	23.10.1894–7.3.1975	1912	100/400R
Morcom, *Gladys Elsie*	31.10.1918	1936	400
Morton, *Anne*	20.5.1937	1956	100Bf
Morton, *Lucy*	23.2.1898–26.8.1980	1924	200Bs
Musgrave, *Pauline Rita*	25.7.1936	1952	100Bk
Nielsen, *Patricia Eleanor*	22.6.1930	1948	100/400/400R
Noakes, *Beryl O*	29.7.1942	1960	400R
Norfolk, *Jill Rosemary*	15.2.1947	1964	100Bk, 400MR
Oldroyd, *Jean*	15.12.1942	1960	100Bf
Osgerby, *Ann*	20.1.1963	1980	100Bf/200Bf/400MR
		1984	100Bf/200Bf
Osgerby, *Janet*	20.1.1963	1980	100Bf/200Bf
Page, *Sharon Louise*	27.6.1971	1988	100Bk
Phillips, *Glenda May*	12.5.1945	1964	100Bf
Preece, *Lillian*	1.4.1928	1948	100/400R
		1952	100/400/400R
Purvis, *Samantha*	24.6.1967	1984	200Bf
Radcliffe, *Charlotte Helen*	3.8.1903	1920	400R
Rae, *AW 'Nan'*	13.1.1941	1960	400
Randage, *Amanda Joy*	27.9.1951	1972	200Bs
Ratcliffe, *Shelagh Hudson*	25.1.1952	1968	200IM/400IM/400R
		1972	200IM/400IM
Read, *Katherine*	30.6.1969	1984	200Bk
		1988	100Bk/200Bk/400MR
Richardson, *Susan Jane*	26.1.1955	1972	200IM/400IM
		1976	400IM
Rose, *Beverley*	21.1.1964	1984	100Bk/400MR
Rudd, *Deborah Lesley*	27.9.1959	1976	200Bs
		1980	200Bs
Samuel, *Judy V*	2.8.1943	1960	400/400R
Sancroft, *Florence*	1903	1920	300
Shearn, *Nicola Maria*	14.10.1966	1988	SS/SSd
Sheppard, *Alison*	5.11.1972	1988	50
Sillett, *Pauline*	22.4.1949	1964	400/400R
Sirs, *Judy*	6.3.1954	1972	400R
Slatter, *Helen Mary*	7.6.1960	1988	200Bk
Slattery, *Jill*	25.5.1945	1964	200Bs
		1968	100Bs/200Bs
Speirs, *Annie*	14.7.1889–10.1926	1912	100/400R

COMPETITOR	DATE OF BIRTH-DEATH	YEAR	EVENT/S
Stanley, *Gaynor*	3.1.1966	1984	200Bs/ 200IM/ 400IM
Steer, *Irene*	10.8.1889–18.4.1947	1912	100/400R
Steward, *Natalie A*	30.4.1943	1960	100/ 100Bk/ 400R/ 400MR
Stewart, *Sarah Gillow Marshall*	19.7.1911	1928	400/400R
Storey, *Doris*	21.12.1919	1936	200Bs
Sutherland, *Diana Margaret*	1.11.1954	1972	200/400/ 100Bk/ 200Bk/ 400R
Tanner, *Irene Vera*	1906	1924	100/400/ 400R
		1928	100/400/ 400R
Treers, *Gillian S*	8.2.1952	1968	100/100Bf
Varcoe, *Helen Gradwell*	18.2.1907	1932	400R
Wadham, *Olive L*	23.3.1909	1936	100/400R
Walker, *Diana Barclay*	2.10.1955	1972	100/ 400IM
Watt, *Sheila*	27.1.1941	1960	100Bf/ 400MR
Wellington, *Margaret Olive*	23.12.1926	1948	100/400/ 400R
White, *Catherine*	26.6.1965	1984	100Bk/ 200Bk
Wilkinson, *Daphne M*	17.4.1932	1952	400
Wilkinson, *Diana Elizabeth*	17.3.1944	1960	100
		1964	100/400R
Wilkinson, *Kim Jacqueline*	21.3.1961	1976	200Bk
Williams, *Susan Elizabeth*	18.3.1952	1968	200/400/ 800/400R
Willington, *Avis*	12.8.1956	1972	800/ 200IM
Willmott, *Jacquelina*	19.3.1965	1980	100/200/ 400/800/ 400R
Wilson, *Carolyn*	11.3.1959	1984	SSd
Wilson, *Lynne*	5.1.1969	1988	200Bf
Wolstenholme, *Cecelia*	18.5.1915	1932	200Bs
Wood, *Grace*	1932	1952	400
Wrigley, *Jean*	1935	1952	200Bs
Yate, *Helen Marie*	1.1.1921	1948	100Bk

Table Tennis

Table tennis was first included in the Olympic programme in 1988.

S = Singles D = Men's Doubles

COMPETITOR	DATE OF BIRTH-DEATH	YEAR	EVENT/S
Andrew, *Skylet*	31.3.1962	1988	D
Cooke, *Alan*	23.3.1966	1988	S/D
Douglas, *Desmond*	20.7.1955	1988	S/D
Prean, *Carl*	20.8.1967	1988	S/D

Tennis *see* Lawn Tennis

Track & Field

MEN

Great Britain, Greece and Australia are the only countries to have been represented in the track & field events at every Olympic Games

AA = All-around b = Both hands CC = Cross-country
Dec = Decathlon DT = Discus fs = Freestyle g = Greek style
h = Hurdles HJ = High jump HT = Hammer JT = Javelin
k = Kilometres LJ = Long jump m = Miles Mar = Marathon
MR = Medley relay Pen = Pentathlon PV = Pole vault
R = Relay s = Standing SP = Shot Put St = Steeplechase
TJ = Triple jump Tm = Team event TW = Tug-of-War
W = Walking event
In 1908, Great Britain entered three teams for the Tug-of-War which have been separately designated:-
(A) = City of London Police (B) = Liverpool Police
(C) = 'K' Division, Metropolitan Police

COMPETITOR	DATE OF BIRTH-DEATH	YEAR	EVENT/S
Abrahams, *Harold Maurice*	15.12.1899–14.1.1978	1920	100/200/ 400R/LJ
		1924	100/200/ 400R
Abrahams, *Sidney Solomon*	11.2.1885–14.5.1957	1906	100/LJ
		1912	LJ
Adams, *Brian*	13.3.1949	1976	20kW
Adcocks, *Willam Arthur*	11.11.1941	1968	Mar
Adedoyin, *Prince Adegboyega Folaranmi*	11.9.1922	1948	HJ/LJ
Ahearne, *Timothy*	18.8.1885–11.1968	1908	110h/sLJ/ LJ/TJ
Ainsworth-Davis, *John Creyghton*	23.4.1895–3.1.1976	1920	400/1600R
Akabusi, *Kriss Kezie Uche Chukwu*	28.11.1958	1984	400/1600R
		1988	400h/ 1600R
Alder, *James Noel Carroll*	10.6.1940	1968	Mar
Allday, *Peter Charles*	27.6.1927	1952	HT
		1956	HT
Allen, *Lawrence*	25.4.1921	1952	10kW
Alsop, *Frederick John*	20.10.1938	1960	LJ/TJ
		1964	LJ/TJ
		1968	TJ
Anderson, *Arthur Emilius David*	30.9.1886–21.10.1967	1912	100/200
Anderson, *Gerard Rupert Leslie*	15.3.1889–9.11.1914	1912	110h
Anderson, *Timothy Donald*	16.10.1925	1952	PV
Anderson, *William Davidson*	–1.1915	1906	400/800
Angus, *Keith*	5.4.1943	1976	Mar
Anthony, *Donald William James*	6.11.1928	1956	HT
Appleby, *Frederick*	30.10.1879–7.4.1956	1908	Mar
Applegarth, *William Reuben*	11.5.1890–5.12.1958	1912	100/200/ 400R
Archer, *John*	10.8.1921	1948	400R
Armstrong, *Gary*	9.4.1952	1972	400
Ashby, *Stanley T*	—	1928	1500
Ashford, *FM*	—	1908	800
Ashington, *Henry Sherard Osborn*	25.9.1891–31.1.1917	1912	sLJ/LJ
Ashurst, *Andrew John*	2.1.1965	1988	PV
Askew, *Henry Edward*	31.12.1917	1948	LJ
Astley, *Arthur*	–1916	1908	400/800
Bailey, *Emmanuel McDonald*	8.12.1920	1948	100
		1952	100/200/ 400R
Bailey, *George William*	29.4.1906	1932	3kSt/5k
Baker, *Benjamin Howard*	15.2.1892–10.9.1987	1912	sHJ/HJ
		1920	HJ/TJ
Baker, *Philip John*	1.11.1889–9.10.1982	1912	800/1500
		1920	800/1500
Bannister, *Roger Gilbert*	23.3.1929	1952	1500
Banthorpe, *Ralph*	6.2.1949	1968	200/400R
Barker, *Henry*		1908	3200St
Barker, *James J*	6.11.1892	1912	100
Barkway, *Raymond Charles*	24.8.1924–1956	1948	110h
Barnes, *E*	—	1908	Mar

COMPETITOR	DATE OF BIRTH-DEATH	YEAR	EVENT/S
Barrett, *Edward*	3.11.1880	1908	SP/DTfs/ JTfs/ TW(A)
(Also see *Wrestling*)			
Barrett, *Henry Frederick*	30.12.1879	1908	Mar
		1912	Mar
Barrett, *John James*	1880	1908	SP
Barry, *Steven John*	25.10.1950	1984	20kW
Beale, *James George*	7.2.1881	1908	Mar
		1912	Mar
Beattie, *Philip Garth*	8.9.1963	1984	400h
Beavers, *Walter James*	1903	1928	5k/10k
Beckwith, *Charles Edward*	12.5.1901	1924	SP
Bedford, *David Colin*	30.12.1949	1972	5k/10k
Bell, *Alan Richard*	10.6.1957	1980	400/1600R
Bell, *Reginald Douglas*	8.1904	1928	1500
Bellerby, *Alfred Courthope Benson*	26.1.1888–10.4.1979	1908	HJ/LJ
Benham, *John C*	1900	1924	CC
Benn, *Maurice*	9.11.1946	1968	1500
Bennett, *Ainsley*	22.7.1954	1976	200/1600R
Bennett, *Charles*	28.12.1870–9.3.1949	1900	1500/ 4kSt/ 5kTm
Bennett, *Todd Anthony*	6.7.1962	1984	400/1600R
		1988	400/1600R
Bicourt, *John Peter*	25.10.1945	1972	3kSt
		1976	3kSt
Biddulph, *NS*	—	1928	3kSt
Bignall, *Herbert James*	28.1.1906–30.10.1989	1928	Mar
Binns, *Stephen John*	25.8.1960	1988	10k
Birrell, *Joseph Robert*	11.3.1930	1948	110h
Birrell, *Robert*	6.3.1938	1960	110h
Black, *Christopher Francis*	1.1.1950	1976	HT
		1980	HT
Black, *David John*	2.10.1952	1976	5k
		1980	Mar
Blackett, *Frederick J*	—	1924	400h
Blagg, *Paul*	23.1.1960	1988	50kW
Blakeney, *Harry Edward Hugh*	6.10.1890	1912	100/110h
Bleadon, *Wilfred Harry*	6.3.1887–30.8.1965	1908	sLJ/LJ
Blewitt, *Charles Edward*	1.11.1895–30.5.1954	1920	3kTm/5k
		1928	3kSt
Blinston, *John Alan*	15.6.1944	1968	5k
Bond, *Laurence Temple*	31.12.1905–1.12.1943	1928	PV
Boosey, *Derek Charles J*	15.7.1942	1956	TJ
Boreham, *Colin Aubrey Geddes*	23.6.1954	1984	Dec
Boulter, *John Peter*	18.11.1940	1964	800
		1968	1500
Box, *Kenneth James*	1.12.1930	1956	100/400R
Boyce, *Edward*	2.6.1913	1936	LJ/TJ
Boyd, *Ian Hugh*	8.12.1933	1956	1500
Boyes, *Max Graville*	6.5.1934	1960	400h
Bradstock, *Arne-Roald*	24.4.1962	1984	JT
		1988	JT
Brasher, *Christopher William*	21.8.1928	1952	3kSt
		1956	3kSt
Braughton, *John*	22.2.1921	1948	5k
Brewer, *Ernest John Aisne*	21.10.1914	1948	DT
Bridge, *Robert*	16.4.1883–1953	1912	10kW
Briggs, *Martin Christopher*	4.1.1964	1984	400h
Brightwell, *Robbie Ian*	27.10.1939	1960	400/1600R
		1964	400/1600R
Britton, *Halland*	18.2.1890–4.2.1975	1924	10k
Brown, *Arthur Godfrey Kilner*	21.2.1915	1936	400/1600R
Brown, *BC*	—	1908	3500W
Brown, *Philip Andrew*	6.1.1962	1984	400/1600R
		1988	1600R
Browne, *Frederick Thomas*	21.2.1890	1912	200
Bryan-Jones, *David Gareth*	25.2.1943	1969	3kSt
Buckley, *FJ*	—	1908	3200St
Buckner, *Jack Richard*	22.9.1961	1988	5k
Bull, *Michael Anthony*	11.9.1946	1968	PV
		1972	PV
Bullivant, *Michael John*	1.3.1934	1964	10k
Bunney, *Elliott John*	11.12.1966	1988	400R

COMPETITOR	DATE OF BIRTH-DEATH	YEAR	EVENT/S
Burghley, *Lord*	9.2.1905–22.10.1981	1924	110h
		1928	110h/400h
		1932	110h/ 400h/ 1600R
Burns, *James Alexander*	5.11.1907	1932	5k
		1936	10k
Burton, *G*	—	1908	400h
Burton, *Leslie Aubrey*	—	1908	400h
Burton, *Robert*	11.4.1885–14.6.1950	1912	800
Butler, *Guy Montagu*	25.8.1899–22.2.1981	1920	400/1600R
		1924	400/1600R
		1928	200
Butler, *John*	–1960	1908	3500W/ 10kW
Butler, *Thomas*	—	1908	TW(B)
Butterfield, *George*	17.10.1917	1908	800/1500
Callender, *Clarence*	16.11.1961	1988	400R
Campbell, *Colin William Ashburner*	20.6.1946	1968	400/1600R
(Also see *Bobsleigh*)		1972	800
Campbell, *James Harper Poynter*	4.11.1901–2.7.1975	1924	PV
Campbell, *Walter Menzies*	22.5.1941	1964	200/400R
Canning, *George*	—	1920	TW
Capes, *Geoffrey Lewis*	22.8.1949	1972	SP
		1976	SP
		1980	SP
Carey, *Denis*	6.8.1872	1912	HT
Carnelly, *Stephen Henry*	22.9.1880	1906	5m
Carr, *Gerald Anthony*	1.2.1936	1956	DT
Carroll, *Timothy J*	8.7.1888	1912	HJ/TJ
		1920	HJ
Carter, *Andrew William*	29.1.1949	1972	800
Carter, *Christopher Sydney*	25.12.1942	1964	800
		1968	800
Carter, *Frank T*	—	1908	10mW
Chaffe, *Walter*	2.4.1870–22.4.1918	1908	TW(C)
		1912	TW
Chapman, *David John*	21.8.1936	1960	3kSt
Chapman, *M*	—	1908	100
Chataway, *Christopher John*	31.1.1931	1952	5k
		1956	5k
Chauncy, *Frederick Charles Leslie*	22.12.1904–4.6.1986	1928	400h
Chavasse, *Christopher Maude*	9.11.1884–10.3.1962	1908	400
Chavasse, *Noel Godfrey*	9.11.1884–4.8.1917	1908	400
Chote, *Morville Vincent William*	6.10.1924	1948	JT
Christie, *Linford*	2.4.1960	1988	100/200/ 400R
Churcher, *Harold George*	21.11.1910–24.6.1972	1948	10kW
Churchill, *Arnold Robertson*	4.3.1883–23.4.1975	1906	1500/5m
Clark, *Arthur*	1900	1924	3kTm
Clark, *Duncan McDougall Munro*	22.6.1915	1948	HT
		1952	HT
Clark, *Frederick Ernest*	—	1924	10kW
Clark, *James Michael*	6.10.1874–29.12.1929	1908	TW(B)
Clark, *Ronald Sydney*	9.3.1930	1956	Mar
Clarke, *William T*	1873	1908	Mar
Clement, *Frank James*	26.4.1952	1976	800/1500
Clibbon, *Charles Thomas*	3.2.1895	1920	10k
		1924	5k/10k
Close, *Frank*	23.4.1913–12.2.1970	1936	5k
Coales, *William*	8.1.1886	1908	3mTm/5m
Coates, *Dennis Malcolm*	11.2.1953	1976	3kSt
Coe, *Sebastian Newbold*	29.9.1956	1980	800/1500
		1984	800/1500
Cohen, *Glendon Howard*	22.4.1954	1976	400/1600R
		1980	400/1600R
Cohen, *Horace James*	6.5.1906	1928	LJ
Coleman, *George William*	21.11.1916	1952	10kW
		1956	20kW
Collins, *M*	—	1908	DT
Connor, *Keith Leroy*	16.9.1957	1980	TJ
		1984	TJ
Constable, *George Charles*	—	1928	10k
Cook, *Gary Peter*	10.1.1958	1984	1600R
Cooper, *John Hugh*	18.12.1940–3.3.1974	1964	400h/

The First British Olympian

The first Briton to actually compete in the Olympic Games was Charles Henry Stuart Gmelin who was fourth in the third heat of the 100 metres in **Athens on 6 April 1896. Gmelin was born on 28 May 1872 and educated at Magdalen College School and Keble College, Oxford. He became Headmaster of Freshfield School,** **Oxford, and held a number of ecclesiastical appointments in the area before his death on 12 October 1950.**

COMPETITOR	DATE OF BIRTH-DEATH	YEAR	EVENT/S
			1600R
		1968	400h
Cormack, *JN*	—	1906	Mar
Cornes, *John Frederick*	23.3.1910	1932	1500
		1936	1500
Cornish, *Lionel John*	25.12.1879	1908	sLJ/LJ
Cottrill, *William*	14.10.1889	1912	1500/ 3kTm
Cox, *Stanley Ernest Walker*	15.7.1918	1948	Mar
		1952	Mar
Crabb, *Stephen Paul*	30.11.1963	1988	1500
Crabbe, *Reginald Percy*	15.7.1883–22.10.1964	1906	800/1500
Cram, *Stephen*	14.10.1960	1980	1500
		1984	1500
		1988	800/1500
Craner, *Walter William*	17.7.1907–12.1.1987	1928	1600R
Cropper, *David*	26.12.1945	1968	800
		1972	800
Cross, *Sidney Ernest*	7.7.1925	1948	TJ
Cruttenden, *Arthur Roy*	18.2.1925	1956	LJ
Cullen, *Peter Sydney*	24.8.1932	1956	JT
Cummings, *David*	1894–9.1986	1924	3kSt
Cummins, *Laurence Michael*	1889	1920	CC
Curry, *Thomas Peter Ellison*	22.7.1921	1948	3kSt
Dalrymple, *James*	2.2.1892–14.5.1960	1924	JT
Dalrymple, *Malcolm James William*	2.12.1922	1948	JT
Daly, *John James*	22.2.1880	1904	2590St
		1906	5m/Mar
d'Arcy, *Victor Henry Augustus*	30.6.1887–1961	1912	100/200/ 400R
		1920	100/200/ 400R
Dauban de Silhouette, *Henri*	1903	1924	JT
Davies, *Howard Granville*	5.8.1944	1968	400
Davies, *John*	17.1.1949	1968	800
Davies, *Lynn*	20.5.1942	1964	100/400R/ LJ
		1968	LJ
		1972	LJ
Davies-Hale, *Paul*	21.6.1962	1984	3kSt
Davis, *CC*	—	1908	400
Deakin, *Joseph Edmund*	6.2.1879–30.6.1972	1908	1500/ 3mTm/5m
Dean, *Graham Alan*	26.1.1942	1964	800
Dear, *David Glyndwr*	8.6.1945	1972	400R
Denley, *Michael John*	21.11.1931	1952	JT
Densham, *John Boon*	2.2.1880–8.1.1975	1908	400h
Dick, *Alan*	15.4.1930	1952	400/1600R
Dickenson, *Derek Paul*	4.12.1949	1976	HT
		1980	HT
Dickinson, *Robert Joicey*	20.5.1901–7.8.1981	1924	HJ
Dineen, *Michael D*	—	1908	TJ
Disley, *John Ivor*	20.11.1928	1952	3kSt
		1956	3kSt
Douglas, *Ewan Campbell Kennedy*	14.11.1922	1948	HT
		1952	HT
Dowler, *Joseph*	1.2.1879–13.2.1931	1908	TW(C)
		1912	TW
Downing, *Thomas*	—	1908	3200St
Dowson, *Charles S*	—	1920	3kW/ 10kW
Drake, *Norman Hercy*	7.7.1912–16.11.1972	1936	HT
		1948	HT
Dugmore, *Cyril Patrick William Francis Radclyffe*	20.5.1882	1908	TJ
Dumbill, *Thomas Henry*	23.9.1884	1912	10kW

COMPETITOR	DATE OF BIRTH-DEATH	YEAR	EVENT/S
Dunbar, *Eric V*	—	1920	110h/HJ
Duncan, *Alexander*	1884	1908	Mar
Duncan, *Robert Cochran*	4.10.1887	1908	100/200
		1912	100/200
Eaton, *William Edward*	20.4.1909–1.4.1938	1936	10k
Ebbage, *Ernest Walter*	1.8.1873–2.9.1943	1908	TW(C)
Edgington, *John William*	5.4.1936	1964	20kW
Edward, *Harry Francis Vincent*	15.4.1895–8.7.1973	1920	100/200/ 400R
			5m
Edwards, *Francis Millward*	1885	1906	5m
Edwards, *Jonathan David*	10.5.1966	1988	TJ
Edwards, *Paul M*	16.2.1959	1988	SP
Eley, *Bryan*	28.1.1939	1968	50kW
Elliot, *Launceston*	9.6.1874–8.8.1930	1896	100
(Also see Gymnastics, Weightlifting & Wrestling)			
Elliott, *Geoffrey Michael*	7.4.1931	1952	PV/Dec
Elliott, *Peter*	9.10.1962	1984	800
		1988	800/1500
Ellis, *Cyril*	23.2.1904–29.3.1973	1924	1500
		1928	1500
Ellis, *Michael John*	3.9.1936	1960	HT
Embleton, *Philip Bruce*	20.12.1948–22.5.1974	1972	20kW
Engelhart, *Stanley Eric*	1905	1932	200/400R
English, *Joseph C*	—	1908	800/3200St
Evans, *Frank*	7.4.1925	1952	800
Evenson, *Thomas*	9.1.1910	1932	3kSt
		1936	3kSt
Eyre, *Leonard*	27.11.1925–1986	1952	1500
Fairbairn-Crawford, *Ivo Frank*	20.12.1884–24.8.1959	1908	800/1500
Fairbrother, *Crawford William*	1.12.1936–11.1986	1960	HJ
Fairgrieve, *John*	18.4.1926	1948	200
Farrell, *Michael Arthur*	27.4.1933	1956	800
Farrell, *Thomas Stanley*	23.9.1932	1956	400h
		1960	800
Farrimond, *Anthony*	1894	1924	Mar
Faulkner, *Stewart*	19.2.1969	1988	LJ
Ferris, *Samuel*	29.8.1900–21.3.1980	1924	Mar
		1928	Mar
		1932	Mar
Finlay, *Donald Osborne*	27.5.1909–18.4.1970	1932	110h/ 400R
		1936	110h/ 400R
		1948	110h
Flaxman, *Alfred Edward*	1879–1.7.1916	1908	sHJ/DT/ DTg/JT
Flynn, *Oliver T*	30.6.1950	1976	20kW
Ford, *Bernard William*	3.8.1952	1976	10k
		1980	Mar
Ford, *Howard*	18.12.1905–28.3.1986	1928	Dec
Forster, *Kevin*	27.9.1958	1988	Mar
Forsythe, *Mark Clifford*	10.8.1965	1988	LJ
Foster, *Brendan*	12.1.1948	1972	1500
		1976	5k/10k
		1980	10k
Francom, *Septimus*	14.9.1882	1912	Mar
Freeman, *Walter*	7.9.1893–10.1987	1920	CC
Fuller, *Stanley Charles*	13.10.1907	1932	100/200/ 400R
Fyffe, *Alan Herbert*	30.4.1884–5.3.1939	1908	HT
Gabbett, *Peter John*	19.11.1941	1968	Dec
		1972	Dec
Gaby, *Frederick Richard*	12.3.1895–7.4.1984	1924	110h
		1928	110h
George, *John Phelps*	1882–26.11.1962	1908	100/200

COMPETITOR	DATE OF BIRTH-DEATH	YEAR	EVENT/S
Giles, *John Alfred*	9.2.1927	1948	SP
		1952	SP
Gill, *Cyril William*	21.4.1902–1.9.1989	1928	100/200/
			400R
Gillingham, *Martin Charles*	9.9.1963	1984	400h
Ginty, *James*	4.4.1908	1936	3kSt
Girvan, *Martin*	17.4.1960	1984	HT
Glover, *Ernest*	19.2.1891	1912	5k/10k/
			CC
Gmelin, *Charles Henry Stuart*	28.5.1872–12.10.1950	1896	100/400
Goodfellow, *Frederick William*	7.3.1874–22.11.1960	1908	TW(A)
Goodwin, *Gordon Reginald*	17.12.1895	1924	10kW
Gordon, *Colin Ernest Sutherland*	24.12.1907–8.1960	1928	HJ
Goudge, *Christopher Edward*	4.3.1935	1960	400h
Gould, *E. Wyatt*	—	1908	400h
Goulding, *Grantley Thomas Smart*	23.3.1874	1896	110h
Gracie, *David Keir*	26.1.1927	1952	400h
Graham, *Derek Austin*	22.9.1941	1964	5k
Graham, *Robert*	4.8.1909–17.4.1963	1936	1500
Graham, *Timothy Joseph Michael*	31.5.1939	1964	400/1600R
Grant, *Dalton*	8.4.1966	1988	HJ
Grantham, *W*	—	1908	3200St
Gray, *George H*	—	1920	110h
Greaves, *Wilbert E*	23.12.1956	1980	110h
		1984	110h
Green, *Arthur William*	27.7.1904–19.8.1981	1928	400
Green, *Brian William*	15.5.1941	1972	100/200/
			400R
Green, *Henry Harold*	15.7.1886–12.3.1934	1912	Mar
Green, *Thomas William*	30.3.1894–29.3.1975	1932	50kW
Greggan, *William*	—	1908	TW(B)
Gregory, *John Arthur*	22.6.1923	1948	400R
		1952	400R
Griffiths, *Cecil Richmond*	20.1.1901	1920	1600R
Groenings, *Oswald E* (later Bickbeck)	—	1908	110h/400h
Gunn, *Charles Edward J*	1885	1920	3kW/
			10kW
Gutteridge, *Jeffrey*	28.10.1956	1976	PV
		1984	PV
Hackney, *Roger Graham*	2.9.1957	1980	3kSt
		1984	3kSt
		1988	3kSt
Haley, *Ernest William*	3.1.1885–20.2.1975	1912	200/400
Hall, *Eric William*	15.9.1934	1956	50kW
		1960	20kW
Halliday, *Donald George*	16.6.1947	1072	100/400R
Halligan, *A*	—	1908	110h
Hallows, *Norman Frederic*	29.12.1886–16.10.1968	1908	1500/
			3mTm
Halswelle, *Wyndham*	30.5.1882–31.3.1915	1906	100/400/
			800
		1908	400
Hambidge, *John Henry*	—	1928	200
Hammond, *Thomas Edgar*	18.6.1878–18.12.1945	1908	10mW
Hampson, *Thomas*	28.10.1907–4.9.1965	1032	800/1600R
Handley, *Francis Richard*	31.10.1910	1936	800
Hanlon, *John Austin Thomas*	18.12.1905–17.10.1983	1928	400
Hardy, *Roland*	3.12.1927	1952	10kW
		1956	20kW
Hare, *Albert*	12.5.1887–23.12.1969	1912	1500
Harmer, *Frederick William*	18.7.1884–13.3.1919	1908	400h
Harmer, *Henry Sutton*	8.7.1883–9.1.1958	1908	100
Harmsworth, *Paul A*	28.9.1963	1988	1600R
Harper, *Ernest*	2.8.1902	1924	10k/CC
		1928	Mar
		1936	Mar
Harper, *Roland St George Tristram*	23.4.1907	1932	110h
Harries, *Philip James Charles*	7.4.1966	1988	400h
Harrison, *Eric George William Warde*	23.3.1893–20.12.1987	1924	110h
Harrison, *Richard*	—	1908	3500W/
			10mW
Hatton, *James*	—	1920	3kTm/10k
Hawkey, *Robert L*	19.3.1915	1948	TJ
Hawkins, *George A*	–1917	1908	200/MR
Hawtrey, *Henry Courtenay*	29.6.1882–16.11.1961	1906	1500/5m

Ernie Harper finishes fourth in the 1924 cross-country race. In 1936 he won a silver medal in the marathon.

Healey, *Alfred H*	—	1906	100/110h
		1908	110h
Heap, *John Crocker*	9.11.1907	1928	100
Heatley, *Benjamin Basil*	25.12.1933	1964	Mar
Hegarty, *A Frank*	—	1920	CC
Hehir, *William*	21.1.1887	1920	3kW/
			10kW
Hemery, *David Peter*	18.7.1944	1968	400h/
			1600R
		1972	400h/
			1600R
Henderson, *Walter Edward Bonhôte*	21.6.1880–2.9.1944	1908	sHJ/sLJ/
			DT/DTg/
			JT
		1912	DT
Henley, *Ernest John*	31.3.1889	1912	400/800/
			1600R
Herbert, *John AA*	20.4.1962	1984	TJ
		1988	TJ
Herriott, *Maurice*	8.10.1939	1964	3kSt
		1968	3kSt
Herring, *John Bryan*	10.4.1936	1964	5k
Hewson, *Brian Stanford*	4.4.1933	1956	1500
		1960	800
Hibbins, *Frederick Newton*	23.3.1890	1912	5k/10k/ CC
Hicks, *Henry John*	6.8.1925	1956	Mar
Higgins, *Francis Peter*	16.11.1928	1956	400/1600R
Higgins, *Terence Langley*	18.1.1928	1952	400/1600R
Higginson, *Jack*	1891	1924	TJ
Hildreth, *Peter Burke*	8.7.1928	1952	110h
		1956	110h
		1960	110h
Hill, *Albert George*	24.3.1889–8.1.1969	1920	800/1500/
			3kTm
Hill, *Michael Christopher*	22.10.1964	1988	JT
Hill, *Ronald*	25.9.1938	1964	10k/Mar
		1968	10k
		1972	Mar

COMPETITOR	DATE OF BIRTH-DEATH	YEAR	EVENT/S
Hill, *William Arthur*	31.10.1896	1920	100/200/400R
Hirons, *William*	15.6.1871–5.1.1958	1908	TW(A)
Hodge, *Percy*	26.12.1890–27.12.1967	1920	3kSt
Hogan, *James Joseph* (né Gregan)	28.5.1933	1968	10k
(Also competed for Ireland in the marathon in 1964)			
Hogan, *John Michael Walter*	9.5.1943	1964	400h
Holdaway, *C Guy*	—	1908	3200St
Holden, *Andrew John*	22.10.1948	1972	3kSt
Holden, *John Thomas*	13.3.1907	1948	Mar
Holding, *Harold Evelyn*	12.4.1883–20.7.1925	1908	800
Hollings, *Stephen Charles*	23.11.1946	1972	3kSt
Hollingsworth, *Roy Anselm*	28.12.1933	1964	DT
Holloway, *John J*	—	1904	AA
Holmes, *Cyril Butler*	11.1.1915	1936	100
Holmes, *Frederick William*	9.8.1886–9.11.1944	1920	TW
Holt, *David John*	18.5.1944	1972	10k
Holtom, *James Mark*	6.2.1958	1980	110h
		1984	110h
Homewood, *Thomas*	25.9.1881	1908	TW(C)
Hooper, *Brian Roger Leslie*	18.5.1953	1976	PV
		1980	PV
Hopkins, *Joseph*	19.2.1902	1936	50kW
Horgan, *Denis*	18.5.1871–2.6.1922	1908	SP
Horne, *John William*	7.11.1877	1906	400/800
Houghton, *Harold*	1901	1924	800
		1928	800
Housden, *Leslie George*	30.10.1894–19.12.1963	1920	Mar
Howell, *John David*	10.4.1936	1960	LJ
Howell, *Rene William*	19.12.1916–1989	1948	3kSt
Howland, *Robert Leslie*	25.3.1905–7.3.1986	1928	SP
Hughes, *Robert Peter*	27.10.1947	1968	20kW
Hulford, *Frederick Henry*	6.2.1883–23.1.1976	1912	800/1500
Humphreys, *Frederick Harkness*	28.1.1878–10.9.1954	1908	TW(A)
(Also see *Wrestling*)			
		1912	TW
		1920	TW
Humphreys, *Thomas Frederick*	8.9.1890–9.4.1967	1912	10k/CC
Hunter, *William Langwill*	15.7.1892	1920	110h/LJ
Hurdsfield, *Samuel*	—	1908	200
Hussey, *Eric Robert James*	26.4.1885	1908	110h
Hutchings, *Timothy Hilton*	4.12.1958	1984	5k
Hutson, *George William*	22.12.1889–10.1914	1912	3kTm/5k
Hyman, *Martin*	3.7.1933	1960	10k
Hynes, *Mathias*	21.1.1883–9.3.1926	1912	TW
Ibbotson, *George Derek*	17.6.1932	1956	5k
Iden, *Geoffrey Lionel*	8.10.1914	1952	Mar
Ireton, *Albert*	15.5.1879–4.1.1947	1908	TW(A)
(Also see *Boxing*)			
Irwin, *Herbert Carmichael*	1894–5.10.1930	1920	5k
Jack, *Thomas*	5.2.1881–9.10.1960	1908	Mar
Jack, *William*	20.12.1930	1952	100/400R
Jackson, *Arnold Nugent Strode*	5.4.1891–13.11.1972	1912	1500
Jackson, *Barry Douglas*	22.8.1941	1960	1600R
Jackson, *Colin Ray*	18.2.1967	1988	110h
Jackson, *John McKenzie*	29.9.1941	1968	3kSt
Jacobs, *David Henry*	30.4.1888–5.6.1976	1912	100/200/400R
Jarrett, *Anthony Alexander*	13.3.1968	1988	110h
Jenkins, *David Andrew*	25.5.1952	1972	400/1600R
		1976	400/1600R
		1980	400
Johnson, *Albert H*	1.5.1931	1956	50kW
		1960	50kW
Johnson, *Derek James Neville*	5.1.1933	1956	800/1600R
Johnson, *Kenneth Edward*	14.10.1928	1952	3kSt
Johnson, *Terence 'Tebbs' Lloyd*	7.4.1900–1984	1936	50kW
		1948	50kW
Johnston, *Herbert Arthur*	16.4.1902–5.4.1967	1924	3kTm
		1928	5k
Johnston, *Timothy Frederick Kendall*	11.3.1941	1968	Mar
Johnstone, *Charles Havard*	1903	1924	5k
Jones, *Arthur John*	5.10.1938	1968	20kW
Jones, *David Henry*	11.3.1940	1960	100/200/400R
Jones, *Kenneth Jeffrey*	30.12.1921	1948	100/400R
Jones, *Michael David*	23.7.1963	1988	HT
Jones, *Robin Evan Hugh*	1.11.1955	1984	Mar
Jones, *Ronald*	19.8.1934	1964	400R
		1968	100/400R
Jones, *Stanley F*	26.12.1914	1948	Mar
Just, *Theodore Hartman*	23.4.1886–13.2.1937	1908	800/MR
Kane, *Harry*	24.5.1933	1956	400h
Keily, *Arthur Patrick*	18.3.1921	1960	Mar
Kellaway, *Henry George 'Tim'*	7.10.1891	1912	Mar
Kelly, *Barrie Harrison*	2.8.1940	1968	100/400R
Kennedy, *Robert Kirk Inches*	20.1.1916	1936	HJ
Kent-Smith, *Brian William*	10.10.1935	1960	1500
Kerr, *Gilbert John Crawford*	—	1924	HJ
Kidd, *Alexander*	—	1908	TW(B)
Kiely, *Lawrence A*	—	1908	110h
Kiely, *Thomas Francis*	25.8.1869–6.11.1951	1904	AA
Kilby, *Brian Leonard*	26.2.1938	1960	Mar
		1964	Mar
Kinahan, *Cecil Edward*	15.4.1879–15.3.1912	1908	110h
Kinchin, *Joseph W*	—	1908	3200St
King, *Barry John*	3.4.1945	1972	Dec
King, *John Stewart*	13.2.1963	1988	LJ
Kingsford, *Philip Cave*	10.8.1891	1912	sLJ/LJ
Kirkbride, *John Christopher*	24.3.1947	1972	1500
Kirkham, *Colin*	30.10.1944	1972	Mar
Kitching, *FO*	—	1908	sLJ
Knott, *Francis Arthur*	1883–24.3.1958	1908	1500
Knyvett, *WA*	—	1908	110h
Kruger, *Alexander Eaton*	18.11.1963	1988	Dec
Langley, *Harold A*	—	1924	TJ
Larner, *Ernest E*	—	1908	3500W/10mW
Larner, *George Edward*	7.2.1875–4.3.1949	1908	3500W/10mW
Leader, *Edward Eastlake*	28.8.1882	1908	110h/HJ
Leahy, *Cornelius*	27.4.1876–1921	1906	HJ/TJ
		1908	HJ
Leahy, *Patrick Joseph*	20.5.1877–1926	1900	HJ/LJ/TJ
		1908	HJ
Lee, *George*	28.12.1886	1912	5k/10k
Lee, *JW*	—	1908	800/1500
Leeke, *Henry Alan*	15.11.1879–29.5.1915	1908	SP/DT/DTg/HT/JT/JTg
Leigh-Wood, *Roger*	16.8.1906–1.3.1987	1928	400/1600R
Lerwill, *Alan Leslie*	15.11.1946	1968	LJ
		1972	LJ
Lewis, *Leslie Charles*	26.12.1924–7.4.1986	1948	400/1600R
		1952	400/1600R
Liddell, *Eric Henry*	16.1.1902–21.2.1945	1924	200/400
Light, *Frederick*	—	1928	5k
Lightman, *Shaun*	15.4.1943	1968	50kW
Lillington, *Alan William*	4.9.1932	1952	100
Lindsay, *Allan Shanks*	5.3.1926	1948	TJ
Lindsay, *Michael Robert*	2.11.1938	1960	SP/DT
		1964	SP
Lindsay, *Robert Alexander*	18.4.1890–21.10.1958	1920	400/1600R
Lindsay-Watson, *Robert Hamilton*	4.10.1886–26.1.1956	1908	HT
Lintott, *JF*	—	1908	800
Liveley, *Charles E*	—	1920	LJ/TJ
Livingston-Learmonth, *Thomas Carlisle*	5.1.1906–24.4.1931	1928	400h
Lloyd, *Edgar William*	31.7.1884–3.1.1972	1912	Mar
London, *John Edward 'Jack'*	13.1.1905–2.5.1966	1928	100/400R
Loney, *E Victor*	—	1908	1500
Long, *David*	21.11.1960	1988	Mar
Longe, *Clive Citreon Olaf*	23.2.1939–27.12.1986	1968	Dec
Lord, *Frederick Thomas*	11.2.1879	1908	Mar
		1912	Mar
Lowe, *Douglas Gordon Arthur*	7.8.1902–30.3.1981	1924	800/1500
		1928	800/1600R
Lucas, *Bernard*	17.8.1907	1928	110h
Lucas, *William Ernest*	16.1.1917	1948	5k
Lucking, *Martyn Taylor*	24.3.1938	1960	SP

For Valour

Only three men have competed in the Olympic Games after being awarded the Victoria Cross. Colonel Paul McKenna and Lieutenant Bryan Lawrence were members of the 1912 equestrian team and in 1924 Lt Colonel Philip Neame uniquely added an Olympic gold medal to the VC he had been awarded in 1914.

The 1908 400 metres runner Noel Chavasse, who became one of only three men to be awarded a bar to the VC, was decorated *after* he had competed in the Olympics. Additionally, Captain Harry Daniels, VC, MC, was a reserve for the 1920 Modern Pentathlon team.

The most highly decorated British team was the No. 1 crew in the four-man bobsleigh event at the 1948 Winter Olympics. Between them the four RAF officers had been awarded two DSOs, three DFCs and three AFCs.

COMPETITOR	DATE OF BIRTH-DEATH	YEAR	EVENT/S	COMPETITOR	DATE OF BIRTH-DEATH	YEAR	EVENT/S
		1964	SP	Miller, *Gordon Albert*	16.12.1939	1960	HJ
McCabe, *Brian Farmer*	9.1.1914	1936	800			1964	HJ
McCafferty, *Ian John*	24.11.1944	1972	5k	Mills, *Arthur Robert*	16.1.1894	1920	Mar
McCalla, *Eric Lloyd*	18.8.1960	1984	TJ			1924	Mar
McCombie, *Ian Peter*	11.1.1961	1984	20kW	Mills, *Edwin Archer*	17.5.1878–12.11.1946	1908	TW(A)
		1988	20kW			1912	TW
McCooke, *Steven H*	4.9.1918	1948	5k			1920	TW
McCorquodale, *Alastair*	5.12.1925	1948	100/200/	Mills, *Roger George*	11.2.1948	1980	20kW
			400R	Milne, *Roderic Bruce William*	15.3.1957	1980	1600R
Macdonald, *Bernard H*	—	1924	3kTm	Misson, *Thomas William*	11.5.1930	1960	50kW
McFarlane, *Michael Anthony*	2.5.1960	1980	200/400R	Mitchell, *Roy R*	1.1.1955	1976	LJ
		1984	100/400R	Montague, *Edwin Herbert*	18.4.1885–1938	1908	400/MR
		1988	400R	Montague, *Evelyn Aubrey*	20.3.1900–30.1.1948	1928	3kSt
McGough, *John*	1887–1967	1906	800/1500/	Moody, *Harold Ernest Arundel*	1.11.1915–12.9.1986	1948	SP
			5m	Moorcroft, *David Robert*	10.4.1953	1976	1500
		1908	1500			1980	5k
Macgregor, *Donald Forbes*	23.7.1949	1972	Mar			1984	5k
Macintosh, *Henry Maitland*	10.6.1892–26.7.1918	1912	100/200/	Moore, *Aston Llewellyn*	8.2.1956	1976	TJ
			400R	Moore, *William Craig*	5.4.1890	1912	1500/
McKean, *Thomas*	27.10.1963	1988	800				3kTm
McKenna, *John 'Jack'*	4.1889–4.12.1973	1924	Mar	Morgan, *Vernon Eversfield*	2.5.1904	1928	3kSt
McKim, *William*	1.10.1941	1964	1500	Morphy, *George Newcomen*	1884	1908	800
MacKintosh, *Charles Ernest*	31.10.1903–12.1.1974	1924	LJ	Morris, *Charles James*	2.1.1915	1948	10kW
Whistler Christopher				Morris, *Richard Arthur*	9.7.1921	1948	1500
McLeod, *Michael James*	25.1.1952	1980	10k	Morton, *John William*	13.2.1879–5.9.1950	1908	100/200
		1984	10k	Morton, *Leslie*	1.7.1958	1988	50kW
		1988	10k	Mountain, *Edgar Donald*	2.4.1901–30.4.1985	1920	800
McLowry, *Daniel*	—	1908	TW(B)			1924	800
McMaster, *Andrew Emyln*	10.5.1957	1980	100/400R	Muggridge, *Arthur Thomas*	12.1904–1933	1928	10k
Macmillan, *Duncan*	1.6.1890–1963	1912	200	Munro, *Alexander*	30.11.1870	1908	TW(C)
McPhee, *Duncan*	1892–1950	1920	1500/			1912	TW
			3kTm	Murphy, *James*	—	1908	5m
McStravick, *Bradley Steven*	25.5.1956	1980	Dec	Murray, *Alistair Fergus*	11.9.1942	1964	10k
		1984	Dec	Murray, *Denis*	1881	1908	100/LJ
Maddocks, *Christopher Lloyd*	28.3.1957	1984	20kW	Murray, *John*	1881	1908	DT/HT
		1988	20kW	Murray, *William*	—	1908	100
Mafe, *Adeoye O*	12.11.1966	1984	200	Nankeville, *George William*	24.3.1925	1948	1500
Manderson, *Floyd*	5.3.1961	1988	HJ			1952	1500
Mann, *Percy Edward*	12.5.1888–1974	1912	800	Naylor, *Mark*	10.9.1957	1980	HJ
Mardle, *Paul Stuart*	10.11.1962	1988	DT			1984	HJ
Marlow, *Peter Frederick*	20.4.1941	1972	20kW	Neame, *Douglas Mortimer Lewes*	9.10.1901–13.6.1988	1928	110h
Marshall, *George*	—	1896	800	Nesbitt, *James*	22.9.1913	1948	DT
(Also see *Lawn Tennis*)				Newey, *Sidney Archibald*	1899	1924	3kSt
Martin, *Eamonn Thomas*	9.10.1958	1984	5k	Newman, *John Lunn*	11.11.1916	1936	HJ
		1988	5k/10k	Nichol, *William Peter*	1901	1924	100/200/
Martineau, *Harold Albert*	24.12.1914	1948	50kW				400R
Matthewman, *Thomas J*	3.1903–8.1990	1924	200	Nichols, *Alfred Hubert*	28.11.1890	1920	5k/CC
Matthews, *Kenneth Joseph*	21.6.1934	1960	20kW	Nicol, *George*	28.12.1886–28.1.1967	1908	400
		1964	20kW			1912	400/1600R
Matthews, *Victor Charles*	23.6.1934	1960	110h	Nicolson, *Thomas Rae*	3.10.1879–18.4.1951	1908	SP/HT
May, *Ernest Edmund Bedford*	14.9.1878–5.1.1952	1908	DT/DTg/			1920	HT
			HT/JT/	Nihill, *Vincent Paul*	5.9.1939	1964	50kW
			JTfs			1968	50kW
Mayberry, *George Mahoney*	1882	1908	TJ			1972	20kW/
Meakin, *Alfred*	30.8.1938	1964	100				50kW
Merriman, *Frederick*	18.5.1873–27.6.1940	1908	TW(A)			1976	20kW
Merriman, *John Linden*	27.6.1936	1960	10k	Noel-Baker, *PJ* see Baker			
Metcalf, *John*	25.2.1934	1960	400h	Nokes, *Malcolm Cuthbert*	20.5.1897–22.11.1986	1924	HT
Metcalfe, *Adrian Peter*	2.3.1942	1964	400/1600R			1928	HT
Middleton, *Raymond Christopher*	9.8.1936	1964	50kW	Norman, *George Jeffery*	6.2.1945	1976	Mar
Mileham, *Matthew D*	27.12.1956	1984	HT	Norris, *Albert James*	5.11.1898–11.6.1990	1936	Mar
		1988	HT	Norris, *Fred*	4.9.1921	1952	10k

COMPETITOR	DATE OF BIRTH-DEATH	YEAR	EVENT/S
		1956	Mar
Norris, *Kenneth Leonard*	11.7.1931	1956	10k
Oakes, *Gary James*	21.9.1958	1980	400h
O'Connor, *Peter*	18.10.1874–9.11.1957	1906	HJ/LJ/TJ
Odde, *Hans Jacob 'John'*	1899	1924	TJ
Oddie, *Brian Cecil Vernon*	1905	1928	5k
O'Gorman, *Denis*	22.5.1928	1960	Mar
Oliver, *Edward Horace*	—	1928	3kSt
Olney, *Henry Alexander*	4.1.1922	1948	5k
Ottley, *David Charles*	5.8.1955	1980	JT
		1984	JT
		1988	JT
Ovett, *Stephen Michael James*	9.10.1955	1976	800/1500
		1980	800/1500
		1984	800/1500
Owen, *Edward*	6.11.1886–24.9.1949	1908	5m
		1912	1500/3kTm
Paddick, *John Chester*	31.8.1943	1964	20kW
Page, *Ernest Leslie*	27.9.1910–9.12.1973	1932	100/400R
Palmer, *Michael John*	6.11.1935	1960	3kSt
Palmer, *William Barclay Livingstone*	2.3.1932	1956	SP
Palmer, *William James*	19.4.1882–21.12.1967	1908	3500W/10mW
		1912	10kW
Pankhurst, *HJ*	—	1908	100/200/MR
Parker, *Alan Bunyard*	5.5.1928	1952	5k
Parker, *Frederick John*	6.9.1927	1952	110h
		1956	110h
Parker, *John Michael*	2.5.1928	1964	110h
		1968	110h
Parlett, *Harold John*	19.4.1925	1948	800
Parsons, *Geoffrey Peter*	14.8.1964	1984	HJ
		1988	HJ
Partridge, *Leopold Frank*	14.6.1901–18.7.1976	1924	110h
Pascoe, *Alan Peter*	11.10.1947	1968	110h
		1972	110h/1600R
		1976	400h/1600h
Paterson, *Alan Sinclair*	11.6.1928	1948	HJ
		1952	HJ
Patterson, *Alan*	12.3.1886–3.1915	1908	400
		1912	400/800
Pavitt, *Ronald Cecil*	15.9.1926–2.1988	1948	HJ
		1952	HJ
Payne, *Andrew Howard*	17.4.1931	1964	HT
		1968	HT
		1972	HT
Payne, *Harry William*	5.9.1892–5.7.1969	1928	Mar
Pennington, *Alan*	4.4.1916–2.6.1961	1936	100/200/400R
Percival, *Lancelot Roger*	14.8.1906–1.9.1964	1928	400h
Peters, *James Henry*	24.10.1918	1948	10k
		1952	Mar
Pharaoh, *Mark*	18.7.1931	1952	DT
		1956	DT
Philbin, *Patrick*	—	1908	TW(B)
Piggott, *Leslie McDonald*	11.5.1942	1972	100/400R
Pike, *Martin W*	12.7.1920	1948	1600R
Pilbrow, *Ashleigh Gordon*	1.7.1912	1936	110h
Piper, *George F*	—	1920	Mar
Pirie, *Douglas Alistair Gordon*	10.2.1931	1952	5k/10k
		1956	5k/10k
		1960	5k/10k
		1964	3kSt
Pomfret, *Ernest*	18.4.1941	1900	Mar
Pool, *Ernest Ion*	1858–26.9.1931	1948	400h
Pope, *Michael Douglas*	25.2.1927	1912	3kTm/5k
Porter, *Cyril Henry Atwell*	12.1.1890–25.6.1977	1924	3kTm
Porter, *WH*	—	1936	10k
Potts, *John Henry*	17.9.1906	1932	800
Powell, *John Vincent*	2.11.1910–27.7.1982	1936	800
Powell, *Kenneth*	8.4.1885–18.2.1915	1908	110h

COMPETITOR	DATE OF BIRTH-DEATH	YEAR	EVENT/S
(Also see *Lawn Tennis*)		1912	110h
Prendergast, *Bernard L*	25.12.1911	1936	DT
Price, *Berwyn*	15.8.1951	1972	110h
		1976	110h
Price, *Jack T*	1884–11.1965	1908	Mar
Pugh, *Derek Charles*	8.2.1926	1948	400/1600R
Quinn, *Patrick*	10.12.1885	1912	SP
Quinn, *Richard*	1882	1908	3500W
Radford, *Peter Frank*	20.9.1939	1960	100/200/400R
		1964	100/200/400R
Ralph, *Michael*	4.7.1938	1964	TJ
Rampling, *Godfrey Lionel*	14.5.1909	1932	400/1600R
		1936	400/1600R
Randell, *Frederick D*	5.2.1864	1900	Mar
Rangeley, *Walter*	14.12.1903–16.3.1982	1924	100/400R
		1928	100/200/400R
		1936	400R
Rawson, *Michael Arthur*	26.5.1934	1956	800
Reavell-Carter, *Laurence*	27.8.1914–4.10.1985	1936	DT
		1948	DT
Reed, *Laurence David George*	22.5.1936	1960	1500
Reed, *Lionel J de B*	—	1908	200
Reed, *Peter Neville*	21.9.1942	1968	LJ
Reed, *Reginald Charles*	1883	1906	100/400
Reeve, *Aubrey Vincent*	19.9.1911	1936	5k
Regis, *John Paul Lyndon*	13.10.1966	1988	100/200/400R
Reid, *Donovan*	31.8.1963	1984	100/400R
Reid, *Frederick Payne*	1909	1932	100
Reid, *John J*	—	1908	3500w
Reitz, *Colin Robert*	6.4.1960	1980	3kSt
		1984	3kSt
Renwick, *George Russell*	7.8.1901	1924	400/1600R
Revans, *Reginald William*	14.5.1907	1928	LJ
Reynolds, *Martin Edward*	22.2.1949	1972	400/1600R
Rice, *Richard Goodenough*	19.3.1886	1912	100/200
Richards, *Gregory Roy*	25.4.1956	1988	Dec
Richards, *Ian William*	12.4.1948	1980	50kW
Richards, *Thomas John Henry*	15.3.1910–19.1.1985	1948	Mar
Ridgeon, *Jonathan Peter*	14.2.1967	1988	110h
Rimmer, *John Thomas*	27.4.1878–6.6.1962	1900	1500/4kSt/5kTm
Rinkel, *John William Joslin*	24.3.1905	1928	400/1600R
Ripley, *Richard Nicholson*	1901	1924	1600R
Robb, *RC*	—	1908	400
Roberts, *William*	5.4.1912	1936	400/1600R
		1948	400/1600R
Robertson, *Arthur James*	19.4.1879–18.4.1957	1908	3200St/3mTm/5m
Robertson, *Donald McNab*	7.10.1905–14.6.1949	1936	Mar
Robertson, *George Stuart*	25.5.1872–29.1.1967	1896	DT
(Also see *Lawn Tennis*)			
Robertson, *Maximilian*	27.12.1963	1988	400h
Robinson, *Sidney J*	1877	1900	2500St/4kSt/5kTm
Roche, *Patrick J*	1886–8.1917	1908	100/200
Rose, *Nicholas H*	30.12.1951	1980	5k
		1984	10k
Rosswess, *Michael*	11.6.1965	1988	200
Rowland, *Mark Robert*	7.3.1963	1988	3kSt
Rowley, *Stanley Rupert*	11.9.1876–1.4.1924	1900	5kTm
(Also competed for Australia in 60,100 & 200 metres)			
Royle, *Lancelot Carrington*	31.5.1898–19.6.1978	1924	100/400R
Ruffell, *Charles Henry*	16.9.1888–9.11.1923	1912	1500/5k/10k/CC
Rushmer, *Alan Trevor*	27.2.1944	1968	5k
Russell, *Arthur*	1886	1908	3200St
Ryle, *Edward Huish*	1.10.1885	1908	400
Salisbury, *John Edward*	26.1.1934	1956	400/1600R

COMPETITOR	DATE OF BIRTH-DEATH	YEAR	EVENT/S
Salvat, *Frank George John*	30.10.1934	1960	5k
Samuels, *Vernon George*	5.10.1964	1988	TJ
Sando, *Frank Dennis*	14.3.1931	1952	10k
		1956	10k
Sandstrom, *Eric Roy*	11.9.1931	1956	100/200/400R
Sarel, *Sydney Lancaster*	1872–23.12.1950	1908	3500W
Saunders, *Frank C*	1899	1924	5k
Savidge, *John Andrew*	18.12.1924–26.12.1979	1952	SP
Saward, *William*	—	1900	Mar
Schofield, *Sydney Charles Apps*	1884–24.3.1956	1908	10mW
Scott, *Angus Weatherit*	16.8.1927–3.1990	1952	400h
Scott, *William*	23.3.1886	1912	10k
Seagrove, *William Raymond*	2.7.1989–25.6.1980	1920	3kTm
		1924	3kTm
Seedhouse, *Cyril Norman*	10.4.1892	1912	200/400/1600R
Segal, *David Hugh*	20.3.1937	1956	100/200/400R
		1960	200/400R
Sewell, *Arthur N*	1903	1924	CC
Sewell, *Harry*	—	1908	3200St
Sewell, *John*	23.4.1882–18.7.1947	1912	TW
		1920	TW
Sharp, *Robert Cameron*	3.6.1958	1980	100/200/400R
Shaw, *Robert Douglas*	27.12.1932	1956	400h
Sheffield, *John*	28.4.1910–30.7.1987	1936	400h
Shenton, *Brian*	15.3.1927–9.5.1987	1952	200/400R
		1956	200/400R
Shepherd, *John James*	2.6.1884–9.7.1954	1908	TW(A)
		1912	TW
		1920	TW
Sherwood, *John*	4.6.1945	1968	400/1600R
		1972	400h
Shirley, *Eric*	3.4.1929	1956	3kSt
		1960	3kSt
Simmons, *Anthony Derek*	6.10.1948	1976	10k
Simmons, *Henry Augustus*	21.2.1911–23.4.1944	1928	HJ
Simpson, *Alan*	22.5.1940	1964	1500
Slack, *David G*	1899	1924	Pen/Dec
Slade, *William*	9.5.1873–30.9.1941	1908	TW(C)
Slaney, *Richard Charles*	16.5.1956	1984	DT
Smedley, *Raymond John*	3.9.1951	1972	1500
Smith, *Barry David*	16.4.1953	1980	5k
Smith, *David*	21.6.1962	1988	HT
Smith, *Geoffrey*	24.10.1953	1980	10k
		1984	Mar
Smith, *George*	1876–14.1.1915	1908	TW(B)
Smith, *John Suttie*	—	1928	10k
Smith, *Joseph M*	—	1908	1500
Smouha, *Edward Ralph*	17.12.1908	1928	400R
Soutter, *James Tindal*	1.1.1885–8.8.1966	1912	400/800/1600R
Spark, *Arthur Percy*	4.6.1894–1.9.1953	1924	Pen/Dec
Speake, *Joseph William*	8.1.1944	1968	400R
Spedding, *Charles*	19.5.1952	1984	Mar
		1988	Mar
Spencer, *Edward Adams*	1876–6.5.1965	1908	10mW
Spencer, *SA*	—	1924	1500
Stacey, *Nicolas David*	25.11.1927	1952	200/1600R
Stafford, *LHG*	—	1908	sHJ/sLJ
Stanes, *Gary Martin*	3.7.1963	1988	5k
Stallard, *Hyla Bristow 'Henry'*	28.4.1901–21.10.1973	1924	800/1500
Stark, *James Primrose*	7.3.1885	1908	100/200
Starr, *Ralph Stewart*	6.3.1903	1924	5k
		1928	800
Staynings, *Anthony Robert*	21.7.1953	1976	3kSt
		1980	3kSt
Steane, *Richard Swift*	26.9.1939	1968	200
Stevenson, *David Deas*	28.11.1941	1964	PV
Stevenson, *Samuel*	—	1908	5m/Mar
Stewart, *Ian*	15.1.1949	1972	5k
		1976	5k
Stewart, *Joseph Laughlin*	22.6.1943	1972	10k
Stiff, *Harold Joseph*	23.10.1881–17.4.1939	1920	TW
Stock, *Keith Frank*	18.3.1957	1984	PV
Stoneley, *Crew Hadlett*	9.5.1911	1932	400/1600R
Storey, *Stuart Ellis*	16.9.1942	1968	110h
Strode-Jackson, *AN* see Jackson			
Sweeney, *Arthur Wellington*	20.5.1909–27.12.1940	1936	100/200
Swindlehurst, *Thomas*	21.5.1874–15.3.1959	1908	TW(B)
Tagg, *Michael John*	13.11.1946	1968	10k
Taitt, *John Lawrence*	28.3.1934	1964	110h
Tammas, *Walter Baldry*	23.8.1870–12.1.1952	1908	TW(C)
Tancred, *Peter A*	20.10.1949	1976	DT
Tancred, *William Raymond*	6.8.1942	1968	DT
		1972	DT
Tarraway, *Harold George*	22.4.1925	1948	800
Tatham, *Wilfrid George*	12.12.1898–26.7.1978	1924	400h
		1928	800
Taylor, *Richard George*	3.1.1945	1968	5k
Teale, *Jeffrey*	20.12.1939	1968	SP
Thomas, *Reginald Heber*	1907–14.3.1946	1928	1500
		1932	1500
Thompson, *Donald James*	20.1.1933	1956	50kW
		1960	50kW
		1964	50kW
Thompson, *Francis Morgan 'Daley'*	30.7.1958	1976	Dec
		1980	Dec
		1984	Dec/400R
		1988	Dec
Thompson, *Frederick Basil Kerr*	1880–19.12.1956	1908	Mar
Thompson, *Ian Reginald*	16.10.1949	1980	Mar
Thorn, *Ernest Arthur*	7.6.1887–18.11.1968	1920	TW
Thornton, *John St Leger*	6.6.1911–18.8.1944	1936	110h
Timms, *Howard William*	9.7.1944	1972	50kW
Toms, *Edward James*	1899	1924	400/1600R
Townsend, *Arthur*	7.4.1883	1912	Mar
Travis, *David Howard*	9.9.1945	1968	JT
		1972	JT
Traynor, *George Terence*	7.11.1915	1936	LJ
Treble, *Arnold Leonard*	8.10.1889–1966	1912	5k
Tremeer, *Leonard Francis*	1875–21.10.1951	1908	400h/JT
Tudor, *Geoffrey David Claude*	29.12.1923	1948	3kSt
Tulloh, *Michael Bruce Swinton*	29.9.1935	1960	5k
Tunbridge, *Donald Arthur*	28.10.1920	1952	50kW
Turner, *Geoffrey*	—	1928	HJ
Tysoe, *Alfred Edward*	21.3.1874–26.10.1901	1900	800/5kTm
Unsworth, *Ronald T*	8.11.1923	1948	400h
Valle, *Paul H*	31.12.1926	1948	200
Vesty, *Philip John*	5.1.1963	1984	20kW
Vickers, *Stanley Frank*	18.6.1932	1956	20kW
		1960	20kW
Voigt, *Emil Robert*	12.1882–16.10.1973	1908	5m
Vose, *Christopher*	27.1.1887–22.8.1970	1920	CC
Walker, *Nigel Keith*	15.6.1963	1984	110h
Wallach, *George Curtis Locke*	20.3.1883–2.4.1980	1912	10k/CC
Walters, *D Wallis*	—	1906	110h
		1908	110h
Ward, *Peter Hans Dudley*	7.12.1913	1936	5k
Warden, *Peter*	7.7.1941	1964	400h
Warhurst, *John*	1.10.1944	1972	50kW
Warren, *David Marlias Jenner*	11.2.1956	1980	800
Watson, *Barrington J*	13.2.1944	1976	Mar
Watson, *Harold*	1883–15.2.1963	1908	100
Watson, *Luke Graeme Lynton George*	19.11.1957	1984	200
Watson, *WFC*	—	1908	LJ
Watts, *Gordon H*	—	1924	10kW
Watts, *John Thomas*	23.4.1939	1972	DT
Webb, *Ernest James*	1872–24.2.1937	1908	3500W/10mW
		1912	10kW
Webb, *John Albert*	21.12.1936	1968	20kW
Webber, *George J*	—	1924	3kTm
Weber, *Henry Guy*	5.11.1885	1906	5m/Mar
Webster, *Albert*	25.5.1925	1952	800
Webster, *Frederick Richard*	31.12.1914	1936	PV
		1948	PV
Webster, *John Edward*	1900–22.8.1945	1924	10k/CC

Track & Field

WOMEN

Track & field athletics for women was introduced into the Olympic programme in 1928. Britain did not compete in 1928 but first sent a team in 1932, since when they have been represented at every Olympics.

DT = Discus   h = hurdles   Hep = Heptathlon   HJ = High jump
JT = Javelin   LJ = Long jump   Mar = Marathon   Pen = Pentathlon
R = Relay   SP = Shot

COMPETITOR	DATE OF BIRTH-DEATH	YEAR	EVENT/S
Wedderburn, *Edison Everton*	6.12.1960	1988	3kSt
Weir, *Robert B*	4.12.1961	1984	DT/HT
Wells, *Allan Wipper*	3.5.1952	1980	100/200/400R
		1984	100/400R
Wells, *Joseph Algernon*	9.9.1885–20.10.1946	1912	200/400
Wells, *Peter*	23.5.1929	1952	HJ
		1956	HJ
Wenk, *John Edward*	14.10.1938	1960	800
West, *Richard A*	27.4.1914	1948	10kW
West, *Stanley Robert*	13.2.1913	1937	HJ
Wheeler, *Michael Keith Valentine*	14.2.1935	1956	400/1600R
Wheller, *Edward William*	23.5.1896	1920	400h
Whetton, *John H*	6.9.1941	1964	1500
		1968	1500
White, *Charles Thomas*	16.11.1917	1948	800
		1952	800
Whitehead, *Joseph Nicholas Neville*	29.5.1933	1960	400R
Whitehead, *Robert John Terence*	10.1.1957	1980	1600R
Whitlock, *George Bernard Rex*	8.9.1910–26.6.1982	1948	50kW
		1952	50kW
Whitlock, *Hector Harold*	16.12.1903–27.12.1985	1936	50kW
		1952	50kW
Whittle, *Brian*	24.4.1964	1988	400/1600R
Whittle, *Harold*	2.5.1922–11.5.1990	1948	400h/LJ
		1952	400h
Wiard, *Charles Arthur*	27.10.1909	1936	400R
Wiggs, *Michael Edwin*	25.4.1938	1960	1500
		1964	5k
Wilkinson, *Richard E*	—	1906	1500W/3kW
Williams, *Barrington Chester*	11.9.1955	1988	100
Williams, *Barry*	5.3.1947	1972	HT
Williams, *Charles Harold*	23.6.1887–15.12.1971	1908	LJ
Williams, *Joseph E*	1897	1924	CC
Willis, *Arthur Gilbert du Laval*	28.8.1893	1924	HJ
Wilmshurst, *Kenneth Stanley David*	9.4.1931	1956	LJ/TJ
Wilson, *David Nicholson*	7.9.1951	1972	110h
Wilson, *Douglas Gordon*	23.1.1920	1948	1500
Wilson, *GH*	—	1908	HJ
Wilson, *Harold Allan*	22.1.1885–1916	1908	1500/3mTm
Wilson, *James*	2.10.1891	1920	10k/CC
Winbolt-Lewis, *Martin John*	14.11.1946	1968	400/1600R
Withers, *Gadwin Robert James*	28.9.1884	1908	10mW
Wolff, *Frederick Ferdinand*	13.10.1910–26.1.1988	1936	1600R
Wood, *Harold*	28.11.1902–27.6.1975	1928	Mar
Wood, *Kenneth*	21.11.1930	1956	1500
Wooderson, *Sydney Charles*	30.8.1914	1936	1500
Woodget, *James Henry*	28.9.1874–3.10.1960	1908	TW(C)
Woods, *Reginald Salisbury 'Rex'*	15.10.1891–21.9.1986	1924	SP
		1928	SP
Worthington-Eyre, *Hedges Eyre*	1900	1920	400
Wright, *Duncan McLeod*	22.9.1896–21.8.1976	1924	Mar
		1928	Mar
		1932	Mar
Wrighton, *John Derek*	10.3.1933	1960	400/1600R
Wyatt, *A*	—	1908	Mar
Yardley, *Harold Malcolm*	23.12.1940	1960	400/1600R
Yates, *William George*	5.8.1880–27.12.1967	1912	10kW
Yeoumans, *Alfred T*	—	1908	10mW
Yorke, *Richard Francis Charles*	28.7.1885–22.12.1914	1908	3200St
		1912	800/1500
Young, *GW*	—	1908	400

COMPETITOR	DATE OF BIRTH-DEATH	YEAR	EVENT/S
Allday, *S see Farmer*			
Allison, *JF see Page*			
Arden, *Daphne*	29.12.1941	1964	100/200/400R
Armitage, *Heather Joy*	17.3.1933	1952	100/400R
		1956	100/200/400R
Augee, *Myrtle Sharon Mary*	4.2.1965	1988	SP
Bailey, *Shireen*	27.9.1959	1988	800/1500
Baker, *Lorraine*	9.4.1964	1984	800
Baptiste, *Joan Jeanetta*	12.10.1959	1984	200
Barnes, *Elizabeth Ann*	3.8.1951	1976	800/1600R
Barnett, *Helen Catherine*	13.5.1958	1984	400/1600R
Barton, *Maureen Anne*	14.12.1947	1968	LJ
(As Chitty in 1972)		1972	LJ
Batter, *Doris*	22.4.1929	1948	100
Beckford, *Patricia*	6.8.1965	1988	400
Bennett, *Audrey Ethel*	1.4.1936	1956	HJ
Benning, *Christine Mary*	30.3.1955	1984	1500
Bernard, *Verona Marolin*	5.4.1933	1972	400/1600R
(As Elder in 1976)		1976	400/1600R
Berkeley, *Mary Andray*	3.10.1965	1988	LJ
Bignal, *Mary Denise*	10.2.1940	1960	80h/400R/LJ
(As Rand in 1964)		1964	400R/LJ/Pen
Birtwistle, *Margaret J*	26.7.1925	1948	SP/DT
Board, *Lillian Barbara*	13.12.1948–26.12.1970	1968	200/400/400R
Boothe, *Lorna Marie*	5.2.1954	1976	100h
		1980	100h
Boxer, *Christina Tracy*	25.3.1957	1980	800
(As Cahill in 1988)		1984	1500
		1988	1500
Boyle, *Janet Margaret*	25.7.1963	1988	HJ
Brown, *Audrey Kathleen*	24.5.1913	1936	100/400R
Brown, *Denise*	1.5.1955	1976	HJ
Budd, *Zola*	26.5.1966	1984	3k
Burke, *Barbara Hannah Anita*	13.5.1917	1936	100/400R
Cahill, *CT see Boxer*			
Callender, *BL see Goddard*			
Carey, *SJ see Taylor*			
Carrington, *Nellie*	27.8.1916	1936	HJ
Cawley, *Shirley*	26.4.1932	1952	LJ
Charles, *Diane Susan*	7.1.1933	1960	800
Cheeseman, *Sylvia*	19.5.1929	1948	200
		1952	200/400R
Chitty, *MA see Barton*			
Clarke, *Gladys M*	15.2.1923	1948	JT
Clarke, *Wendy Patricia*	17.12.1957	1976	400R
Coates, *Diana*	25.6.1932	1952	JT
Colyear, *Sharon*	22.4.1955	1976	100/100h/400R
(As Danville in 1984)		1984	100h
Connall, *Kathleen I*	8.6.1912	1936	JT
Coomber, *Margaret Teresa*	13.6.1950	1972	800
Cooke, *KJ see Smallwood*			
Creamer, *Angela Mary*	30.1.1956	1976	800
Crehan, *Susan Sarah*	12.9.1956	1988	Mar
Critchley, *Margaret Ann*	4.4.1949	1972	200
Cropper, *PB see Lowe*			
Crowther, *Bertha*	9.12.1921	1948	80h/HJ

Top Schools

With 32 old boys having won gold medals, Eton easily heads the list of schools which have produced British Olympic champions. The top six schools are:

Eton	**32**
Harrow	**8**
Marlborough	**6**
Rugby	**6**
Blundells	**5**
Westminster	**5**

The six most successful Oxford and Cambridge Colleges are:

Trinity, Cambridge	**25**
Magdalen, Oxford	**16**
Trinity Hall, Cambridge	**6**
Christ Church, Oxford	**5**
Gonville & Caius, Cambridge	**5**
Merton, Oxford	**3**

COMPETITOR	DATE OF BIRTH-DEATH	YEAR	EVENT/S
Danville, S see Colyear			
Davies, DC see Elliot			
Desforges, *Jean Catherine*	4.7.1929	1952	80h/400R
Devine, *Patricia Yvonne*	25.4.1932	1952	200
Dimmock, *Penelope Ann*	28.12.1954	1972	HJ
Dunn, *Paula*	3.12.1964	1988	100/200/
			400R
Edwards, *Diane Dolores*	17.6.1966	1988	800
Elder, *VM* see Bernard			
Elliot, *Diana Clare*	7.5.1961	1984	HJ
(As Davies in 1988)		1988	HJ
Erskine, *Margaret*	31.7.1925	1948	LJ
Farmer, *Suzanne*	26.11.1934	1952	DT
(As Allday in 1956 & 1960)		1956	SP/DT
		1960	SP/DT
Few, *Rosaline*	20.1.1955	1972	HJ
Foulds, *June Florence*	13.6.1934	1952	100/400R
(As Paul in 1956)		1956	100/200/
			400R
Furniss, *Jane Elizabeth*	23.8.1960	1984	3k
Gardner, *Dora Kathleen*	6.5.1912	1948	HJ
Gardner, *Maureen Angela Jane*	12.11.1928–2.9.1974	1948	80h/400R
Gibson, *Sharon Angelia*	31.12.1961	1984	JT
Goddard, *Beverley Lanita*	28.8.1956	1976	200
(As Callender in 1984)		1980	200/400R
		1984	400R
Golden, *Helen*	16.5.1953	1976	200
Green, *Josephine Mary*	10.11.1943	1968	400
Grievson, *Elizabeth Joy*	31.10.1941	1964	400
Gunnell, *Sally Jane Janet*	29.7.1966	1988	100h/
			400h/
			1600R
Hagger, *Kim*	2.12.1961	1984	Hep
		1988	LJ/Hep
Hall, *Loreen Doloris*	12.10.1967	1988	400
Halstead, *Nellie*	2.1911	1932	400R
Hanson-Nortey, *Yvonne W*	18.2.1964	1988	SP
Hartley, *D-ML* see Murray			
Hearnshaw, *Susan Christina*	26.5.1961	1980	LJ
		1984	LJ
Hiscock, *Eileen May*	25.8.1909	1932	100/400R
		1936	100/400R
Hiscock, *Hilary Jean*	9.4.1939	1960	200
Hodson, *Mary*	28.10.1946	1964	800
Hopkins, *Thelma Elizabeth*	16.3.1936	1952	HJ
		1956	HJ/LJ
Hoskin, *Sheila Hilary*	14.10.1936	1956	LJ
Hoyte-Smith, *Joslyn Yvonne*	16.12.1954	1980	400/
			1600R
		1984	1600R
Hunte, *Heather Regina*	14.8.1959	1980	100/400R
(As Oakes in 1984)		1984	100/400R
Hunter, *Jill*	14.10.1966	1988	3k
Hyman, *Dorothy*	9.5.1941	1960	100/200/
			400R
		1964	100/200/
			400R
Inkpen, *Barbara Jean*	28.10.1949	1968	HJ
		1972	HJ
		1984	400R
		1988	100/200/
			400R
Jacobs, *Kim Simmone Geraldine*	5.9.1966		

COMPETITOR	DATE OF BIRTH-DEATH	YEAR	EVENT/S
James, *Della Patricia*	28.3.1949	1968	100
(As Pascoe in 1972)		1972	200/400R
Jamieson, *Louise Alexander*	31.3.1942	1964	LJ
Jeal, *Wendy*	12.11.1960	1988	100h
Jenner, *Elizabeth Ann*	30.8.1941	1960	100
Jennings, *Joanne*	20.9.1969	1988	HJ
Johnson, *Ann Elaine*	28.9.1933	1952	200
Johnson, *Ethel*	8.10.1908–30.3.1964	1932	100
Jones, *Patricia Ann*	20.6.1942	1968	80h
Jordan, *Joy Wilhelmina*	13.11.1935	1960	800
Jordan, *Winifred Sadie*	15.3.1920	1948	100
Keough, *Linda*	26.12.1963	1988	400/1600R
Kinch, *Beverly*	14.1.1964	1988	400R
Kippax, *Patricia Ann*	23.9.1941	1964	400
Knowles, *Linda Yvonne*	28.4.1946	1964	HJ
Laidlow, *Simone*	28.7.1965	1988	400h
Lannaman, *Sonia May*	24.3.1956	1972	100
		1976	200
		1980	100/200/
			400R
Lee, *Lorna*	16.7.1931	1948	LJ
Lerwill, *Sheila W*	16.8.1928	1952	HJ
Littlewood, *Angela Mary*	24.9.1949	1980	SP
Livermore, *Judith Earline Veronica*	14.11.1960	1980	Pen
(As Simpson in 1984)		1984	Hep
Long, *Marian Katherine Rosalie*	24.9.1920	1948	JT
Longdon, *Susan Jane*	22.1.1950	1976	Pen
		1980	Pen
Lowe, *Patricia Barbara*	15.9.1943	1968	800
(As Cropper in 1972)		1972	800
Lynch, *Andrea Joan Caron*	24.11.1952	1972	100/400R
		1976	100/400R
		1988	10k
McColgan, *Elizabeth*	24.5.1964	1980	400/1600R
MacDonald, *Linsey Tarrel*	12.2.1964	1984	1500
MacDougall, *Lynne*	18.2.1965	1988	DT
McKernan, *Jacqueline*	1.7.1965	1988	400h
McLaughlin, *Elaine*	17.11.1963	1976	800
McMeekin, *Christine*	1.12.1956	1948	100/400R
Manley, *Dorothy Gladys*	29.4.1927	1980	1500
Marlow, *Janet*	9.12.1958	1972	LJ
Martin-Jones, *Ruth*	28.1.1947	1964	HJ
Matthews, *Gwenda Mary*	6.6.1944	1988	LJ
May, *Fiona Marcia*	12.1.1969	1988	100
Miles, *Helen Louise*	2.3.1967	1980	HJ
Miller, *Louise Ann*	9.3.1960	1984	400h
Morley, *Susan Anita Jayne*	6.1.1960	1988	Hep
Mulliner, *Joanne C*	18.8.1966	1972	200
Murray, *Donna-Marie Louise*	1.5.1955	1976	400/1600R
(As Hartley in 1980)		1980	1600R
Murray, *Yvonne Carol Grace*	4.10.1964	1988	3k
Neil, *Anita Doris*	5.4.1950	1968	100/400R
		1972	100/400R
Nimmo, *Myra Alexander*	5.1.1954	1976	LJ
Nutting, *Patricia Anne*	4.1.1942	1960	80h
(As Pryce in 1964 & 1968)		1964	80h
		1968	80h
Oakes, *HR* see Hunte			
Oakes, *Judith Miriam*	14.2.1958	1984	SP
		1988	SP

COMPETITOR	DATE OF BIRTH-DEATH	YEAR	EVENT/S
Odam, *Dorothy Jennifer Beatrice*	14.3.1920	1936	HJ
(As Tyler in 1948, 1952 & 1956)		1948	HJ
		1952	HJ
		1956	HJ
Olney, *Violet R.*	22.5.1911	1936	400R
Packer, *Ann Elizabeth*	8.3.1942	1964	400/800
Page, *Joan Florence*	10.6.1947	1968	800
(As Allison in 1972)		1972	1500
Pain, *Angela Joyce*	8.2.1962	1988	Mar
Parkin, *Sheila Hilary*	22.10.1945	1964	LJ
(As Sherwood in 1968 & 1972)		1968	LJ
		1972	LJ
Paul, *JF* see Foulds			
Pascoe, *DP* see James			
Pashley, *Anne*	5.6.1935	1956	100/400R
Payne, *Christine Rosemary*	19.5.1933	1972	DT
Peat, *Valerie*	30.4.1947	1968	100
Perkins, *Phyllis Elsie Maureen*	22.2.1934	1960	800
Persighetti, *Christina May*	6.7.1936	1968	LJ
Peters, *Mary Elizabeth*	6.7.1939	1964	SP/Pen
		1968	Pen
		1972	Pen
Piggford, *Angela Mary*	17.8.1963	1988	1600R
Platt, *Susan Mary*	4.10.1940	1960	JT
		1964	JT
		1968	JT
Pletts, *Muriel*	23.2.1931	1948	400R
Pryce, *PA* see Nutting			
Porter, *Gwendolina Alice*	—	1932	100/400R
Probert, *Michelle*	17.6.1960	1980	400/1600R
Quinton, *Carole Louise*	11.7.1936	1956	80h
		1960	80h/400R
Ramsden, *Denise Irene*	11.2.1952	1976	400R
Rand, *MD* see Bignal			
Reeve, *SD* see Scott			
Reid, *Bevis Anael*	13.6.1919	1948	SP/DT
Ritchie, *Margaret Elizabeth*	6.7.1952	1980	DT
		1984	DT
Roscoe, *Janette Veronica*	10.6.1946	1972	400/1600R
Rowell, *Sarah Louise*	19.11.1962	1984	Mar
Sanderson, *Theresa Ione*	14.3.1956	1976	JT
		1980	JT
		1984	JT
		1988	JT
Scott, *Susan Diane*	17.9.1951	1968	Pen
(As Reeve in 1976 & 1980)		1976	LJ
		1980	LJ
Scrivens, *Jean Eileen*	15.10.1935	1956	200/400R
Scutt, *Michelle*	17.6.1960	1984	400/1600R
Seaborne, *Pamela Georgina*	16.8.1935	1952	80h
Shepherd, *Joan CE*	5.5.1924	1948	LJ
Sherwood, *SH* see Parkin			
Shields, *Jane Elizabeth*	23.8.1960	1988	10K
Shirley, *Dorothy Ada*	15.5.1939	1960	HJ
		1968	HJ
Shivas, *Isobel BA*	19.4.1925	1952	100
Short, *Sallyanne*	6.3.1968	1988	400R
Simpson, *Janet Mary*	2.9.1944	1964	200/400R
		1968	400/400R
		1972	400/400R
Simpson, *JEV* see Livermore			
Skeete, *Lesley-Ann*	20.2.1967	1988	100h
Slaap, *Frances Mary*	25.6.1941	1960	HJ
		1964	HJ
Sly, *Wendy*	5.11.1959	1984	3k
		1988	3k
Smallwood, *Kathryn Jane*	3.5.1960	1980	100/200/400R
(As Cook in 1984)		1984	200/400/400R
Smart, *Jennifer Ann*	19.2.1943	1960	100/200/400R
Smith, *Anne Rosemary*	31.8.1941	1964	800
Simth, *Joyce Esther*	26.10.1937	1972	1500
		1984	Mar

COMPETITOR	DATE OF BIRTH-DEATH	YEAR	EVENT/S
Stewart, *Mary*	25.2.1956	1976	1500
Stirling, *Rosemary Olivia*	11.12.1947	1972	800/1600R
Stoute, *Jennifer Elaine*	16.4.1965	1988	1600R
Strong, *Shirley Elaine*	18.11.1958	1980	100h
		1984	100h
Stuart, *Katherine Louise*	18.5.1967	1988	200
Taylor, *Gladys*	5.3.1953	1976	400/1600R
		1984	400h/1600R
Taylor, *Sheila Janet*	12.8.1946	1968	800
(As Carey in 1972)		1972	1500
Thomas, *Shirley*	15.6.1963	1984	100
Threapleton, *Pauline Anne*	16.10.1933	1952	80h
(As Wainwright in 1956)		1956	80h
Tiffen, *Kathleen Margaret*	15.7.1912–5.1986	1936	80h
Tooby, *Angela Rosemary*	24.10.1960	1988	10k
Tooby, *Susan Julia*	24.10.1960	1988	Mar
Tranter, *Maureen Dorothy*	7.5.1947	1968	200/400R
Tyler, *DJB* see Odam			
Upton, *Joan M*	16.12.1922	1948	80h
Vernon, *Judith Ann*	25.9.1945	1972	100h/400R
Wade, *Kirsty Margaret*	6.8.1962	1988	800/1500
Wainwright, *PA* see Threapleton			
Walker, *Margaret*	2.1.1925	1948	200/400R
Walls, *Moira Lindsay*	4.5.1952	1976	HJ
Webb, *Violet B*	3.2.1915	1932	80h/400R
		1936	80h
Welch, *Priscilla*	22.11.1944	1984	Mar
Whitaker, *Sandra*	29.1.1963	1984	200
Whitbread, *Fatima*	3.3.1961	1980	JT
		1984	JT
		1988	JT
Whitehead, *Grethe*	24.6.1914	1936	80h
Whyte, *Elspeth A*	24.12.1926	1948	SP/DT
Williams, *Averil Muriel*	14.3.1935	1960	JT
Williamson, *Audrey Doreen Swayne*	28.9.1926	1948	200
Willoughby, *Constance Lydia*	6.1.1930	1952	LJ
Wilson, *Ann Shirley*	29.9.1949	1968	80h/LJ/Pen
		1972	100h/Pen
Wray, *Yvette Julie*	18.10.1958	1980	Pen
Yule, *Penelope*	7.6.1949	1976	1500

Water Polo

Water polo has been held at every Olympic Games except those of 1896 and 1906. Great Britain competed in the first tournament in 1900 and, apart from 1904 and 1932, took part in every Olympics up to 1956. From 1960 onwards, Britain has not progressed beyond the qualifying rounds.

COMPETITOR	DATE OF BIRTH-DEATH	YEAR
Ablett, *Leslie*	6.3.1904–22.4.1952	1928/1936
Annison, *Harold Edward*	1895	1924
(Also see *Swimming*)		
Beaman, *Nicholas Victor*	—	1928
Bentham, *Isaac*	27.10.1886	1912
Blake, *Ernest*	31.3.1912	1936
Brand, *Charles William*	16.1.1916	1948/1952
Budd, *John Ernest Cloud*	1900	1924/1928
Bugbee, *Charles*	29.8.1887–18.10.1959	1912/1920/1924
Coe, *Thomas*	1880	1900
Cornet, *George Thomson*	15.7.1877–22.11.1952	1908/1912
Dean, *William Henry*	6.2.1887–2.5.1949	1920
Derbyshire, *John Henry*	29.11.1878–30.7.1938	1900
(Also see *Swimming*)		
Ferguson, *John Andrew*	4.4.1930	1952/1956
Forsyth, *Charles Eric*	10.1.1885–24.2.1951	1908
Garforth, *Roy Russell*	30.4.1918	1948
Gentleman, *Robert Forbes*	28.8.1923	1948
Grady, *Arthur Robert*	5.8.1922	1956
Grogan, *David*	7.7.1914	1936

COMPETITOR	DATE OF BIRTH-DEATH	YEAR EVENT/S
Hardie, *Peter*	—	1948
Hatfield, *John Gatenby*	15.8.1893–30.3.1965	1928
(Also see *Swimming*)		
Hawkins, *Stanley*	24.11.1924	1952
Hill, *Arthur Edwin*	9.1.1888	1912
Hodgson, *Richard*	24.12.1892–13.9.1968	1924/1928
Hunt, *Arthur William James*	27.8.1886–24.9.1949	1924
Johnston, *Ian Thompson*	—	1948/1952
Jones, *Christopher*	23.6.1886–18.12.1937	1920
Jones, *John Shaw*	17.4.1925	1952/1956
Kemp, *Peter*	1878	1900
(Also see *Swimming*)		
Knights, *Robert Edwin*	22.7.1931	1956
Lewis, *Trevor J*	—	1948
Lister, *William Haughton*	1882	1900
McGregor, *David Blane*	7.2.1909	1936
Martin, *William*	20.12.1906	1936
Miller, *Terence Charles*	2.3.1932	1952/1956
Milton, *Frederick George Matt*	2.10.1906	1936
Mitchell, *Robert*	14.12.1913	1936
Murray, *David Young*	13.6.1925	1948/1952
Nevinson, *George Wilfred*	3.10.1882–13.3.1963	1908/1912
North, *Alfred Sydney*	7.2.1908	1936
Palmer, *Leslie*	17.6.1910	1936
Pass, *Peter Walton*	8.3.1933	1956
Peacock, *William*	6.12.1891–14.12.1948	1920
Peter, *Edward Percival*	28.3.1902	1928
(Also see *Swimming*)		
Potter, *Reginald P*	—	1948
Purcell, *Noel Mary*	14.11.1891–31.1.1962	1920
(Also competed for Ireland in 1924)		
Quick, *William S*	—	1928
Radmilovic, *Paul*	5.3.1886–29.9.1968	1908/1912/1920/
(Also see *Swimming*)		1924/1928
Robertson, *Arthur G*	1879	1900
Robinson, *Eric*	1878	1900
Smith, *Charles Sydney*	26.1.1879–6.4.1951	1908/1912/1920/
		1924
Spooner, *Edwin Clifford*	21.12.1933	1956
Sutton, *Reginald James Cushing*	10.5.1909	1936
(Also see *Swimming*)		
Temme, *Edward Harry*	16.9.1904–20.6.1978	1928/1936
Thould, *Thomas Henry*	11.1.1886–15.6.1971	1908
Turner, *Ronald Frederick*	11.6.1929	1952/1956
Wilkinson, *George*	3.3.1879–7.8.1946	1900/1908/1912
Worsell, *Gerald Albert*	1.5.1930	1952/1956

Weightlifting

With the exception of 1900; 1908 and 1912, weightlifting events have been held at every Olympic Games. Great Britain did not compete in 1904, 1906 and 1932.

B = Bantamweight   Fe = Featherweight   Fl = Flyweight
H = Heavyweight   H(1) = First heavyweight
H(2) = Second heavyweight   L = Lightweight
LH = Light-heavyweight   M = Middleweight
MH = Middle-heavyweight   SH = Super-heavyweight
1h = One-handed lift   2h = Two-handed lift

COMPETITOR	DATE OF BIRTH-DEATH	YEAR EVENT/S
Arthur, *Peter John Henry*	4.4.1939	1968 LH
		1972 MH
Attenborough, *Charles Frederick*	1902	1924 M
		1928 M
Austin, *John S*	1900	1924 M
Barnett, *Joseph Melvin*	3.11.1920	1952 MH
Baxter, *Alfred*	1898	1924 Fe
		1928 Fe
Blackman, *Sylvanus Timotheus*	1.7.1933	1960 LH
		1964 LH
		1968 MH

COMPETITOR	DATE OF BIRTH-DEATH	YEAR EVENT/S
Blenman, *Blair*	23.11.1933	1960 M
Boxell, *Keith*	6.5.1958	1984 MH
		1988 MH
Bryce, *Jeffrey*	28.4.1948	1980 Fe
Burns, *John*	21.12.1948	1976 H(1)
		1980 H
Burrowes, *Newton*	5.6.1955	1980 M
		1984 LH
Caira, *Philip Mario*	24.2.1933	1956 LH
		1960 LH
Chaplin, *Ricki*	24.8.1964	1988 M
Creus, *Julian*	30.6.1917	1948 B
		1952 Fe
		1956 Fe
Cummins, *Augustus*	1881	1924 Fe
Daniels, *Victor*	9.10.1951	1976 Fe
Davies, *Andrew*	17.7.1967	1988 H(2)
Drzewiecki, *Andrzej*	9.11.1947	1980 H(2)
Eland, *Ronald*	—	1948 L
Elliot, *Launceston*	9.6.1874–8.8.1930	1896 1h/2h
(Also see *Gymnastics, Track & Field* and *Wrestling*)		
Evans, *Yorrie*	16.4.1923	1952 L
Ford, *Michael Anthony*	19.5.1939	1972 LH
Greenhalgh, *Abraham*	—	1948 B
Griffin, *Alfred*	31.5.1909	1936 L
Hallett, *Denis W*	—	1948 Fe
Halliday, *James*	19.1.1918	1948 L
		1952 L
Hancock, *David*	11.12.1945	1972 H
Harrington, *Sydney*	16.11.1926	1956 MH
Helfgott, *Benjamin*	22.11.1929	1956 L
		1960 L
Hillman, *Dennis*	6.4.1933	1960 H
Holroyd, *Norman*	8.5.1914	1936 Fe
Hopkins, *Alfred H McDonald*	16.5.1900–16.4.1986	1928 Fe
Isaac, *Leo*	8.11.1954	1980 L
Kemble, *Sidney*	23.1.1914–10.4.1979	1948 Fe
Kennedy, *Kevin see Welch*		
Knight, *Alfred J*	1916	1948 H
Langford, *Gary*	14.3.1953	1976 MH
		1980 MH
Laurance, *Harold Edward Kirby*	1.7.1915	1936 M
Laws, *Geoffrey*	19.12.1956	1980 Fe
		1984 Fe
Lowes, *R Frederick*	1904	1924 M
McKenzie, *Precious*	6.6.1936	1968 B
		1972 B
		1976 Fl
Manners, *George Russell*	25.1.1938	1964 LH
Marsh, *Frederick*	4.5.1910	1936 Fe
Martin, *Louis George*	11.11.1936	1960 MH
		1964 MH
		1968 MH
May, *Peter*	18.6.1966	1988 H(1)
Megennis, *Maurice*	16.11.1929	1952 B
		1956 Fe
Mercer, *David*	16.4.1961	1984 MH
		1988 MH
Mills, *Percival*	—	1920 L
Morgan, *David*	30.9.1964	1984 M
		1988 LH
Newton, *George*	13.8.1936	1964 Fe
		1972 L
Owen, *Ieuan Wyn*	12.2.1941	1972 L
Paine, *John G*	—	1920 Fe
Pearman, *Michael*	22.5.1941	1964 M
		1968 LH
		1972 LH
Peppiatt, *Ernest James*	—	1948 M
Perdue, *Terrence Robert John*	10.11.1938	1968 H
		1972 SH
Perrin, *Gerald*	17.11.1946	1968 Fe
Pinsent, *Peter*	25.11.1960	1984 H(1)
Pinsent, *Stephen*	5.3.1955	1980 LH
		1984 M

Age Records

Although the precise date of birth has not been established for every British Olympian, the following age records **have been compiled from all available facts. An asterisk indicates** **an age which has been estimated with only the year of birth known.**

SUMMER GAMES

Men: Oldest

Gold medallist:	*58 yrs 236 days	Jerry Millner	1908 Shooting
Medallist:	61 yrs 246 days	John Butt	1912 Shooting
Competitor:	66 yrs 8 days	Charles Lucas	1952 Shooting

Men: Youngest

Gold medallist:	18 yrs 6 days	William Foster	1908 Swimming
Medallist:	16 yrs 134 days	Brian Phelps	1960 Diving
Competitor:	15 yrs 94 days	Fred Hodges	1936 Diving

Women: Oldest

Gold medallist:	53 yrs 275 days	Queenie Newall	1908 Archery
Medallist:	As above (Newall)		
Competitor:	70 yrs 3 days	Lorna Johnstone	1972 Dressage

Women: Youngest

Gold medallist:	17 yrs 266 days	Bella Moore	1912 Swimming
Medallist:	15 yrs 113 days	Sarah Hardcastle	1984 Swimming
Competitor:	13 yrs 43 days	Margery Hinton	1924 Swimming

WINTER GAMES

Men: Oldest

Gold medallist:	39 yrs 1 day	Carl Erhardt	1936 Ice Hockey
Medallist:	45 yrs 225 days	Edgar Syers	1908 Figure Skating
Competitor:	53 yrs 297 days	John Coats	1948 Skeleton

Men: Youngest

Gold medallist:	18 yrs 224 days	John Kilpatrick	1936 Ice Hockey
Medallist:	As above (Kilpatrick)		
Competitor:	15 yrs 352 days	Rodney Ward	1956 Figure Skating

Women: Oldest

Gold medallist:	*27 yrs 128 days	Madge Syers	1908 Figure Skating
Medallist:	38 yrs 246 days	Ethel Muckelt	1924 Figure Skating
Competitor:	42 yrs 330 days	Ethel Muckelt	1928 Figure Skating

Women: Youngest

Gold medallist:	21 yrs 150 days	Jeannette Altwegg	1948 Figure Skating
Medallist:	15 yrs 79 days	Cecilia Colledge	1936 Figure Skating
Competitor:	11 yrs 76 days	Cecilia Colledge	1932 Figure Skating

COMPETITOR	DATE OF BIRTH-DEATH	YEAR	EVENT/S
Price, *Kenneth*	6.1.1941	1972	H
		1976	MH
Randall, *William Albert*	1888	1924	L
Robinson, *Allan*	19.6.1935	1960	Fe
Roe, *Ernest*	—	1948	LH
Saxton, *Andrew*	4.5.1967	1988	H(1)
Strange, *Brian*	29.1.1954	1976	H
Supple, *Anthony*	15.12.1961	1984	LH
Taylor, *Gary*	14.10.1960	1984	H(2)
Taylor, *Thomas*	1889	1924	Fe
Thomas, *Mark*	17.4.1963	1988	H(2)
Tooley, *JH*	1899	1924	L
		1928	M
Vine, *Matthew*	7.9.1959	1988	SH
Walker, *Ronald*	22.12.1907 – 25.10.1948	1936	H
Watson, *G William*	—	1948	M
Welch, *Kevin*	13.12.1952	1976	L
(Competed as Kennedy in 1980)		1980	M
Willey, *Dean*	9.6.1962	1984	L
		1988	M
Winterbourne, *Alan*	1.4.1947	1976	L
		1980	L
Wood, *Harold*	1890	1924	H
		1928	H
Wyatt, *WP*	1893	1924	L

Wrestling

Apart from 1900, wrestling has been featured on the programme at every Olympic Games. Britain were not represented in 1904 and 1906 but competed on every other occasion.

B = Bantamweight Fe = Featherweight Fl = Flyweight
H = Heavyweight L = Lightweight LF = Light-flywieght
LH = Light-heavyweight M = Middleweight S = Super-heavyweight
W = Welterweight

Contests in the Greco-Roman style are denoted by the suffix (GR). Britain competed in these events only in 1896, 1908, 1912 (when there were no freestyle events) 1936 and in 1948.

COMPETITOR	DATE OF BIRTH-DEATH	YEAR	EVENT/S
Adams, *WT*	—	1908	Fe
Allan, *Maurice*	30.10.1945	1976	LH
Allen, *Leonard John*	22.5.1931	1964	W
Amey, *Peter*	3.8.1935	1960	W
Angus, *H*	—	1928	Fe
Aspen, *Albert*	1.3.1934	1960	Fe
		1964	Fe
Aspen, *Brian*	6.4.1959	1980	Fe
		1984	B
Bacon, *Ernest Aubrey*	1893	1924	L
Bacon, *Edgar Hugh*	9.10.1887	1908	M/M(GR)
		1912	M(GR)
		1920	M
		1924	M

BRITISH OLYMPIC COMPETITORS

COMPETITOR	DATE OF BIRTH-DEATH	YEAR	EVENT/S
Bacon, *Stanley Vivian*	13.8.1885–13.10.1952	1908	M/M(GR)
		1912	M(GR)
		1920	M
Baillie, *H*	—	1908	L
Banbrook, *A*	—	1908	H/LH(GR)
Barraclough, *Richard William*	6.3.1943	1972	M
Barrett, *Edward*	3.11.1880	1908	H/H(GR)
(Also see *Track & Field*)		1912	H(GR)
Bayliss, *Steven*	5.9.1959	1984	L
Beck, *Frederick*	—	1908	M/M(GR)
Bernard, *PW*	—	1920	Fe
Bissell, *Stanley John*	—	1948	M(GR)
Blount, *EJ*	—	1908	L(GR)
Bowey, *Edward*	—	1948	M
Bradshaw, *GA*	—	1908	M/M(GR)
Brown, *CH*	—	1908	H/LH(GR)
Bruce, *L*	—	1908	H
Buck, *Anthony Jude Joseph*	29.12.1936	1964	LH
Butts, *A*	—	1960	M
Cazaux, *Raymond*	3.7.1917	1936	B
		1948	B
Cheetham, *Leslie*	8.10.1926	1952	Fl
Chenery, *HE*	—	1908	M
Clempner, *Matthew*	20.5.1956	1980	S
Cockings, *Percy Horatius*	19.12.1885	1908	Fe
		1912	Fe(GR)
Coleman, *Aubrey*	1888	1908	M
Cook, *R*	—	1928	W
Couch, *R*	—	1908	Fe
Cox, *JE*	—	1908	B
Cox, *WJ*	—	1908	B
Darby, *H*	1902	1924	B
Davis, *F*	—	1908	B
Davis, *JW*	1893	1924	W
Dawes, *Kenneth George*	17.1.1947	1972	Fe
		1976	Fe
Doyle, *Martin*	16.11.1958	1988	M
Dunbar, *Mark Anthony*	1.6.1961	1980	Fl
		1984	Fe
Elliot, *Launceston*	9.6.1874–8.8.1930	1896	H(GR)
(Also see *Gymnastics, Track & Field* and *Weightlifting*)			
English, *Graeme*	25.9.1964	1988	LH
Farquhar, *George Hardy*	14.12.1929	1956	M
Faulkner, *GA*	—	1908	L/L(GR)
Foskett, *Harold J*	—	1908	H/LH(GR)
Fox, *William*	9.8.1912	1936	W
Gardner, *G*	1900	1924	L
Gilligan, *Joseph*	7.11.1954	1972	L
		1976	L
Gingell, *Albert*	1883	1908	L
Goddard, *AJ*	—	1908	Fe
Gould, *Arthur Edwin*	31.1.1892	1912	L(GR)
Grinstead, *Ronald Sydney*	25.12.1942	1968	M
		1972	LH
Hall, *Herbert Henry*	16.3.1926	1952	Fe
		1956	Fe
Haward, *Keith*	28.6.1951	1976	W
Hawkins, *AE*	—	1908	L(GR)
Hayes, *William Ernest*	20.4.1891	1912	L(GR)
Henson, *WJP*	—	1908	L
Hoy, *J*	—	1908	L
Humphreys, *Frederick Harkness*	28.1.1878–10.8.1954	1908	H/H(GR)
(Also see *Track & Field*)			
Inman, —		1920	Fe
Irvine, *Donald*	—	1948	W
		1952	W
Irvine, *Kenneth H*	12.2.1923	1948	B/B(GR)
		1952	B
Jeffers, *Leslie Herbert Arthur*	8.1.1910	1936	M
Jones, *WF*	—	1908	Fe
Knight, *FW*	—	1908	B
Kurpas, *Stefan Otto*	22.2.1955	1984	M
Lay, *VC*	1896	1924	LH
Loban, *Noel*	28.4.1957	1984	LH
		1988	H
Luck, *PG*	—	1948	L
Lupton, *William Thomas*	—	1912	L(GR)
McCourtney, *John*	—	1968	Fe
McDonald, *Andrew*	1895	1920	H
		1924	H
MacGuffie, *W*	—	1948	Fl(GR)
MacKenzie, *George*	21.11.1888–1957	1908	L/L(GR)
		1912	L(GR)
		1920	L
		1924	Fe
		1928	L
McKenzie, *J*	—	1908	L
McKie, *William*	1886	1908	Fe
McNamara, *Denis*	27.8.1930	1964	H
Mason	—	1920	H
Moores, *Gary*	4.4.1959	1984	F
Morrell, *Norman*	17.7.1912	1936	F/F(GR)
Mortimer, *J*	—	1948	Fe(GR)
Myland, *Raymond*	30.7.1927	1948	L(GR)
		1952	L
Nixson, *EE*	—	1908	H/LH(GR)
Oberlander, *Frederick*	23.5.1911	1948	H
Ogden, *David*	30.3.1968	1988	B
O'Kelly, *George Cornelius*	29.10.1886–3.11.1947	1908	H
Parker, *H*	—	1948	Fl
Parsons, *Arnold S*	—	1948	Fe
Peache, *Keith*	10.8.1947	1976	H
		1980	LH
Peake, *SJ*	—	1908	Fe
Phelps, *Robert Edward*	21.7.1890	1912	L(GR)
Pidduck, *Leonard J*	—	1948	H(GR)
Pilling, *Walter*	18.4.1935	1960	B
		1964	B
Press, *William J*	—	1908	B
Rabin, *Samuel*	—	1928	M
Reid, *Joseph*	—	1932	B
de Relwyskow, *George Frederick William*	18.6.1887–9.11.1942	1908	L/M
Rhys, *Noel Raymond*	23.2.1888	1912	M(GR)
		1920	LH
		1924	M
Richmond, *Kenneth Alan*	10.7.1926	1948	LH(GR)
		1952	H
		1956	H
		1960	H
Rose, *AE*	—	1908	L(GR)
Rowe, *BJ*	—	1924	M
		1928	M
Ruff, *William*	30.1.1883	1908	L(GR)
		1912	L(GR)
Sansom, *B*	—	1908	B
Sansum, *HE*	1883	1924	B
		1928	B
Saunders, *GJ*	—	1908	B
Schwan, *GH*	—	1908	B
Shacklady, *Anthony Max*	26.12.1945	1968	W
		1972	W
		1976	M
Shepherd, *WH*	—	1908	L
Singh Gill, *Amrik*	24.4.1951	1972	B
		1976	B
		1980	B
Singh Tut, *Ravinder*	23.5.1969	1988	Fe
Slim, *James P*	—	1908	Fe
Sprenger, *Harry Osmond*	1882–1957	1908	B
Stephenson, *Kenneth*	12.6.1938	1960	L
		1964	L
Stott, *George Henry*	1888	1924	Fe
Sullivan, *John*	—	1948	LH
Tagg, *W*	—	1908	Fe

COMPETITOR	DATE OF BIRTH-DEATH	YEAR	EVENT/S
Taylor, *Alfred William*	8.2.1889	1912	Fe(GR)
Taylor, *James*	7.3.1932	1956	L
Taylor, *Joseph William*	—	1932	Fe
Thompson, *Arthur*	24.11.1911	1936	L
Till, *Roger Michael*	4.9.1947	1968	L
Tomkins, *F*	—	1908	B
Walker, *Fitzlloyd Dean*	7.3.1959	1980	W
		1984	W
		1988	W
Wallis, *AE*	—	1908	M
Ward, *Thomas Ian Murray*	29.6.1907	1936	LH
Webster, *JA*	—	1908	Fe
West, *W*	—	1908	H/LH(GR)
White, *JG*	—	1908	Fe
Whittingstall, *AJ*	—	1908	L(GR)
Wilson, *JA*	—	1948	W(GR)
Wilson, *WG*	1884	1920	LH
		1924	LH
Witherall, *HP*	—	1908	B
Wood, *William*	1888	1908	L/L(GR)
Wright, *Peter*	—	1920	L

Yachting

MEN

The yachting events scheduled to be held at the 1896 Olympics were cancelled because of bad weather and there were no yachting events at the Games of 1904 and 1906. Apart from 1912 and 1980 Great Britain have been represented on every occasion.

0.5–1 = 0.5 to 1 ton class (1900) 2–3 = 2 to 3 ton class (1900) 3–10 = 3 to 10 ton class (1900) 10–20 = 10 to 20 ton class (1900) 20+ = Over 20 tons class (1900) OP = Open class (1900) 5.5 = 5.5 metre class 6 = 6 metre class 7 – 7 metre class 8 – 8 metre class 12 – 12 metre class 470 = 470 class Di = Dinghy Dr = Dragon FD = Flying Dutchman Ff = Firefly FM = Finn Monotype Sh = Sharpie So = Soling St = Star Sw = Swallow Te = Tempest To = Tornado WG = Wind Gliding

In 1908 there were two British entries in the 6 metre, 8 metre and 12 metre classes. The crews of these yachts have been identified as follows:
 6 metre D = Dormy S = Sibindi 8 metre C = Cobweb
 S = Sorais 12 metre H = Hera M = Mouchette

COMPETITOR	DATE OF BIRTH-DEATH	YEAR	EVENT/S
Adam, *JM*	—	1908	12(M)
Aisher, *Robin Allingham*	24.1.1934	1960	5.5
		1964	5.5
		1968	5.5
Allam, *Peter*	26.7.1959	1984	FD
Anderson, *Paul Richard*	26.2.1935	1968	5.5
Aspin, *John Symington*	31.3.1877–19.2.1960	1908	12(H)
Backus, *Ronald*	28.3.1932	1956	Dr
Banks, *Bernard Bruce*	5.4.1918	1952	St
		1956	St
Baker-Harber, *Michael*	4.10.1945	1976	So
Barrington-Ward, *John Craig*	28.8.1928	1952	Dr
Baxter, *James*	8.6.1870–4.7.1940	1908	12(M)
Belben, *Jason*	13.9.1965	1988	470
Bellville, *Miles Aubrey*	28.4.1909–27.10.1980	1936	6
Bingley, *SS Norman*	—	1908	7
Blackall, *Jasper Roy*	20.7.1920	1956	Sh
Boardman, *Christopher Alan*	11.6.1903–29.9.1987	1936	6
Bond, *David John Were*	27.3.1922	1948	Sw
Bowker, *David Graham*	15.3.1922	1956	5.5
Brooke Houghton, *Julian*	16.12.1946	1976	FD
Brown, *GH*	—	1948	Dr
Buchanan, *John*	1.1.1884–25.11.1943	1908	12(H)
Bunten, *James Clark*	28.3.1875–3.1.1935	1908	12(H)
Calverley, *John Selwin*	4.7.1855–30.12.1900	1900	20+

COMPETITOR	DATE OF BIRTH-DEATH	YEAR	EVENT/S
Campbell, *Charles Ralph*	14.12.1881–19.4.1948	1908	8(C)
Campbell-James, *David*	29.12.1949	1984	To
Childerley, *Stuart*	12.2.1966	1988	FM
Clark, *Derek EC*	12.6.1951	1976	470
Cochrane, *Blair Onslow*	11.9.1853–7.12.1928	1908	8(C)
Coleman, *Robert Henry Schofield*	1888–1.1.1960	1920	7
Compton, *Joseph Neild*	25.9.1900	1936	8
Creagh-Osborne, *Richard Pearson*	5.4.1928–20.8.1980	1956	FM
Crebbin, *Philip J B*	10.11.1951	1976	470
Crichton, *Charles William Harry*	7.7.1872–8.11.1958	1908	6(D)
Currey, *Charles Alistair*	6.11.1947	1972	Dr
Currey, *Charles Norman E*	26.2.1916	1952	FM
Currie, *Lorne Campbell*	25.4.1871–21.6.1926	1900	0.5–1/OP
Davidson, *WP*	—	1908	12(M)
Davies, *Christopher*	29.6.1946	1972	FD
Dawes, *William Lancelot*	16.3.1904–8.12.1985	1960	FD
Denham, *Eric*	20.9.1929	1964	5.5
Dillon, *John Desmond*	24.3.1921–17.10.1988	1952	5.5
		1956	5.5
Dixon, *Richard Travers*	20.11.1865–14.11.1949	1908	7
Downes, *Arthur Drummond*	23.2.1883–12.9.1956	1908	12(H)
Downes, *John Henry*	18.10.1870–1.1.1943	1908	12(H)
Dunlop, *David*	—	1908	12(H)
Dunning, *Barry Frank*	17.3.1946	1972	So
		1976	So
Dyson, *Edward*	10.10.1919	1952	Dr
Eddy, *John Noel*	14.3.1915	1936	8
Exshaw, *William Edgard*	15.2.1866–16.3.1927	1900	2–3
Falle, *Philip Vernon Le Goyt*	19.3.1885–2.6.1936	1928	8
Farrington, *Sloan Elmo* (Also represented the Bahamas in 1956)	17.5.1923	1948	St
Fowler, *Harold Gordon*	4.1.1886	1924	Di/8
		1928	Di
Gaydon, *Harold R*	—	1928	Di
Glen-Coats, *Thomas Coats Glen*	5.5.1878–7.3.1954	1908	12(H)
Goody, *Simon*	19.11.1966	1988	WS(II)
Gretton, *John, Jr*	1.9.1867–2.6.1947	1900	0.5–1/OP
Grogno, *Keith Leslie*	4.11.1912	1936	St
Hackford, *David*	3.3.1964	1984	WG
Hannay, *Ian Morton*	23.8.1935	1960	Dr
		1972	Dr
Hardie, *BG*	—	1948	6
Hardie, *HG*	—	1948	6
Harmer, *Russell Thomas*	5.11.1896–31.10.1940	1936	6
Harris, *Jeremy David*	17.12.1942	1964	Dr
Hemmings, *Andrew*	9.8.1954	1988	470
Hore, *Edward*	—	1900	10–20
Howlett, *David J*	24.11.1951	1976	FM
Hughes, *Alfred Collingwood*	1868–17.2.1935	1908	8(S)
Hughes, *Frederick St John*	22.2.1866–3.11.1956	1908	8(S)
Hume, *JD Howden*	1928	1948	6
Hume, *James Howden*	30.3.1903	1948	6
Hunloke, *Philip* (né Percival)	1868–1.4.1947	1908	8(S)
Hunt, *David Charles Gower*	22.6.1934	1972	Te
		1976	Te
Hunter, *HA*	—	1948	6
Jacob, *Edwin Ellis*	1878	1924	8
Jaffe, *Peter*	—	1932	St
Janson, *Jonathan*	5.10.1930	1956	Dr
		1960	Dr
Jardine, *Adrian*	23.8.1933	1964	5.5
		1968	5.5
Jardine, *Stuart*	23.8.1933	1968	St
		1972	St
Jellico, *JF*	—	1908	12(M)
Judah, *Robin David*	18.6.1930	1968	Dr
Kenion, *JG*	—	1908	12(M)
Kennedy-Cochrane-Patrick, *Neil Aylmer*	5.5.1926	1952	5.5
		1956	5.5
Knowles, *Durward Randolph* (Also represented the Bahamas in 1956, '60, '64, '68, '72, '76 and 1988)	2.11.1917	1948	St
Law, *Christopher*	5.7.1952	1984	So
Laws, *Gilbert Umfreville*	6.1.1870–3.12.1918	1908	6(D)

COMPETITOR	DATE OF BIRTH-DEATH	YEAR EVENT/S
Leaf, *Charles Symonds*	13.11.1895–19.2.1947	1936 6
Leask, *Edward*	18.5.1947	1984 So
		1988 So
Leuchars, *JW*	1852–8.9.1920	1908 6(S)
Leuchars, *W*	—	1908 6(S)
Littledale, *TAR*	—	1908 12(M)
McDonald, *Arthur William Baynes*	14.6.1903	1948 Ff
McDonald, *Neal*	22.7.1963	1988 FD
MacDonald-Smith, *Iain Somerled*	3.7.1945	1968 FD
		1976 So
McIntyre, *Michael*	29.6.1956	1984 FM
		1988 St
MacIver, *Charles*	28.11.1866–21.2.1935	1908 12(M)
MacIver, *CR*	—	1908 12(M)
Mackenzie, *John*	21.9.1876–9.12.1949	1908 12(H)
McLeod Robertson, *C*	—	1908 12(M)
McMeekin, *Thomas D*	—	1908 6(D)
Maddison, *WJ*	—	1920 7
Maddocks, *John Leyshon*	7.1.1958	1984 St
Mann, *Graham Hargrave*	26.6.1924	1956 Dr
		1960 Dr
Martin, *Albert*	—	1908 12(H)
Martin, *Leonard Jack*	24.11.1901	1936 6
Maudslay, *Algernon*	10.1.1873–2.3.1948	1900 0.5–1/OP
Maynard, *Michael John*	23.2.1937	1968 FM
Mellor, *SM*	—	1900 10–20
Mitchell, *John Frederick Roy*	6.4.1913	1960 St
Morgan, *Arthur William Crawford*	24.8.1931	1964 FD
Morris, *Stewart Harold*	25.5.1909	1948 Sw
Murdoch, *Frank John*	1.2.1904	1952 6
Musto, *Franklyn Keith*	12.1.1936	1964 FD
Newlands, *Peter*	31.10.1953	1984 470
Newman, *Jeremy*	16.2.1961	1988 To
Nicholson, *George Ian*	23.4.1937	1960 5.5
Oakeley, *John Digby Atholl*	27.11.1932	1972 So
Osborn, *John*	8.9.1945	1972 To
Parry, *Edwin Martin*	14.3.1935	1964 Dr
Pattisson, *Rodney Stuart*	5.8.1943	1968 FD
		1972 FD
		1976 FD
Perry, *Robert Stanley Grosvenor*	4.5.1909–3.4.1987	1952 5.5
		1956 5.5
Potter, *Stanley Arthur*	3.6.1914	1952 St
		1956 St
Preston, *Francis Richard Walter*	6.6.1913	1936 8
Preston, *Kenneth Huson*	19.5.1901	1936 8
		1952 6
Pym, *Patrick Ernest*	6.9.1936	1972 FM
Quentin, *Cecil*	1852–29.10.1926	1900 20+
Ramus, *James Pickering*	14.4.1935	1960 FD
		1968 Ft
Ratsey, *George Colin*	1905–3.1984	1932 ST/FM
Ratsey, *George Ernest*	1875–25.12.1942	1908 8(S)
Reade, *Peter John Chorley*	14.1.1939	1964 Dr
Reynolds, *Charles Lewis*	18.3.1943	1968 Dr
		1972 So
Rhodes, *John Edward*	13.2.1870–6.2.1947	1908 8(C)
Richards, *Jeremy*	30.1.1956	1984 So
		1988 So
Richards, *Jonathan*	31.3.1954	1984 FD
Riggs, *Thomas Cooper*	1903	1924 8
		1928 8
Riggs, *Walter*	1.1.1877	1924 8
		1928 8
Rivett-Carnac, *Charles James*	18.2.1853–9.9.1935	1908 7
Roney, *Ernest John*	1900	1924 8
		1928 8
Roney, *Esmond Y*	—	1928 8
Ruggles, *John K*	12.4.1934	1960 5.5

COMPETITOR	DATE OF BIRTH-DEATH	YEAR EVENT/S
Saffrey-Cooper, *Brian Linford*	9.7.1934	1964 FM
Scott, *Peter Markham*	14.9.1909–29.8.1989	1936 FM
Sharp, *Martin*	1917	1952 6
Smith, *FB*	—	1908 6(S)
Smith, *Lawrie*	19.2.1956	1988 So
Smith, *Terence James George*	18.10.1932	1956 Sh
Somers, *Thomas Vivian*	1909	1952 Dr
Spence, *JFD*	—	1908 12(M)
Steele, *Robert*	26.2.1893	1936 8
		1952 6
Strain, *William Eric Hamilton*	1.12.1915	1948 Dr
Stratton, *Vernon Gordon Lennox*	26.10.1927	1960 FM
Sutton, *Henry Cecil*	26.9.1868–24.5.1936	1908 8(C)
Tait, *Simon*	31.10.1932	1972 Dr
Tait, *Thomas Gerald*	7.11.1866–19.12.1938	1908 12(H)
Taylor, *J Howard*	—	1900 3–10
Tucker, *David Ernest George*	22.9.1941	1968 Dr
Vaile, *Philip Bryn*	16.8.1956	1988 St
Wallace, *TP*	—	1948 Dr
Ward, *William Dudley*	14.10.1877–11.11.1946	1908 8(S)
Warren, *Alan Kemp*	13.12.1935	1972 Te
		1976 Te
Wastall, *John Andrew*	23.6.1928	1972 St
Welpy, *William Rupert*	25.12.1912	1936 St
White, *Reginald J*	28.10.1935	1976 To
White, *Robert*	23.4.1956	1984 To
		1988 To
Wood, *Arthur Nicholas Lindsay*	29.3.1875–1.6.1939	1908 8(C)
Woodroffe, *Frankin Ratsey*	1918	1952 6
Woolward, *Iain*	3.4.1940	1984 St
Wright, *Cyril Macey*	17.9.1885–26.7.1960	1920 7
Yeoman, *Roger*	15.1.1957	1988 FD

In the Dinghy class in 1924, HR Gaydon was injured and withdrew after two races. He was replaced for the remaining races by HG Fowler.

Virtually every Olympic reference source gives FA Richards and T Hedberg as the winners of the 18 foot dinghy event in 1920 sailing *Brat*. As theirs was the only entry, Richards and Hedberg withdrew and should not be considered as Olympic winners – or even Olympic competitors.

Yachting
WOMEN

Separate yachting events for women were introduced in 1988. Prior to the Seoul Olympics, women were entitled to sail in the same events as the men.

COMPETITOR	DATE OF BIRTH-DEATH	YEAR EVENT/S
Foster, *Catherine*	28.2.1956	1984 470
Hay, *Susan*	13.9.1964	1988 470
Jarvis, *Debbie*	16.1.1964	1988 470
Mitchell, *Jean MAC*	9.7.1912	1960 St
Preston, *Beryl Wilmot*	2.11.1901	1936 8
Rivett-Carnac, *Francis Clytie*	1875–1.1.1962	1908 7
Roney, *MH*	—	1928 8
Wright, *Dorothy Winifred*	19.8.1889	1920 7

In order to ensure that Great Britain was suitably reprsented against foreign challengers at the 1908 Olympics, the Duchess of Westminster purchased *Sorais*, which was one of the finest 8 metre yachts of the time. Although her Grace sailed aboard her new boat during the Olympic Regatta, her role was strictly that of a spectator and she cannot be considered as an Olympic competitor.

Winter Games

Alpine Skiing
MEN

Alpine Skiing was first included in the Olympic Games in 1936 when an Alpine Combined event was held. The combined event was again on the programme in 1948 but was not held for a third time until 1988.

The Downhill and Slalom events were added in 1948, the Giant Slalom in 1952 and the Super Giant Slalom in 1988.

Great Britain has been represented in Alpine Skiing on every occasion.

AC = Alpine Combined (known as the Combined Competition from 1988 onwards)   CD = Combined Downhill   CS = Combined Slalom
Dh = Downhill   GS = Giant Slalom   SGS = Super Giant Slalom
Sl = Slalom

COMPETITOR	DATE OF BIRTH-DEATH	YEAR	EVENT/S
Appleyard, *Ian*	—	1948	Dh/Sl
Bartelski, *Konrad*	27.5.1954	1972	Dh/GS/Sl
		1976	GS
		1980	Dh/GS/Sl
Bell, *Graham*	4.1.1966	1984	Dh
		1988	Dh/GS/SGS/CD/CS
Bell, *Martin*	6.12.1964	1984	Dh/GS
		1988	Dh/GS/SGS/AC/CD/CS
Blyth, *Ross*	30.4.1961	1980	Dh/GS/Sl
Borradaile, *David*	16.9.1945	1968	Dh
Boumphrey, *P*	—	1948	Dh
Boyagis, *John*	26.1.1928	1948	Sl
		1952	Dh/GS/Sl
Brock-Hollinshead, *John*	1928	1956	Dh
Burton, *Frederick*	15.3.1959	1984	Dh/GS
Cargill, *David*	15.4.1957	1980	Dh
Duncan, *Ronald*	4.9.1962	1988	Dh/CD
Finlayson, *Iain*	19.12.1951	1972	Dh/GS/Sl
Fitzsimmons, *Stuart*	20.12.1956	1976	Dh/GS
Fuchs, *Peter*	28.10.1955	1976	Dh/GS/Sl
Gardner, *Nigel*	1933	1956	Dh/GS
Garrow, *Donald*	—	1948	Dh/Sl/AC
Harrison, *Noel*	29.1.1934	1952	Dh/GS/Sl
		1956	GS/Sl
Hooper, *Robin*	1934	1956	GS
Hourmont, *Robbie*	21.4.1969	1988	Sl/GS
Hudson, *Christopher S*	1.8.1900	1936	AC
Jones, *Morgan*	29.1.1968	1988	GS/Sl
Langmuir, *Roderick*	8.6.1960	1980	GS/Sl
de Larringa, *Rupert*	19.11.1928	1952	GS
Lunn, *Peter Northcote*	15.11.1914	1936	AC
Mackintosh, *Charlach*	1.6.1935	1956	Dh
		1960	Dh/GS
Mackintosh, *Douglas*	1931	1956	Dh
Mapelli-Mozzi, *Alex*	7.5.1951	1972	Dh/GS/Sl
Mercer, *David*	4.8.1960	1984	GS/Sl
Oakes, *John W*	23.9.1932	1960	Dh/GS
O'Brien, *Connor*	4.2.1961	1984	Dh
O'Reilly, *Luke*	21.6.1944	1968	Dh/GS/Sl
Palmer-Tomkinson, *Charles A*	4.1.1940	1964	Dh/GS
Palmer-Tomkinson, *James Algernon*	3.4.1915–7.1.1952	1936	AC
		1948	AC/Dh

COMPETITOR	DATE OF BIRTH-DEATH	YEAR	EVENT/S
Palmer-Tomkinson, *Jeremy James* (Also see *Luge*)	4.11.1943	1968	Dh/GS/Sl
Parkinson, *Stuart*	—	1948	Dh
Pitchford, *Geoffrey*	13.8.1936	1960	Dh/GS/Sl
Riddell, *William James*	27.12.1910	1936	AC
Rigby, *A John*	25.4.1942	1964	Dh/GS
Seilern, *Peter*	1936	1956	Sl
Skepper, *Robert B*	3.4.1938	1960	Dh/GS/Sl
Smith, *Nigel*	31.1.1964	1988	SGS
Stewart, *Alan*	15.9.1955	1976	Dh/GS/Sl
		1980	Dh/GS/Sl
Taylor, *Harold*	—	1948	AC/Sl
Taylor, *Jonathan*	12.10.1943	1964	Dh
Todd, *Ian*	26.6.1947	1968	Dh/GS/Sl
Torrens, *J Peter*	1934	1956	Sl
Varley, *Royston*	27.1.1952	1972	Dh/GS/Sl
Vasey, *Julian*	26.4.1950–5.1979	1968	GS/Sl
Waddell, *PL*	—	1948	Dh
de Westenholz, *Charles*	1946	1964	Dh/GS/Sl
de Westenholz, *Piers*	10.12.1943	1964	GS
Whitelaw, *G Alexander*	1930	1956	GS/Sl
Wison, *Nicholas*	9.6.1960	1984	GS/Sl

Alpine Skiing
WOMEN

The women's Olympic alpine skiing programme has always been identical to that of the men. Great Britain has been represented in the women's events at every Games since the Alpine Combined event was introduced in 1936.

COMPETITOR	DATE OF BIRTH-DEATH	YEAR	EVENT/S
Asheshov, *Anna Margaret C*	8.7.1941	1964	Dh
Beck, *Lesley*	10.7.1964	1984	Sl
		1988	GS/Sl
Blackwood, *Carol*	27.10.1953	1972	Dh/GS/Sl
Blane, *Helen*	5.9.1913	1936	AC
Booth, *Clare*	19.9.1964	1984	Dh
		1988	Dh/SGS/CD/CS
Cairns, *Kirstin*	11.1.1963	1980	GS/Sl
		1988	Sl
Campbell, *Fiona*	12.5.1929	1952	Dh/GS
Cargill, *Moira*	10.12.1958	1980	Dh
Duke-Wooley, *Bridget*	—	1948	Sl
Duthie, *A Birnie*	11.6.1905	1936	AC
Easdale, *Fiona*	11.3.1959	1976	Dh/Gs/Sl
Farrington, *M Wendy*	2.1.1941	1960	Dh/GS/Sl
		1964	GS
Field, *Felicity*	4.3.1946	1968	Dh/GS/Sl
Galica, *Davina Mary*	13.8.1944	1964	Dh/GS/Sl
		1968	Dh/GS/Sl
		1972	Dh/GS/Sl
Gibbs, *Josephine M*	21.5.1938	1960	Dh/GS/Sl
Gissing, *Jane Eleanor*	9.6.1943	1964	GS/Sl
Grant, *Ingrid*	16.10.1964	1988	GS
Greenland, *B*	—	1948	Sl
Hathorn, *Georgina Melissa*	6.7.1949	1964	Dh/GS/Sl
		1968	Dh/GS/Sl
		1972	Dh/GS/Sl
Heald, *Tania Elizabeth*	28.5.1943	1964	Dh/Sl
Hutcheon, *Hazel*	18.8.1960	1976	Dh
Holmes, *Susan Renate*	30.8.1929	1956	Dh/GS/Sl
		1960	Dh/GS/Sl
Iliffe, *Serena*	6.1.1960	1976	GS

COMPETITOR	DATE OF BIRTH-DEATH	YEAR	EVENT/S
Iliffe, *Valentina Dorcas*	17.2.1956	1972	Dh/GS/Sl
		1976	Dh/GS/Sl
		1980	Dh/GS/Sl
Jamieson, *Helen*	9.12.1946	1968	Dh/GS
Kessler, *Jeannette Anne*	4.10.1908–1972	1936	AC
Laing, *Jocelyn Hilary Mary*	21.9.1927	1952	Dh/GS/Sl
Lewis, *Sarah*	29.11.1964	1988	GS/Sl
Lumby, *Wendy*	13.6.1966	1988	Dh/GS/ SGS/AC/ CD/CS
McCaskie, *Sonia*	19.2.1939	1960	GS
Mackintosh, *Sheena*	10.1.1928	1948	AC/Dh/Sl
		1952	Dh/GS/Sl
Mackintosh, *Vora*	2.6.1919	1952	Dh/GS
Nowell, *Marjorie Alexandra 'Zandra'*	1936	1956	Dh/Sl
Pinching, *Evelyn A*	18.3.1915	1936	AC
Pryor, *Adeline Margery*	1939	1956	GS/Sl
Robb, *Anne*	27.7.1959	1976	Sl
		1980	GS/Sl
Roe, *Isobel M*	—	1948	Dh/Sl/AC
Ryder, *Xanthe*	—	1948	AC/Dh
Sandford, *Jeanne Ethel*	1929	1956	Dh/GS
Sparrow, *Rosemary*	—	1948	AC/Dh
Tomkinson, *Diana*	23.4.1943	1968	Sl
Wallis, *Theresa*	3.6.1957	1976	Dh/GS
Wardrop-Moore, *Jocelyn Avril*	1932	1956	GS/Sl

Biathlon

From 1924 to 1948 the Biathlon, which combines cross-country skiing and shooting skills, was included in the Olympics as a demonstration event and was known as the Military Ski Patrol. As it was felt that the military nature of the event was not compatible with the Olympic ideal it was dropped as a demonstration event after the 1948 Games but was reinstated, under its current name, as an official event in 1960.

No British representatives took part in the Military Ski Patrol demonstration event but Great Britain has been represented in the Biathlon on each occasion since its introduction in 1960.

From 1960 to 1976 the 20km was the only individual event but in 1980 a second individual event of 10km was included. The 4 × 7.5km relay was added to the programme in 1968.

10k = 10 kilometres – individual   20k = 20 kilometres – individual
Ry = 30 kilometres – relay (4 × 7.5km)

COMPETITOR	DATE OF BIRTH-DEATH	YEAR	EVENT/S
Andrew, *Frederick* (Also see *Nordic Skiing*)	28.4.1940	1968	20k/Ry
Bean, *Roger*	18.11.1945	1968	20k/Ry
Davies, *Carl*	30.7.1964	1988	10k/20k/ Ry
Dent, *John Robin* (Also see *Nordic Skiing*)	15.2.1938	1964	20k
Dixon, *Michael*	21.11.1962	1988	10k/20k/ Ry
Ferguson, *Graeme*	17.6.1952	1976	20k/Ry
		1980	20k/Ry
		1984	10k
Gibbins, *Paul* (Also see *Nordic Skiing*)	3.1.1953	1976	Ry
		1980	10k/Ry
Halliday, *Marcus*	15.7.1937	1968	20k/Ry
Hirst, *Malcolm*	13.6.1945	1972	20k/Ry
		1976	20k/Ry
Howdle, *Patrick*	24.4.1963	1984	Ry
King, *Trevor*	28.5.1969	1984	10k
		1988	10k/20k/ Ry
Langin, *Mark*	18.5.1962	1988	10k/20k/ Ry
MacIvor, *Charles* (Also see *Nordic Skiing*)	23.1.1957	1984	20k/Ry
McLeod, *Anthony*	29.4.1959	1984	20k/Ry

COMPETITOR	DATE OF BIRTH-DEATH	YEAR	EVENT/S
Moore, *John Arthur G* (Also see *Nordic Skiing*)	18.5.1933	1960	20k
		1964	20k
Notley, *Alan Graham*	10.4.1940	1964	20k
		1968	20k/Ry
		1972	10k/Ry
Oliver, *Keith Anthony* (Also see *Nordic Skiing*)	27.10.1947	1972	20k/Ry
		1980	10k/20k/ Ry
Shutt, *Norman L* (Also see *Nordic Skiing*)	9.11.1929	1960	20k
Stevens, *Jeffrey Stanley*	26.7.1945	1972	20k/Ry
		1976	20k/Ry
Tancock, *Peter* (Also see *Nordic Skiing*)	22.7.1940	1968	Ry
Tuck, *Roderick* (Also see *Nordic Skiing*)	28.5.1934	1964	20k
Wood, *James E*	13.10.1952	1980	10k/20k/ Ry
		1984	10k/20k/ Ry

Bobsleigh

The four-man bobsleigh event was included in the first Olympic Winter Games in 1924. With the exception of 1960, when no bobsleigh events were held, the four-man event has remained on the programme ever since, although in 1928 a five-man event was held in its place. The two-man event was introduced in 1932 and, with the exception of 1960 (see above), has been held at every subsequent Games. In 1928 and 1948 a Skeleton (one-man bob) event was held.

With the exception of 1932 and 1952 Great Britain has been represented on every occasion that bobsleigh events have been held.

2 = 2 man bob   4 = 4 man bob   5 = 5 man bob   Sk = Skeleton
The letters (A) and (B) indicate if the competitor was a member of the first or second crew.

COMPETITOR	DATE OF BIRTH-DEATH	YEAR	EVENT/S
Agar, *Hon Mark Sydney Andrew*	2.9.1948	1976	2(B)/4(B)
Armstrong, *David*	2.7.1964	1988	2(B)/4(A)
Arnold, *Thomas Alfred*	1901	1924	4(B)
Birch, *Walter*	—	1928	5(B)
Blockley, *John William*	2.4.1932	1968	2(B)/4(B)
Bott, *Richard EA*	—	1948	SK
Brandt, *Rollo*	1934	1956	4(A)
Broome, *Ralph Howard*	5.8.1889	1924	4(B)
Brown, *Harold John Catleugh*	21.4.1935	1968	4(A)
Brown, *Peter William 'Corrie'*	16.8.1949	1980	4(A)
		1984	4(A)
Browning, *Frederick Arthur Montague*	20.12.1896–14.3.1965	1928	5(A)
Brugnani, *Peter*	28.10.1958	1984	2(B)/4(B)
Campbell, *Colin William Ashburner* (Also see *Track & Field*)	20.6.1946	1976	4(A)
Cardno, *James Farquhar*	25.5.1912	1936	2/4
Clarke, *T*	—	1948	SK
Clifford, *Peter Michael*	11.4.1944	1972	2(A)/4(B)
Coates, *James Stuart*	13.4.1894–26.10.1966	1948	SK
Coles, *William Edward*	26.7.1913–7.6.1979	1948	2(A)/4(A)
Collings, *Raymond William Pennington*	23.9.1908–13.11.1972	1948	2(A)/4(A)
Crabbe, *Archibald Douglas*	7.3.1903	1924	4(A)
Crammond, *John Gordon*	5.7.1906–18.9.1978	1948	SK
Dalrymple, *John Aymer*	9.10.1906	1928	5(B)
De La Hunty, *Thomas*	4.7.1956	1984	2(A)/4(B)
		1988	2(A)/4(B)
Dixon, *Hon Thomas Robin Valerian*	21.4.1935	1964	2(A)/4(A)
		1968	2(A)/4(A)
Dugdale, *Guy Carol*	9.4.1905	1936	4
Evelyn, *John Patrick Michael Hugh*	16.10.1939	1972	2(A)/4(A)
Fairlie, *Francis Gerard Louis*	14.9.1899	1924	4(A)

COMPETITOR	DATE OF BIRTH-DEATH	YEAR	EVENT/S
Freeman, *Roy Edward Michael*	30.6.1937	1968	2(B)/4(B)
		1972	4(A)
Gadd, *Anthony*	26.10.1917	1948	2(B)
Gee, *John*	—	1928	5(B)
Green, *Charles Patrick*	30.3.1904	1936	4
Griffith, *David*	—	1928	5(A)
Hall, *Edward Ramsden*	1900	1928	5(B)
Hammond, *John Maurice*	4.8.1933	1972	2(B)/4(B)
Hedges, *Andrew*	16.9.1935	1964	2(B)/4(B)
Holliday, *George Stanley Charles*	14.2.1917	1948	4(A)
Horton, *William Gray*	24.8.1897–13.7.1974	1924	4(A)
Howell, *John*	17.6.1955	1980	2(A)/4(A)
Iremonger, *James Henry*	31.3.1918	1948	4(B)
Jeffery, *Richard Robert*	24.11.1917	1948	4(B)
Jones, *Alan*	25.10.1946	1972	4(B)
Leonce, *Alec*	19.4.1962	1988	2(A)/4(B)
Lewis, *Walter David*	3.9.1936	1964	4(A)
Lloyd, *Denys Malcolm*	26.2.1947	1972	4(A)
		1976	2(A)/4(A)
		1980	4(B)
		1984	2(B)/4(B)
Lund, *Peter*	24.2.1955	1984	2(A)
McCowen, *William*	31.3.1937	1964	2(B)/4(B)
McEvoy, *Frederick Joseph*	12.2.1907–7.11.1951	1936	2/4
McKenzie, *Angus Carl Alexander*	29.12.1954	1984	4(A)
McLean, *William John*	9.7.1918–9.11.1963	1948	4(A)
Mann, *Rodney K*	1929	1956	4(B)
Martineau, *Henry C*	—	1928	5(B)
Meddings, *Edgar James*	5.6.1923	1948	4(B)
Nash, *Anthony James Dillon*	18.3.1936	1964	2(A)/4(A)
		1968	2(A)/4(A)
Northesk, *David Earl of*	24.9.1901–7.11.1963	1928	SK
Norton, *Anthony*	27.2.1950	1976	4(B)
Ogilvy-Wedderburn, *Andrew John Alexander*	4.8.1952	1976	4(B)
		1980	4(B)
Parkinson, *W Stuart*	1929	1956	2(A)/4(B)
Paul, *Leonard*	25.5.1958	1988	4(A)
Phipps, *Nicholas D*	8.4.1952	1980	4(B)
Pim, *George Cecil*	14.1.1899	1924	4(A)
		1928	5(A)
Potter, *Roger*	14.3.1945	1980	2(B)
Powell-Sheddon, *George Ffolliott*	1.4.1916	1948	4(B)
Price, *Michael John*	15.8.1950	1972	4(B)
		1976	2(A)/4(A)
		1980	4(B)
Pugh, *Michael*	20.7.1953	1980	2(B)
		1984	4(A)
Raffles, *Ralph*	1920	1956	4(A)
Rainsforth, *John*	1934	1956	2(B)/4(A)
Rattigan, *Colin*	12.11.1961	1988	4(B)
Read, *John*	1926	1956	4(A)
Renwick, *Guy Philip*	5.11.1936	1964	4(A)
		1968	4(A)
Richards, *Audley*	24.2.1960	1988	4(A)
Richardson, *Alexander Whitmore Colquhoun*	11.5.1887–22.7.1964	1924	4(B)
Robertson, *George E*	19.12.1958	1988	4(B)
Schellenberg, *Clifford Keith W*	1929	1956	2(B)/4(A)
Seel, *Robin Edward*	20.2.1940	1964	4(B)
Smith, *Howard*	29.9.1956	1984	4(B)
Soher, *Rodney E*	1893	1924	4(B)
Sweet, *Graham*	26.10.1948	1976	4(B)
Sweet, *Michael William*	12.4.1947	1972	2(B)/4(A)
		1976	2(B)/4(A)
Thorn, *Timothy*	21.9.1942	1968	4(B)
Tout, *Mark John*	24.1.1961	1984	4(A)
		1988	2(B)/4(A)
Tracey, *M*	—	1928	5(A)
Wallington, *Anthony E*	5.10.1948	1980	4(A)
		1984	4(A)
Warner, *TS*	—	1928	5(A)
Wellicome, *Basil William*	28.12.1926	1948	2(B)
Widdows, *Robin Michael*	27.5.1942	1964	4(B)
		1968	4(A)

COMPETITOR	DATE OF BIRTH-DEATH	YEAR	EVENT/S
Williams, *Christopher Charles Ulysses*	1927	1956	2(A)/4(B)
Woodall, *Jonathan William Agnew* (Also see *Luge*)	25.1.1946	1980	2(A)/4(A)

The composition of the 5-man crews in 1928 given in the above list is taken from the programme and the Official Report of the Organizing Committee, ie, Crew No. 1 FAM Browning, D Griffith, GC Pim, (Captain), M Tracey and TS Warner; Crew No. 2 W Birch, JA Dalrymple, J Gee, E Hall and HC Martineau (Captain). However, it should be noted that the Official Report of the British Olympic Association gives G Gordon in place of M Tracey in Crew No. 1 and lists M Tracey as a *sixth* member of Crew No. 2.

Figure Skating
MEN

Figure skating events were held as part of the Summer Games of 1908 and 1920 and have subsequently been included at every Winter Games. In 1908 a 'Special Figures' event for men was held in addition to the regular figure skating competition. Ice Dancing first became an Olympic event in 1976.

With the exception of 1932, Great Britain has been represented in the men's figure skating events on every occasion.

D = Dance   P = Pairs   S = Singles   SF = Special Figures (1908 only)

COMPETITOR	DATE OF BIRTH-DEATH	YEAR	EVENT/S
Askham, *Paul*	20.10.1962	1988	D
Beaumont, *Kenneth Macdonald*	10.2.1884–24.4.1965	1920	S/P
Booker, *Michael Robert*	16.4.1937	1956	S
Bowhill, *Ian Home*	1974	1928	S
Burman, *Albert Proctor*	10.3.1893–11.5.1974	1928	P
Cannon, *Malcolm Rogar*	22.6.1944	1964	S
Clarke, *Herbert James*	1879–5.9.1956	1924	S
Clements, *David William*	8.8.1939	1960	S
Cliff, *Leslie Harold Talbot*	5.6.1908–2.8.1969	1936	P
Cousins, *Robin John*	17.8.1957	1976	S
		1980	S
Cumming, *Arthur Warren J*	8.5.1889–8.5.1914	1908	SF
Curry, *John Anthony*	9.9.1949	1972	S
		1976	S
Cushley, *Neil J*	23.2.1967	1988	P
Daw, *Robert J*	6.1.1964	1980	P
Dean, *Christopher Colin*	27.7.1958	1980	D
		1984	D
Dunn, *John Edward Powell*	28.3.1917–16.7.1938	1936	S
Evans, *Hywel Lloyd*	9.1.1945	1964	S
Foster, *Kenneth J*	16.6.1951	1976	D
Greig, *John Keiller*	—	1908	S
Hall-Say, *Geoffrey Norman Ernest*		1908	SF
Holles, *Anthony Frederick*	8.2.1939	1956	P
Howarth, *Christopher*	25.12.1960	1980	S
Jenkins, *Ian Roger*	18.5.1962	1984	P
Johnson, *James Henry*	1874–15.11.1921	1908	P
Jones, *Christopher Robin*	17.6.1943–30.3.1986	1960	S
Jones, *Glyn*	22.8.1953	1976	S
Lockwood, *Raymond Charles*	12.12.1928	1952	P
March, *Albert*	—	1908	S
Maxwell, *Warren D*	15.12.1952	1976	D
Naylor, *Andrew*	12.8.1965	1988	P
Nicks, *John Allen Wisden*	22.4.1929	1948	P
		1952	P
Oundjian, *Haig Bertrand*	16.5.1949	1968	S
		1972	S
Page, *John Ferguson*	1900–14.2.1947	1924	S/P
		1928	S/P
Richardson, *Thomas Dow*	16.1.1887–7.1.1971	1924	P
Robinson, *Paul*	10.4.1965	1984	S
		1988	S
Sharp, *Henry Graham*	19.12.1917	1936	S
		1948	S

COMPETITOR	DATE OF BIRTH-DEATH	YEAR	EVENT/S
Silverthorne, *Dennis Alfred*	1.2.1923	1948	P
Slater, *Nicholas Mark*	6.4.1958	1980	D
		1984	D
Syers, *Edgar Morris Wood*	18.3.1863–16.2.1946	1908	P
Taylforth, *Colin*	16.9.1953	1972	P
		1976	P
Tomlins, *Frederick William Edwin*	5.8.1919–20.6.1943	1936	S
Wallwork, *Sydney*	—	1920	P
Ward, *Rodney*	12.2.1941	1956	P
Watts, *Glyn Robert*	16.3.1949	1976	D
Williams, *Basil J*	—	1920	S/P
Williams, *Michael Thorpe*	23.3.1947	1968	S
Williams, *Stephen Gordon*	23.5.1960	1984	D
Wilson, *Raymond Edward*	22.5.1944	1968	P
Yates, *Ernest Henry Charles*	18.1.1915	1936	P
Yates, *Geoffrey Sidney*	16.5.1918	1936	S
Yglesias, *Herbert Ramon*	1867–20.8.1949	1908	S

Figure Skating
WOMEN

With events being held in conjunction with the 1908 and 1920 Summer Games and at the first Winter Games in 1924 the women's Olympic figure skating programme runs parallel to that of the men.

Great Britain has been represented in the women's events on every occasion.

COMPETITOR	DATE OF BIRTH-DEATH	YEAR	EVENT/S
Adams, *Bridget Shirley*	4.5.1928	1948	S
Altwegg, *Jeannette Eleanor*	8.9.1930	1948	S
		1952	S
Barber, *Karen*	21.6.1961	1980	D
		1984	D

COMPETITOR	DATE OF BIRTH-DEATH	YEAR	EVENT/S
Barsdell, *Kathleen Irene*	10.11.1952	1976	D
Batchelor, *Erica Anne*	10.8.1933	1956	S
Beaumont, *Madelon St John*	—	1920	P
Bernard, *Linda Christine*	7.12.1950	1968	P
Butler, *Gweneth Leigh*	1.6.1915	1936	S
Cliff, *Violet Hamilton*	2.11.1916	1936	P
Clifton-Peach, *Diana Cynthia*	17.3.1944	1964	S
Coates, *Joyce Pamela*	14.12.1939	1956	P
Colledge, *Magdalen Cecilia*	28.11.1920	1932	S
		1936	S
Connolly, *Linda C*	30.4.1952	1972	P
Conway, *Joanne*	11.3.1971	1988	S
Cushley, *Lisa*	12.4.1969	1988	P
Davies, *Marion Tiefy*	12.10.1928	1948	S
Devries, *Patricia*	6.7.1930	1952	S
Dix, *Joan*	1920	1932	S
Dodd, *Patricia Ann*	7.4.1948	1968	S
Fulton, *Gina*	13.2.1971	1988	S
Garland, *Susan Jane*	30.4.1966–10.4.1987	1980	P
		1984	P
Green, *Hilary*	29.12.1951	1976	D
Greenhough-Smith, *Dorothy Vernon*	1875–9.5.1965	1908	S
Horne, *Peri Victoria*	21.4.1932	1952	P
Jackson, *Susan-Ann*	30.11.1965	1984	S
Jepson-Turner, *Belita Gladys Olive Lyne*	21.10.1923	1936	S
Johnson, *Phyllis Wyatt*	12.1886–2.12.1967	1908	P
		1920	S/P
Jones, *Sharon*	24.4.1964	1988	D
Krau, *Carolyn Patricia*	18.8.1943	1956	P
		1960	S
Linzee, *Maidie Jill L Hood*	18.10.1928	1948	S
Lovett, *Kathleen Marion*	–23.3.1969	1928	P
Lycett, *Gwendolyn*	—	1908	S
Muckelt, *Ethel*	30.5.1885–13.12.1953	1920	P
		1924	S/P
		1928	P

The youngest ever competitor at the Winter Olympics – Cecilia Colledge took part in the 1932 Games less than three months after her 11th birthday.

The First Flag Bearer

The distinction of being the first woman to carry her country's flag at an Olympic Opening Ceremony is held by Mollie Phillips, who led the British team onto the ice at the 1932 Winter Games at Lake Placid.

In later life Miss Phillips, who studied law at Lincoln's Inn, achieved other notable 'firsts'. In 1953 she was the first woman referee in a world championship when she was in charge of the Ice Dance event, and in

1961 she became the first woman to be appointed High Sheriff of Carmarthenshire. As her father had held the appointment in 1938, she was also the first daughter to succeed her father in office.

COMPETITOR	DATE OF BIRTH-DEATH	YEAR	EVENT/S
Nicks, *Jennifer Mary*	13.4.1932–21.8.1980	1948	P
		1952	P
Osborn, *Valda Rosemary*	17.9.1934	1952	S
Pauley, *Patricia Ann*	27.9.1941	1960	S
Peach, *Dianne Carol Rosemary*	25.12.1940	1956	S
Peake, *Cheryl*	30.3.1966	1988	P
Phillips, *Mollie Doreen*	27.7.1907	1932	S
		1936	S
Richardson, *Fannie Mildred*	19.7.1893–28.6.1987	1924	P
Richardson, *Karena*	12.10.1959	1976	S
		1980	S
Scott, *Jean Atkinson*	15.3.1951	1972	S
Sessions, *Wendy*	3.1.1959	1984	D
Shaw, *Gertrude Kathleen*	1903	1924	S
		1928	S
Silverthorne, *Winifred Ellen*	3.3.1925	1948	P
Stapleford, *Sally-Anne Martine*	7.7.1945	1964	S
		1968	S
Stewart, *Rosemarie*	22.6.1914	1936	P
Sugden, *Yvonne de Montfort Boyer*	14.10.1939	1956	S
Syers, *Florence Madeline 'Madge'*	1882–9.9.1917	1908	S/P
Taylforth, *Erika Leslie*	22.11.1956	1976	P
Taylor, *Megan Devenish*	25.10.1920	1932	S
Thompson, *Janet A*	15.3.1956	1976	D
Torvill, *Jayne*	7.10.1957	1980	D
		1984	D
Waghorn, *Frances Muriel*	5.6.1950	1968	S
Warner, *Carol-Ann*	13.7.1945	1964	S
Wyatt, *Barbara Florence Amelia*	17.7.1930	1952	S

COMPETITOR	DATE OF BIRTH-DEATH	YEAR	EVENT/S
Fawcett, *Bernard Harold*	—	1928	
Foster, *James*	13.9.1905	1936	
Green, *Arthur*	12.5.1921	1948	
Green, *Frank*	1919	1948	
Greenwood, *Harold Gustave Francis*	15.11.1894	1928	
Holmes, *George*	1894	1924	
Hurst-Brown, *Wilbert*	24.9.1899–1964	1928	
Jardine, *Frank*	—	1948	
Jukes, *Hamilton D*	1895	1924	
Kilpatrick, *John*	7.7.1917	1936	
Melland, *Frederick Nevill Shinwell*	3.4.1904	1928	
Murray, *John*	—	1948	
Oxley, *John Arthur*	21.1.1923–1.6.1976	1948	
Pitblado, *Edward Bruce*	23.2.1896–2.12.1978	1924	
Rogers, *GEF*	—	1928	
Sexton, *Blane N*	1892	1924	
		1928	
Simon, *Stanley*	—	1948	
Smith, *William*	—	1948	
Speechley, *William Grove*	5.7.1906	1928	
Stinchcombe, *Archibald*	17.11.1912	1936	
		1948	
Syme, *Thomas William*	24.8.1918–1984	1948	
Tait, *Victor Herbert*	8.6.1892–27.11.1988	1928	
Wyld, *Charles John*	—	1928	
Wyman, *James Robert*	27.4.1909	1936	

CB Boulden and G Holmes are not listed as team members in the 1924 Report of the British Olympic Association but both are shown in the team photograph which appears in that volume. The Official Report of the Organizing Committee indicates that Holmes did, in fact, play but that Boulden was only a reserve. Hence, Holmes has been included in the above list but Boulden has been omitted.

Ice Hockey

Ice Hockey was introduced into the Olympics in 1920 as part of the Summer Games. From 1924 Ice Hockey has been held regularly at the Winter Games and Great Britain has competed in 1924, 1928, 1936 and 1948.

COMPETITOR	DATE OF BIRTH-DEATH	YEAR EVENT/S
Anderson, *William Harding*	1901	1924
Archer, *Alexander 'Sandy'*	1.5.1910	1936
Baillie, *George*	1921	1948
Baker, *Leonard*	13.9.1918	1948
Borland, *James Andrew*	25.3.1911	1936
Brenchley, *Edgar*	10.2.1912–1975	1936
Brown, *Wilbert Hurst* see Hurst-Brown		
Carr-Harris, *Lorne Howland*	13.12.1899	1924
Carruthers, *Colin Gordon*	17.9.1890	1924
		1928
Carruthers, *Eric Dudley*	11.10.1895	1924
		1928
Chappell, *James*	25.3.1914–4.1.1973	1936
		1948
Clarkson, *George Elliott 'Guy'*	1.1.1891	1924
Coward, *John*	28.10.1910	1936
Cuthbert, *Cuthbert Ross*	6.2.1892	1924
		1928
Dailley, *Gordon Debenham*	24.7.1911–3.5.1989	1936
Davey, *John Gerald*	5.9.1914	1936
		1948
Dunkleman, *Frederick*	—	1948
Erhardt, *Carl Alfred*	15.2.1897–3.5.1988	1936

Luge
MEN

Luge became an Olympic sport in 1964 and Great Britain has been represented at every Games.

The letters (A) and (B) indicate whether the competitor was a member of the first or second crew in the two-man event.

S = Single   2 = Two man

COMPETITOR	DATE OF BIRTH-DEATH	YEAR	EVENT/S
Brialey, *Stephen*	8.10.1963	1988	S/2(A)
de Carvalho, *Michel Rey*	21.7.1944	1972	2(B)
		1976	S/2(A)
Deen, *Rupert Frank Frenan*	14.11.1938	1972	S
Denby, *John*	16.8.1946	1980	2(B)
Dyason, *Christopher*	13.3.1948	1980	2(A)
Howard, *Anthony Michael*	18.5.1958	1984	S
Liversedge, *Richard Lorton*	31.8.1940	1968	S
		1972	S
		1976	S/2(B)
Manclark, *James William McKinnon*	3.12.1939	1968	S
Marsh, *Stephen Alastair*	2.6.1947	1972	2(A)
Nicol, *Macleod*	18.10.1958	1988	S
Ovett, *Nicholas*	4.1.1967	1988	S/2(A)
Palmer-Tomkinson, *Jeremy James*	4.11.1943	1972	S/2(B)
(Also see *Alpine Skiing*)		1976	S/2(A)
		1980	S/2(B)

COMPETITOR	DATE OF BIRTH-DEATH	YEAR	EVENT/S
Porteus, *Gordon John Pulham*	16.11.1935	1964	S
Prentice, *Christopher*	4.5.1953	1984	S
Prentice, *Derek*	13.6.1950	1980	S/2(A)
Schellenberg, *Clifford Keith W*	13.3.1929	1964	S
Tapp, *Russell*	15.4.1943	1976	2(B)
Townshend, *Neil William*	29.5.1955	1980	S
Usborne, *André Charles*	16.10.1952	1984	S
Woodall, *Jonathan William Askew* (Also see *Bobsleigh*)	25.1.1946	1972	S/2(A)

Luge
WOMEN

Women's Luge first became an Olympic sport in 1964 but Great Britain has only been represented in 1980, 1984 and 1988.
Women only compete in the Singles at the Olympics.

COMPETITOR	DATE OF BIRTH-DEATH	YEAR EVENT/S
Sherred, *Claire*	4.11.1956	1984
Walker, *Avril*	8.5.1954	1980
Weaver, *Joanna*	11.3.1957	1980
Wreford, *Alyson*	19.2.1959	1988

Nordic Skiing
MEN

Nordic skiing events have been held at every Winter Games. Great Britain first competed in 1936 and after missing the next two Games (1948 & 1952) has been represented regularly since 1956.
It was not until 1988 that a Briton first competed in the ski jumping event.

15k = 15 kilometre cross-country   30k = 30 kilometre cross-country
50k = 50 kilometre cross-country
Ry = 40 kilometre cross-country relay (4 × 10km)
NC = Nordic Combined   SJ = Ski jumping

COMPETITOR	DATE OF BIRTH-DEATH	YEAR	EVENT/S
Andrew, *Frederick* (Also see *Biathlon*)	28.4.1940	1964	15k
Aylmer, *Richard*	1932	1956	50k
Cairney, *Thomas*	1932	1956	30k/50k
Daglish, *Steven*	1.6.1957	1984	30k
Dakin, *Victor*	30.1.1943	1968	15k
Dent, *John Robin* (Also see *Biathlon*)	15.2.1938	1964	Ry
Dixon, *Michael*	21.11.1962	1984	15k/RY
Edwards, *Michael Thomas 'Eddy'*	5.12.1963	1988	70mSJ/ 90mSJ
Elliott, *Douglas Mitchell*	14.2.1950	1976	15k
Fielder, *Aubrey*	1929	1956	15k/Ry
Gibbins, *Paul* (Also see *Biathlon*)	3.1.1953	1976	15k
Goode, *Michael*	22.8.1952	1980	15k
Gover, *Maurice*	1932	1956	15k/Ry
Graham, *Dominick S*	24.7.1920	1956	50k
Howden, *Ronald*	23.6.1967	1988	15k
Jacklin, *Philip*	20.9.1952	1980	15k
Legard, *Charles Percy Digby* (Also see *Modern Pentathlon*)	17.6.1906	1936	NC
MacIvor, *Charles* (Also see *Biathlon*)	23.1.1957	1980	15k
McKenzie, *Ewan*	11.1.1959	1988	30k/50k/ Ry
Moore, *John Arthur G* (Also see *Biathlon*)	18.5.1933	1956	15k/30k
		1960	15k/30k/ 50k
		1964	15k/Ry

COMPETITOR	DATE OF BIRTH-DEATH	YEAR	EVENT/S
Moore, *Mark*	28.9.1961	1984	15k/30k/ 50k/Ry
Morgan, *Andrew John M*	24.3.1934	1956	15k/30k/ Ry
		1960	15k/30k
		1964	15k
Oliver, *Keith Anthony* (Also see *Biathlon*)	27.10.1947	1972	30k
		1976	15k
Palliser, *Terence*	22.3.1948	1972	15k/30k
Rawlin, *Andrew*	14.7.1960	1984	30k/Ry
Rees, *David Edgar*	29.12.1940	1964	15k
Shutt, *Norman L* (Also see *Biathlon*)	9.11.1929	1960	30k
Spencer, *James*	1926	1956	30k/Ry
Spotswood, *John*	26.8.1960	1984	15k/30k/ 50k/Ry
		1988	15k/30k/ Ry
Strong, *Peter*	23.5.1946	1972	15k
Tancock, *Peter* (Also see *Biathlon*)	22.7.1940	1968	15k
Tobin, *Harold James*	26.11.1944	1972	15k
Tuck, *Roderick* (Also see *Biathlon*)	28.5.1934	1964	30k/Ry
Walter, *Francis Joseph*	28.5.1909	1936	NC
Watkins, *Martin*	24.1.1962	1984	15k
		1988	15k/30k/ 50k/Ry
Winterton, *Patrick*	15.9.1961	1988	15k/30k
Wylie, *Andrew*	6.9.1961	1988	Ry

Nordic Skiing
WOMEN

Nordic Skiing was first introduced as an Olympic sport for women in 1952. Great Britain has only competed in 1972, 1984 and 1988.

5k = 5 kilometre cross-country   10k = 10 kilometre cross-country
20k = 20 kilometre cross-country   Ry = 20 kilometre cross-country relay (4 × 5km)

COMPETITOR	DATE OF BIRTH-DEATH	YEAR	EVENT/S
Brittan, *Caroline Susan*	9.3.1959	1984	5k
Coats, *Ros*	17.1.1950	1984	5k/10k/ 20k/Ry
Jeffrey, *Lauren*	23.6.1960	1984	10k/Ry
Lavery, *Nicola*	19.11.1960	1984	5k/10k/ 20k/Ry
Lutken, *Francis*	2.10.1950	1972	5k/10k
McKenzie, *Louise*	31.3.1964	1988	5k/10k/ 20k
Trueman, *Doris*	23.5.1953	1984	5k/10k/Ry
Watson, *Jean*	29.10.1960	1988	5k/10k

Speed Skating
MEN

Speed skating events have been held at every Winter Games and, with the exception of 1932 and 1936, Great Britain has been represented on each occasion.

COMPETITOR	DATE OF BIRTH-DEATH	YEAR	EVENT/S
Blewitt, *John B*	19.12.1945	1968	5k
		1972	1500/5k/10k
Bodington, *David George*	30.7.1947	1968	500/1500
Blundell, *Dennis*	17.6.1921	1948	500/1500/5k
Bullen, *Anthony F*	2.8.1931	1964	1500/5k/10k
Carbis, *Bryan*	23.4.1961	1984	1500/5k
Connel, *Alexander*	1930	1956	500/1500/5k
Cronshey, *John D*	7.7.1926	1948	500/5k/10k
		1956	500/1500/5k/10k
Dawson, *Thomas Bryce*	15.2.1942	1964	500/1500
Dix, *Frederick Walter*	1883–18.2.1966	1924	500
		1928	500/1500/5k
French, *John*	22.12.1955	1980	5k/10k
Green, *Julian*	3.11.1965	1988	1000/1500/5k/10k
Hampton, *David*	16.12.1947	1972	500/1500/5k/10k
Hearn, *John Graham*	27.12.1929	1952	1500/5k/10k
		1956	500/1500/5k/10k
Holwell, *L Norman*	6.9.1928	1952	500/1500/5k/10k
Horn, *Cyril Walter*	1905	1924	500
		1928	500/1500/10k
Howes, *Henry J*	11.11.1928	1948	500/1500/5k/10k
Jones, *William Ashford*	18.3.1923	1952	500/1500/5k
Luke, *Alan*	17.6.1959	1980	1500/5k
Mcnicol, *Craig*	11.4.1971	1988	1000/1500/5k
Malkin, *Thomas Alfred T*	20.9.1935	1960	500/1500/5k
		1964	500/1500/5k/10k
Marshall, *Archibald*	23.10.1952	1976	500/1000
		1980	500/1000
Monaghan, *Terence A*	20.9.1955	1960	500/1500/5k/10k
Peppin, *Bruce*	26.8.1933	1948	500/1500
Ross, *Thomas C*	1.9.1927	1948	1500/5k
Sandys, *Geoffrey*	9.6.1951	1976	1500/5k/10k
		1980	1500/5k
Stewart, *Leonard*	—	1928	500/1500/5k
Stockdale, *Geoffrey Robert*	—	1968	500/1500
Sutton, *Bernard Harold 'Tom'*	1892	1924	500
Tebbit, *Albert E*	26.12.1872	1924	5k
Tipper, *A John*	16.9.1944	1968	500/1500

The 1948 Official Report of the British Olympic Association incorrectly lists A Holt instead of HJ Howes as placing 19th in the 5km event.

Speed Skating
WOMEN

A demonstration of women's speed skating was held in 1932 but it did not become an official Olympic sport for women until 1960.
Great Britain has only been represented in 1968 and 1980.

COMPETITOR	DATE OF BIRTH-DEATH	YEAR	EVENT/S
Farren, *Kim*	10.1.1958	1980	500/1000/1500
Horsepool, *Amanda*	18.5.1959	1980	1000/1500/3k
Tipper, *Patricia*	—	1968	1000/3k

Index of Biographies

MEN

WOMEN